DATE			

BAKER & TAYLOR BOOKS

Being familiar with Goethe's Faust story, students of Western thought will not be surprised to learn that Goethe was also a scientist, philosopher, and historian. This book is about the interdisciplinary activities of his mid-life (1790–1810) when he researched optics, color theory, and plant morphology, and at the same time contributed to the growing literature in the history and philosophy of science.

In Goethe's writings, Karl J. Fink finds a scientist examining the junctures of nature, the boundary conditions where growth and change occur. These topics of transition also define his approach to the history of science, where the gaps between visible states challenge the historian to search for metaphors that bridge discontinuities. Written in the idiom of Thomas Kuhn, Fink discovers how this pioneer in the historiography of science investigated the shared exemplars, common metaphors, and topoi of thought that shape scientific traditions.

In *Goethe's History of Science* Fink examines the birth of a discipline. He describes how Goethe distinguished science from the history of science; how, in dialogue with Friedrich Schiller, Goethe applied Kantian categories of the mind to his project on color theory; how Goethe confronted Newtonian science with the strategies of polemics; how he organized science from antiquity to the Enlightenment into epochs of authority and canonicity; and how, as poet and critic, he linked the scientist's language, style, and personality to the development of schools of thought. Fink concludes his study with Goethe's views on the possibility of a teleology of science, looking at those writings in which Goethe explores how the scientist of today projects and directs the science of tomorrow.

Goethe's history of science

Chalk drawing of Johann Wolfgang von Goethe (1749–1832) at age fifty-one, by Friedrich Bury, Weimar, 1800. From the Nationale Forschungs- und Gedenkstätten, Weimar.

Goethe's history of science

KARL J. FINK
St. Olaf College

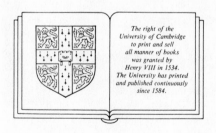

The right of the
University of Cambridge
to print and sell
all manner of books
was granted by
Henry VIII in 1534.
The University has printed
and published continuously
since 1584.

CAMBRIDGE UNIVERSITY PRESS

Cambridge
New York   Port Chester   Melbourne   Sydney

Published by the Press Syndicate of the University of Cambridge
The Pitt Building, Trumpington Street, Cambridge CB2 1RP
40 West 20th Street, New York, NY 10011, USA
10 Stamford Road, Oakleigh, Melbourne 3166, Australia

First published 1991

Printed in the United States of America

Library of Congress Cataloging-in-Publication Data

Fink, Karl J., 1942–

    Goethe's history of science / Karl J. Fink.

      p. cm.

    Includes bibliographical references and index.

    ISBN 0-521-40211-5

    1. Goethe, Johann Wolfgang von, 1749–1832 – Knowledge – Science
2. Science – History. 3. Science – Philosophy – History. 4. Science –
Historiography. I. Title.
Q143.G53F56   1991
509 – dc20   91–8631
                                                              CIP

British Library Cataloging in Publication Data

Fink, Karl J.

    Goethe's history of science.
    1. Goethe, Johann Wolfgang von, 1749–1832
    I. Title
    509.2

ISBN 0-521-40211-5 hardback

For Alene
Charles, Brian, and Melissa

We would rather confess our
moral mistakes, errors, and defects,
than our scientific ones.

(Wir gestehen lieber unsre
moralischen Irrtümer, Fehler, und Gebrechen,
als unsre Wissenschaftlichen. LA, I, 11, 341)

Contents

Contents

Preface

Many people have drawn inspiration from Goethe's writings on science and history, including some of the greatest minds of the nineteenth and twentieth centuries. Two early responses came from Friedrich Nietzsche (1844–1900) and Oswald Spengler (1880–1936), both of whom struggled with the conflict of Goethe's organic optimism and their own existential pessimism. A different temperament, Thomas Mann (1875–1955), drew from the symbolic potential of Goethe's life and works, referring to the centerpiece of the present study, Goethe's *Geschichte der Farbenlehre* (1810), as "a novel in European thought" (*The Permanent Goethe*, 1948, xxvii). From James Gleick's account, *Chaos: Making a New Science* (1987), we learn that some of our most creative minds continue to look to Goethe's works for inspiration in the study of life's mysteries, and in Gleick's book for clues to understanding patterns of disorder.

Goethe spent most of his adult life in search of ways to shape the amorphous states of nature. Thus, this book begins with Goethe's science, first as represented in his poetry, and then as found in essays ranging from formal scientific treatises to aphoristic fragments on natural philosophy. From a study of his scientific writings we learn that in content and composition he focused on the transitions in life processes, on the fluid and ambiguous junctures between form and function. From his study of nature, Goethe learned that dynamic processes are not to be discovered in the obvious features of structure, but at the borders between states of order, at the threshold of change. Goethe established this theme early in life, and by the time he began serious writing in historiography, the border-experience had become a way of life, a way of life in his search for the patterns of organic process, in his style of scientific composition, and in his interdisciplinary relationship to professional colleagues.

The book is focused on the two decades of his mid-life during 1790–1810, the period of his most intense research in science and history. In these years he learned the ways in which science develops. He came to understand the power of science, the communities and schools of theory, the authority of the scientist, and the process by which a document takes shape and becomes a canon of culture. Goethe advanced the view that, properly understood, the study of science is a study of language, for it is in the idiom of the text where we find the patterns of change that shape history. Goethe's history of color theory is a "novel"; it comes closer to literature than to science; but so does science, for in the final analysis science is embedded in language, and, in Goethe's view, all language is tropological.

Acknowledgments

Study and writing for this book was concentrated in three periods, one in Weimar during 1981, supported jointly by the American Philosophical Society and the Research Center for Classical Studies in Weimar, the Nationale Forschungs- und Gedenkstätten (NFG), and another in 1986, with additional support from the American Philosophical Society. The last phase of the project began in 1988 on an ACM Visiting Professorship at the University of Chicago, and ended during the summer of 1990 at the Research Center in Weimar on a grant from the International Research and Exchange Board (IREX), with funds provided by the Andrew W. Mellon Foundation, the National Endowment for the Humanities, and the U. S. Department of State. I wish to extend special appreciation to these institutions for their support, and to St. Olaf College for financial assistance from the Faculty Development Program for summer research from 1983 to 1987.

Special thanks also go to Professors Harry G. Haile, who introduced me to Goethe's writings in science and history, James W. Marchand for his attention to questions on the philosophy of language and science, and Hans Henning for supporting research in Weimar. It has been a privilege to work with these scholars, for their interest and insights have kept alive my own enthusiasm for research on Goethe as an historian of science.

Although the project could not have been completed without the support and encouragement of these individuals and organizations, none of them is responsible for the views expressed in this book.

Abbreviations used in text and endnotes

Akad.   Immanuel Kant. *Kant's Gesammelte Schriften.* Published by the
         preussische Akademie der Wissenschaften. 29 vols. Berlin:
         Reimer and de Gruyter, 1910–.

BA   Johann Wolfgang Goethe. *Goethe. Poetische Werke.* 22 vols.
         Berlin: Aufbau-Verlag, 1961–.

GA   Johann Wolfgang Goethe. *Gedenkausgabe der Werke, Briefe
         und Gespräche.* 24 vols. Ed. E. Beutler. Zurich: Artemis-
         Verlag, 1949.

LA   Johann Wolfgang Goethe. *Die Schriften zur Naturwissenschaft.*
         Vollständige mit Erläuterungen versehene Ausgabe
         herausgegeben im Auftrage der Deutschen Akademie der Natur-
         forscher Leopoldina. 2 pts., 11 vols. Ed. Rupprecht
         Matthaei, Wilhelm Troll and K. Lothar Wolf. Weimar: Böhlau,
         1947–. Pt. I, Texte; pt. II, Ergänzungen und Erläuterungen.

NA   Friedrich Schiller. *Schillers Werke.* Nationalausgabe. 42 vols.
         Ed. K. H. Hahn. Weimar: Böhlau, 1943–.

SA   Johann G. Herder. *Sämtliche Werke.* Suphan-Ausgabe. 33 vols.
         Ed. B. Suphan. Hildesheim: Georg Olm, 1967. Repr., 1877–
         1913.

WA   Johann Wolfgang von Goethe. *Goethes Werke.* Herausgegeben
         im Auftrag der Grossherzogin Sophie von Sachsen. 4 pts., 133
         vols. in 143. Weimar: Böhlau, 1887–1919. Pt. I, Werke; pt. II,
         Naturwissenschaftliche Schriften; pt. III, Tagebücher; pt. IV,
         Briefe.

Introduction

Johann Wolfgang Goethe was born on Aug. 28, 1749, in Frankfurt, an imperial city and coronation site for the emperors of the Holy Roman Empire of the German Nations. In 1774, following studies in law at the universities in Leipzig and Strasbourg, Goethe wrote *Die Leiden des jungen Werthers,* a novel in letter form about the pains of an unsuccessful love affair and the anxieties of a young man seeking his place in German society. In other works from the early 1770s, Goethe discovered his Germanic roots, writing a play about *Götz von Berlichingen,* a minor political figure of the Martin Luther era, folk poems such as "Heidenröslein," and essays on Shakespeare and Gothic architecture. At the age of twenty-five, Goethe's literary success prompted an invitation from Duke Karl August to visit the small duchy of Saxony–Weimar. Here he stayed, soon becoming an administrator in the economic, political, social, and cultural affairs of the state.[1] Poet, scientist, and thinker, Goethe became Germany's most famous writer, internationally known for the breadth of his knowledge and the universality of his genius.[2]

Goethe was a prolific writer, ranging in forms of expression from the essay for his research in geology, comparative anatomy, botany, and color theory; to dramas about human rights, political intrigue, and wars; and novels about marriage and the development of the artist.[3] He is best known for the richness of his poetic verse, which includes some of the finest lyrics in the German language, as in the poems "Mailied," "Wanders Nachtlied," and "Der König in Thule." Many of his intellectual and personal experiences are woven together in his most famous work, *Faust,* begun in the restless period of his youth and completed a year before he died. This dramatic poem of 12,111 lines was written in two parts, the first focused on the life of the adventurer and magician in the small world of love and learning, and the second on the way he engaged the broader forces of science, politics, and culture. In both parts the hero was seeking ultimate knowledge about life and nature, a vision of modern scientific man that Goethe shared during the 1790s with friends and colleagues at the Friday Round Table discussions held in the Wittumspalais of Duchess Anna Amalia.

A watercolor of the "Round Table" (Tafelrunde), a Friday discussion group sponsored by Duchess Anna Amalia of Weimar–Saxony at the Wittumspalais in Weimar. Duchess Amalia is seated at the center behind the table and Goethe is seated to her right at the end of the table, partly hidden from view by a colleague to his right. Painted by Georg M. Kraus about 1795. From the Nationale Forschungs- und Gedenkstätten, Weimar.

Goethe traveled extensively, but left Weimar only once for an extended period, 1786–8, which he spent in Italy in study of classical art and literature. In the two decades, 1790–1810, relieved of many of his administrative duties, he devoted much of his time to studying the history of science and doing research on plant morphology and color theory, and at the same time writing classical German verse. And in 1809 he published *Die Wahlverwandt-schaften,* a novel about marriage cloaked in the symbolism of the language of chemistry.

During the last two decades of his life, he continued these parallel interests in the arts and sciences, in both dimensions reflecting on the processes that move the creative spirit of the human being. In these decades he began his autobiographical writings, completed the stories of Wilhelm Meister, the hero of the artist's drive to shape life, and Faust, the hero of the modern drive to know all of life. Between 1810 and 1820, the synthesis of these urges drove him to study oriental literature, resulting in a collection of critical essays and in a cycle of love poems, the *West–östlicher Divan*. This blend of Eastern and Western themes, stimulated by one of many close relationships with a woman, put a global stamp on his life and works. Goethe, the author of the concept of

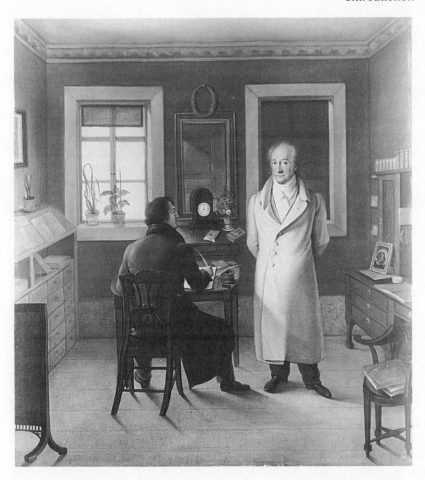

An oil painting of Goethe in his study, dictating to his scribe, John, by Johann J. Schmeller, 1829–31. From the Nationale Forschungs- und Gedenkstätten, Weimar.

world literature, continued writing into the last years of his life, in his study living the legend of the Faustian quest for knowledge.

When he died on March 22, 1832, Goethe left posterity a collected edition of forty volumes edited in his own hand (1827–30), with instructions for the posthumous publication of twenty additional volumes (1832–42). He also left an archive of unpublished notes and manuscripts, a museum of scientific instruments, works of art, cabinets of flora, fauna, and minerals, and a personal library of over five thousand books. And from this depository, heirs of Western culture have shaped their concept of his effects, ranging in approach from new scholarly editions of his writings, to displays of artifacts in muse-

3

ums, to audiovisual versions of his works, indeed, to the dramatization of his way of life.[4]

Even though Goethe left few technical marks on the pages of modern science, scholars, scientists, artists, and students remain fascinated by his nature studies. By 1940 this fascination had generated the 4,500 items listed in Günther Schmid's bibliography, and by the estimation of one of the leading critics of Goethe's science, Dorothea Kuhn, "the 5000th title has probably long since been passed."[5] Also adding to the interest in Goethe's scientific work is a collection of over 50,000 artifacts on nature and culture, a small museum of scientific instruments from his era,[6] and well over a dozen volumes of published and archival writings on scientific topics.

For the scholar and critic, study of the scope and richness of these writings is challenging and intriguing, for at least half of his collected volumes consists of unpublished research notes, letters, diary comments, book reviews, and sketches and outlines he wrote in preparation of his published works. From these published and unpublished materials the critic has the opportunity to study Goethe's science in the context it took shape, adding social and biographical background to examination of the scientific text. Until recently this holistic approach to the study of Goethe's science would have been a very tedious affair, for it would have required work with the cumbersome Weimar edition (WA) and with various other isolated resources, such as with the collections of his letters.

After 1947 the fragmented picture of Goethe's scientific writings began to change with the regular publication of new volumes of his works in the Leopoldina edition (LA). The edition was planned in two parts, the first including Goethe's primary writings, published and unpublished, and the second comprising contextual materials that contain the biographical and archival background to his scientific work.[7] It is the more recent appearance of the volumes in Part II, the first two in 1959 and 1961 and the other three in 1973, 1977, and 1986, that has made less tedious the task of examining Goethe's scientific writings as a whole. It is also easier to work with this new edition because it has been organized chronologically and topically, beginning with two volumes on his studies in mineralogy and geology. Volumes three to seven are devoted to his work in color theory, while eight and nine are published notebooks, one on science in general and another on morphology. The last two volumes repeat this separation, each focusing on fragments and essays not published elsewhere in the edition. Thus, in each field of inquiry the reader can follow Goethe's development as writer, thinker, and scientist, roughly from age twenty-one to eighty-two.

The present study of Goethe's historiography of science is focused on volume six of the Leopoldina edition, on the *Materialien zur Geschichte der Farbenlehre,* although discussion in the early chapters is based on materials from the entire collection of his scientific writings. Much of this material is considered primary, although it comprises many pages never published in Goethe's lifetime, materials printed in recent years as a convenience to the scholarly world. This editorial approach has opened the doors to new examinations of Goethe as a scientist,[8] and to his views on the history of science, a field that matured with Goethe's interest in science in general and in color and optics in specific. But the picture is still broader than the writings contained in the Leopoldina edition, for to these one must relate the poetry and prose of his imaginative writings, which also comprise views on nature, science, and the history of science.

A look at the entire spectrum of Goethe's writings on science brings several perspectives to our understanding of his theory of the history of science, including the fact that in most of his nature studies he tended to review the history of the problem on which he was working. Secondly, there are certain views from his approach to science that also conditioned his estimation of documents in the history of science. These views are embedded in his science, and understanding them gives us some insight into the development of his theory of the history of science. And finally, a look at the entire range of his nature studies, including primary and secondary, published and unpublished works, provides a basis for examining Goethe as a scientific writer, a point of view important to his history of science, for he, too, based his view of scientists from the past on the documents they left posterity.

Part I

The real joints of nature

Basic characteristic of an individual organism: to divide, to unite, to merge into the universal, to abide in the particular, to transform itself, to define itself, and as living things tend to appear under a thousand conditions, to arise and vanish, to solidify and melt, to freeze and flow, to expand and contract. Since these effects occur together, any or all may occur at the same moment.[1]

1

Goethe's romantic science

When Goethe matriculated at the University of Strasbourg in 1770, he enrolled in a liberal arts curriculum with courses in political science, history, anatomy, surgery, and chemistry. He had planned a doctorate in law, following his father's wishes, but only achieved the "licentiate" to practice law. He had written a dissertation on "The Legislature, On the Power of the Magistrate to Determine Religion and Culture" (De legislatoribus, über die Macht der Gesetzgeber, über Religion und Kultus zu bestimmen), but it was an attack on orthodoxy and the thesis was rejected.[2] The thesis itself is not extant, but from a letter written by one of his professors, we learn that, among other controversial assertions, Goethe contended that "Jesus Christ was not the author of our religion, but that a number of other wise men composed it in his name. The Christian religion, he avers, is merely a rational, political institution."[3] The episode is not atypical for the annals of higher education, but in Goethe's case is significant, because in it we find early evidence of the exception he took to tradition, apparently "puffed up over his store of knowledge, but chiefly by reason of a few undesirable traits he has got from M. Voltaire."[4]

Following the rejection of the dissertation, Goethe showed his contempt for the authorities of the university by offering a series of theses for disputation, fifty-six in all, some thought extremely simplistic, others conservative, and still others liberal and progressive, collectively written without logical order.[5] But from this list of disputations, we see questions about life that were to fall within the pale of his literary and scientific works during the next sixty years. In the first thesis, for example, in the one considered simplistic by the law faculty, he proposed that "natural law is what nature has taught all creatures" (Jus naturae est, quod natura omnia animalia docuit, WA, I, 37, 119), a statement that bore the seeds of his romantic science, which said that the lessons of life can be found in nature itself, that science should interpret nature, not serve technology.[6] From this perspective he asked in disputation fifty-five about the rights and responsibilities of a mother in childbirth, raising an issue that was to emerge later in his Faust story: "Should the woman who kills her newly born child suffer the death penalty? There is no unity among the learned on this point" (An foemina partum recenter editum trucidans capite plectenda fit? quaestio est inter Doctores controversa, p. 125).

The red thread running through his formal educational experience was shaped by questions about human nature, about the rights of individuals and states, about patterns of life and death. With these questions Goethe gave vent to his distaste for learned authority, casting about for new ways of looking at the relationship of human beings to nature, society, and tradition, challenging a world order that had become dated.[7] And in this quest he drew inspiration from a small circle of friends in Strasbourg that gave birth to the movement that became known as the German Storm and Stress, a movement considered by some an analogue to the French Revolution.[8] These emergent writers set a course for the revival of science and literature in Germany, a course grounded in the quest for a science of human beings, for study of their nature, culture and history. By the end of the decade, Friedrich Schiller (1759–1805) repeated Goethe's search for new definitions of human nature when he succeeded in writing a dissertation "On The Relationship of Man's animal and spiritual Nature" (Ueber den Zusammenhang der tierischen Natur des Menschen mit seiner geistigen).[9] Here Schiller, after having his first dissertation on a philosophy of physiology rejected, found a thesis that captured the central issue of Storm and Stress anthropology.

By 1771 Johann G. Herder (1744–1803), Goethe's mentor and the intellectual leader of the Storm and Stress movement, had completed his "Treatise on the Origins of Language," arguing that language developed from within the human being, disputing the view of some that it was God-given and of others that it was animal imitation.[10] Then in 1774 he further challenged intellectual orthodoxy with "Another Philosophy of History for the Formation of Mankind," initiating ideas that brought about the demise of divine providence in interpretation of the history and origin of peoples of the globe.[11] In this effort, Herder was arguing for a new kind of historiography, one grounded in a teleology of cultural forms, like other participants in the Storm and Stress decade, introducing ideas that would emerge in the next decades as mature statements, as finished versions of earlier notions.

Immanuel Kant (1724–1804), Herder's teacher at the University of Königsberg, also set the parameters for the fields of Goethe's interest. He began his lectures on anthropology in the Winter Semester of 1772–3, by the middle of the decade announcing his traditional course on physical geography with an essay "On the Different Races of Mankind."[12] Here Kant argued that the races of mankind were of a single species, a definition he grounded in the "Buffon test" (Büffonsche Regel),[13] which said that animals that mate and produce fertile offspring belong to the same species. With this essay Kant introduced a biological connection between man and animal, in the same year that Johann Blumenbach (1752–1840) completed his dissertation "On the Natural Varieties of Mankind" (1775), dividing the peoples of the globe into four groups, the Americans, Caucasians, Mongolians, and Ethiopians.[14] With Kant, he argued the unity of the human species according to the "Buffon test" and, while both agreed that this test confirmed the blood relationship of all peoples of the globe, they also understood that this relationship neither explained the diversity nor the origins of the various peoples of the globe. This question remained open, surfacing again in the middle of the next decade when Goethe began research in human and animal anatomy.

By 1775, the first steps had been taken toward a unified theory of anthropology grounded in teleology of organic forms, by Herder in history and Kant and Blumenbach in biology. Together they confronted popularized versions of Linnean anthropology, as found, for example, in Voltaire's (1694–1778) *Philosophy of History* (1765), in which he argued that "none but the blind can doubt that the whites, the negroes, the Albinoes, the Hottentots, the Laplanders, the Chinese, the Americans, are races entirely different."[15] Others in the Storm and Stress decade (1770–80), like Georg Forster (1754–94), participated in the search for new definitions of the peoples of the globe, but none so systematically documented the myths behind racial prejudices and so convincingly argued for the unity of the human species as did Blumenbach in his dissertation on the varieties of peoples of the globe. And in the years that followed, he continued to improve this definition, by 1779 assimilating the new ethnographic materials on Polynesian cultures into his famous theory of the five races of mankind. Then, in 1781, he published his second major contribution to the biology of the human being, his theory of the "forces of formation" (Bildungstrieb).[16]

These developments in physical anthropology entered Goethe's writings in science early in the next decade. In 1775 he had taken an appointment in the administration of the small duchy of Saxony-Weimar, beginning a career at first limited to cultural affairs, but one that soon required research for decisions on mining, engineering, economics, education, and financial management. In 1776 he brought Herder to Weimar to serve as general superintendent of education, thus, staying in touch with the emerging author of historical teleology and cultural pluralism. By 1783 he met Blumenbach in Weimar, remaining in close contact with him the rest of his life, joining him and Kant in the search for definitions of the human being.[17]

In a series of short essays, "On Morphology" (1817–22), Goethe recalled the way developments in physical anthropology entered his intellectual framework, emphasizing particularly the influence of Kant's "teleology of judgment" (teleologische Urteilskraft, p. 92) and Blumenbach's "theory of epigenesis" (Theorie der Epigenesis, p. 99).[18] In these essays Goethe expressed appreciation for Blumenbach's energized versions of organic development (Bildungstrieb), but also explained that he viewed the concept of "force" (Kraft), and particularly "drive" (Trieb), as highly anthropomorphized. In his view, these terms assume something "physical" (physisch) and "mechanical" (mechanisch), and while they bring vitality to organized matter, they still leave us with a gap in the understanding of organic development, with "a dark incomprehensible point" (ein dunkler unbegreiflicher Punkt). Nor were terms like "evolution" (Evolution), "epigenesis" (Epigenese), and "preformation" (Präformation) of any help. These, too, he argued, could not be understood without a concept of forms in process, of "metamorphosis" (Metamorphose), the science that emerged from the first phase of Goethe's struggles with the way of nature.[19]

In defense of nature's unity

An incision into Goethe's topography of nature begins at that point when he began to articulate a detached view of his relationship to his environment, or at least when he began to recognize that it was possible to write about nature in an intimate or detached manner. These beginnings can be found in his poetic writings, as in the poem "Maysong" (Mailied), written in 1771 during the Storm and Stress period of literary and cultural revival in Germany.[20] This celebration of nature in the month of May is on the surface a light song of nine stanzas, each one advancing toward the center, where the infatuation with nature is supplanted by that for his "sweetheart" (Mädchen, p. 12). This symmetry in structure corresponds to the thematic balance of the poem. In the first four stanzas Goethe sings to the joys of nature, and in the fifth he signals a transition in the celebration from nature to lover, the focus of the closing four stanzas.

The point, in this introduction to Goethe's maturing views as a scientist, is that even in his earliest poems Goethe recognized a subject–object relationship in writing about nature. Most importantly he recognized that the relationship could be turned off and on, that there is a threshold between the author's feelings for nature and the thoughts springing from them. Indeed, a transition stanza in the poem marks the border between the two topics, but also unites them with a personal pronoun, "you" (Du), which refers back to nature and forward to his sweetheart. Passion and intimacy underscore the relationship to nature and to lover, but in this particular poem, feelings for nature precede, or maybe even are the source of those for the lover, at least so it would appear, based on the sequence presented in the written form.

The author–nature, or the subject–object relationship, and a clearly marked transition is again central to the structural symmetry of the poem "On the Lake" (Auf dem See) from 1775, a poem written shortly before he began his professional career in the administration of Duke Karl August in Weimar.[21] Here the middle stanza marks the transition from the author's feelings for nature to a detached description of a scene on a lake in Switzerland. Indeed, here Goethe makes the transition experience the central message of the poem.

The opening lines show how nature nutures his soul: "And fresh nourishment, new blood / I suck from a world so free; / Nature, how gracious and how good, / Her breast she gives to me."[22] And in the transition stanza, a pair of rhyming couplets located between two sets of eight-line stanzas, he refers directly to the organ of observation, the eye, asking why his own are sinking, lulled into a dreamlike state by the rocking boat on the lake. In the second couplet he answers his own question, shedding the golden dreams and recognizing a new presence in life at hand. The second stanza of eight lines then offers a discriminating description of the lake, the stars, and the shaded shore.

In this poem, "On the Lake," the threshold between intuitive and critical experiences seems more essential than either the author's intimacy with nature in the first part or the clarity of description in the last. And indeed it was, for this focus on borders and transitions became central to Goethe's study of nature as he entered formal scientific writing in the last two decades of the eighteenth century. In fact, the last two lines of the poem signal awareness of his development toward higher levels of critical thinking. In this context, these lines yield a double meaning, one describing the maturing fruit in the scene on the shore, and one reflecting the maturing mind of the observer in the boat: "And in the water mirrored / The fruit is ripening."[23]

The poem "Permanence in Change" (Dauer im Wechsel) from 1803 illustrates a new level of critical thinking attained by Goethe at the turn of the century.[24] Between 1775 and 1800 he had devoted most of his scientific work to the study of plant and animal forms and to patterns of color, light, and vision. The central issue in most of this scientific activity was the question of locating those junctures of nature which showed "Permanence in Change," a poem of five stanzas written with full attention to understanding nature as forms in process. And in this poem, too, the middle stanza serves as a turning point, in this case where attention is shifted from the observed to the observer. In the first part of the poem Goethe describes the transitoriness of blossoms, leaves, fruits, and the waters of the river, in which no one can swim twice, "so quick the changes come."[25] However, in this poem the subject–object question in the transition stanza reaches a new high in which Goethe observes that "You yourself!" (Du nun selbst!) change, so that you view your environment "with an ever-changing eye" (Stets mit andern Augen).

In the second half of the poem, on the other side of the border, after establishing the constancy of change, first in the observed and then in the observer, there Goethe discovered a second kind of "permanence," namely, the relationship between the designed and the designer. Here he examined the source of "the web of life" (das gegliederte Gefüge, WA, I, 1, 119), the articulated, observable patterns of matter. In the opening line of the second part, Goethe introduced a teleological agent into the process that shapes our world, connecting "that hand" (jene Hand), that architect, to the organization of the natural world. He did not specify the agent, leaving ambiguous the source of the design, although in the last stanza, as a final statement, he opened the ambiguity to creative acts of poets and scientists, to those who shape the world. Indeed, the last stanza is a call to integrate the "beginning with the end" (Anfang mit dem Ende), an appeal to articulate a teleology of organic forms. In closing, Goethe expressed appreciation for the source of the designing hand of the creator, giving thanks to the muse that shapes "content" (Gehalt), which issues from the heart, and gives "form" (Form), which is controlled by the mind.

In later writings Goethe often wrote on behalf of a science that would preserve the harmony and integrity of nature. In his poem "True Enough: To the Physicist" (Allerdings: Dem Physiker) from 1820 he captured this point.[26] In fact, here Goethe gave the topic broader perspective by placing it in the context of the sociology of science. Once again the theme of the poem is the relationship of the subject and object, although this time the subject is Goethe the scientist and the object is the guild of physicists. He introduced the poem with reference to the "philistine" (Philister) observation that "Into the core of Nature / . . . No earthly mind can enter," asking that dissenters, namely, that he and his kind, be spared this label, for they believe they are in every place "at the center" (im Innern).[27] Again in the middle of the poem, Goethe inserts a transition statement. Here he announces that for sixty years he has been saying that nature has neither "core" (Kern) nor "outer rind" (Schale), that it is unified and is "all things at once" (Alles ist sie mit einemmale). The last lines then point to one of the central tenets in his theory of the history of science, namely, that the field is essentially study of the scientist: "It's yourself you should scrutinize to see / Whether you're center or periphery."[28]

Granite, the archetypal rock

The first two volumes of the Leopoldina edition (LA) include most of Goethe's writings on geology and mineralogy, fields of interest that originated from his practical duties as an administrator in the small duchy of Saxony-Weimar. On Sept. 22, 1775, at five in the morning, he arrived in Weimar following an invitation for a visit from Duke Karl-August earlier that fall. And by the next summer this young poet, who had gained instant fame throughout Europe for his novel, "The Sufferings of Young Werther" (Die Leiden des jungen Werthers, 1774), was accompanying the equally young Duke and engineers on expeditions to the Ilmenau valley in Thüringen, in the hopes of reviving copper and silver mines there. These sojourns in the countryside of Thüringen, trips to the Harz Mountains in 1777 and to the Swiss Alps in 1779, as well as contact with Abraham G. Werner (1750–1817), the newly appointed lecturer on mining and mineralogy at the nearby Freiberg

Mining Academy in Saxony, all contributed to his preoccupation with the theories and details of geology over the next half-century.

Most of Goethe's ideas on geology are tightly synthesized in his essay "On Granite" (Ueber den Granit, LA, I, 1, 57–63) from 1784. Today this text is generally recognized as representative of his geological studies, although it could hardly have played a significant role in the scientific community of his day, as the essay was not published and was planned as part of a larger work on the history of the earth's development.[29] And by itself it reads more like a hymn to nature than like a scientific essay. Yet, it does contain the essence of the descriptive and theoretical work which has gained him recognition as a practicing geologist.[30] And it also illustrates once more his view of the au-thor–object relationship in the study of nature as is the case in many of his nature poems. For the present introduction to his theory of the history of science the essay also shows his approach to scientific writing and ultimately to his way of evaluating a historical document. In addition, we once more see in this essay, how his search for shape and form in nature was really a search for borders and transition, for in them he saw the source of dynamics and change in nature.

Goethe began the essay with explanation of the term granite as used in ancient and modern writings, at the same time admitting to the pursuit of his study of granite "with a passionate inclination" (mit einer recht leiden-schaftlichen Neigung, p. 58). He also anticipated reproach for moving from poetry, from topics of the heart, that most recent and fragile organ of creation, to granite, the oldest and most secure "son of nature" (Sohn der Natur, p. 58). In this tone he introduced the reader to the idea of granite as the bottom of the primeval world and the "first firmest beginnings of our existence" (die ersten festesten Anfänge unsers Daseins, p. 59). In this subjective introduction, he proclaims that among rocks, granite remained "the one solid to the core" (die Grundfeste) when "new scenes of destruction" (neue Szenen der Zerstörungen, p. 60) from time to time reshaped the earth's topography.

As discussion moves toward the center of the essay, so does the reader's awareness of an intensifying passion and of an approaching transition to objectivity and distance. In the middle of this display of enthusiasm for the topic, Goethe opened a paragraph by revealing that he had come to these views sitting "on a high naked peak" (auf einem hohen nackten Gipfel, p. 59), reemphasizing the personalized view, which he intensified in the same paragraph by writing it in the first person. As in the poem "On the Lake," the author reveals that at this point he was radically awakened to reality, however, this time, in the essay, by "the burning sun, thirst and hunger" (die brennende Sonne Durst und Hunger, p. 60). From these heights he envisioned the raging waters, the emerging islands of land and the formation of mountain peaks; he saw how, with time, everything before him began to emerge, how in earlier times the earth began to "teem with life" (von Leben zu wimmeln, p. 60). But

15

before the paragraph is out, he has returned to his "study" (Studierstube, p. 60), where he reviews the literature on the earth's formation and on the definition of granite.

The survey of opinions following his rhapsodic introduction to the topic reads like a refrain to the stanza of a hymn, a refrain that retains syntactic harmony through repeated use of the conjunction "at times" (bald, p. 61), at the same time retaining disharmony in the array of scientific opinions on the topic. Namely, at times he reads that the earth's core consists of one solid rock, at times it is layers of diverse rocks, and still at other times it is viewed as consisting of many large independent and unrelated masses of stone. And concerning granite itself he points out that among the Germans as well as foreigners, there is still much confusion: The Italians confuse it with lava, the French with gneiss, and even the Germans had of late confused it with graywacke, a geologically recent mixture of quartz and slate. With this refrain, with these opinions from geologists of the day, Goethe presented the title and argument of the second part, the technical part, of his essay on granite: "Granite as the Basis of all Geological Formation" (Der Granit als Unterlage aller geologischen Bildung, p. 61).

The scientific statement on granite is simply his view that granite is the type of rock that extends both the depths and the heights of the earth. All other rock forms either lie beside it or on it, and it in turn lies on no other rock forms. With regard to the possible depths of the rock he states that, even if it does not contain the entire core of the earth, it is at least "the deepest crust" known to us (die tiefste Schale, p. 62). On the technical side he further defines the form of the rock as consisting of quartz, feldspar, mica, and occasionally schorl, or black tourmaline. These three minerals, he observed, are not united by an outside medium and are by themselves a united whole, which reflects their common origin: "thus one clearly sees, that granite developed from an active crystallization which was compressed inwardly at its origins."[31]

Following this brief description of granite he offered several concluding remarks which essentially project his research in geology and mineralogy over the next decades. First he observed how people generally assume that massive geological formations resulted from catastrophic actions, and secondly that this tendency to equate massive structures with violent forces is common even though daily life gives evidence to the contrary. This tendency he attributed to poets, who imagine in the beginning a raging chaos, at the same time assuring us that his own "spirit has no wings" (Mein Geist hat keine Flügel, p. 62). Goethe, writing in the second, objective part of the essay, pointed out that he is standing on granite and is asking how it developed (entstanden) and how it is constituted (beschaffen, p. 63). Thus, he opened the essay with speculations about granite as a primeval rock and he closed it with plans to study both the form and development of its present state. This essay marks the beginning of his research on an amorphous state of nature, and it also set the course of his

16

search for explanation of the transitional forms which evolve from a primal phenomena of nature.[32]

The search for transition forms is the topic of many sketches, outlines, letters, reports and drawings issuing from Goethe's pen between 1784 and his death in 1832, as in the undated and unpublished essay on "Comparative Suggestions to Unite the Vulcanists and Neptunists on the Origins of Basalt" (Vergleichs-Vorschläge die Vulkanier und Neptunier über die Entstehung des Basalts zu vereinigen, LA, I, 1, 189–91), written between 1788–90. While this essay has served scholars in arguing Goethe's unified theory of geology,[33] the main point of the essay is that basalt represented a problem in Goethe's scheme of geological change, which he hoped to locate in transition forms of granite, a problem somewhat like that of the whale in the transition between mammals and fish, or the polyp between animal and plant forms.

Goethe opened the essay on vulcanism and neptunism by observing the various reasons why basalt had come to be viewed as a product of volcanic action. Supporting this view was the similarity of basalt and lava in their component parts and in their outward appearances, as well as the location of both types of rock in mountainous regions. Confusion, however, set in when in some instances the craters usually associated with volcanic action could not be found. In explanation of their absence Goethe compromised the theories of the Vulcanists and Neptunists by proposing that basalt was the result of both aqueous and igneous action, the product of a "general volcanic ocean" (Ausgeburten eines allgemeinen vulkanischen Meeres, p. 190). Goethe explained away the missing craters by hypothesizing "a period of hot-melt" (in dieser heissen Epoche, p. 190) in which combustible materials had settled next to crystallized basalt, giving source to ever new periods of volcanic flow. He speculated that layers and seams of it should run to the earth's surface where active volcanoes would be visible in "large oceanic bays" (ungeheure Meerbusen) and in "whole volcanic shorelines" (ganze vulkanische Uferreihen, p. 190). Only here, in more recent volcanic flow, would one expect to see the remains of craters created by violent igneous action.

In these speculations on the origin of basalt, Goethe's flight of imagination led him to visualize large regions of volcanoes, such as those in the Pacific basin known to us as the "ring of fire." But this ingenious suggestion of a "general volcanic ocean" was not the only result of his efforts to compromise the thinking of the Neptunists and Vulcanists. Equally significant is the language which he developed for this synthetic reasoning, a language which labels transition and integration in the formation of rocks. In this case he found terms that admit the transitions between molten and solid states of lava, for he argued that one can no longer deny the "close relationship" (nahe Verwandtschaft, p. 190) of basalts and lavas. And so he suggested that, "even if the basalts were not volcanic in origin, the lavas would be basaltic," (Waren also die Basalte nicht vulkanisch, so wären doch die Laven basaltisch, p.

190), a suggestion he grounded in the noun–adjective relationship of basalt and lava. Today it has become common practice to think of the adjective forms, granitic and basaltic, as defining the molten state of lava and the noun forms, granite and basalt, as defining the crystallized form.

As in other essays, the most scientific and technical part of the comparison of vulcanism and neptunism appears in the second half, following a transition statement, in this case a paragraph of only one sentence: "Here, therefore, lies the relationship of basalts and lavas" (Hier läge also die Verwandtschaft der Basalte und Vulkane, p. 190). This relationship Goethe enumerated in four short statements. In the first he argued that basalt could have formed from a general volcanic ocean and could exist where there is no longer volcanic action; second, that new volcanoes could have melted existing basalt deposits; and third, new volcanoes could have emerged from combustible deposits not previously ignited. His fourth point reaffirms the adjective–noun relationship of basalt and lava and refers to the possible results of points one and two as "a basaltlike lava" (basalt-ähnliche Laven, p. 191).

Into middle and old age Goethe pursued his search for explanation of geological change grounded in a view of gradual processes, such as in the weathering of rock clusters illustrated in Figure 1.1. In the essay "Dynamism in Geology" (Der Dynamismus in Geologie, LA, I, 1, 378–81) from 1811, he attempted to explain such processes, distinguishing them from atomistic and mechanical "phases" (Momenten, p. 378), in which the results of a process are frozen. Dynamism focuses on change and development, on "the lively play of elements" (das lebendige Spiel der Elemente, p. 378), and it assumes that all matter is "capable of change" (verwandlungsfähig, p. 379), varying according to the conditions of the time. Dynamism, Goethe argued, "permits an inner development, that is, it permits a collection and attraction of similarities and correspondences to emerge."[34]

With granite he illustrated this principle of dynamism, for granite's mark of distinction is that it "contains nothing and is contained by nothing" (kein Continens und Contentum, p. 379). Rather, it is an integration, "a complete trinity of its parts" (eine vollkommene Dreieinigkeit seiner Teile, p. 379). And when granite yields this distinguishing characteristic, it admits only that one of its component parts has taken dominance, and where granite yields this balanced trinity, there it exhibits the role of dynamism in the metamorphoses of form.

The second half of the essay on dynamism deals with the transition forms that issue from the potential of granite to give up its most distinctive feature, "to yield its character," a "metamorphosis" (Metamorphose) that "can be viewed as an escape from the self, a transition."[35] This he illustrates with the model of a ball that, if one views it from the center, permits "radii in all directions" (Radien nach allen Enden, p. 380).

Goethe concludes the essay by describing the initial metamorphosis of

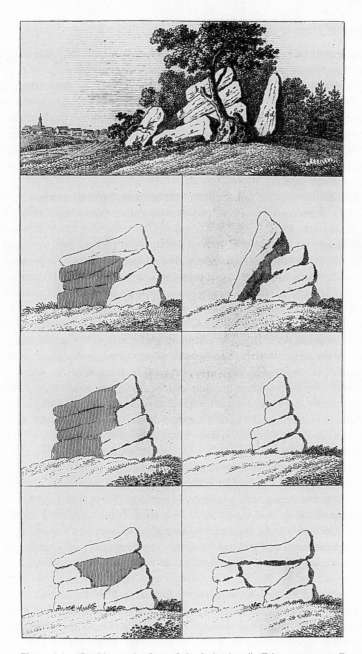

Figure 1.1. "Boulder at the foot of the Luisenburg" (Felsengruppe am Fuss der Luisenburg, LA, I, 1, 112 and LA, I, 8, 168) illustrates the weathering effects on granite. In the top image, Goethe placed a small letter in each piece of the cluster so that he could show how "b" falls forward to the position of "bb" when "a" weathers away, and "d" to "dd" after "c" disappears. In time, only "e" would remain in its original position. Reading from left to right, Goethe shows three other cluster arrangements that could emerge from the effects of weathering. From the Nationale Forschungs- und Gedenkstätten, Weimar.

granite into metal formation and the later ones as mostly fixed compounds resulting from mechanical and atomistic action, nevertheless, forms still susceptible to change from sedimentary processes, such as weathering. But for his theory of granite as the archetypal rock, his closing observation is central, namely, there where he argues that crystallized granite is "the first successful individualization of nature" (das erste gelungene Individualisieren der Natur, p. 381). In second-level transitions organic forms emerge, ranging from corals to ferns, and here Goethe breaks the essay, at the juncture between inorganic and organic studies.

Two further essays, one entitled "Problematic" (Problematisch, LA, I, 2, 154–9), written around 1820, and another called "Geological Problems and an Essay on their Solution" (Geologische Probleme und Versuch ihrer Auflösung, LA, I, 2, 385–9) from 1829, three years before his death, give evidence of his continued struggle with transition and change in geology.[36] He began the former essay by reaffirming his "primary maxim" (Hauptmaxime), that all geological observations begin with granite, but immediately proceeded to the question of "transitions" (Uebergänge, p. 154) in rock forms from granite to one of its varieties. A rich source of such varieties came from the "transition mountains" (Uebergangsgebirge, p. 155) surrounding Karlsbad in Bohemia, where he often sojourned to the watering resorts of the region. The problem discussed in the essay is the taxonomic order of these transition forms, which he tried to arrange according to his theory of granite as the archetypal rock. He gave particular attention to hornstone, a rare stone similar to quartz, observing that at times it seems to contain, and at others to be contained by granite. Feldspar, limestone, and various other "transition rocks" (Uebergangs-Gestein, p. 159) are the focus of the problem, for these forms he hoped also to enter into Joseph Müller's mineral collection, which had been organized according to his theory of granite.[37]

In the second essay on "problems of geology" from 1829, he treated global questions issuing from his concept of granite as the archetypal rock of geological formations. In this essay he serendipitously became among the first to write extensively of a general "ice age" (eine Epoche grosser Kälte, p. 388). But the essay is hardly designed as an argument for a general ice age in geological history. Rather, it is focused on a problem relating specifically to his theory of granite as an archetypal rock and to the related concept of dynamism. In this case he is puzzled by the isolated and erratic deposits of granite masses he had encountered in his travels. These unexplained deposits as well as topographical inconsistencies farther south, around Lake Geneva, had to be attributed to a period of glacier activity greater than those which had been extrapolated from ice flows observed in his day. But "the wings of his imagination," at age eighty, did not stop with description of glacial deposits alone, for he assumed a further distribution of deposits resulting "from the thaw" (beim Auftauen, p. 386) of the imagined ice.

And it is with this speculation of a general ice age that Goethe's search for phenomena of form and change in geology ended. He had devoted nearly a half a century to saving the appearances of his theory of granite as an archetypal rock, and in most of this activity has left us with much more than a description of varieties in rock formation. His legacy lies in the search for those junctures in which a hidden form of kinetics is located.

The intermaxillary bone, a connecting link

Goethe's research in osteology and comparative anatomy also extends a lifetime of effort to preserve the appearance of the harmony of nature. As in geology, stimulation came in the year of his arrival in Weimar, but in this case during travels to Switzerland, where he met the theologian Johann K. Lavater (1741–1801). Lavater introduced Goethe to the field of physiognomy, a field in which the shape and structure of the human skull is examined and correlated with the study of character types, an approach to form integrating art and science in a single act of perception. At that same time Goethe was studying Carl Linnaeus's (1707–78) work on facial bones as the distinguishing features in zoological types, learning the critical tools of analysis and description from the master scientist of the era. And to the physiognomy of the skull and the anatomy of the face, we must add Goethe's studies with Herder in culture and in the anthropological basis of man's relationship to nature, studies dating back to student days at the University of Strasbourg in the early seventies.[38]

The year 1784 marks the beginning of serious writing in the field of comparative anatomy, which began with an essay on osteology in which he asserted in the title that "An Intermaxillary Bone is to be Ascribed to the Upper Jaw of Man and Animals" (Dem Menschen wie den Tieren ist ein Zwischenknochen der obern Kinnlade zuzuschreiben, LA, I, 9, 154–61). The essay bears many of the characteristics of Goethe's other scientific writings, including signs of enthusiasm for the subject, comments recognizing the author–object relationship, reference to the notion of the unity of nature, and evidence of research on the history of the topic. But it also differs significantly from the earlier one on granite, and reflects some of the stylistic features typical of scientific essays of the period. In addition the context of the essay differs in that the scientific community had immediate access to the work, both in its original form and in letter summary, which Goethe distributed to a number of friends, including Herder and Karl L. Knebel (1744–1834), and colleagues, including Justus C. Loder (1753–1832) and Johann H. Merck (1741–91). Through Merck the essay reached the leading comparative anatomists of the period, Blumenbach and Samuel T. Sömmerring (1733–1808) in Germany and Peter Camper (1722–89) in Holland.[39]

Written specifically for the scientific community, Goethe clearly presented his study in the style of an argument rather than in that of a hymn, as was the case in his first essay in geology. He began his argument by announcing that he had made a discovery in comparative anatomy and by stating his thesis that the bones of the upper animal jaw were also present in the jaw of the human being, as shown in Figure 1.2. The "intermaxillary bone" (Os intermaxillare, p. 154), he pointed out, had become significant because it was the "distinguishing mark" (Unterscheidungszeichen, p. 154) between man and ape, a distinction in which the bone was denied the facial structure of the former and ascribed to that of the latter. Thus, in three short introductory paragraphs, in straightforward prose, Goethe announced his discovery, described the topic, and stated his thesis, turning the intermaxillary bone from the status of a distinguishing mark to that of a connecting link, a reversal of tremendous magnitude in an era in which the primacy of divine order as announced in the Hebrew book of Genesis held firm.

And following this bold announcement, Goethe interjected a transition paragraph that begins in the first person, attesting both to his enthusiasm for the topic and to the desire to report his assertion as concisely as possible. The effect of this subjective intrusion exposed his personalized approach to science, in a sense reducing it to the mere opinion of a poet and amateur, a fate he had anticipated in the essay on granite, yet one that may have been designed to soften the potential shock of an assertion linking man and ape. But the impact of the essay was also reduced in ways external to the text, particularly by the informal approach in which the manuscript was distributed, and the selective manner in which colleagues quoted from it.

This initial response to the essay was somewhat out of Goethe's control, because he had asked Merck to serve as a mediator, an individual through whom the study could be channeled to leading scientists in the field. Yet, it was also conditioned by Goethe's mode of presenting the original manuscript. He listed no author, the contents were sent in abridged versions to friends in letter form, and the full document, including all the plates and illustrations did not appear until almost fifty years later, in 1831, in Volume 15, Part I, of the scientific journal, *Nova Acta Leopoldina*.[40] As the text did not appear in print until well after the turn of the century, it was given attention only for isolated examples of comparative anatomy, namely, Goethe was recognized only for having discovered the intermaxillary bone in various animals, such as the walrus. Thus, the thesis of the connecting link was lost in an age not yet ready for the implications of the anatomical relationship of man and animal.[41]

Following the transition paragraph, in the technical part of the essay, Goethe gave a description of the intermaxillary bone, which appears between the two main bones of the upper jaw, and is the one containing the four incisor teeth of the jaw. The sutures defining the bone run between the incisor and canine teeth and upward to the nasal passages, where they connect to the main part of the skull. At the outset Goethe noted that it is difficult to recognize the bone as an independent structure, because the upper jaw varies in overall

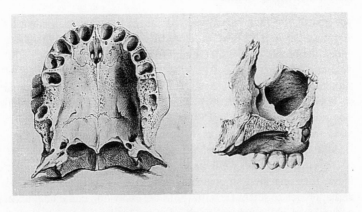

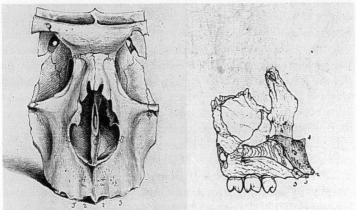

Figure 1.2. "Parts of the human skull" (Teile des Menschenschädels, LA, I, 9, XXVIII). These four images show a three-dimensional view of the intermaxillary bone in the human skull. Other figures from Goethe's collection show the same arrangement in the skull of an ape and in a variety of domesticated and wild animals. From the Nationale Forschungs- und Gedenkstätten, Weimar.

structure from one animal to the next, sometimes stretching forward, sometimes drawn back into the face as in that of man and the ape. Secondly, he examined the inadequacy of the existing terminology for capturing the variation in form: "It contains so many difficulties when it is supposed to fit all animals."[42] Thus, in the main part of the essay, he narrated the search for sutures, for the borders of the bone, in animals ranging from the domestic oxen to the lion of the jungle. In some animals, particularly in the human, the bone has disappeared visually, leading some to conclude it did not exist there. This then became the challenge to Goethe: to illustrate that it is there, even if less visible in some animals than in others.

As conclusive evidence in support of this theory, he argued that the sutures of the bone are most obvious in embryonic forms, where the bones have not yet grown together. He also cited the cleft palate as evidence of fissures denoting the independent structure of the bone. And to these arguments he added the record of history dating back to Claudius Galen (ca. 130–200) and Andreas Vesalius (1514–64), who had recorded the presence of the main sutures in various animal forms. But Goethe also noted contemporary sources, such as John Hunter's *History of the Human Teeth* (1771–8), in which there is "no trace" (keine Spur, p. 158) of the sutures, even though they are "more or less" (mehr oder weniger, p. 159) visible in every skull.

Although the essays on granite and the intermaxillary bone were conceived in the same year, and while he tried to preserve the unity of nature in both of them, they appeared on opposite ends of the scale in terms of Goethe's style and approach to scientific writing. In the essay on granite he proceeded from a general and philosophical point of view, beginning with a theory about the origins of rock formations, a theory to which he devoted a lifetime in search of examples and illustrations. In the essay on the intermaxillary bone, he began with the specific bone from which he proceeded in the next decades to formulate broader approaches to comparative anatomy. Yet, studies in bone and mineral structures remained incomplete, despite a massive collection of artifacts in both fields, for only later, in the study of plants and colors, did he bring his data base into successful integration with a theory of morphology from which he could present a complete topography of nature.

By the middle of the 1790s Goethe's search for the connecting links in nature began to take the shape of a general theory of morphology. In January of 1795, he wrote the "First Draft of a General Introduction to Comparative Anatomy, Proceeding from Osteology" (Erster Entwurf einer allgemeinen Einleitung in die vergleichende Anatomie, ausgehend von der Osteologie, LA, I, 9, 119–53), an outline of his theory of "type" (Typus) and the basis of his comparative methods. Here he proceeded from examples in osteology, particularly from his research on the intermaxillary bone, but in the dozen years following his initial study of the bone, he had extended his search for transition patterns and connecting links into other fields. By 1796, when he prepared the "Lectures" (Vorträge, LA, I, 9, 193–209) for the "General Introduction," he put the study of bone structure into the context of organic and inorganic studies, looking at the question of change and form in minerals, plants, insects, and in a wide range of zoological species. And in part it is this generalized approach to a definition of "type" which marks Goethe's transition from romantic to classical science, to an approach more formal in thought, style, and presentation.[43]

Goethe opened his "Lectures" with the observation that a better understanding of type in geology must come from chemical analysis of minerals, but, in his view, organic studies had not yet come that far and required improved methods of comparative study. He thought new approaches were needed particularly in the study of mammals, for too much of zoology was being studied from the top down. Too often lower animal forms were measured against the human being, and in his view comparative anatomy should first discover "the simple animals" (das einfache Tier, p. 195), and then should seek these forms "in the composite human being" (im zusammengesetzten Menschen, p. 195). The construction of a theory of types, he thought, would facilitate studies in comparative anatomy and bring order to the field.

Goethe attempted to bring order to organic studies through a theory of types, which would be applied equally to the study of fish, amphibians, birds, and mammals. These animal forms, he argued, are all shaped "according to one primeval form" (nach einem Urbilde, p. 198), which varies "more or less" (mehr oder weniger, p. 198) only in its component parts. And once "the idea of this type" (die Idee von diesem Typus, p. 199) is formed, it should be impossible to set a single species up "as a canon" (als Kanon, p. 199) against which all others are measured. Such a canon-free "construction of a type" (Konstruktion des Typus, p. 201) would have to comprise all existing modes of comparison, including those for the comparison of animals among each other, of animals to humans, and more recently those for the comparison of the various human races.

Goethe concluded his lecture on a unified theory of comparative anatomy with discussion of "the concept of organic beings" (der Begriff organischer Wesen, p. 202). These he distinguished from inorganic matter by observing that the latter seem not to exhibit "borders" (Grenze) and "order" (Ordnung, p. 202) as readily as is found in plants and animals. In his view it was the "indifference" (Gleichgültigkeit, p. 203) of minerals that distinguished them from organic bodies. Biological forms of life always exhibit "a kind of inclination" (eine kleine Neigung, p. 203); they show an inherent purpose, a direction even when the "relationships" (Verwandtschaften, p. 203) between organs and organisms are based only on "outward determinations" (äussere Determinationen, p. 203).[44]

Particularly the organs of plants and insects, simple forms of life, supplied illustration of Goethe's concept of forms in process, of structures that exhibited similarity in borders and in patterns of transition. Such organs would illustrate Goethe's "concept of a successive change" (der Begriff einer sukzessiven Verwandlung, p. 208). The vertebrae of animals, for example, were really one organ. But here would lie the difficulty, for when one compares a vertebra of the neck with one of the tail, there seems to be little trace of "form similarity" (Gestalt-Aehnlichkeit, p. 208), a paradox both pleasing and perplexing, for the beauty of an organism lies in its ability to generate new forms, in its telos. Thus, the search for the "modification" (Modifikation, p. 208) of the organs of nature, and the identification of thresholds of change, came to define the mature work of Goethe as a scientist, research generally referred to as studies in morphology.

2

Goethe's classical science

No phenomenon can be explained in and of itself; only many comprehended together, methodically arranged, in the end yield something that could be regarded as theory.[1]

The leaf, an organ in transition

Goethe's search for the principles of structure and change in nature began with a theory of granite and a discovery of the intermaxillary bone, two unlikely topics for a young scientist interested in the kinetics of structural change in nature. However, not long after 1784 his interests began to extend the range of organic and inorganic sciences. He soon admitted insufficient training in chemistry to advance his studies in geology, and from his work in osteology, a science equally plagued with evidence of a static nature, he learned of the limits to which narrated illustrations can aid the presentation of a dynamic nature. Thus, it was in botany, a field of interest dating back to days of gardening with his father and to university studies in Leipzig, where he formalized most clearly his theory of the metamorphosis of types in nature.

In 1790, at the age of forty-one, the results of his studies in botany were published in a document called "The Metamorphosis of Plants" (Die Metamorphose der Pflanzen, LA, I, 9, 23–61). The first printing of the work appeared as a single text complete with all of the tables and illustrations. And almost thirty years later (1817–22) it appeared again as the first section of his "Morphological Notebooks" (Morphologische Hefte, LA, I, 9, 23–61), this time surrounded by shorter essays written in retrospect on the "History of my Botanical Studies" (Geschichte meines botanischen Studiums, pp. 15–19). This second printing also included a follow-up essay on the "Fate of the Printed Text" (Schicksal der Druckschrift, pp. 65–72). Thus, the "Metamorphosis of Plants," the crowning achievement of Goethe's study in the morphology of nature, is in its final form a text set in context. This was a bond established by Goethe's own design, one which became a model for his later research in the theory of colors in 1810, and one that became basic to his theory of the historiography of science as well.[2]

The text–context relationship in Goethe's botanical studies emerged over several decades, beginning with the publication of the scientific text itself, "The Metamorphosis of Plants," in 1790, and ending with the sociology of the text as printed in the "Morphological Notebooks," in 1817–22. Thus, Goethe formalized a pattern observed in his earliest scientific writing, a pattern in which the subject–author became an integral part of the research and writing on the object, at times separated and distanced, at other times integrated and at one with the topic. The difference between this text on plant metamorphosis and earlier ones in other sciences is that it was written in a style conforming completely to the expectations of the scientific community. Only later did he add to the text short essays on topics of a personal and social nature. That is, despite Goethe's separation of text and context in 1790, by 1817 he wished them wedded as in his earlier scientific writing, a point of view that evolved between 1790–1810 from observations on the reception to his text on plant theory and from research in the history of science.

The "Metamorphosis of Plants" follows a strict taxonomic style and is organized into eighteen sections labeled with roman numerals and one hundred and twenty-three paragraphs, each labeled with arabic numerals. In the margins he listed corresponding illustrations numbering a total of sixteen plates. Although the structure is much more rigid than his essay on granite and the intermaxillary bone, it is also aesthetically and scientifically more complete. Indeed, the goal of the total essay is to present the reader with a series of written pictures that illustrate the phases of plant life from dormant seeds to ripening fruit. This series displays plant life as if in the continuity of a motion picture, as an uninterrupted narration similar to the one in his first drama on a human life, on that of Götz von Berlichingen (1773).[3]

Goethe began the essay in the standard fashion with an introduction and definition of terms, distinguishing three types of metamorphosis, regular, irregular, and accidental. In Section I he illustrated the "gradual process" (Stufenfolge) of "plant growth" (Pflanzen-Wachstum, p. 25), beginning with the "seed leaves," or "cotyledons" (Samenblätter, Kotyleden, p. 25), and concluding with the fruit encapsulating the seed. In the main part of the text, from paragraph ten to eighty-one, Goethe illustrated his concept of "the leaf-shape" (die Blattgestalt, p. 45) as a form in process and development, at times more static and at others more dynamic, but always retaining its fundamental shape. This form in process he further explained as visible in six alternating phases of "expansion" (Ausdehnung) and "contraction" (Zusammenziehung, p. 37): The contracted seed leaves, visible to the naked eye when split open, expand to the axis leaves, which contract in the calyx. The calyx in turn expands into the corolla. The third and last phase begins with the contracted stamens and pistils, which expand into the fruit, where new seeds are contained, the source of another cycle in plant growth. The text is richly illustrated with examples from the growth of corn, beans, peas, tulips, roses,

gladioluses, carnations, irises, and narcissuses, namely, with plants of the
garden variety, all showing the "leaflike" structure (Blattähnlichkeit, p. 46) as
the basic pattern of an organism in transition.[4]

Goethe's theory of plant morphology is the realization of goals to which he
had aspired in his research in geology and osteology. He had approached those
fields with the same enthusiasm as he did botany, but the study of plant life
was simply more compatible to his approach, as was the case in later studies
in color theory. In botany the archetypal leaf is readily visible to the naked eye
in the axis leaves, calyx, and corolla, and only in the reproductive organs does
the observation of forms in process require special attention. This he addressed with a number of illustrations focused on the leaflike patterns in the
development of the stamens and pistils, as is shown in Figure 2.1. Goethe had
struggled with this problem in earlier research on granite and the intermaxillary bone, where the forms of a series were not readily visible and where it was
more difficult to acquire the necessary artifacts needed for evidence. Yet, in a

Figure 2.1. "By Goethe in illustration of the stamens which are contained in the
corolla formations" (Von Goethe für Staubblattandeutungen gehaltene Kronen-
bildungen, LA, I, 9, XI). The image at the top, left, shows the nectars of the gladiolus,
and at the bottom the leaf of the sweet William with emerging secondary corolla
formations. The middle image is the corolla of the morning glory with emerging
anthers, and the one on the right shows how the petals of the rose have begun to
withdraw into an anther. From the Nationale Forschungs- und Gedenkstätten, Weimar.

sense, it was in these early studies that Goethe developed his approach and acquired his talents in form perception, his vision of structure in process, and his sense of shape, even though they were for the first time applied successfully and completely in plant theory.

The success of Goethe's plant theory goes beyond his aesthetic sensibilities of perception. It rests also on his relentless search for border experiences in nature. Indeed, he followed this interest into the pathological and aberrant variations, namely, to that juncture at which the abnormal serves an argument in understanding regular patterns. As the cleft palate became proof of a suture in the upper jaw of the human being, so the "Proliferous Rose" (Durch-gewachsene Rose, p. 53) served Goethe as proof that the leaflike structures are at the base of the phases of plant growth. In Paragraph 103, nearing the end of his essay on plant morphology, Goethe wrote that "everything we have tried to grasp to this point with the powers of imagination and with understanding is shown us most clearly by the example of a proliferous rose."[5] Namely, there where we expect the contracted reproductive organs, the plant axis continues upward in a mixture of red and green colors, a mixture of foliage and flower leaves. With the illustration in the top, left corner of Figure 2.2, we see how Goethe tried to show that the extended axis even exhibits "traces of anthers" (die Spur der Antheren, p. 54), evidence of the potential for a normal successive pattern of plant growth.

Also in conclusion to his essay on the theory of plant growth, Goethe included a discussion of "Linnaeus' Theory of Anticipation" (Linnés Theorie von der Antizipation, pp. 55–6). Here he explains that with this concept Linnaeus had observed the successive stages of plant growth as the realization of potential forms of life cycles. But, Goethe pointed out, Linneaus did not advance his theory of plant dynamics because he had based his study on perennial plants, which require lengthier periods for observation of the same growth phases of annual plants. Therefore, Goethe had limited his study to annuals, where the processes are magnified by a constriction of time, and where the life processes can be observed on the surface, rather than under layers of growth hardened with age. With this limitation to annual plants Goethe also held firm to a principle developed earlier in his study of the intermaxillary bone. There he had learned of the advantages of proceeding from simple to complex forms of life. That is, if the study locates archetypal forms in simple organisms of nature, then one can expect these to exist in complex ones as well.

Goethe's theory of plant growth brought mixed reviews, leaving a trail of responses from the scientific community and counter-responses from Goethe that stretched over the next several decades and culminated in the publication of his "Morphological Notebooks" in 1817 (LA, I, 9, 5–83).[6] The first "Notebook" contains ten essays, with "The Metamorphosis of Plants" positioned as number six, the centerpiece of the "Notebook," surrounded by

Figure 2.2. "Proliferous Rose from the front and the back" (Durchgewachsene Rose von vorn und hinten, LA, I, 9 XII). From the Nationale Forschungs- und Gedenkstätten, Weimar.

essays on the sociology of the text. He began the series with an apology for the project (Das Unternehmen wird entschuldigt, pp. 5–6), and in the second and third essays he explained the purpose of the study and gave an introduction to the topic. In the fourth and fifth he documented first the history of his botanical studies and then the development of the scientific text itself.

The four essays following the centerpiece are equally predictable, treating first the fate of the manuscript, then that of the publication of the text, and third his discovery that Caspar F. Wolff (1734–94) was a precursor to his theory of plants.[7] In the last of the ten essays called "A Fortunate Event" (Glückliches Ereignis, 79–83), he ended his discussion of a lukewarm response to his theory of plants on a positive note. He recalled how he had spent time on his trip to Italy in 1786–8, in search of a leaf that would embody the conceptual basis to his theory of plant growth. He recalled primarily how he met Friedrich Schiller (1759–1805) after a lecture in Jena, and how they later came into a conversation on Goethe's theory of plant morphology. From this account we learn that it was Schiller who informed him that the leaf he had symbolically sketched on paper was "no experience" (keine Erfahrung), that it was "an idea" (eine Idee, p. 81), an observation which contributed significantly to the maturation of Goethe's theory of morphology in the 1790s.

The sociopsychological context into which Goethe placed his theory of plants is simply the attempt of an author to record his version of the life of a scientific text. The structure of the essays in the "Notebook" shows in clear lines the patterns of his early scientific essays, particularly the focus on the subject–object relationship and the history of the topic. New and clearer in the "Notebook" is the understanding of his audience, the scientific guild, and of the reception of a text, the recognition that a text has a life independent of the author. Indeed, recognizing the independent life of a text is perhaps his prime motivation for reprinting the essay on plant theory in the context of the "Notebook," for this was an opportunity to condition the reception of the text and to interpret his own study of plant life. From his research in the history of science between 1790–1810, he had learned that the fate of a text was often different from the intention of the author and here he took the opportunity to play a role in determining the fate that would eventually fall to his "Metamorphosis of Plants." Here we see an attempt to preserve a scientific document for its proper place in the history of science, as intended by the author, Goethe.

Colors, the borders of black and white

Goethe's research on optics and color theory forms the fourth and last field of inquiry to which he devoted significant effort. His familiarity with Newtonian optics dates back to university studies in Leipzig, although serious investigation in the field did not begin until several decades later, after publication of his research in botany. In 1791 he rushed the first results of his "Contributions to Optics" (Beiträge zur Optik, LA, I, 3, 6–53) to the publishing house of a local entrepreneur, Friedrich J. J. Bertuch (1747–1822), quickly publishing his research in a style and format similar to the one used in his essay on plant morphology. However, this urge to publish left him with another fragmented piece of scientific writing, for the investigation soon expanded from study of optics to one on all aspects of color. The project ended in 1810 with the publication of a three-volume work "On Color Theory" (Zur Farbenlehre, LA, I, 4, 5, 6). The first volume includes his own theory of colors, "The Didactic Part" (Didaktischer Teil), the second his "Disclosures on Newton's Theory, The Polemical Part" (Enthüllung der Theorie Newtons, Polemischer Teil), and the third his "Materials on the History of Color Theory, The Historical Part" (Materialien zur Geschichte der Farbenlehre, Historischer Teil).

In color theory and optics Goethe followed the pattern of other scientific writings by framing the text in a context and by clearly delineating subject–object relationships. Also, the search for nature's junctures became the central theme in Goethe's efforts to present a complete topography of color. It seems that at this point in his career the focus on boundary experiences became a blinding preoccupation, one in which the errors of a significant part of his optical studies is grounded.[8] In fact, the two publications from 1791 and 1810 are textually related as they are grounded in the same anecdote of Goethe's life, an anecdote narrated in the "Confessions of the Author" (Konfession des Verfassers, LA, I, 6, 412–29), the final chapter of his "Materials on the History of Color Theory." It is in this anecdote that we learn of the source of the border-experience in color theory which led to Goethe's errors in physical optics and his polemics with Newton.

From the "Confessions" of 1810, we learn that he, one day by chance early in the 1790s, happened to "quickly glance through a prism" (geschwind durch ein Prisma sehen, p. 419), rather than letting light fall through it in the manner of standard prismatic experimentation. This serendipitous event, with both fortunate and unfortunate results, explains the direction of research in the "Contributions to Optics," where he records his first experiments with the prism. These are all organized around procedures in which the scientist looks through the prism: "One takes the prism, observes the objects of the room and the landscape through the same."[9] And from this primal act followed the observation fundamental to his theory of colors, namely, the observation that no matter what the position of the prism, everywhere there are bright colors, especially "at the horizontal edges" (an horizontalen Rändern, p. 8) of small objects.[10] Thus, early in his research on optics he came to focus on the borders, on the juncture where darkness and light meet, where colors emerge, namely, at an intersection of polarities, that point where nature is in tension, dynamic and energized.

The "Contributions to Optics" is of particular significance in Goethe's scientific writings as it forms a link between his 1790 essay on plant morphology and the 1810 volume on his theory of colors, a twenty-year hiatus in scientific publication. In structure and style it repeats the pattern of the "Metamorphosis of Plants," including sections with roman numerals and paragraphs with arabic numbers. The similarity is there even in terms of length, the whole work comprising eleven sections and one hundred and twenty-two paragraphs, one paragraph less than in the earlier work on plant theory.

But the "Contributions" also look forward and serve as a primer to Goethe's research on colors,[11] even though plans for publication of further issues stopped with the second one in 1792. At this point, Goethe's research interests began to transcend the narrow boundaries of optics, and a new definition of the field, as he understood it, consumed his scientific interests for the next two decades. In these two decades he expanded the primer to six parts, fifty-six sections, and 920 paragraphs. But it was hardly the quantitative change that made the difference, for the work had changed radically, not in its initial presentation of physical optics, but in its dimensions as an interdisciplinary work, organized according to the phenomena of nature, one ignoring the traditional boundaries of the scientific guild.

In the mature work of 1810, Goethe organized his topography of color so that it proceeded from the eye of the beholder to the artifacts of nature and back to the effects of color on society in general. The physiological, physical, and chemical colors, the scientific parts, make up the bulk of the text, including 680 paragraphs, and the remaining 240 paragraphs cover a range of topics that relate research on colors to scientific method, to mathematics, to industrial applications of color theory, and to the psychological and social effects of color. Thus, his topography of colors is an ordered series of phenomena, radiating from those most immediate to the scientist to those most distant from the scientist, a series moving from the subject to the object and finally to the environment of both. That is, he presents first those colors originating in the physiology of the eye, then those originating outside the eye (those observed through optical mediums), and third, those located in the substances of the environment, in the object itself.

But all instances of color, physiological, physical, and chemical, are organized according to his concept of a primal phenomenon, the polarity of light and darkness. As the plant was organized according to an ideal leaf, so colors were only manifestations and modifications of the polarity of black and white. The polarity of black and white, he argued, was to color theory as attraction and repulsion to magnetism, minus and plus to electricity, and major and minor to music. And with this concept of polarity in color theory, he organized the transitions between disciplines, the variation in color, the possible fabrication of dyes, the reaction of the retina to light and darkness, the colors of shadows, and, alas, the colors of the solar spectrum. His topography of colors is minute and is marked by emphasis on transitions between disciplines, encouraging, if not enticing, the reader to explore further phenomena and to add to the well-narrated taxonomy of colors.

The title to the first paragraph of the text tells the whole story of his theory, "Light and Darkness to the Eye" (Licht und Finsternis zum Auge, LA, I, 4, 26). It is also in this section, in the arrangement of his physiological colors, that Goethe's theory continues to hold the respect of scientists.[12] Unfortunately it is also this bias, this organization of color theory from the eye of the beholder, that limits the value of his discussion of optical color phenomena.

By 1810, when Goethe's color theory appeared in its final form, Joseph Fraunhofer (1787–1826) was already preparing his map of the absorption lines in the solar spectrum, setting a course of specialization in spectroscopy that became a tool of research in many fields of science. In a brief aphoristic essay called "More on Mathematics and Mathematicians" (Ferneres über Mathematik und Mathematiker, LA, I, 11, 367–71), Goethe even discussed the Fraunhofer "cross-lines" (Querlinien, p. 369), but thought they only complicated experiments in color theory, adding distance between scientist and

33

nature. With mounting evidence at his fingertips, we can only wonder why Goethe continued his search for a unified theory of colors that ignored the study of light as a substance.

In Goethe's topography of color the prism represented only one of several "colorless mediums" (farblose Medien, LA, I, 4, 62). In his scheme it was "a turbid medium" (trübes Mittel, p. 158), the first beginnings of opacity which allows the passage of light with resistance, and through which the spectral colors can be observed. In the physical series, colors arise from three different conditions of light, when light is reflected as from an ordinary pane of glass (catoptric colors), when it is refracted as in a prism (dioptric colors), and finally when it is absorded at the surface as on a piece of solid glass, or on a mass of ice (epoptric). He arranged these mediums in a series, beginning with those mediums that do not condition light, those closest to the eye, and ending with those most distanced, those that hide light: "so we find that the catoptric colors connect most closely to the physiological ones" and "the epoptric ones, even though they are in their origins only apparent, make the transition to the chemical colors."[13] Thus, if one accepts Goethe's goal of describing and ordering color phenomena in a series, extending from the most subjective ones occurring in the eye to the most objective ones occurring on the surface of substances, then physical colors are logically arranged as a series, beginning with clear glass and ending with solid glass.[14] However, this goal has little to do with advances in spectroscopy, or with the analysis of light as a substance.

The concept of the polarity of light and darkness seemed to work best as an organizing principle in the topography of physiological colors. Here the eye functions much like a plant, as an organism in a continual state of transition. In this case the transitions range between the two extremes of light and darkness, which in their modifications produce the range of basic colors. In addition, the "retina" (Netzhaut, p. 26) is in a continual state of receptivity to the entire range of colors between the extremes, so that if either light or darkness dominates, the eye is ready also to generate an image of the polarized form. Thus, a bright light would create in the retina a corresponding image of darkness, and so through the range of colors. For this reason Goethe began his topography of colors with black and white images and proceeded to colored ones, repeating the sequence with variations created by the changing conditions in which colors are observed, as in shadows and on gray surfaces.

Although the conditions of vision vary, the range of physiological colors remain located in the eye itself, where Goethe discovered a pattern of complementary colors, each one stimulating in the retina its counterpart. The pattern consisted of three sets of complementary colors, including purple (red-violet) and green, blue and orange (yellow-red), and violet (blue-red) and yellow.[15] These three sets of complementary colors also remained basic to his concept of prismatic colors. In his view these could occur only there where light and darkness come together, for example, next to the slats between the panes in a window frame, at the border between light and darkness, there where he first observed spectral colors as narrated in the anecdote in his "Confessions." In chemical colors, these complementary sets could only be explained with additional theoretical terms such as "intensification" (Steigerung, p. 162), in which a pure version of blue, for example, under certain conditions changes to violet, or yellow to orange.

Saving the appearances of polarity was the most problematic in Goethe's experimentation with prismatic colors.[16] He had found that an object viewed through the prism yields the same set of complementary colors as is found in the physiology of the eye, although they appear only when the environment of the boundaries between black and white is manipulated. Where the boundary faces one way, the colors are violet and blue, and where it faces the other way, orange and yellow appear, as is shown in Figure 2.3. Green and purple complete the complementary set of six colors, but only when the black and white backgrounds, namely, the borders between them, approach each other and are closed as is illustrated in the middle and bottom images in Figure 2.4. Here we see that, where yellow of one boundary approaches and overlaps blue of the other, green appears as in the left sequence, and in the right sequence, where violet and orange meet and overlap, the sixth color, purple, appears. By manipulating the black and white background, or the aperture between them, Goethe was able to create the green and purple found in the solar spectrum, saving the appearances of his theory that colors originate at the threshold between black and white.[17]

Goethe's topography of colors does not account for advancements in special fields like spectroscopy, but it does remain consistent with observations proceeding from those most immediate to the eye of the beholder, and extending to those affecting society at large. In this extension he found linkages to the established disciplines of mathematics, philosophy, physics, and physiology, as well as to practical applications such as in the manufacture of dyes, and finally also to the sociopsychological and aesthetic effects of colors in everyday life.[18] By disregarding traditional disciplinary boundaries, and at the same time, through a focus on the borders and transitions between phenomena, fields, institutions, and societies, Goethe succeeded in bringing the study of colors to a level in which it represented a topography of nature.

In geology this approach to a full topographical description ended where chemical analysis of minerals should have begun. In comparative anatomy it remained a fragmented search for a general theory of bone structure in all zoological species, and in botany it achieved a certain state of completeness, but remained limited to annual plants with assumed implications for perennials. Only in the study of colors did Goethe achieve his goal of writing a complete topography of a science, grounded in a primal phenomenon from which all modification forms could be derived.

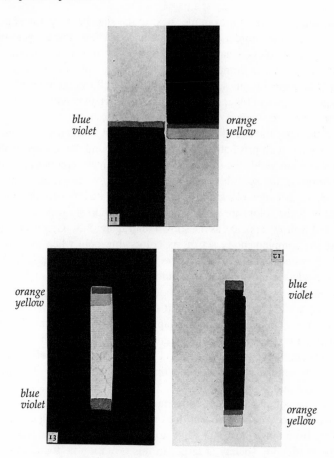

Figure 2.3. "Contributions to Optics" (Beiträge zur Optik, I, 3, 1–53). Goethe attached a collection of loose-leafed cards to his first work on optics so that his experiments on color could be repeated. His card includes the three images used to manipulate black and white borders and backgrounds in the production of prismatic colors. The additive and subtractive mixing used to create purple and green would be carried out by overlapping the squares at the top of the figure. From the Nationale Forschungs- und Gedenkstätten, Weimar.

The experiment, a mediator of continuity

In the organization of the "Metamorphosis of Plants" in 1790 and the "Contributions to Optics" in 1791, Goethe overcame the rhapsodic style and looser structure of the essays in geology and osteology from the 1780s. However, the change was located more in the taxonomic arrangement of the narration itself than in his philosophy of science. Also, although he retained his original concept of contextual writing, he kept it more rigidly separate from his science per se. In this sense, his color theory stands at the highest level of his

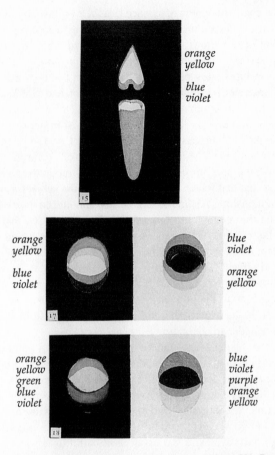

Figure 2.4. "Contributions to Optics" (LA, I, 3, 1–53). Goethe repeats the experiment from Figure 2.3, this time making the borders circular and illustrating more clearly the process of closing the aperture and creating the overlap in the middle and bottom images. Here he shows how the overlap creates the additive and subtractive mixing necessary for purple and green to emerge between violet and orange on the right and yellow and blue on the left. From the Nationale Forschungs- und Gedenkstätten, Weimar.

scientific writing, for he clearly distinguished his description of physiological, physical, and chemical colors from topics peripheral to the phenomena of colors, namely to questions about the inner form of colors, the relations of colors, and the effects of colors. Indeed, to the volume on his color theory he added one on polemics and another on history, retaining the text–context structure of his earlier scientific writing, but parsing the idea into new fields of study, into separate volumes on science, the sociology of science, and the history of science.[19]

The real joints of nature

In addition to the contextual view of science Goethe's philosophy of science was grounded in an understanding of the experiment as a tool for the non-metrical ordering of observations. In 1793, after he had adopted a classical style of scientific writing, he wrote the only essay in which he tried to establish the relationship of his philosophy of science to his science. This essay on "The Experiment as Mediator of the Object and Subject" (Der Versuch als Vermittler von Objekt und Subjekt, LA, I, 8, 305–15) was not published until twenty-nine years later, between 1817–24 in the series of six "Scientific Notebooks" (Naturwissenschaftliche Hefte, LA, I, 8), which appeared concurrently with the "Morphological Notebooks" (Morphologische Hefte, LA, I, 9). In the title of the essay we immediately recognize the pattern of previous writings that had focused on the question of the subject–object, or scientist–nature relationship. Yet, in the title he also announced a new level of consciousness about the relationship. Namely, in the title we see that he has generalized from his previous experiences in scientific research and has attached to the concept of the experiment the role of "mediator" (Vermittler) of both the subject and object.[20] The experiment, in Goethe's view, serves as a vehicle for transmitting the subject and his object of investigation. That is, Goethe is not subscribing to the popular notion that the scientist is dispassionate and detached from his experiment. His view assumes passion and enthusiasm for the object under investigation.[21]

In this essay on the "experiment" Goethe is subscribing to a point of view also found in his early essays, that the experiment does not transmit information about nature alone, but does so equally about the designer of the experiment.[22] Secondly, there is a double edge in the meaning of "Versuch," which means at the same time "experiment" and "essay."[23] Goethe's use of the term is consistent with his approach to scientific writing, for the experiment is incomplete without narrative, and the essay as a narration always remains unfinished. It is a trial, an attempt, a third meaning carried primarily by the verb form, "versuchen." In this sense, the term also explains the fragmentary nature of most of Goethe's scientific writing, and his efforts from late in life to fit them into a constructive whole, as in the two sets of "Notebooks" on science and morphology. That is, his scientific writings are mostly fragmentary, excepting the three-volume publication on color theory, which, in a certain sense, is also gleaned from many fragments, notes, reports, reviews, outlines, and "attempts."

The topic of the essay on the "experiment" is, therefore, the essay itself, as understood in scientific or critical writing. As in much of Goethe's scientific writing, he treats simultaneously science, the sociology of science, and the history of science, in this essay focusing on the latter two and beginning with the sociology of science. He began at the most fundamental level of the philosophy of science, by observing that the human being is usually positively or negatively disposed toward the objects of nature surrounding him. This

38

posture Goethe finds necessary and correct, for it is the source of motivation which stimulates investigation. Yet, at this level the work of the scientist is grounded in his particular bias, which can lead him to a "thousand errors" (tausend Irrtümer, p. 305). For this reason the scientist must overcome the self as a "measure" (Masstab, p. 305), and in its place must organize the "data of judgement" (Data der Beurteilung, p. 305) according to the "spheres of things" (Kreise der Dinge, p. 305) from which they are taken.[24] This requirement of scientific investigation and presentation is the central theme of the essay and of Goethe's philosophy of science.

In the introductory paragraph Goethe acknowledged the scientist's subjective relationship to the object. And in the thesis paragraph he stated his view that objectivity might be gained if the scientist were to use the sphere of nature, rather than the self, as the measure of experimental organization. In Goethe's view, the experiment–essay itself is primarily a reconstruction of experiences in which phenomena discovered and creatively designed, are presented to the scientific community. Thus, the major part of Goethe's philosophy of science is focused on how phenomena are arranged and presented in written form. Because it is a human tendency to measure phenomena against the self, the experiment is primarily an attempt to overcome the self, which, even in its purest form, is only a process of bringing objects of nature into a conceptual relationship, "which they, strictly speaking in themselves never have" (das sie, streng genommen, unter einander nicht haben, p. 310). Although the inclination to devise "hypotheses" (Hypothesen), "theories" (Theorien), "nomenclature" (Terminologien), and "systems" (Systemen, p. 310) is entirely human, resisting these temptations is also the mark of difference between objectivity and subjectivity. In Goethe's mind objectivity is achieved when materials are ordered in serial description and when the abstractions of theories, systems, and hypotheses have been overcome.

And because nature is unified, because nothing happens in nature that is isolated from the whole, the scientific representation, the "experiment–essay," must also illustrate "the connection of these phenomena" (die Verbindung dieser Phänomene, p. 312). Thus the "multiplication" (Vermannigfaltigung) of each experiment–essay is the "real duty of the scientist" (die eigentliche Pflicht eines Naturforschers, p. 312). And so the real charge to the scientist is to record all facts and leave no details to the reader's imagination, to give a holistic representation of nature, even at the risk of creating boredom.[25]

Then with reference to his first attempt at a theory of colors, the "Contributions to Optics" of 1791–2, Goethe explained his understanding of the experiment as a tool for nonmetrical ordering. In essence the experiment–essay is a process of serialization, of placing items next to each other in a natural sequence, not one necessarily isomorphic to nature, but one natural to the environment of the object under investigation. This process of serialization

Goethe compares to the method of continual justification by proofs used in mathematics, a method that relies more on "demonstration" (Darlegung) and recapitulation" (Rekapitulation), than on "arguments" (Argumente, p. 313).[26] Goethe emphasized the difference between this model of mathematical demonstrations, which focuses on the "linkage" (Verbindung, p. 313) and those of the rhetorician, whose arguments can focus on "completely isolated relationships" (ganz isolierte Verhältnisse, p. 313). Goethe concluded the essay in defense of the serial demonstrations as a higher level of science than the formulations of hypotheses and theories based on isolated experiments. This criticism of the "Experimentum Crucis" was made without mentioning the name of Newton, but was a point that would over the next two decades become a central conflict in Goethe's polemics against Newtonian science.

In various essays Goethe came back to the topic of nonmetrical ordering, in some focusing more clearly on a non-Aristotelian, on nondiscrete, aspects of re-presentation of nature's forms in transition. In the essay on the experiment he had found in mathematics a model for his approach to serial description of nature, but, to solve the problem of natural or genetic connections, he was left to his own devices, for in mathematics the relationships between entities did not necessarily lead to borders with natural transitions, to organic nodes between life forms. That is, his mathematical model of serial demonstrations brought him to a point of understanding descriptive proofs with logical but not necessarily natural connections. It is therefore in his writings on the idea of morphology where we find a deeper understanding of his experiment as a tool for nonmetrical ordering.

In an essay simply called "Problem and Response" (Problem und Erwiderung, LA, I, 9, 295–306), he further examined the problem of nonmetrical ordering. Here he located the problem in the paradox inherent in the concept of a "natural system" (natürliches System), for this is a contradiction in terms as "nature has no system" (Die Natur hat kein System, 295). Nature emerges "from an unknown center" (aus einem unbekannten Zentrum) and evolves "to an unrecognizable border" (zu einer nicht erkennbaren Grenze, 295). And for this reason he repeatedly returned to the "idea of morphology," an approach he admitted was grounded in a talent, a "gift" (Gabe) through which the scientist–author gives shape to the amorphous states of nature, which is without center and borders. Thus, overcoming the paradox requires intuitive sensibilities which grasp and define forms in process.[27] But the problem is even more complex, for in Goethe's view, possession of such talents can be a "dangerous gift" (gefährliche Gabe), because with the idea of morphology, namely in the search for forms in transition, one easily moves from the realm of nature into abstractions of the mind, to that point at which the paradox between "natural" and "system" is not easily resolved.

Goethe took the problem of nonmetrical ordering one step beyond recognition of the dangers, or trap, of abstractions. He saw that the paradox was really one in both directions, a richness–ambiguity dilemma. There is, on the one hand, a "centrifugal" (vis centrifuga) and on the other a "centripetal" (vis centripeta) force at play in the description of nature. In the former we are confronted with the problem of overemphasizing the forms of nature, so that the results dissipate into infinity, leaving us with vague abstractions and generalities. And in the case of the latter there is the "urge to specification" (Spezifikationstrieb, p. 295), where excessive detail no longer yields distinctive features, as for example in the genus Erica, shrubs of the heath family with a name but without character.

Thus, Goethe at the same time elevates the idea of morphology to the instrument of the experiment–essay, and reduces it to the status of "a dangerous talent." To this paradox he added irony by observing that both forces of the richness–ambiguity tension operate at the same time, each serving as a "counterweight" (Gegengewicht, p. 295), which adds to the problem, because any attempt to formalize the process didactically would have to show them functioning in concert.[28] But the brief essay does not end here, nor does the dilemma. Closer definition of the synthetic techniques underlying the morphological process would, according to Goethe, require recourse to comparisons and, hence, to an "artificial method" (künstliches Verfahren, p. 296), a recourse to abstractions, which Goethe abhorred. And, he asked, even if a mode of discourse, "a symbolism" (eine Symbolik, p. 296) describing the process, were found, who would recognize it once it is established.

In the paradoxical depths of this essay, Goethe retained his critical posture, but he was unable, or unwilling, to offer a pedagogy of methods in the science of morphology. However, he did conclude the essay with advice against prescriptive approaches to "systematizing" (systematisieren) and "schematizing" (schematisieren, p. 297) nature, suggesting instead that we learn to read between the lines in our study of nature. As he had learned, the real sutures and joints of nature are not on the surface, they are elusive, disappearing and appearing seemingly at random, requiring approaches as unobtrusive as the subject is elusive. Thus, in this essay he simply suggested that rather than forcing nature into the abstractions of our mind, we might try to "overhear" (ablauschen) her secrets, for in this way we neither make her obstinate through our "prescriptions" (Vorschriften), nor are led astray by her "whims" (Willkür, p. 297).

3

Goethe's re-presentation of nature

Symbolism. The anthropomorphism of language. In history in general, but
particularly in philosophy, science and religion, we notice how poor limited
individuals do not find it unworthy to transfer their darkest subjective feelings, their apprehension of confined conditions, into observations on the
universe and its higher noble appearances.[1]

Language, the limits of science

In Goethe's writings there is no major essay or book that would suggest he
gave attention to the topic of language and science. But a reading of his
collected writings in the Leopoldina edition (LA) suggests otherwise. Here in
published and unpublished materials, in sketches and outlines, research notes
and book reviews, essays and monographs, we find that he gave persistent
attention to the topic. And in surveying the material, we find also that his
views on the language of science changed over the years, maturing from early
efforts to systematize technical terminology to later study of the symbolic and
metaphoric nature of scientific language. Running parallel to this maturation
was a shift in his discussion from the language of a particular field of study to
one of science in general, so that over time a metalanguage of science began
to emerge.[2]

   In one of the earliest documents in which he treated scientific language, in
study of the intermaxillary bone, he noted some of the fundamental problems
of language in classification schemes, pointing out that the confused technical
terminology in comparative anatomy was due both to the transition in language from Latin to the vernacular and to the subtle differences in observation
recorded by various individuals in the history of that science:

With the help of Councillor Loder I have prepared the Latin nomenclature which is
appended here as an aid. It was difficult to make this nomenclature applicable to all
animals for in some animals certain parts recede or merge, while in others they may
disappear entirely. Thus, this table would certainly be subject to improvement if
pursued in more detail.[3]

This rather elementary but fundamental recognition of the need for improved technical language persisted through a lifetime of scientific criticism, particularly in his study of color. There he observed that when colors are labeled and abstracted, and then observed in context, they are exposed to a thousand variables: "thereby a diversification into infinity arises, where no language, indeed, all languages of the world together will not reach."[4]

But Goethe's commentary on the language of science matured beyond criticism of the inadequacy of technical terminology. It advanced to questions concerning the social and psychological basis of scientific language, to questions about the prejudices of the mind (Bacon-idols), modes of conception (Leibniz, Wolff, Kant-Vorstellungsart), and canons of thought (Goethe-Autorität), to mention a few topics important to his historiography of science.[5] After his initial contact with the technical language of science in the 1780s, he more often tended to look at the sources of language, at the scientists and at the human dimension of science. This was the focus of his essay on "The Experimenter as Mediator of the Object and Subject" from 1793, an essay summarizing his view of the anthropomorphic basis of science in the thesis that "man takes more pleasure in the idea than in the thing; or rather, man takes pleasure in a thing only insofar as he has an idea of it."[6] In his scientific writings, there is a persistent focus on the individuation of science, as in his review of Athanasius Kircher's (1601–80) "Pyrophylacium," of pyro and hydro processes in geological formations: "In observations on nature, in general and in specific, I have without exception asked the question: is it the object or is it you that is speaking here. And in this sense I observed precursors and colleagues."[7]

The kinds of documents in which Goethe wrote down his observations on precursors and colleagues are varied, as are the themes and topics they contain. But criticism of the imposition of the scientist and the mark of individuality in science and in the scientific text remained central to his views on language and the representation of nature. When he began serious study of documents in color, optics, and vision, around 1800, there followed an increased tendency to specify this discussion with questions on the language of the scientist. The introduction to his "History of Color Theory" from 1810, for example, sets the tone of his view on the logocentric basis of science. Here he observes that scientists are usually predisposed to one or the other "way of thinking" (Gesinnung), but that their "individuality" (Individualität), their form of "discourse" (Vortrag), the "peculiarity of the idiom" (Eigentümlichkeit des Idioms), indeed, "the change of times" (Wendung der Zeit, LA, I, 6, VIII) will modify this predisposition.

Goethe's view that the anthropomorphisms of science were embedded in language evolved gradually, roughly between 1790–1810. Around 1800 he began serious study of documents in the history of science, and it is in this research where we begin to note more formal attention to the language of science and scientist.[8] This is not to say that he dropped earlier questions about the nomenclature of taxonomies, or questions about schools of thought, idols of the mind, and modes of conception, but is to emphasize that after 1800 he refined his perspective on the role of language in shaping the structure of science. Indeed, after 1810 he reduced most observations on science to questions about language, as for example in his critique of the debates centered around Etienne Geoffroy de Saint-Hilaire (1772–1844) and Georges Cuvier (1769–1832) in the French Academy of Sciences.[9] Concerning "The Discussion of Debates on the Principles of Zoology at the Royal Academy in Paris, 1830" (Principes de philosophie zoologique discutés en mars 1830 au sein de l'académie royale des sciences par Mr. Geoffroy de Saint-Hilaire Paris 1830, LA, I, 10, 373–403) Goethe wrote:

We want to try and explain this situation constructively, for we do not want to miss this opportunity to show how word usage in French discourse, indeed, in the polemics of admirable men, leads to significant misunderstandings. We think we are speaking in pure prose and are already speaking tropologically, the tropes are applied differently, are used in a related sense, and in this way the quarrel becomes endless and the riddle insoluble.[10]

Thus, a good starting point for study of Goethe's mature views on the language of science is his work "On Color Theory" (Zur Farbenlehre, LA, I, 4, 5, 6), which includes a section on "Language and Terminology" (Ueber Sprache und Terminologie, LA, I, 4, 221–3). Here he observed that "One never considers fully enough that language is actually only symbolic, only figurative, and never directly, but only in reflection, expresses an object."[11] He goes on to emphasize his particular view of nature, arguing that the "objects" of nature (Gegenstände) are better described as "acts" of nature (Tätigkeiten), which cannot be held fast, but in our need to speak about them, we do so using "all kinds of expressions" (alle Arten von Formeln, p. 221), and thereby approach them symbolically.[12] Then, in the next paragraph, Goethe listed the five "types of expressions" he found to persist in studies in color theory, including metaphysical, mathematical, mechanical, corpuscular, and moral formulas. These, he added, we usually apply with partisan loyalty, making it difficult to avoid identifying with the "sign" (Zeichen) and the "thing" (Sache), to avoid replacing the living being with the word, and "not to kill it through the word" (es nicht durch das Wort zu töten, p. 222).

Goethe went on to explain that, because the "acts" of nature are so easily frozen through language, scientists might designate them with a language drawn from the sphere (Kreis) in which they occur. They ought to use a language and specific forms of expression commensurate with the events of nature. The simplest phenomena should be expressed with primary formulas, while the more complicated ones could be deduced and developed from them, and articulated in a language appropriate to the level of abstraction and degree of departure from the acts of nature. Polarity, for example, he considered a primary term, one appropriately used to describe the primal acts of nature, such as the negative and positive of electricity. The concept was used by Goethe to designate elementary phenomena of nature and in his writings on science, it stands as an example of his understanding of the first order of gradation in the link between nature and language. It stands at the level in which nature is "more or less" represented by language, "where the principal sign expresses the phenomenon itself" (wo das Grundzeichen die Erscheinung selbst ausdrückt, p. 222).

In another text, Goethe specified more systematically the gradations in the representation of nature in language. In his "Outline of Lectures on Physics" from 1805–6, he included a section on symbolism, where he took the more radical position that "through words we neither express completely the objects nor ourselves. Through language a new world emerges which consists of things necessary and accidental."[13] He went on to confirm the view expressed elsewhere that there are various levels in the relationship between language and nature. But here he distinguished the degrees of differences, suggesting a relationship something like the gradations found in a monetary system based on gold, silver, copper, and paper: "In the first ones there is more or less reality; in the last one only convention" (In den erstern ist mehr oder weniger Realität, in dem letzten nur Konvention, LA, I, 11, 56).[14]

Goethe often elaborated upon this view of symbolism in science, at one point stating that in ordinary life we get along without thinking about the inadequacy of language, because our communication is essentially superficial. But "as soon as the talk is about deeper relationships, a new language emerges, a poetic one" (Sobald von tiefern Verhältnissen die Rede ist, tritt sogleich eine andere Sprache ein, die poetische, LA, I, 11, 56). Thus, in three different ways Goethe expressed his view of language as re-presentation, namely, that through language "a new world" emerges, secondly that language only "more or less" relates to the stream of reality, that it tends toward "convention," and finally that in meaningful studies of nature "a poetic" language emerges.[15]

After introducing his essay on "symbolism" with the metaphor of money, Goethe elaborated upon this scheme of four levels of gradation by which language represents nature. In the first he found terms which are "physically real" (physisch real), such as those that express the polarity observed in electricity, and in the second terms that are "aesthetically ideal" (ästhetisch ideal), like the simile that only seems to be related to reality. In the next level of representation, the terms are "mnemonic" (Mnemonik), namely, devices serving completely arbitrary designs. The fourth level consists primarily of terms from mathematics that are "identical with appearances" (identisch mit den Erscheinungen, p. 57) in the most radical sense, because they are grounded in the perception, not in an object. Thus Goethe qualifies the relationship of language to nature as "more or less" and in general as "convention," in effect subscribing to a moderate form of nominalism. But in some of the notes to his research on the history of color theory, this graduated form of nominalism takes on a more radical tone: "All appearances are inexpressible for language, too, is in itself an appearance, which only has a relationship to the others, but cannot reproduce them (express them identically)."[16]

Thus, Goethe argued primarily two points in his view of the representation of nature, namely, that there are gradations in the relationship of language to the stream of reality, and secondly, that scientific expressions can be grouped in typologies as "modes of conception" (Arten der Vorstellung, LA, I, 4, 221). These views brought him to a point at which he saw a close connection between the language of poetry and science, a point at which both were faced with the richness–ambiguity paradox, one which he hoped to solve with the idea of morphology and the experiment as a tool of nonmetrical ordering. Here Goethe raised questions about the role of metaphors in scientific language, an issue in modern philosophy of science precipitated by a gradual loss of faith in the literal language of logical positivism.[17] This abandonment of hopes for a literal language of science, for a sense-datum language, hopes for an adequate technical taxonomy of a field of inquiry, has in our century given rise to an increased tendency to ask with Goethe, as Thomas Kuhn has, whether science is indeed "zeroing in on nature's real joints."[18]

Twentieth-century critics seem to have come to the same point to which Goethe arrived after a lifetime of observing and doing science, to that point, when we realize that the language of science and the "acts" of nature are not identical, when we begin to understand the richness–ambiguity paradox in scientific discourse. It is at this point that we begin to realize with Goethe that science and poetry share tropological properties of language. That is, when Kuhn writes of "acquiring exemplars" and of "a learned similarity relationship in science," and when Max Black defines metaphors as "conceptual archetypes," or as "creating similarities," they parallel the views of the literary critic, Ernst Curtius, who described literary topoi as aids in poetic composition, as "storehouses of trains of thought."[19] And the perspective of all three, Black, Kuhn, and Curtius, seems to be a refrain from Goethe's observation on the Saint-Hilaire–Cuvier debates in 1830 that "we think we are speaking in pure prose and are already speaking tropologically" (LA, I, 10, 398). That is, the language of science is human, it is individual, and, as Goethe observed in his research notes on the history of color theory, it is the language of anthropomorphism that provides the symbolic basis of science. The dark subjective feelings, which Goethe observed in the opening passage, are the anthropomorphisms that surface in language, which we tend to praise in poetry but ignore in the sciences, where we believe we speak in "pure prose," and as Goethe put it in his analogy of money and language, "words are as strong as money. But there is a difference in money" (Verba valent sicut nummi. Aber es ist ein Unterschied unter dem Gelde," LA, I, 11, 56).

Concepts, the richness–ambiguity tension

In studying documents from the history of science, Goethe became particularly aware of how a field of inquiry could become saturated with terms of specification, eventually reaching a point at which it no longer functioned synthetically.[20] Especially the terminology used by tradesmen and craftsmen in the manufacture of colors and dyes had become problematic, for in an attempt to accommodate the increasing variation in shades of color, the terminology had become richer and the terms more discrete (ein unendliches Heer von Farbenindividualitäten, LA, I, 4, 183). But at the same time they had become more difficult to master, they were less flexible and applicable to changes in science and society. From this trend Goethe observed "that man has always sought more exact determinations, and through language has also tried to hold firm and isolate the fixed and specified."[21]

According to Goethe, the trend in the history of color theory was toward stabilizing phenomena and toward controlling the language needed to express color phenomena. This constriction of the stream of reality, he observed, was more characteristic of some writers, languages and epochs than of others. He felt Greek documents, for example, showed a flexible language as their terms did not compartmentalize colors, for they tended to capture the borders, fringes and levels of intensification of a phenomenon.[22] In that particular culture, the language included expressions for colors in the verb form, so that yellow, for example, might be related to red as an inclination, and just as yellow can "redden" (röteln), so red can "yellow" (gelbeln, LA, I, 6, 37). German color designations had the advantage of originating from four monosyllabic terms; that is, *gelb, blau, rot,* and *grün,* and as these terms are etymologically primary, like the *incunabula verborum* of the Stoics, ergo can no longer be traced etymologically, they represent only the most general idea of color without reference to specific modifications (LA, I, 4, 183). Goethe found most favorable a terminology that showed the vitality of, the continuity between, and the aura around, phenomena of nature, and in his history of color theory he evaluated texts accordingly.

In his observation on scientific documents, Goethe also explored the extent to which the writer distinguished between words, concepts, and objects, and the role of experimentation in making these distinctions.[23] In the writings of the ancients he observed that they had no clear conception of the function of an experiment, which led to the mixing of ideas, concepts, and phenomena. In his view "experiments are mediators between nature and concept, between nature and idea, between concept and idea,"[24] they are aids in the nonmetrical ordering of the objects and phenomena of nature. Thus, Goethe noted from the "language usage" (Sprachgebrauch, LA, I, 6, 37) of Greek and Roman writers, that they often reversed general and specific color terms, and sometimes the nuances of color were labeled with the species term and sometimes with the genus. The mark of the modern scientist, wrote Goethe, is possession of sufficient reflective skills (philosophische Bildung) to distinguish between himself, his language, and the object of his investigation: "He must avoid turning perceptions into concepts and concepts into words and then operating with these words as if they were objects."[25]

The richness–ambiguity problem, which Goethe observed in scientific language, had begun to emerge early in his century as two distinct traditions.[26] Those in one tradition, of which Christian Wolff became representative, attempted to correlate words with events, seeking an isomorphic relationship of language, object, and experience. Those in this tradition preferred that individual words be sharply defined and that they be distinguished from other terms so that there would be no vagueness as to the specific value of the term. Thus, words became a series of discrete signs identified with even more closely limited objects. And, for those who viewed words as discrete entities, there were Aristotelian procedures to uniquely assign one phenomenon to one term, "per genus et differentiam."[27] It was in the scientific work of this tradition, where Goethe observed an "urge to specification," where he observed the tendency toward increased quantification of language and nature. It is in contrast to this tradition that we see how his own approach was a search for language diversification and for alternative modes of discourse.[28]

Goethe prized the contribution of those like Linnaeus for enriching the language of science by specifying each newly discovered discrete entity.[29] But he also recognized his own talent for creating a language that focused on the object and captured the aura surrounding the object, for defining the thresholds between objects, namely, the transitions where he attempted to locate the kinetics of organic life. And, while this attempt to bridge the richness–ambiguity tension clearly placed him outside the guild of professional scientists, it also identified him as a language philosopher in the tradition of the "romantics," like the philosopher Johann G. Hamann (1730–88), who had emphasized a language of vitalism, a language that probed areas of ambiguity and vagueness without sacrificing fixed correlations between terms and events.[30] Within the romantic tradition of language philosophy, there was the tendency to focus on a phenomenon and at the same time to use language as a way to multiply the correlations between symbol and reality; the concern was to characterize the essential qualities of an event. Thus, concepts were not sharply delimited, indeed, they were left open-ended as a means of capturing relationships to other terms, concepts, and phenomena, as a way of engaging the totality of experiences with a living and dynamic world.

For writers like Hamann, Herder, and Goethe, words correlated with specific phenomena, but they also overlapped in meaning, had fuzzy edges, thus allowing flexibility in specification of the phenomena of nature and culture. It is said of Herder that his concepts were "more painted than logically drawn,"[31] and that his critical terms had not only a focus of meaning, but also fringes of meaning. Indeed, it is the aura of meaning surrounding the terminology of these writers that makes translation of their expository prose so difficult, for their terms often defy singular explanation, and consequently defy technical application. The writers from this tradition may be studied best for their words of centrality, their ability to focus without delimiting, for characterizing that which cannot be specified and quantified.

Thus, Goethe, in searching for a descriptive language of historiography, looked beneath the chronological structure of history for meaningful tendencies in science, emphasizing that an historical description cannot be divided quantitatively by centuries, for human lives and actions overlap from one century into the next, and yet, "all classifications, if one looks at them closely, are derived from some kind of tendency" (aber alle Einteilungsgründe, wenn man sie genau besieht, sind doch nur von irgend einem Ueberwiegenden hergenommen, LA, I, 6, 109).

Goethe was not alone in this understanding of the language of history,[32] for particularly the histories of literature written during his day reflected methods of nonmetrical ordering. Johann G. Eichhorn (1752–1827), for example, wrote that "the history of the arts and sciences, their beginning, continuation, and their various changes can never be presented as separate from the history of social conditions. For culture and literature are twin sisters of a common father, who through mutual accomplishments incessantly support each other."[33] Indeed, Franz C. Horn (1781–1837) not only advocated a holistic history but also recognized like Goethe that a qualitative language was central to writing such history. He developed vitalistic concepts such as "formability" (Bildsamkeit) and "originality" (Genialität) and, like Goethe, he emphasized the need for gradations in the relationship between language and the stream of reality: "The spirit of a language is not found in its quantitative perimeter, but like in the life-principle of the human being, it is found in its center, from which it determines its range and obtains its color and complexion."[34]

Herder, too, tried to capture the heartbeat of a culture, the voice of a people, with a language that penetrated the events of a dynamic world and captured values that extended beyond the artifacts of history. Thus, one of the key concepts of his historiography, "empathy" (Einfühlung),[35] expressed the idea that a writer must have an affinity and understanding for a subject in order to evaluate it properly. In it he located his dictum that "language is a tool of science and a part of the same: Whoever writes on the literature of another nation cannot ignore its language."[36] It is this perspective Goethe took seriously in his evaluation of the science of other cultures, a perspective important to questions in historiography, one that he shared with Herder and applied to his own theory of the history of science.[37]

Goethe's attention to the language of scientific texts was born in a broader movement, in which the potential of the German language for literary and scientific discourse was realized for the first time in the history of Western civilization.[38] But his observations on the idiom of scientific texts were unique, for it was through his universal genius as poet, scientist, and historian that he came to recognize the biographical and logocentric basis of developments in science.[39] Indeed, he learned, after many years, how language hardens with use, confining both mind and matter: "Experiments continued over many years have taught me something else, taught me: that phrases continuously repeated in the end ossify into conviction and completely numb the organs of perception."[40] And because the text is the measure of science, he put the study of an author at the center of his research in the history of science. He explained that his approach is grounded in the assumption that study of a text yields an understanding of its author as a whole person, as a sociological and psychological being: "for when one has claimed that the style of an author is the whole man, then even more so the whole person should contain the whole author."[41]

Polemics, bridging science and history

Goethe's science was shaped by a search for the elusive sutures, the hidden borders, the key linkages, namely, by the recognition of thresholds in nature, where the study of static forms yielded to a science of dynamics. He believed in the study of a vital and unified nature,[42] one focused on the search for the serial relationships in nature, at each turn putting emphasis on a border–experience, on that juncture where the "real joints of nature" are located, on that point where lines and connections show that nature was in a continuous state of flux. Science, then, was the re-creation of the border experience, the "attempt" to narrate nature, an "experiment" in the re-presentation of growth, of nuances in change. At this level science became the task of those individuals who are at the same time poet and scientist, of those who synthesize imagination, observation, and thought in the act of language.

Goethe's science was a narration of the acts of nature as he had found them in the transformation of rocks, in the linkages of bones, in the transitions of the leaf, and in the generation of colors. But these acts of nature could only be approximated by the poet–scientist, they could only be presented anew, as a mere version of the original. In this view, he acknowledged the limits of language as well as the tensions in concept formation. Here, namely, in the inadequacy of scientific instrumentation, Goethe located polemics, which, he thought, had to materialize, because the language and concepts of individuals and whole schools of thought cannot fully re-create the acts of nature, a situation ultimately leading to competing languages of science.

Goethe found evidence of competing versions of nature in all of his scientific work, in geology, botany, anatomy, and optics, and, in the boundaries between versions of these fields, he located polemics, the conflict over interpretation, but also that juncture at which truth begins to crystallize. That is, science began to achieve clarity at the point at which the language of the self and that of others, where communication, argumentation, and rhetoric met in criticism, a form of scientific progress supported more by debate than by a system of logic.[43]

In the rhetoric of scientific authorship, Goethe found a new border–experience, one located between the science of the self and that of the other, the latter belonging to historiography, for the science of the self was current, it was alive and immediate, because it was in reaction to that of others. And so it was in polemics that Goethe found the juncture at which science and historiography met, that state of science marked by competing narrations of nature.[44] Thus, Goethe came to learn, particularly from his research in chromatics, that science was like nature, that it had its own elusive sutures, namely, junctures at which differences in language marked the stress, tension, and conflict in the human drives to knowledge.[45]

For Goethe, scientific discourse gained its weight and consistency with "attempts" to describe and explain the full range of phenomena, the entire spectrum of collected acts of nature, for at this point observation became theory, as for example in his own metamorphosis of plants. That is, here the leaf was no longer an isolated object of nature, but gradually emerged as an ideal type concept, a concept not defined but one narrated as a series of phenomena. And it was at this level at which science also became a social phenomenon, a point at which opposing theories met and conflicted, giving rise to scientific polemics, the genre defining the border–experience between his and Newton's approach to the study of chromatics. To this juncture, Goethe dedicated the second of his three-volume work on chromatics, a line-by-line critique of Newton's optics, focusing the differences on competing languages, and shaping a transition in the narration from the didactic to the historical sections of his project in chromatics.[46]

Goethe's volume of polemics with Newton was organized in the style of his classical science, consisting of 680 numbered paragraphs, in total forming a bridge between his science and history, in detail examining the language and concepts of a competing approach to chromatics. In structure it also followed the pattern of his scientific writings, near the middle, in paragraphs 231–8, interrupting his line-by-line critique of the first book of Newton's *Opticks* (1704) with an "overview of the following" (Uebersicht des Nächstfolgenden, LA, I, 5, 86–8). Here he explained the origins of the text and the theory, distancing himself by examining the main issue, by focusing on "the central statement" (der Hauptsatz, p. 86), namely, "that the homogeneous lights which are separated from the white heterogeneous light, are unchangeable" (dass die aus dem weissen heterogenen Licht geschiedenen homogenen Lichter unveränderlich seien). Then he pointed to the origins of the polemical battles, to Edme Mariotte's (1620–84) response to Newton's first publication on light and color in 1672, to Mariotte's attempt to repeat the "experimentum crucis," the central issue in the conflict between Goethe and Newton, an issue of approach and method as much as one of the results of science.[47]

In the introduction and in the conclusion to his volume, Goethe addressed the question of the function of his polemics, recognizing in it a bridge between his science of colors and his history of the field. In the second half of the introduction, he explained the transition with an "interruption" (Zwischenrede, p. 5), eight paragraphs explaining that the volume was written as a way to distinguish his science from "that which originated with Newton and spread through the educated and uneducated world" (die von Newton herstammend sich über die gelehrte und ungelehrte Welt verbreitet hat). He emphasized at the outset that Newton's "way of thinking" (Denkweise) was not that of his own, "not one characteristic of us" (uns nicht etwa eigentümlich angehört), and nor for that matter was it a way of thinking original with Newton. Indeed, he argued, it was one with traces found "in the earlier times" (in den frühern Zeiten, p. 6), one that stayed alive "so many centuries" (so manche Jahrhunderte) "and from time to time has resurfaced, of which history will instruct us more" (und ist von Zeit zu Zeit wieder ausgesprochen worden, wovon uns die Geschichte weiter unterrichten wird).

In the "conclusion" (Abschluss, pp. 193–4) to the volume on polemics, Goethe observed that many years of experience had taught him that in "conflicts of opinions" (im Konflikt von Meinungen, p. 194), what matters is not how you spare your opponent, but how you overcome him, "that no one lets himself be flattered and complimented from his position of advantage, rather that he, if it cannot be otherwise, at least wants to be thrown out."[48] This view of the ruthless conditions of scientific life was grounded in experience with many opponents, of whom he found none more obstinate than those of "the Newtonian party" (als die Newtonische Partei). But then in the final paragraph, at the edge of the transition from the polemics with Newton to the history of color theory, Goethe softened his own combative posture, observing that, to a certain extent, "the battle" (der Streit) will be resumed "in the succeeding historical section" (in dem folgenden historischen Teile), where the reader will be introduced "to this milder treatment" (zu dieser milderen Behandlung). Here he explained how he could detach himself from the battle, because one needed only to show how "such an extraordinary man" (ein so ausserordentlicher Mann) came to his errors, and how "so many remarkable people" (so viele vorzügliche Menschen) came to his support. This account, he pointed out, must excuse rather than accuse the "founder" (Urheber), the "students" (Schüler), and the "chiming and persevering century" (das einstimmende und beharrende Jahrhundert).

By the time Goethe began his project in chromatics, Newtonian optics was a tradition, it was almost a century old, it stood as a canon of thought, so that Goethe's own publication of a volume on "polemics" primarily served to close a gap between science and tradition.[49] It served him as a heuristic device, as a literary approach to distinguish and to connect his own work to the history of optics and color theory. Goethe did not limit the concept of "polemics" to its traditional meaning, as a confrontation among contemporaries, as for example in the debate between Newton and Leibniz on the discovery of calculus.[50] That is, Goethe brought new significance to the meaning of polemics by using it in the history of science as a narrative technique, giving life to history by framing it in a dialogue. In this way, he not only focused the differences in competing languages of science, but he also added new value to the concept by using it as linkage between science and history.

Most opponents in scientific polemics, in retrospect, rue the day of public engagement in debates,[51] and by the time Goethe published his project on color theory, polemics, as a form of public behavior directed at a specific colleague, had gone out of style, even in the form of book reviews, the most popular source of polemical materials.[52] But Goethe's decision to publish a volume focused on the distinction between his theory of colors and that of Newton was not a feud with a contemporary figure, it was a confrontation with a tradition, with a canon of the field.[53] His polemics with Newtonian optics was primarily a way to confront a legacy and to legitimate his own approach as a competing science of color. And in this effort, Goethe maximized polemics as a rhetorical device to defend the old truths about color, to shift emphasis from laboratory control of colors, from Newtonianism, to the study of the phenomenon of color itself.

Goethe used the concept of polemics as a rhetorical device to link his science to scientific tradition. And between his science and that of the canon, at the border, he found the real issues of science, indeed, there he saw the vitality, the driving force of the history of science, not in the finished laws of science, but in the confrontations which arise from different ways of thinking and presenting science. Thus, he did not propose "to stand on the shoulders of giants," as Newton had, but in keeping with the revolutionary spirit of the turn of the century, he chose to confront tradition, to "storm the Bastille," to turn the tide of time.[54] From Goethe's point of view, Newton's optics was a problem of historiography and science, it was a canon of history with power reaching into his own day and conflicting with his own experiences in chromatics. In Goethe's view, science is always current, hence, in conflict with tradition, and thus the boundaries between science and tradition become the focus of studies in the historiography of science.

Goethe's "polemics" with Newton's optics was a discussion of competing languages, one, that of Newton, located in the texts of history and the other in his own writings. This juncture was a miniature version of major transitions in history, for example, between the science of the ancients and that of the moderns. Here he found the Middle Ages, a period of history largely unexplored in his day, a gap Goethe solved with another heuristic device, the aphorism. He closed the gap with a series of terse statements on historiography, thus bridging ancient and modern science with a discussion of his theory of the history of science, a substitute for discussion of medieval science. Indeed, the theme of these statements is the gap itself, providing him with the opportunity to recognize the missing link in the history of science, namely, medieval science, and with the possibility of discussing a way in which the threshold between science and tradition might be approached.

In this series of statements on the boundary between science and tradition, Goethe observed that "there are two kinds of experiences, those of absence and those of presence" (Es gibt zweierlei Erfahrungsarten, die Erfahrung des Abwesenden und die des Gegenwärtigen, LA, I, 6, 86); that is, we are continually exposed to the "transmission" (Ueberlieferung, p. 87) of foreign experiences, namely, to those of other scientists, past and present, thus, in science we are continually "in battle" (im Kampfe). In Goethe's view, it was the urge to follow experiences on "our own authority" (auf eigene Autorität) that often draws us into "debate" (Streit). Thus, "the conflict of the individual with immediate experience and with distant tradition is the actual history of science; for, in the final analysis, that which happens refers to the diligent individual, who is supposed to gather, separate, edit, and collate everything; whereby it really does not make much difference whether contemporaries support or resist such an effort."[55]

Science, for Goethe, was nature re-created in the experience of an individual who was at the same time scientist, poet, and historian. It was a process in which the author mediated between his experience and those of others with competing views. And at that juncture, between him and others, Goethe found the genre of scientific polemics, a genre shaped by the gap between the science of the self and that of the other.[56] In this gap, Goethe recognized that boundary where he saw how scientists tend to differ in the way they use language, the instruments of mediation, some forming concepts contributing to the specificity of the word-referent relationship, and others to the generality of the word-environment relationship, the former losing itself in a richness of terms, in terms correlated with data, and the latter losing itself in an ambiguity of symbolism, in terms of variance and flexibility. In these two observations, in the limits of language and in the richness–ambiguity tension,

Goethe located his understanding of the rhetoric of scientific polemics, a genre of writing that connected his science to the history of science, a discipline that Goethe pursued apart from his research in geology, osteology, botany, and color theory.

Part II

The shifting map of history

There is no longer any doubt in our day that the history of the world must from time to time be rewritten. However, such a necessity does not develop because many new events have been discovered, but because new perspectives are being expressed, because the companion of a progressive era is being led to a position from which the past can be viewed and evaluated in a new way.[1]

4

Goethe's narrative strategies

Goethe, like many of his contemporaries, was well aware of the changing views of man, time and history. With others he actively participated in the revolution in historiography, an event centered in eighteenth-century Germany and roughly spanning his lifetime, commencing with the appearance of Georges Buffon's (1707–88) *Natural History* in 1749 and concluding with the first publication of Charles Lyell's (1797–1875) *Principles of Geology* in 1830–3.[2] Within this period global schemes of history began to appear in Germany; Immanuel Kant (1724–1804) wrote his theory of the origin and constitution of the universe (1755), Gotthold E. Lessing (1729–81) conceived the notion of two elementary phases in the progress of man toward immortality (1780), August Ludwig von Schlözer (1735–1809) defined the field of universal history (1772), and Herder wove into a single composition the story of the birth of the universe and the diffusion of national cultures across the face of the earth (1784–91).[3] The period was pregnant with historical concepts in which the earth began to acquire a history, the literal truth of the Old Testament was challenged, man became anthropological, and space and time took on dimensions no longer expressible in ordinary language.[4] These were the new perspectives which came about at the turn of the century and in the decades 1790–1810 they formed the intellectual background to Goethe's independent contribution to the revolution in historiography.[5]

Goethe was particularly impressed by Buffon's *Natural History* for its views on man's past; two years after the 1778 edition appeared, he wrote a defense of Buffon's attempt to define the epochs of the earth's history numerically:

The *Epochs of Nature* by Buffon are excellent. I agree with it and will not allow someone to call it an hypothesis or a novel. No one should say something against him concerning details unless a more unified and comprehensive picture can be offered. At the very least the book appears to me to be less of an hypothesis than the first chapter of Moses.[6]

This bold and perhaps impudent comparison shows the effect writings in natural history, like the work by Buffon, had upon the young Goethe. These impressions were documented later in life in the essay on the polemical debates between Cuvier and Saint-Hilaire: "how early an affinity to natural history, vaguely but persistently, affected me" (Wie früh ein Anklang der Naturgeschichte, unbestimmt aber eindringlich, auf mich gewirkt hat, LA, I, 10, 382).

Goethe's own work in natural history does not have the scope of that by Buffon. Goethe focused more on the development of structure and form in nature, on the processes visible in the formation of bones, rocks, and particularly in plants. From this kind of work Goethe developed his understanding of time and process, as in a sketch of the epochs of the earth's formation, an organic process he compared to logarithmic progression (Neperische Stäbchen).[7] Early in his life Goethe recognized the necessity of collecting fauna and flora in order to better establish the epochs of natural history and in 1782, in a letter to Merck, he anticipated the day when fossil collections would be recorded more systematically and would be ordered "relative to the epochs of the world" (verhältnismässig zu den Epochen der Welt, WA, IV, 6, 77). As director of the museums in Weimar and Jena he followed this development closely, particularly in paleontology and stratigraphy, fields of study that eventually brought such order to natural history.

Focusing the questions of history

Through his studies in morphology Goethe came to new ways of thinking in which the static structures of nature were viewed in process.[8] Goethe, like others in his day, recognized the inadequacy of classical taxonomies for a description of dynamic processes in nature. It is this urge to represent organic and inorganic nature as living and vital which gave his writings developmental overtones and eventually contributed to his understanding of form and process in historiography. These overtones were evident early in his life, as in his essay on the intermaxillary bone, where he observed in the jaw of animals and human beings the appearance, disappearance, and reappearance of the sutures that identify the bone, a fluctuation in variables respective to the age and species under observation. Recognition of the bone as a form in process meant a great deal to Goethe, for it supported the changing conception of man suggested in writings like those by Buffon. To Goethe the bone meant a link between man and animal and it is to Herder, the emerging author of historical anthropology, that he reported this discovery: "I have found – neither gold nor silver, but what gives me untold pleasure – the 'os intermaxillare' in man!" (Ich habe gefunden – weder Gold noch Silber, aber was mir eine unsägliche Freude macht – das *os intermaxillare* am Menschen, WA, IV, 6, 258).

Goethe's approach to the study of the intermaxillary bone soon became typical for his nature studies. He tended to view science from the perspective of man, to relate the phenomena of nature to the history of man's search for an understanding of them. Thus, the "discovery" of the bone was less significant for the field of comparative anatomy than for the anthropological and philosophical perspective it gave to views on human history. At least half of the essay is devoted to the significance of the bone and to the history of the "discovery," to individual contributions in this discovery, such as those by Galen and Vesalius. And so one of Goethe's earliest investigations of nature shows concomitant interests in the history of science.

Equally important to the development of Goethe's concept of time were studies in culture, particularly in biblical and oriental criticism. Here again others like Buffon, Herder and Eichhorn established the broad philosophical framework for Goethe.[9] Buffon's seven epochs of the earth's history ranged from 3,000 to 35,000 years, defining variously the length of each of the seven days of Hebrew Genesis. And Herder's panhistory placed the dawn of human civilization in the general area of Asia, embracing in a single study the development of stars, planets, and all living species on the face of the earth. Many in this period recognized the need to reevaluate notions about time and, indeed, in his survey of historical scholarship (1812–20), Ludwig Wachler (1767–1838) listed over thirty studies in chronology alone, including James Ussher's (1581–1656) *Annales Veteris et Novi Testament; a prima mundi Origine deducti* (1650), the popular measure of historical time, even to the end of the eighteenth century.

In culture studies Goethe also understood, but avoided, expanding upon the broad conceptual schemes of history. Instead he favored investigation of issues focused in specific events, from which broader implications of the concept of time could be derived. Like in the study of the intermaxillary bone, that of Hebrew chronology was controversial, and at the same time fundamental to new conceptions of man and history. When Goethe began critical examination of the Bible in 1797, the field had already been the source of polemical debates for almost a century, first between Hermann Reimarus (1694–1768) and Johann M. Goeze (1717–86), then at mid-century between Johann D. Michaelis (1717–91) and Hamann, and again in the early decades of the nineteenth century between Josef von Hammer-Purgstall (1774–1856) and Heinrich F. Diez (1751–1817).[10] At issue in these debates was the formal criticism and scientific authority that began to dominate interpretations of the Bible.[11] Goeze protested Reimarus's rationalism, while Hamann reproached Michaelis for not understanding the symbolic value of oriental writing in general, that is, both were criticized for narrow and factual philological treatment of the Bible and Eastern forms of literature. In the last round of debates between Hammer-Purgstall and Diez, in the second decade of the nineteenth century, the issues were no longer strictly theological. By this time the debates, and Goethe's participation in them, focused on technical questions, primarily on the theory and methods of translation.[12]

Between 1810–20, following publication of his history of color theory, Goethe researched the history of Arabic literature as background study for his cycle of poetry, which he published in 1819 as the "West–Eastern Divan" (West–östlicher Divan, BA, 3, 9–160). However, the first evidence of concentrated research into Eastern cultures came at least a decade earlier, in 1797, at a time shortly preceding research on sources in the history of color theory.[13] Here, in an exegetic experiment on the "Israelites in the Desert" (Israel in der Wüste, BA, 3, 256–75 and Vorstufen und Vorarbeiten zu einzelnen Abschnitten, 381–400), we find a focus on the specific question of how long the Israelites actually wandered in the desert on the return from Egypt to their homeland.

In the essay Goethe asserted that they could not have spent forty years there, as it is not possible to account for at least thirty-six years and for eighteen to twenty place names. Goethe explained that the entire story of the Israelites in the desert is best understood in symbolic terms. He thought that a time span of forty years simply represented a basic human fear of the future (Drohung der 40 Jahre, BA, 3, 388), a fear that they might end up spending a lifetime there, a fear that was real enough, but was never fulfilled. Goethe argued that forty is a convenient number, a number with anthropological origins representing the years usually considered to span an individual's lifetime: "I consider the thirty-six year interpolated, an expedient custom of the following era, space which they were to cover" (Ich halte 36 Jahre für eingeschoben, als ein zweckmässiges Kommentum der folgenden Zeit. Raum, den sie zu durchziehen gehabt, BA, 3, 388). Thus, the story in the desert was not fact (Faktum), but poetry (Poesie) and, indeed, "writings in which old traditions are brought together always remain a kind of poetry, not to mention that they were in large part, even in form, song; thus their content is mostly poetic, that is, only the sense is *true,* the expressed fact is mostly fable."[14]

Goethe's observations on the Israelites in the desert are generally considered correct by today's standards of philology and history.[15] His analysis includes information typical for studies of older cultures such as discussion of the condition of the historical materials, the character of the hero and his god, and the peculiarities of sociopolitical life and of the historical situation. It is significant that Goethe was able to balance study of broad cultural questions with specific problems in historiography. On the question of Hebrew history, he looked particularly at the poetic and symbolic value of the numbers forty and seven, the latter more commonly used to show process, action, and change, and the former appearing more often as a static concept marking phases, stages, and periodicity (BA, 3, 272).

Creating realistic illusions of the past

Goethe never lost sight of the individual who created the sources of history, be it Galen, Moses, or, in an earlier century, Newton. According to him it is neither talent nor fate but personality that is the source of an individual's creations and deeds: "And so we gladly confess that Moses' personality, from the time of the first assassination, through later horrors, up to his disappearance, casts a highly significant and worthy image" (Und so gestehen wir gern, dass uns die Persönlichkeit Mosis von dem ersten Meuchelmord an durch alle Grausamkeiten durch bis zum Verschwinden ein höchst bedeutendes und würdiges Bild gibt, BA, 3, 274). But Goethe's resources for re-creating the personality of the individual are grounded in earlier writings, in those from the 1770s and 1780s, when he attempted to dramatize the life of historical figures. In these efforts he tried to vitalize the events comprising the life, not necessarily of great men, but of ordinary individuals, who were heroic precisely because they were ordinary and persevered in the face of great adversity. Two such individuals re-created by the younger Goethe were Gottfried von Berlichingen (1480–1562) and Duke Lamoraal von Egmont (1522–68), both historical figures of minor significance, minor political figures in whom Goethe saw representation of an entire age, of another time and culture.

Goethe took the material basis of the historical Götz and shaped it into the form of a drama, which he published in 1773 under the title of "Götz of Berlichingen with the Iron Hand" (Götz von Berlichingen mit der eisernen Hand, WA, I, 8, 1–169).[16] The historical Götz had begun his adult life in the military service of Duke Friedrich of Ansbach. He had lost his right hand in battle, became a robber baron, later feuded with the Swabian Union, and in 1525, after spending some time in prison, assumed command of revolutionary forces in the Peasant's War in the hopes of containing some of the radical elements in the revolution. After being taken prisoner a second time he spent most of his adult life in the service of Charles V, a life limited in freedom and movement.

From these historical details Goethe created, in dramatic form, the realistic illusion of a sixteenth-century man; it was an illusion because the events in the drama are fictive, realistic because the fictive events re-create the spirit of the times, the environment and the climate in which the historical Götz lived. That is, the characters and events surrounding the Götz of Goethe's drama are fiction. And yet they symbolize typical activities, namely, imprisonment, battle, violation of law, feuding, intrigue, and solitude. This symbolic relationship to the historical Götz continues to the end; in real life he spent the last years of his life confined and trapped in the service of the emperor. As an illusion of this reality Goethe ended the drama by portraying Götz in prison, a broken man, who in his dying breath called out the cry of the age, "freedom" (Freiheit, WA, I, 8, 169).

The techniques for re-creation of historical personalities reached a new high in the drama *Egmont, A Tragedy in Five Acts* (Egmont. Ein Trauerspiel in fünf Aufzügen, WA, I, 8, 171–305) from 1788. Here Goethe again reconstructed from the materials of history a drama about an ordinary individual, documented in time, but lost in the archival past.[17] In the year in which the drama appeared, Schiller argued as the main point of his review that Goethe had created the illusion of a real historical figure.[18] As the author of a classical study on the period of Egmont's life, the period of the struggle for freedom in the Netherlands and the decline of Spanish rule there, Schiller observed that "in history Egmont was no great character, nor is he in the tragedy."[19] In arguing the concept of realistic illusion, Schiller focused on one of the most obvious differences between Goethe's Egmont and the historical figure; on the fact that the historical figure had nine children and for this reason remained in the Netherlands, refusing to leave his homeland and hoping to avoid subjecting his family to difficulties abroad greater than those threatened by the Spanish suppression at home. In Goethe's drama, Egmont's love for family, Schiller observed, is replaced by a love for country and fellowman, a love tangible and concentrated in Egmont's relationship to Clärchen, the woman willing to incite a riot as a means of saving her lover. Thus, Schiller argued that Goethe, like Shakespeare, was able to draw on the fragmentary nature of political records, on diverse social and cultural events, and with genius (Genie) re-create the individual, making him appear to live and act before our very eyes.[20]

Yet, according to Schiller, Goethe did not permit the reader to substitute the illusion for reality: "The higher the illusion is driven in the drama, the more incomprehensible one will find it that the author himself mischievously destroys it."[21] In his view, Goethe destroyed the fictive development by ending the drama with Egmont in prison. Here he awaited his execution, drifting into a state of dreams in which he had visions of the significance of his death for the life of his people and country. In these final scenes, Schiller argued, Goethe displaced the reality of Egmont's death with a vision of freedom that appeared to him in the figure of Clärchen, in this figure allegorically uniting Egmont's two dominant feelings, his love for Clärchen and for personal freedom. In this vision, Goethe replaced the reality of Egmont's impending death with a vision of the future, indeed, with a truth about the place of Egmont in history: "I die for freedom" (Ich sterbe für die Freiheit, WA, I, 8, 305). Thus, in Schiller's view, the reality of the historical Egmont, as presented by Goethe, existed not in overt political and social life, but in the feelings, thoughts, passions, and moods, in the internal motivations, namely, in the spirit that moved his outward life.

The progression of Goethe's ideas on historical reality, on the development of his view of man's past, had reached a significant state in the publication of *Egmont,* a work refined and completed while he was in Italy (1786–8). Shortly thereafter, around 1790, a new phase began, a phase that emerged from his work in botany and color theory, from an increased effort to represent reality acceptable to the scientific community. In 1790 he published his "Metamorphosis of Plants," in which he attempted to re-create the reality of plant growth. He did this by describing the inner, structural changes in plant life, by describing the modification of forms from the young cotyledons to the mature fruit of the plant.[22] Thus, Goethe came to realize that not only historical events but also natural events, like the growth of plants, can be re-created as illusions of reality, in this case through the representation of plant growth as the alternating stages of expansion and contraction of structures with leaflike characteristics. That is, the leaf became an ideal type, fundamental to the structure of the cotyledons as well as to the stamen and pistil, giving his narrative on the morphology of plants visual structure, providing the reader with the illusion of seeing forms in the process of growth.

Yet the relationship of Goethe's morphology to historiography does not exist in any attempt on his part to give history the same structure he gave plant growth; it does not lie in the six alternating stages of expansion and contraction, in the diastolic and systolic processes of life. Its significance for historiography lies in the recognition that narration can give the illusion of growth and development and, therefore, provide a more realistic description of organic development than can schemes of classification and analysis. In the language of narration, the laws of nature can be described so that things natural and fictive can be related, and from them one can create something "refreshingly probable."[23]

5

Goethe's reconstruction of amorphous states

> Little comes to us through time as a complete monument; much comes as remnants; much as techniques, as practical manual; some things because of their close affinity to man, like mathematics; other things because they are always encouraged, like astronomy and geography; other things because of man's needs, like medicine; and finally some things, because the human being, without wanting to, continues to produce them, like music and the other fine arts.[1]

Drawing lines between law and chance

In Goethe's view there is something incalculable and incommensurate about the way events of the past relate. From the materials of history he was not assured of the same kind of continuity and regularity found in studies on nature. In history he found gaps in the evidence relating events, documents, and individuals, so that statements about the past were exposed to a greater degree of the author's opinions than in writings on nature. A history was not a re-presentation of phenomena as he had experienced writing in nature studies, rather it was a reconstruction of events, only to a degree reflecting the stream of reality. Thus, he argued that history is a product of "law and chance" (Gesetz und Zufall), and that the relationship of the laws of history to the stream of reality are both regular and random, "proportionate" and "disproportionate" (proportionierlich und unproportionierlich, LA, I, 6, 85).[2] That is, in his view history consists of bits and pieces, of fragmentary evidence, and a thoroughly connected view of history could exist only in the mind of the historian who ignores the ambiguous relationship of law and chance: "The observer often confuses the two, as is especially noticeable among partisan historians, who mostly unconsciously, but nevertheless artistically enough, make use of this uncertainty to their advantage."[3]

The tension between chance and design, and the question of truth in historical records, is a central problem in Goethe's historiography of science. They were also issues of debate among professional historians of the day, as is recorded in Goethe's conversation with Heinrich Luden (1780–1847), a Jena

University historian with whom Goethe discussed the differences between mathematical and historical truth. In this conversation Goethe argued that events of the past might be explained, if one had the appropriate instruments of research, tools of criticism, and access to materials. But because this is usually not the case, there will remain a difference between the truth of mathematics and history: "not between that which is really true, but between that which can be demonstrated as true and that which is assumed as true."[4] Goethe's discussion with Luden touched on several aspects of the question of historical truth,[5] although in essence the distinctions come back to the same problem, to the discontinuity in evidence and to the high degree of subjectivity required in the interpretation of historical materials. In Goethe's view the transmission of the artifacts of history is fortuitous, so the historian must of necessity become a subjective participant in the process of history. Thus, history is murky waters and, while each historian may arrive at a truth, it will remain individual, lacking the foundation of proofs that gives universality to the statements of mathematics: "The difference is that mathematics can force everyone to recognize, that all right angles are the same; in historical things, on the other hand, you can never force me to be of your opinions."[6]

The tension between history as a product of design and of chance is also recorded in the title of Goethe's work, "Materials on the History of Color Theory" (Materialien zur Geschichte der Farbenlehre). On the one hand the title includes the word "Materials," which suggests an unstructured collection of resources and on the other it includes the word "History," implying a narration in which the events of the past are given direction and interpretation. Both dimensions are represented in the title, and the work as a whole is compatible with this paradox in his theory of historiography. With the word "Materials" he implies that he did not construct a "complete monument," or formulate a history based on "mathematical proofs." With this word he emphasized the amorphous nature of the tradition represented in the work. Thus the title points to the fragmentary condition of traditions and to the possibility of finding patterns in the record of human activities. This possibility Goethe explored by holding design and chance in tension on the one hand, and on the other by searching for sources and events that would shape and connect studies in color theory into an organic whole.[7]

Goethe's history of color theory is an attempt to balance the fragmentary and amorphous nature of traditions with the structure and form that arises from the subjectivity of historiography. In this effort Goethe left the field of historiography a rich legacy of tools, techniques, and methods, which may not yield the universality of mathematical proofs, but nevertheless reconstructed and gave meaning to a piece of man's past. Although this perception admitted to the amorphous condition of the human archives, it also showed that there is a continuity and a pattern in the way human achievements of the past are related to those of the present. More importantly it showed that, if these patterns are presented in an idiom that reflects both "law and chance," then the historian has achieved a measure of truth in the reconstruction of something that does not necessarily exist, but is at least true to the sources, and perhaps also "refreshingly probable."[8]

Setting the parameters of research

In attempting to structure the history of color theory, Goethe had to develop the full range of techniques available to trained philologists of today, including the acquisition of source materials, authentication of documents, editing and translating of texts, as well as an understanding of basic principles of semantics and textual linguistics.[9] As a pioneer in the historiography of science he had no canon of texts with which to work; the scientific tradition was amorphous. The first step in overcoming this condition was the acquisition of source material, and this Goethe did through various friends and acquaintances, particularly through those associated with the libraries in Weimar and Göttingen.[10]

Goethe's work in Göttingen was particularly important to his effort in shaping the discontinuities of scientific tradition and via one of Göttingen's professional historians, Georg Sartorius (1765–1828), Goethe received Thomas Birch's (1705–66) *History of the Royal Society of London* (London, 1756) as well as various issues of the *Philosophical Transactions,* the official journal of the Royal Society. As late as 1809, one year before publication of his history, Goethe requested from Sartorius volumes twenty-nine and thirty-two of the *Transactions* so that he might for a last time review the context of some of the materials he excerpted for his history (LA, II, 6, 384). In his visits to Göttingen, Goethe also became acquainted with science as a social movement, not only through study of the Royal Society but through analysis of the Göttingen Academy and its reception of British science. For this study he made use of Johann S. Pütter's (1725–1807) history of the academy. He studied the institution's catalog of offerings, noted the institution's strong emphasis on applied research, and learned of the institution's emphasis on historical studies, on empirical methodology, and its devotion to specialized training in the sciences.[11]

In the introduction to his history of color theory, Goethe summarized the types of materials he acquired for his history, including books, memoirs, journals, and various other kinds of collections. His study of these materials varied; from some he made more copious notes than from others. For many of the older documents Goethe made detailed outlines of what he considered important content, as in the case of Seneca's (ca. 4–65) *Naturalium Quaestionum,* which he divided into sections on God and the heavenly fires, air, water, the source of the Nile, and on winds, earthquakes, and comets (LA, II, 6, 25–7). Goethe noted such details as Seneca's account of the destruction of

Pompeii, Thales's opinion that the earth is afloat, and the attribution of earthquakes to demonic forces. In each of the sections he noted Seneca's penchant for emphasizing the practical value of science (Nutzanwendung). And with this observation Goethe shaped his view of the science of Seneca, his interpretation of Seneca's writings and Roman science: "The difference between him and the true physicist is his constant, often forced, application and connection of the highest natural phenomena to the needs, enjoyment, fancy, and wantonness of mankind."[12]

Goethe prized some works, not so much for their information on color, but because they contributed to a holistic, to a total understanding of scientific life. One such source was Roger Bacon's (1214–94) *Opus majus.* He valued it because he saw in it the combined genius of mathematician, philosopher, scientist, and writer: "He [Bacon] valued authority but did not underestimate the intricacy and fluctuation in transmission" (Er schätzt die Autorität, verkennt aber nicht das Verworrene und Schwankende der Ueberlieferung, LA, II, 6, 34). Goethe viewed Bacon both as a scientist and practical thinker, one able to articulate a realistic relationship between man and nature and at the same time creative enough to visualize instruments of technology before they were constructed. Goethe's research notes show particular concentration on Bacon's optics, on his description of instruments like the "camera obscura," "the magic lantern" (Die Zauberlaterne), and the "solar microscope" (Sonnenmikroskop, p. 103). From an analysis of Bacon's language and style Goethe concluded that such tools of science had never been seen by Bacon, only visualized and therefore to be admired as a contribution to the continuity of science, as a linkage of scientific epochs grounded in prophetic thoughts and visions: "Only those who recognize how the human mind can anticipate technology will find nothing shocking in Bacon's writings" (Allein wem bekannt ist, wie der Menschengeist voreilen kann, ehe ihm die Technik nachkommt, der wird auch hier nichts Unerhörtes finden, p. 103).

Diogenes Laertius's (ca. 250 B.C.) collection of materials was of particular significance for Goethe's search for linkage in the history of color theory, for it was the most complete resource for study of ancient thought.[13] Goethe made copius notes from the seventeenth-century edition by Marcus Meibomius (d. 1711), which appeared with the title *Diogenis Laertii di Vitis, dogmatibus et apophthegmatibus clarorum philosophorum, libri X, graece et latine* (Amsterdam, 1692), as well as from the German translation of this edition (Vienna, 1807) by August C. Borhek (1751–1816). Much of Diogenes Laertius's work contains second- and third-hand material, although it is significant that precisely the writings of the Stoics and Epicureans were well preserved as near originals. Goethe was particularly attracted to the writings of early atomists and subsequent to publishing his history of color theory, he did considerable philological work on Lucretius's (96–56) *De natura rerum.* Indeed, Goethe is to be counted among those late eighteenth-century Germans who recognized atomism as an independent tradition and who contributed to our understanding of the way it helped shape the development of science and thought.[14]

Goethe also found Plutarch's (46?–127) *De placitis philosophorum* to be a useful source in shaping early scientific thought.[15] In chapters one and four of this work he found extensive materials on color theory. He observed in his notes that the writings of the ancients reveal many examples of intuitive perceptions (Aperçüs) and good empirical statements (gute empirische Enunciationen, LA, II, 6, 8). In this source Goethe found early speculation on whether light was material, whether it was essential or accidental (Substanz or Accidenz, p. 9), marking one of the fundamental questions in the development of color theory in his day. With this source Goethe was able to follow one of the basic threads of research which was to run through his materials on color theory, giving it shape, structure, and continuity.

Legitimating a canon of history[16]

Goethe's research on Theophrastus's (ca. 372–288), or better (vielmehr, LA, I, 6, 16–36), on Aristotle's *De coloribus,* is a lesson in the philological methods Goethe developed in his attempt to reconstruct a history of color theory. The text had been attributed to Aristotle by both Plutarch and Georgius Pachymeres (ca. 1242–1310), whereas Simon Portius (1497–1554) left the question open, as is indicated in the title of his Latin translation: *Aristotelis vel Theophrasti de coloribus libellus a Simone Portio neapolitano latinitati donatus* (Paris, 1549). Goethe, too, left open the question of authorship, making the philological work on ancient texts, that is, on the reception of ancient science, the main focus of his fourth chapter on sixteenth-century science.

Before making a decision on the status of *De coloribus,* Goethe tried to establish its author through analysis of the text and through comparison of the text with other writings by Aristotle, such as his *De anima, De sensu et sensili,* and *De somno et vigilia* (LA, II, 6, 8–15). In this comparison, Goethe observed Aristotle's use of black and white as theoretical principles basic to all colors.[17] In *De coloribus* yellow was given the same status, leading Goethe to question Aristotle's authorship and to ascribe the text also to Theophrastus. But the centrality of this text to his search for linkage in the history of color theory gave him reason to seek advice on the matter from leading authorities in the emerging field of philology.

As diary records show, Goethe obtained Portius's 1549 edition of *De coloribus* from the Weimar library; he then studied the work at various intervals beginning in the winter of 1798 (LA, II, 6, 319). In 1801 he began to translate it into German and, as he wrote to Schiller a few years later, at this point he consulted one of Germany's foremost philologist, Friedrich A. Wolf (1759–

1824), on the issue of authorship and the means for establishing the authenticity of the document: "With Wolf I have already gone through the little book on colors. The primary result, namely, that also according to his criteria the work is genuine, old, and worthy of the Peripatetics, pleased me greatly as you can imagine. Indeed, he would rather ascribe it to Aristotle than to his students."[18]

Thus, Goethe discovered a text that was genuine and original and could serve as a organizing principle in his history of color theory. His enthusiasm in this discovery was comparable to his joy in discovery of the "os intermaxillare" twenty years earlier. Namely, *De coloribus,* like the intermaxillary bone, represented for Goethe a real discovery, for he had established it as a primal text from which links to a unified history of color theory could be developed. In his view, the text gave shape and synthesis to the amorphous condition of transmissions in color theory.

Goethe traced the life of *De coloribus* to the Renaissance period, when it was examined by Antonius Thylesius (1482–1533), Simon Portius (1497–1554), and Julius Scaliger (1484–1558). He observed how Thylesius studied the etymology of Greek color terms, how Portius translated *De coloribus* into Latin, and how Scaliger expanded the work of Thylesius to include the etymology of color terms from other Greek sources. Goethe then included Thylesius' text on etymology in his history in the original Latin without alteration, recognizing the semantic problems that arise in the translation of color terms: "We wanted to translate it, but soon found that one cannot treat the etymology of a language in another language: thus we decided to reprint it in the original."[19]

Goethe observed that many of the Arabic and Latin translations of Greek color terminology had been done carelessly and had contributed greatly to the amorphous condition of writings on color theory. But, he added, even the most careful translation introduces something foreign into a term, for the "difference in language usage" (Verschiedenheit des Sprachgebrauchs, p. 126) itself introduces changes. He noted that the Latin use of nouns (Substantiva), for example, added a rigidity to the thoughts and ideas expressed in the original Greek language in which verbal forms (Verba) dominate: "The Latin language on the other hand becomes decisive and authoritative through its use of nouns. The concept is set up in the word, solidified in the word, with which one then operates as with a real being."[20]

In Goethe's view, translation difficulties, semantic diffusion, and authoritative language were only a few of the explanations for the amorphous state of the tradition of color theory. He found no standardized editorial principles, and there was little sense for establishing the authenticity of a text, or for translations true to the original text. Portius's treatment of *De coloribus,* for example, was not really a translation for he added extensive commentary to the text, made interlinear notations, rephrased definitions, expanding *De coloribus* far beyond its original state:

The form of the presentation, writing notes to a text, necessitates repetition and reference, everything said is worked and reworked into confusion, so that as a whole it does not lack internal clarity and consequence, as in a card or board game; after reading everything again and again, one knows more than before, but precisely not that, which one expected or wanted.[21]

After Goethe, Carl Prantl, in 1840 again took up the question of the authorship of *De coloribus,* approaching the problem by studying Aristotle's narrative style; he found that Aristotle's criticism of other writers was missing in the text, which he thought supported the view that the document belongs to the Peripatetic school rather than to Aristotle alone.[22] Nevertheless, Prantl proceeded to incorporate the work into Aristotle's writings on color theory, and today standard editions of Aristotle's writings include *De coloribus,* usually noting the same reservations found in the conclusions reached by Goethe, Wolf, and Prantl.[23] Thus, Goethe, with others of his age, found in the methods of classical philology the means for legitimating a canon in the historiography of science.

Filling gaps in the historical terrain

Thus, with attention to law and chance in history, Goethe varied his approach to evaluating materials on color theory. He edited and translated texts, he compared texts by the same author, from other texts he took copious notes, and some he simply examined as generally important to the history of science. And from this philological effort he organized a unified body of materials, which more or less followed a thin line of continuity from ancient to modern science.

But narrative techniques also brought unity to his history and helped bridge discontinuity in his materials. Particularly helpful was recourse to the language of theatrics and his experience in directing the Weimar Theatre. Organizational terms in his history, like "Interim" (Zwischenzeit, p. 83), were common parlance in techniques of staging in his day, for it was considered in poor taste to allow gaps in the performance on the stage.[24] The obvious interval in Goethe's history was the medieval period and to cover this period he looked to the language of theatrics. Although Goethe had researched the period and had found it not without evidence of scientific activity, as in the case of the writings by Roger Bacon, it was in his day "a hiatus" (eine Lücke, p. 83), "an opaque period" (eine trübe Zeit, p. 95), a weak link in the continuity of his studies on color theory.

As Goethe also knew of the link which Arabic writings formed between the ancient and modern epochs of science, he could not ignore the medieval period. His dilemma was that he found no sources from the period with direct linkage to texts like *De coloribus*. And so that "the stage may never be empty,"[25] Goethe inserted into this chapter a series of aphoristic statements and essays on his theory of the historiography of science. With his "Interim" he was asking the reader to reflect on the principles of historical organization, on such issues as the role of authority in the history of science, on the relationship of truth and error in science, and on the relationship of science to history and tradition. The chapter in effect represents the essence of Goethe's theory of historiography, a theory not presented as a complete system of thought, but as a collection of aphorisms, of loosely connected statements about history, science, tradition, and man's relationship to the past.

Yet, there is a pattern in the collection of statements found in this intermission in the drama of science: first in discussion of the "hiatus" (Lücke, p. 83) itself, and then in the two well-structured essays on transmission (Ueberliefertes) and authority (Autorität, pp. 88–95), two fundamental organizing principles in Goethe's historiography.[26] Then following this discussion of problems in historical reconstruction, he offers pioneering research on the history of medieval science, including a study of Roger Bacon's writings on optics, as well as brief references to ibn al-Hai-tham Alhazen (ca. 965–1039), Aurelius Augustinus (354–430), and Themistius (320–90), the Latin, medieval, and Arabic links in the continuity between ancient and modern science.

Goethe explained also that filling space in the medieval period with thoughts on the historiography of science, was similar to the way in which early geographers of Africa would label unknown territory with exotic symbols, such as with an elephant or a lion. He explained that the unexplored areas of the earth were like history, a map that was incomplete but was not to be ignored as insignificant. Goethe had used a gap in the map of history as an opportunity for stating his theory of historiography, fully realizing that, just as in geography the map is not the territory, so also in history the structure is not the tradition.[27]

Goethe realized that both the map of geography and the structure of history are mental constructs, that they are a product of the human mind held in tension with the accidents of time, with the chance appearance of texts and sources in the scholar's efforts to reconstruct history. But Goethe did not imply by this paradox of chance and design that a morphology of history could never be achieved. Rather he saw in the resolution of the dilemma definition of the human being, as expressed in the poem "The Godlike" (Das Göttliche) from the early 1780s: "Yet man alone can / Achieve the impossible: / He distinguishes, / Chooses and judges; / He can give lasting / Life to the moment."[28]

As in his studies in geology, osteology, botany, and color theory, so, too, did his research in history focus on the junctures of difficulty. Indeed, into the weakest link of his history, into the period of medieval science, he poured most of his ideas on the historiography of science, demonstrating truth about the state of research on the period. Goethe researched and prized the scientific accomplishments of the period; he looked at the writings of individuals like Robert Grosseteste (1175–1253) and Averroës, ibn Roschd (1126–98). He saw life in the period and in the idiom of his theory of plants he compared it to the seed from which the plant emerges: "That time, which the seed spends in the soil, belong very much to the life of the plant" (Diejenige Zeit, welche der Same unter der Erde zubringt, gehört vorzüglich mit zum Pflanzenleben, LA, I, 6, p. 83).

6

Goethe's transition from history to historiography

It would have been good, if Bacon had not poured the child out with the bath water, if he had seen the value of existing tradition and had advanced this point of view, if he would have known how to value and to make use of existing experiences, rather than in his style to refer to that which is indeterminable and infinite. He knew of Gilbert's work on magnetism, for example, but seemed to have no idea of the monumental worth which already existed in this discovery.[1]

A dialogue on a priori histories

Goethe's historiography of science crystallized in the period 1798–1801, a period that began with a brief but rich exchange of letters with Schiller and ended with an equally brief and stimulating contact with the Göttingen school of history. In Schiller, Goethe found an irreplaceable friend, one whose "reflective power" (reflektierende Kraft, LA, I, 6, 429) quickly focused his project in chromatics, yet, "nowhere was I advanced so quickly as in Göttingen where I was with great generosity and active support permitted use of the invaluable collection of books."[2] With Schiller's assistance Goethe gained clarity in his project on chromatics, making distinctions first between chemical, physical, and physiological colors, and later between science, polemics, and history. Yet, with Schiller these distinctions were worked out primarily in the abstract, for it was in Göttingen where he met the professional historians, who were writing histories of a particular branch of science, and where his own study of the sources led him to the view that the history of science was an independent discipline, one quite apart from study in a particular branch of science. Reconciling this contradiction between a historiography of science and the history of a particular branch of science, was both the challenge and the product of Goethe's encounter with Schiller and the Göttingen professors.

Although Goethe's perception of history developed over many years, reaching at least as far back as his student days at Strasbourg, his theory of the history of science seems to have had its clearest beginnings in the exchange of ideas with Schiller. On Jan. 13, 1798, he wrote to him that he had been studying "various writings in physics" (verschiedene physische Schriften, LA, II, 6, 291), and that it suddenly occurred to him how most scientists use the phenomena of nature as an opportunity "to apply the powers of their individuality" (die Kräfte ihres Individuums anzuwenden) and "to practice their craft" (ihr Handwerk zu üben).

In this letter on the scientists' projection of the self, Goethe explained how Newton turned optics into a geometer, how mechanists turned light into particles, how chemists attributed everything to "caloric" (Wärmestoff, p. 292), and more recently to oxygen, how George S. Klügel (1739–1812) hesitated with a sense of doubt, while Lichtenberg joked about the "modes of conception" (Vorstellungsarten) of others. Goethe outlined for Schiller the whole range of scientific life as he found it in texts from the physical sciences, finding in Christian E. Wünsch (1744–1828) an hypothesis more amazing "than a chapter from the apocalypse" (als ein Kapitel aus der Apokalypse), and in Friedrich A. K. Gren (1760–98) a refrain sung like "a symbolic confession of faith" (ein symbolisches Glaubensbekenntnis). To Schiller he expressed the view that writings in the physical sciences are a mirror of the scientists' self, and that it is his intention to write "an *aperçu* on all of it" (ein Aperçu über das Ganze).

A few days later, on Jan. 20, 1798, Goethe recorded further work on "the history of color theory" (die Geschichte der Farbenlehre, p. 292), both in his journal and in another letter to Schiller, to which he also attached a "draft of the history of color theory" (Entwurf zur Geschichte der Farbenlehre), a schema that is missing, but one that can be reconstructed from the exchange of letters between Goethe and Schiller during the next few months. In this first communication, Goethe began to formulate a theory of the history of science, observing that from the "draft" one could make "some nice observations on the development of the human mind" (schöne Bemerkungen über den Gang des menschlichen Geistes). Here Goethe also began to connect a central thesis from his philosophy of science to his theory of the history of science, observing that the sources he had studied exhibited a "common" (gemeine) form of empiricism and rationalism, and very little of this material had advanced to a level where experiments show "a pure connection of phenomena" (Versuche einer reinen Zusammenstellung der Phänomenen).[3] Based on this inadequacy of scientific method, he concluded that history itself teaches us a lesson on the task at hand.

Schiller responded three days later, concurring with Goethe that "the little schema" (das kleine Schema, p. 293) contained some "basic trends" (Grundzüge) for a "history of science and of human thinking" (Geschichte der Wissenschaft und des menschlichen Denkens). Schiller's comments on Goethe's "draft," showed other themes from Goethe's historiography of science, particularly his references to Goethe's views on "authority" (Autorität) and "dogma" (Dogma), and to other concepts important to his evaluation of science, including the passion with which scientists mount "a meth-odologically serious attack" (ein methodisch ernstlicher Angriff). Goethe wrote back the following day that he already had "a better schema for a future history of color theory" (ein besseres Schema einer künftigen Geschichte der Farbenlehre, p. 294). He also referred to Schiller's comment, that his "draft" showed signs of a history of "human thinking," observing that "writing a history a priori" (eine Geschichte a priori zu schreiben) should be taken seriously, for everything in the history of science can be traced back to the "characteristics of the human mind" (Eigenschaften des menschlichen Geistes).[4]

During the month of February, Goethe and Schiller focused their attention on writing an "a priori history," primarily examining the value of the Kantian categories of the mind for Goethe's project in chromatics. As the dialogue progressed, the value of the word "history," too, began to change. It changed from its original meaning of description into a concept of historiography, gradually moving from the Greek term "historia" as a narration of the present state of human affairs, to a theory of the origins and development of human science and thought, a distinction Kant had made in 1788 in his essay "On the Uses of Teleological Principles in Philosophy."[5] Here Kant distinguished between "natural history" (Naturgeschichte) and "natural description" (Naturbeschreibung, p. 161), emphasizing that the physical status of nature can be reduced to theory, but that study of life processes must be subjected to different measures, namely, to principles of teleology. That is, this essay is really about a central problem of historiography, about a distinction between "history" as narration of the present state of events, namely, the natural sciences, and a narration about the origin and development of life, the biolog-ical and social sciences.

Kant had distinguished between "history" as a descriptive mode of writing and historiography as a theory of development, but it was Schiller who edu-cated Goethe in this distinction, for it was a theme in his inaugural address as professor of history at the University of Jena in 1789. In this lecture on the question as to "Why and to what end do we study universal history?,"[6] Schiller focused on the differences between the scientific activity of "the bread-academician" (der Brotgelehrte) and "the philosophical head" (der philosophische Kopf, p. 360), emphasizing, as Kant had done a year earlier, the service of philosophy in science.[7] But Schiller went beyond this distinc-tion to argue for a historiography that was more than narration and descrip-tion, for one guided by concepts of purpose and freedom, for a history written from the perspective of Kant's secularized version of a telos, one which would organize the historical past with visions of the future, with a perception of Kant's principles of teleology.[8] It was this background in Kantian philosophy which Schiller, ten years later, introduced into the discussion with Goethe on writing "a priori histories," a discussion which gradually moved from the organization of Goethe's concept of chromatics, to a discussion of histories of thinking, and finally to Goethe's historiography of science.

A series of Goethe's letters to Schiller in the first two weeks of February 1798, showed his struggles with new border experiences, with the search for the lines between approaches in the sciences, between categories of thinking, between the disciplines of chromatics, and in general between "the two cultures" of science and history, differences which he helped create and attempted to bridge. On February 3, he reported to Schiller that he was using his spare time partly "for a purer schematizing of [his] future essay" (zum reineren Schematisieren meines künftigen Aufsatzes, p. 295), partly "for pruning and simplifying his earlier work" (zum Verengen und Simplifizieren meiner frühern Arbeiten), and partly "for studying the literature" (zum Studieren der Literatur) and "the history of the same" (zur Geschichte derselben). In this period, he requested from colleagues materials for his project, mentioning as an aside to Wilhelm von Humboldt, for example, that his work on "the schema" was progressing well and that the history of color theory could be interesting for it was "the history of the human mind in miniature" (die Geschichte des menschlichen Geistes im Kleinen, p. 296).[9]

At this time, Goethe reported to Schiller how "philosophy is becoming increasingly valuable" (die Philosophie wird mir immer deshalb werter, p. 297), for example, how it was helping him understand Newton's penchant for theoretical science as a reaction to Baconian empiricism. Here Goethe observed how Robert Boyle had advanced color theory "according to Bacon's good advice" (nach des Baco guten Rat), but that Newton had "tyrannized" (tyrannisierte) this progress and the whole field with his "antibaconian" (antibaconisch) hypotheses. At this time Goethe also recorded in his journal that he had completed an "application of the categories" (Anwendung der Kategorien, p. 298) to Giovanni Rizzetti's (d. 1751) theory of colors.[10] And, in a letter to Schiller on the same day, he wrote that he was enclosing the first version of his theory of colors "set up according to the categories" (nach den Kategorien aufgestellt, p. 298), as well as "an explanation of the terminology for his tripartite division" (eine Eklärung der Terminologie meiner dreifachen Einteilung).

Thus, by February 15, Goethe had tried to apply the Kantian categories of thinking to a division of his color theory, and to a text in color theory by Rizzetti, and he also had noted the difference between Baconian and Newtonian forms of empiricism. Indeed, by this time he was also beginning to respond to a strong urge to study the historiography of the field. In the letter in which he enclosed the "terminology" for his "tripartite division," he also reported to Schiller "that no name in the whole literary history of this discipline should remain a mere name" (dass mir kein Name in der ganzen Literaturgeschichte dieses Faches ein blosser Name sei). Yet, at this point in the discussion on "a priori histories," clarity was only emerging between the various branches of his theory of colors, and the one between science and history had not yet become an issue.

The new version of Goethe's border experiences in chromatics, the one listing a "tripartite division," is also missing, although from Schiller's letter of Feb. 16, 1798, there is concrete evidence that Goethe had tried to apply "the 12 categories" (die 12 Kategorien, p. 299) to his theory of colors. Yet, based on Schiller's comments, it is clear that Goethe did not understand the process, and that he must not have defined his "tripartite division" clearly, for Schiller went to great lengths to explain how the Kantian categories might be applied to his project in chromatics. Thus, in the course of his letter, Schiller specified his criticism of the materials thus far collected on color theory, in his opening comments assuring Goethe that "all possible essential questions" (alle mögliche Hauptfragen) about an "object" (Gegenstand) would follow from the application of the categories, "if correctly embraced" (wenn richtig subsumiert worden).

In this critique of Goethe's application of the Kantian categories of thinking, Schiller confessed that he had no "feeling of satisfaction" (Gefühl von Befriedigung) in Goethe's presentation. But he also thought this dissatisfaction was due more to the material itself than to the form of presentation, that the material, namely, that the state of color theory still had too much of a "rhapsodic and therefore arbitrary appearance" (rhapsodistisches und daher willkürliches Ansehen). Indeed, he feared that he would always regard the material of this project as "an unmanageable mass" (eine unübersehbare Masse), especially when seeking in it an inner form which meets the "demand of totality" (Forderung der Totalität).[11]

Nevertheless, Schiller proceeded to advise Goethe on the application of Kant's twelve categories to his theory of colors. He began by suggesting that, if Goethe were to apply the "categorical test" (Kategorienprobe), he should begin by separating the most general phenomena of color from the most simple. Secondly, Schiller observed that in his sample from Rizzetti's theory of color, Goethe had failed to focus on a subject, that at times he was applying a category to "light" (Licht, p. 300), and at other times to "color" (Farbe). He advised him "that the categories must always yield a predicate" (dass die Kategorien immer nur die Prädikate hergeben), and that the subject "being acted upon" (von welchem prädiziert wird) must remain constant. On this point Schiller promised future conversation, but he did add one example, applying the category of "relation" (Relation) to the question of "whether color produced a positive, independent energy, or whether it is only a limited light energy?" (ob die Farbe als positive eigene Energie oder nur als limitierte Licht-Energie wirkt?).[12]

In application of the category of "relation," Schiller explained that it would be possible to determine whether color is an "accident" (Accidens) of light, if color is only an "effect" (Wirkung) of light, and therefore not substantial.

Here Schiller suggested to Goethe a way by which he might arrive at sharper distinctions in his materials, distinctions grounded "in tripartite relations" (in dreifacher Beziehung), namely, colors in relationship to light and darkness, to the eye, and to material bodies. In other words, here Schiller was examining Goethe's claim to a "tripartite division" of his materials on chromatics, in effect, correcting the one Goethe proposed, using a more exacting application of Kant's category of relations. That is, from the "tripartite division" attached to Goethe's letter of February 14, Schiller saw only two divisions, physical and chemical colors, and from his critique of Goethe's application of the Kantian category "Of Relation," he came to the "tripartite" distinction.

Goethe's response to Schiller's advice was nothing less than enthusiastic. The day after receiving his letter, he wrote back explaining that Schiller's outline of "tripartite relations" corresponded to his own divisions of physiological, physical, and chemical colors, a distinction that was for the first time clearly expressed in Schiller's previous letter. It might seem that the origins of the clarity is perhaps less significant than the agreement and than Goethe's sense of progress in establishing the divisions of his chromatics, a step allowing him to proceed with the project. Yet, Goethe's version of the origins is significant for he observed that what brought him to his schema, indeed, what necessitated the division, even as he saw it, was "the history of color theory" (die Geschichte der Farbenlehre, p. 301), the "description" and "narration" of materials, "the literary history of this discipline" (Literaturgeschichte dieses Faches, p. 298), not the categories of Kantian philosophy.

After achieving clarity in his division of color theory, Goethe quickly moved to confirm another border experience, the one between a description of chromatics, namely, "a history of experiences" (die Geschichte der Erfahrungen), a description in the Baconian sense of empiricism, and a discussion of the hypotheses in chromatics, namely, "the history of opinions" (die Geschichte der Meinungen), a discussion in the Newtonian sense of a theory. In the distinction between "histories of experiences" and "histories of opinions," Goethe came a step closer to forming a theory of historiography, a step in the direction of defining scientific polemics, the bridge between science and tradition. In his view the Kantian categories should be applied only to the "history of opinions," namely, that all hypotheses must stand "under the categories" (unter den Kategorien), a comment referring to Goethe's distinction between a narration about experience and one about hypotheses, the former a description of the "acts of nature," and the latter about "the condition of the human mind."[13]

In conclusion to this letter of response to Schiller's lesson on applied Kantian philosophy, Goethe expressed caution against completing any part of the schema until the entire project on color theory was finished. He also admitted a lack of confidence in any procedure involving philosophy, expressing delight in being able to return to his growing urge to study the literature of the field. Here he mentions that he had surveyed the writings of a dozen authors hoping to find a few "salient monuments" (Hauptmonumente, p. 302) for his history. Thus, Goethe, at this point, was beginning to distinguish historiography from the two kinds of histories, the one a description of empirical data, phenomena of experience, and the second a description of opinions, hypothetical statements about that data. With his search for "salient monuments," he began to seek key documents, important nodes in the development of science, a first step in establishing concepts of periodization in historiography.

Schiller observed in a letter from Feb. 20, 1798, that he was confident that Goethe's application of the categories will be "fruitful" (fruchtbar, p. 303), for it will force Goethe to "strict determinations" (strenge Bestimmungen), to "border distinctions" (Grenzscheidungen), indeed, to "tough opposition" (harte Opposition). Schiller was convinced that with the categories of "reciprocity" (Wechselwirkung), "limitation" (Limitation), "totality" (Allheit), and "necessity" (Notwendigkeit), Goethe would be well served, especially in polemics, which Schiller thought Goethe could not avoid, but also would give him a "decisive advantage" (einen entscheidenen Vorteil). And in conclusion Schiller also referred to the promise which this "categorical test" (Kategorien-Probe) holds for an "overview of the historical part" (Uebersicht des historischen Teils), a promise that was not realized until after Goethe's visits in Göttingen and after almost another decade of research and work on the project.

In the last exchange of letters from February 1798, Goethe expressed his continued interest in "rational empiricism" (die rationelle Empirie, p. 303). He was particularly eager "to be clear about it" (damit aufs reine kommen) before he returned to Bacon "in whom he again has gained a great confidence" (zu dem ich abermals ein grosses Zutrauen gewonnen habe). Schiller responded by confirming the advantage of an approach to empiricism controlled by the Kantian "categorical test," emphasizing that "insight into the phenomenon" (Einsicht in den Gegenstand) and "insight into the operation of the mind" (Einsicht in die Operation des Geistes) will yield "a beautiful double gain" (den schönen doppelten Gewinn), indeed, the latter is even the greater gain, for insight into the "tools of the mind" (Geisteswerkzeuge, p. 304), to a certain extent, made people "master over all objects" (zum Herrn über alle Gegenstände).

In this last exchange of ideas, Goethe focused on the impact that his transition to "rational empiricism" had on his emerging study of the literature of the field, how "in the entire history of color theory" (in der ganzen Geschichte der Farbenlehre) the greatest error was the failure to come to a tripartite division of the field, an error he thought came from the attempt to extend theories over too broad a range of phenomena. By the end of the year,

Goethe's journal entries reflected a clear transition to questions about the historiography of science, questions again discussed with Schiller: "The order and division, in which the history of color theory is supposed to be presented, were studied by epochs, as were the individual writers, also the theories themselves were weighed carefully and discussed with Schiller."[14] And by Feb. 8, 1799, he noted in his diary that he had developed a new scheme for the historical section of his project, one that no longer was shaped according to the categories of science. By this time he was beginning to distinguish between his interest in scientists and science, as well as to recognize the need for integration of both in a historiography of science: "I worked more on the outline of the history of color theory and then briefly summarized the character of individual scientists from memory."[15]

The structure of Goethe's color theory was shaped from a combination of discussions on the categories of the mind, and from research in the amorphous collection of historical materials on the topic, although he claimed the shape of the entire project had its origin in the broader literature of the field. That is, he thought the particular state of color theory in the eighteenth century necessitated a review of past writings as a means of gaining perspective on his own theory of color. Then once the parameters of his color theory were established, a new phase emerged in which he could distinguish between the traditional meaning of "history" and a historiography, a phase that focused on the social, psychological, and biographical development of science. This phase was for the first time broadly outlined in a sketch done in Jena in 1799 (LA, II, 6, 258–67), and in that year Goethe spent considerable time with Schiller in discussions on the philosophy of science, in particular in discussion of theoretical questions concerning the historiography of color theory.

On Dec. 24, 1800, Goethe announced with conviction that he had divided his enterprise on chromatics into three separate volumes, distinguishing systematic, polemical, and historical aspects of the topic (LA, II, 6, 311). This separation of historiography from his science was a pioneering effort in the history of science, the result of theoretical discussions with Schiller, a plan formulated while he was on a visit to Jena, where Schiller was employed at the university as a professor of history (LA, II, 6, 311). This pioneer effort emerged from an exchange of ideas that began with the possibility of writing "a history a priori," and ended with a clear recognition that the history of science is not necessarily a catalog of scientific discoveries and theories, but is a narrative about the human search for knowledge.

Although the distinction between "a priori histories" and a historiography of science was clear from the sketch of 1799, Goethe wavered in his resolution to write a history in which the latter was emphasized. And so, while he was on a visit to the library in Göttingen on Aug. 2, 1801, he wrote a new outline for the historical part of his project, the "Göttingen–Schema" (LA, I, 3, 335–38), a formal outline by disciplines, suggesting a return to the "tripartite divisions" of color theory he had discussed earlier with Schiller. In the university library, Goethe discovered, and studied, "a priori histories," descriptions of science written by professional scientists for the series on the "History of the Arts and Sciences" (Geschichte der Künste und Wissenschaften) sponsored by the publishing houses of Göttingen. Yet, the Göttingen–Schema became only a brief alternative to the Jena-sketch, which called for the present division of his work into separate volumes on color theory, polemics and history. The Göttingen–Schema of 1801 called for a radically different approach. Rather than a self-contained history, each division of Goethe's color theory would have concluded with a historical study, for example, after Goethe's theory of physiological colors, there would have been a history of physiology. The same plan was proposed for chemical and optical colors. The result would have meant an emphasis on science rather than on scientists and history.

The difference between the two outlines represents the differences between Goethe's view of the history of science and that of other pioneers in the field, most of whom were also professional scientists. Goethe's final choice was to present the historiography of color science separately, thereby illustrating the historical value, whereas in general his contemporaries looked to the history of science for systematic advancement of the respective sciences. The defunct Göttingen–Schema of 1801 followed the pattern typical for those histories written at Göttingen. It can be safely assumed that Goethe considered the histories of science by Abraham G. Kästner (1719–1800), Johann F. Gmelin (1748–1804), Johann K. Fischer (1760–1833), as well as those from abroad, such as the one by Jean Etienne Montucla (1725–99), more valuable as contributions to the respective fields of mathematics, chemistry and physics than as statements about the historiography of science.[16] One may conclude from this observation that, in Göttingen, Goethe reaffirmed prior convictions rather than establishing a real alternative for his historiography of science. That is, Goethe clearly prized the history of science quite aside from any putative scientific accomplishments.

The fundamental difference between Goethe's historiography and the "histories" of his contemporaries is reflected in the way Goethe used their works as source material for scientific detail in his own "history of color theory."[17] The historians of science in Göttingen were more interested in organizing the discoveries, theories and systems than in an understanding of the context in which science develops. Even the personal letters accompanying Fischer's newly published *Geschichte der Physik* (1801–8) elicited no comments from Goethe, who could only appreciate such histories for their contribution to science and not for their historical value.

The Goethe–Schiller dialogue on "a priori histories" and the difference in points of emphasis existing between Goethe's history and those by the Göttingen professors, has continued into twentieth-century debates in the historiography of science. The aim of one kind of history of science is not exclusively history, but is devoted at least in part to the study of science. A second kind of history seeks to understand why a historical event happened as it did.[18] Indeed, the former kind was discussed by Goethe and Schiller as "a priori histories," and only recently was it again given full attention by Joseph Agassi, who labeled the work of those concerned with the findings of science "inductive history."[19] He traces this ahistorical point of view back to the Baconian injunction that scientists collect into "histories" all "true" facts known in various branches of science, emphasizing that the concerns of a modern "inductivist historian" are then limited to "chronological problems," "priority problems," and "authorship problems."[20] Agassi is thus arguing with Goethe that by listing only the true facts, laws, and theories, and by sifting these from fancy, legend, error and from other human factors, the writer will obtain an up-to-date science textbook, not a history of science.[21]

These "inductivist" histories were prominent among Goethe's contemporaries. Joseph Priestley (1733–1804), in the preface to *The history and present state of discoveries relating to vision, light and colours* (1772), voiced the typical notion that by listing in "histories" all discoveries related to a branch of science, new discoveries will result: "In order to facilitate the advancement of all branches of useful science, two things seem to be principally requisite. The first is, an historical account of their rise, progress, and present state; and the second, an easy channel of communication for all new discoveries . . . so that, in the present state of science, such histories as these are, in a manner, absolutely necessary."[22] Montucla, too, in the preface to his *Histoire des mathématiques* (1799–1802), stated that it is his goal to write an up-to-date scientific textbook: "I am particularly eager to present a clear idea and the true principles of all the theories of some importance which make up the system of mathematics."[23]

Presenting the findings of science in true Baconian fashion were, in addition to Priestley and Montucla, the Göttingen historians Kästner, Fischer, and Gmelin. Fischer, for example, wrote in the preface to his *Geschichte der Physik* (1801–8) that he is proud to offer his history to the scientific community for the purpose of learning physics (Erlernung der Physik, Vol. 1, p. xii). Its usefulness, he continued, lies in its presentation of the step-by-step development of science and in its value for acquainting the reader with those, to whom we owe all the discoveries of science. Fischer sent his eight volumes to Goethe as they appeared from the press, requesting comments from him. Goethe did not respond to the request, but we can speculate that he considered Fischer's history more a scientific textbook than a statement on the historiography of physics.

Thus, it was in Göttingen where Goethe experienced a dramatic difference between his interests in scientific life, in the process of science, and the interests of professional historians in scientific accomplishments, in the state of science. There systematic histories gave the impression that the sciences accumulated in logical patterns, a picture radically different from the one Goethe found when he began research into the traditions of color, vision, and optics. He found one in which there was no common denominator, no scientific procedure for mapping out the development of science. Goethe pictured the historiography of science as a "labyrinthine garden" (der labyrinthische Garten, p. 94), a view of history with distinct lines of movements, but one in which the origins, directions, and flow of events were vague, and at times deceptive: "Unfortunately the entire background of the history of science to the present day consists of moving specters that drift into each other but do not unite. They confuse our view to such a degree that it is hardly possible to get a clear picture of prominent and worthy figures."[24]

Goethe's decision to rise above the scientific data, to investigate the human drama behind science, was unique for this pioneer's stage in the historiography of science. The decision was based on his view that the historiography of science should show:

how one gropes and falters when one wants to dedicate himself to knowledge, how in the sciences one tends to take the back for the front and the bottom for the top; this is to be presented in the history of color theory, which, by treating a specific realm, must present symbolically the destiny of many other human efforts.[25]

This view of the historiography of science did not exclude "a priori histories," rather it embraced both the "histories of experiences" and the "histories of opinions," indeed, it comprised both "the object" and "the operation of the mind," making the historian "master over all objects." Yet, to be "master over all objects" meant developing a theory of historiography, above all it meant developing a concept of periodization, a task he had begun when he announced to Schiller his search for "salient monuments" in the literature of the field.

A discourse on paradigm shifts

The Weimar tendency to focus on the human factors in the history of science continued beyond Goethe's discussions with Schiller, although Schiller remained a central figure in this dialogue until his death in 1805. In this period Goethe was also in contact with various other historians, philologists, and intellectuals of the Weimar community, seeking further clarification of his theory of historiography.[26] In some cases Goethe worked closely with life-long friends, as with Knebel with whom he translated into German Lucretius's (96–56) *De rerum natura,* the primary source of their study in the history of atomism.[27] Based on this intimate understanding of Goethe's history, Knebel observed in 1810 that the work merited special attention as a human history, for it focused on science and on scientific life. In his view the book showed deep insight into humanity which challenged "scientific man" (der wissenschaftliche Mensch) above all to be a "human being" (Mensch, LA, II, 6, 404). It was also in a letter to Knebel that Goethe first clearly labeled his history "a symbol of the history of all sciences" (ein Symbol der Geschichte aller Wissenschaften, LA, II, 6, 331).

Goethe's goal then was to establish a relationship between the growth of knowledge and the human factors important to that development. As he explained in his chapter on Greco-Roman science, he hoped to couch the details of science in their social and humanistic context by integrating the history of color theory with (1) the history of other sciences, (2) the history of philosophy, and (3) the life and character of individuals and nations: "The history of color theory is only understandable in the context of the history of all natural sciences. For insight into the specific requires the overview of the whole."[28] By relating the development of color theory to philosophy and to human personality and national character, Goethe felt his history should symbolically present the fate of many other human activities.

Goethe's search for an integration of factors intrinsic and extrinsic to the development of science stood in contrast to the Göttingen emphasis on the intellectual development of science, on the logical and rational structure of science. The dialogue on this fundamental conflict in the historiography of science has in recent decades contributed significantly to better understanding of the dilemma confronting Goethe in 1810. Today there are those like Thomas Kuhn who continue to argue that until external and internal factors are treated as complementary concerns, "each drawing from the other, important aspects of scientific development are unlikely to be understood."[29] Yet, others like Rupert Hall, take the position that external factors, particularly socioeconomic factors, have limited interpretive capacity and tell us little about science itself. In his view external factors are concerned with science as a movement rather than as a system of knowledge.[30]

During the last two decades, greater clarity on Goethe's position has emerged through studies on the language, symbols, and metaphors used in various epochs of the history of science.[31] Although this shift is new to recent historiography, interest in the nature of scientific language has been central to the philosophy of science for several centuries, coinciding with the rise of modern science in the sixteenth and seventeenth centuries. In the philosophy of science, writers have at various times entertained the possibility of developing a sense-datum language, as in the classical taxonomies of Linnaeus, for example. At other times they have abandoned such hopes and given attention to the formation of correspondence rules that relate words to other words, but not necessarily to the individual's experience or to nature.[32]

Today there is interest in concept formation in historiography, an interest that has surfaced along with discussion of Thomas Kuhn's concept of a "paradigm" in the history of science.[33] Margaret Masterman's analysis of the twenty-one different ways Kuhn used the term, as well as subsequent attempts to specify the nature of a scientific paradigm, has brought the field to its present discussion on the way models and metaphors have functioned in scientific discourse during different periods of history.[34] It is this convergence in historiography, this common concern for understanding the relationship of language, science, and history, which brings the field full circle to Goethe, a pioneer in historiography who did not need to discover the linguistic basis of changes in the growth of knowledge because, as a writer, as a poet and a thinker, he assumed it.

The present shift of interest in historiography, this attempt to understand the linguistic value of scientific texts, has focused more clearly the difference between Goethe's historiography of science and the "histories" of his own contemporaries. Although there were others, like Georg C. Lichtenberg (1742–99), who perceived paradigm changes in the history of science, Goethe's perception of the linguistic basis of that change seems to be unique.[35] To a certain extent Goethe's long life, namely, his many years of participation in the process of science, made it possible for him to directly experience at least one significant paradigm shift, the shift in emphasis from a taxonomy to a morphology of plants. He documented this paradigm change in two essays he wrote in the last years of his life, "The Author shares the History of his Studies in Botany" (Der Verfasser teilt die Geschichte seiner botanischen Studien mit, LA, I, 10, 319–38), and "The Discussion of Debates on the Principles of Zoology at the Royal Academy in Paris, 1830" (LA, I, 10, 373–403). In the discussion of debates in Paris, Goethe observed how his own studies in botany paralleled a shift in the history of botany. That is, using his own biography as a mirror of science, he observed structure, "synchronic with his life" (synchronisch mit meinem Leben, p. 382), in the development of a specific field of science.

In the "History of his Studies in Botany" Goethe began with an attempt to define the structure of the "epoch" (Epoche, p. 319) of studies in botany that paralleled his life. In his view the first step in establishing such a structure was to identify the inventions and discoveries, the phenomena and appearances (Erscheinungen) central to all inquiries on a particular topic. And the next was to form the line of thought that proceeded from one writer to the next: "One takes great pains to determine who first gave attention to a particular event, how he behaved toward it, when and where certain appearances were first observed; one does so to the extent that new views emerge from one thought to another, which when generally applied, finally define the epoch."[36]

In Goethe's view the shift in botany ran parallel to his own career as a scientist, a period of science characterized by a change in emphasis from taxonomies to morphologies of plant life. He located the shift primarily in the work and effort of Rousseau, who developed the language needed for an alternative to Linnaeus's classification of plant life.[37] He considered Rousseau a "dilettante" (LA, I, 10, 329–30) and a stranger to professional scientific guilds, but also one who came to the study of botany with a fresh look, not a look at a more efficient instrumentation of the Linnean system, but with a look at the ontology of nature and the reality of current descriptions of organic life.[38]

When Goethe arrived in Weimar in 1775, he entered the "realm of science" (die Sphäre der Wissenschaft) in the company of miners, hunters, foresters, noblemen, poets, and intellectuals, "the noble Weimar circle" (der edle Weimarische Kreis, LA, I, 10, 320). In this company taste and knowledge and science and poetry were socially united in a pleasant and congenial manner, reflecting in a sense the style of Rousseau's approach to nature studies. In this context Goethe recalled how Linnaeus's taxonomy of plants and regular visits to the nursery at the academy in Jena remained the source of his systematic study of plant life. Yet, Goethe remembered, too, that it was not in his character to master the Linnean system, to quantize and quantify nature: "we often had to hear, that all of botany, a field which we so eagerly followed, was nothing more than nomenclature, and a whole system founded, although incompletely, on numbers."[39]

In this context Rousseau's approach to plant life was a refreshing change for the Weimar circle, for he included descriptions of plants by family and by regions, descriptions that were aesthetic, useful, and indigenous, and where they lacked richness in taxonomic specification, they gained clarity through selective illustration. In Goethe's view, it was Rousseau's effort that marked a crisis and a new stage in the science of botany: "Thus, we might well mention from our perspective, that there are advantages to entering a field of science which is in a state of crisis, and in which we also find an active, extraordinary person. We are young with young methods, our beginnings reach into a new epoch."[40]

Goethe's own response to the crisis in botanical studies came on a trip across the Alps to Italy (1786–8), where he was exposed to new forms of vegetation, particularly to exotic plants in the botanical gardens of Palermo. It was on this trip to the south, in search of an original plant (Urpflanze, LA, I, 10, 333), namely, in search of an ideal plant whose structure might be basic to all other plant forms, that Goethe developed his own theory of the morphology of plants. It was also in morphological studies where Goethe observed that the shifts in this paradigm of science were marked by a particular use of models, metaphors, and language. This tendency he recognized particularly in the debates between Saint-Hilaire and Cuvier in the Royal Academy of Science in Paris.

In his "Discussion" of those debates Goethe observed how the lines of argument reflected two distinct modes of thought (zwei verschiedene Denkweisen) that were beginning to divide the scientific world: "The former [Cuvier] proceeds from the individual to the whole, which is assumed, but is viewed as never recognizable; the latter [Saint-Hilaire] nourishes the whole inwardly and lives in the conviction that from it one can with time develop the specifics."[41] Goethe discussed many aspects of the debates, elaborating further on Saint-Hilaire's a priori and Cuvier's empirical approach, as well as on their personal lives and careers, on their forty years as colleagues in the Royal Academy. He observed the points of tension and stress, how the one emphasized a static description of nature, namely, items in arrangement (das Geregelte), and the other the changing forms of nature, namely, items in process (das Werdende). The former approach Goethe labeled stationary (stationär) and the latter he called developmental (entwickelnd, LA, I, 10, 385–7).[42]

Goethe found at least four terms that became central to the crisis in French zoological description: "materials" (Matériaux), "construction" (Composition), "branch" (Embranchement), and "design" (Plan, pp. 398–9). In one way or another, these words were intended as aids for understanding structures and relationships in organic life, but in Goethe's view, they had limited value because they originated in the crafts of ordinary life. Such words convey static images and especially the word "composition," even when applied to music, was a problem, for it gave the false impression that a work of art is "set together," as if it were of pieces to be joined. Rather, the work of art "develops" (entwickeln, p. 399), as does the organ of nature. And the word "branch" was particularly limited, for it came from carpentry and called forth a static view of nature, reflecting the joints in the structure of a building rather than describing the dynamics of change typical of organic life, where "nothing stands still" (Nichts ist stillstehend, LA, I, 6, VII).

In Goethe's view this crisis in French zoological language could be traced to a history of preoccupation with the physical aspects of nature and to the exclusive use of an atomistic, mechanistic terminology. That is, the French scientific language was inadequate for the description of subtle organic processes, transitions, growth, and change. From this crisis he further observed that an "inherited language usage suffices in common discourse, however, when the conversation becomes intellectual, it obviously stands in conflict with the higher views of excellent men."[43] And so Goethe's discussion of this crisis focused on the misunderstandings that arose in the use of metaphors grounded in concrete and tangible images of technology and everyday life.

In his view the debates of 1830 in Paris came to represent a new crisis in the history of organic studies in which the French language of morphology and structure had run its course. Even broader concepts in the dialogue, terms like "unity of structure" (Unité du Plan) eventually became inadequate because they, too, served only as "analogy" (Analogie): "Thus they used the word design, but were immediately brought to the concept of a house, of a city, which, even when applied reasonably, cannot serve as an analogy to an organic being."[44]

Goethe, like others in the Weimar circle, particularly Herder, recognized that the models and metaphors of scientific discourse were not identical with nature. This circle of thinkers understood language as a reflection of man and did not assume that language could be made to accommodate the world. Whereas Herder, a seminal thinker for the Weimar circle, exclaimed in his psychology of the human mind that "what we know, we know only through analogy," Goethe argued that through language we create "a whole new world," emphasizing that the best we can do is select our metaphors and concepts well, namely, from that "sphere of life" we are describing.[45]

Goethe's discourse on paradigm shifts was grounded in the view that an epoch of science was defined by competing languages none of which accommodate nature, and secondly that epochs of science were characterized by the use of particular sets of metaphors, which eventually run the course of adequacy and rise to a state of crisis. These perceptions of the development of science set his historiography apart from that emerging elsewhere at the turn of the century, particularly as it was practiced in Göttingen. In Goethe's view an epoch of science reaches a crisis when individuals no longer can tolerate the language and thought of those from another tradition. Thus, central to Goethe's theory of historiography was a concept of scientific biography, and secondly an analysis of the patterns of authority. In addition, Goethe developed a theory of scientific discourse based on the view that individuals differ in their ways of thinking, indeed, he argued that each individual observes the edifice of nature in accordance with his particular situation (seine Konvenienz) and therefore: "The tower of Babel lives on, they are not to be united. Every man has his quirk, Copernicus had his too."[46]

Part III

The logocentrism of scientific movements

When observing Epicurus and Lucretius we come to the general observation, that the founders of a doctrine are still aware of the difficulty of their task, and try to approach it in a naive, supple manner. The followers soon become didactic and then dogmatism intensifies to intolerance. Democritus, Epicurus, and Lucretius relate in this manner. In the last we find the way of thinking of the first, but already solidified as conviction and transmitted with partisan passion.[1]

7

Goethe's theory of biography

In the course of his scientific studies, Goethe became convinced that "the fine thread, which wafts and woofs through the web of knowledge, through the sciences in all periods, even through the darkest and most confusing ones, is drawn by individuals."[2] The scientist's stages of growth, his response to an inherited tradition, his location in society, in short, the scientist's socio-psychological development became the focus of Goethe's history of science. In his view it was in the final analysis the skillful and diligent individual (ein tüchtigeres Individuum) who must collect, sort, analyze and interpret scientific information,[3] although he recognized those times when science becomes a movement, a process beyond the influence of an individual: "Knowledge, like flowing water pent up, gradually rises to a certain niveau, where the finest discoveries do not occur so much on account of individuals as on account of the times."[4] Thus Goethe's history of color theory is an account of individuals riding the tide of science, an approach recognizing both the creative energies of the individual and the support of communities, scientific and cultural.[5]

Goethe's scientific biographies follow a pattern in which the individual's personality and stages of development are related to his scientific contributions. And these dimensions, namely, personality, stages of growth, and scientific activity, are usually cloaked in external materials, in information on the individual's environment, on his habitat, and on his social context, for Goethe thought it is the climate of the times that conditions the scientist and his work.[6] As scientists are usually unaware of these external influences on personality and development, they normally do not question the effects of environment upon their work; indeed, the individual is often quite satisfied with the status quo; he allows emotional, intellectual, and biographical functions to be conditioned by the commonplaces (Gemeinplätze, WA, I, 37, 331) of ordinary life.[7] Schools in particular condition the individual in this manner, for there students are introduced to many phenomena, but it is also these phenomena that condition the individual's perception of the world about him so that he sees only what he has been taught to see. This cycle can hardly be changed and "of course the masses are always on the side of the ruling school" (Freilich ist die Menge immer auf der herrschenden Schule, LA, I, 3, 152).

The individual, prototypes of an era

As a biographer Goethe attempted to focus on those perspectives conditioned by a particular school of thought; he tried to articulate the extent to which a scientist held views in common with those of other thinkers and writers. In his history of color theory, Theophrastus's theoretical statements, for example, were connected easily to the school of Aristotelian thought, as were the views of Franciscus Aguilonius (1566–1617) and Franciscus Grimaldi (1618–63) in later centuries. But Goethe also showed how individuals were influenced by their own century, as in the case of Grimaldi who participated in the epochal change, in which Aristotle's view that light was accidental was replaced with the idea that it was a substance. Goethe saw too that such changes in schools of thought were gradual, for Grimaldi was not permitted to express publically the view of light as a substance and, hence, his treatise on the topic turned into a strange mixture of theories, expressions, and experiences, in the end submitting to the traditional view that "light is accidental" (das Licht sey ein Accidens, LA, II, 6, 260).

Because Goethe made the individual the prime mover in the origins of a school of thought, he made the study of personality central to his study of scientific biographies. In this Newton was his object lesson, for in his view Newton's success as a scientist was grounded both in his own genius and in the conditions of English society at the time. In part it was England's philosophy of education that allowed each child to develop in its own manner, to become independent. This included the permission to react against public opinion and to ignore the commonplaces of tradition. This England, into which Newton was born, was bursting with life; there was political upheaval, change in government, and conflict between state and church. Goethe found it hard to believe that anyone could have avoided being swept up and drawn into the activity of the era.

He found it even more remarkable that in this environment certain individuals were able to retain their particular personality and character. In his view Newton was able to because he blocked out the outer world and dedicated his talents to more introspective aspects of science: "Newton was a well-organized, healthy and good-tempered man, without passion, without desires. His mind was of a constructive nature, in the most abstract sense; therefore advanced mathematics became the true vehicle through which he constructed his inner world and with which he attempted to dominate the outer world."[8] With these personality traits Goethe proceeded to explain the thoroughness with which Newton presented his optics, his tendency to idealize, formalize, and mathematize his perceptions, which led to his conception of nature and to the operations that he performed on the world around him. Thus, it was quite natural that Newton's color theory should reflect abstractions of the mind rather than the data (Faktum, LA, I, 3, 156) of sensory experience.

Goethe also discussed the social and cultural influences on the science and personality of other individuals. He observed that Roger Bacon, for example, was born into an environment (Kultur) that had inherited traditional Christian attitudes toward man and nature but at the same time showed progressive social and political ideals such as were represented in the Magna Carta (1215). This and the security of the monastery in which Bacon lived gave his work composure, circumspection, and clarity: "Even though Roger was only a monk and kept himself inside the monastery, the atmosphere of such surroundings penetrated through the walls, and certainly he owes it to national tendencies that his mind was able to rise above the dreary prejudices of the times and hasten forward in advance of the future."[9]

Goethe compared some individuals with their contemporaries, showing the extent to which two individuals from the same period differed in their scientific efforts because of the conditions in which they lived. Georg Agricola (1494–1555), for example, was born and raised in a German mining community and his entire scientific effort focused on related problems. Francis Bacon on the other hand was an islander and belonged to a nation whose shipping industry put him in touch with the rest of the world. And because this industry was vital to the interests of the country, Bacon identified wind as one of the most critical scientific problems of the day (LA, I, 6, 149). In other cases Goethe explained that an individual's genius was enhanced by the tide of events, so that Galileo, for example, came "like a diligent reaper to a rich harvest" (wie ein tüchtiger Schnitter zur reichlichsten Ernte, p. 154), and with his telescope opened up the sky.

Goethe's scientific biography generally included discussion of the individual's development and his personality. However, the depth of analysis varied with the availability of documents and with the significance of the individual for a particular period of history. That is, Goethe made comprehensive coverage essential to those cases where the individual was of general significance to the development of science: "For insight into the smallest part requires the overview of the whole" (Denn zur Einsicht in den geringsten Teil ist die Uebersicht des Ganzen nötig, p. 69). By locating the scientist's total being in the context of the historical process, Goethe developed models in which the life of that individual would represent scientific work of an entire epoch. Thus, in many cases the individual served as an ideal type, or better, as a prototype, for Goethe did not turn the individual into an abstraction consisting of qualities compiled from all other scientists of the epoch. Instead, he looked primarily for those qualities the individual had in common with most other scientists from his era: "We think of Lucius Annaeus Seneca here not for his work in colors, since it is very little and is only mentioned casually, but more because of his general relationship to science."[10]

In discussing Seneca as a prototype of Roman science, he began with observations on his personality. He observed that Seneca was a diligent individual, as were many of his contemporaries and, although he showed a great liveliness and interest in nature, he was often overwhelmed by those monumental events that have intrigued man since the beginning of time: the rainbow, eclipses, comets, and earthquakes. He thought that Seneca's discussion of these events digresses and regresses at random, consistently showing evidence of activity but also showing little evidence of critical standards of science. Although he interacted well with other members of the scientific community, he also took issue with those asserting obviously false views, such as the view that comets are transitory phenomena; he chided some of his contemporaries for their gullibility and superstitions (Leichtgläubigkeit und Aberglauben, p. 80).

According to Goethe, Seneca was particularly disturbed by the general decadence of Roman society (das Verderbnis der Römer, p. 81). But Goethe concluded that, although Seneca was critical of the excess of Roman society, its utilitarian attitudes and its lack of critical judgments, he was still a child of the times, the best representative of a period diverse in interests, divisive in action, and limited in success. Although Seneca possessed a serious attitude toward the study of nature, Roman society did not seem to provide an environment in which such attitudes could support the development of scientific methods and discovery. The general desire for luxury (Luxus and Pracht, pp. 80–1) was an outgrowth of an uneducated society, whose material wealth had far exceeded the cultural sophistication necessary to properly administer it. This same inconsistency between technology and culture also explained Roman scientific interest in the exotic, in the extraordinary events of nature. In fact, wrote Goethe, it led to excesses such as one which he called a second Roman population (das zweite Volk, p. 81), which consisted solely of statues. Thus, in Goethe's study of Seneca the individual explained the whole society, just as generalizations about Roman science served better understanding of Seneca. In the essay Seneca's inner and outer being, his social environment, and his national heritage all came together to form a composition on the typical scientist in Roman times.[11]

In addition to the scientific personality and the prototypes of a scientific era, Goethe looked at developmental phases in the life of scientists. In his view "the life of every significant individual, which has not been marked by an early death, can be divided into three phases, into that of the first formation, that of the actual striving, and into that of arriving at the goal, at completion."[12] The first and the last phases, the formative years and the years of accomplishment, are usually without conflict. But the transition period consists of problems generated by the individual's tendency to assert his own views. Thus, the period of striving toward achievement becomes critical, for it is marked by general confusion, by obstacles, and by the attempt of authorities to control and entrench the norms of scientific thought.[13]

During the first phase of a scientist's life, everything is done to enhance and develop the young scientist's capabilities, and each significant step is recognized with rewards. The individual is supported with a great deal of enthusiasm. However, as the scientific community becomes aware of his aggressions, everything is done to restrain him, for he has suddenly challenged the experiences and beliefs of the established scientists: "This epoch is generally one of conflict, and one can never say that this era gains honor through his person. The honor belongs to the individual, to him alone and to those few who encouraged him and stood by him."[14] In the third phase, in the period of completion, there is less conflict, although this more subdued and peaceful phase does not always grant the aspiring individual any more respect than was granted during his phase of striving. In the third phase the individual may simply be tolerated while resistance remains latent.

Newton's biography, perhaps more than that of most individuals discussed in Goethe's history, illustrated these stages of growth. In the chapter on "Newton's Relationship to Society," Goethe described the first stage of his young adulthood (Jüngling, LA, I, 6, 262), which began with connections to established members of the scientific community, such as Heinrich Oldenburg (1615 or 1627?–78). Newton's aggressive phase became apparent when he presented the catoptric telescope to the Royal Society and claimed a patent to its discovery, challenging technical and theoretical work in dioptrics. According to Goethe the theory of color and optics underlying the fabrication of the telescope was not discussed initially and only later did it become an issue in the scientific community. Goethe described Newton's reaction to the controversy issuing from the first opponents: "He did not actually controverse, he only repeated to his opponents: conceive the topic as I do, approach it in my way, organize everything the way I have, see as I do, conclude as I do, and so you will find what I have found."[15] Newton engaged his opponents with an unusual steadfastness and his success, Goethe thought, was grounded in a confidence in his methods and a belief in the accuracy of his discoveries.

Newton, Newtonians, and anti-Newtonians

In Goethe's view, innovation in science originates in the individual, but is advanced in schools of thought; that is, it emerges from within the individual's being but usually is integrated into large philosophical movements associated with the names of the original thinker. For centuries these schools of thought endured, but around the sixteenth century, they were replaced by the efforts of new authorities: "The epochs of science in general and of color theory in particular will show such an oscillation in several ways. We will see how the warehouse of the past becomes burdensome for the human mind in a period, when the new, the present, also begins to emerge with force."[16]

Schools of thought, as understood by Goethe, were a function of the manner in which they received documents.[17] At times old documents would become a hindrance to the advancement of science, as in the case of British science. Here Goethe found that a rejection of the past and a partisan interest in the present provided the tide upon which science was carried during most of the eighteenth century. From Newton's efforts emerged the Newtonians (Newtonianer), a school of thought social in structure and normative in impact: "On British Patriotism. He who challenges Newton in the fields of physics and mathematics is not treated as an opponent, but as a rebel. Argumentation in color theory, as well as in differential and integer-calculus, is taken personally by the academy, indeed, by the whole nation. The entire populace, like Newton himself, is a *noli me tangere*."[18]

The longest chapter in Goethe's history covers a period entitled "From Newton to Dollond" (Von Newton bis auf Dollond, pp. 238-360). The chapter includes over a hundred pages on the development of color theory from Newton's innovation to the Newtonian standardization, coming full circle to crisis and change of emphasis in research on color theory. He began his discussion of this epoch with a description of Newton's education, his attainment of the master's degree in 1667 and with his appointment in 1669 as professor of mathematics at Trinity College, Cambridge. And he ended the period with Leonhard Euler's (1707–83) theoretical and John Dollond's (1706–61) technical demonstration that the color aberrations in the dioptric telescope could be remedied, challenging Newton's justification for the technology of the reflector telescope. The period ended with the observation that Newton's initial claim to scientific accomplishment was unfounded; it ended with proof that refraction and dispersion were not proportional and that it was possible to correct chromatic aberrations in objectives.

With the Newton–Dollond episode in the history of color, vision, and light, Goethe demonstrated all aspects of his theory of the historiography of science. Here he formalized his view that the standardization of language is both evidence of science as a movement and the source of inadequacy leading to the crisis of the movement. That is, his analysis of the Newtonian paradigm showed that through the individual's initiative schools of thought are established, and that through the schools of thought language is standardized and science is normalized.

A reconstruction of Goethe's research notes and of the narrative in his history illustrates his attention to the writings of Newtonians and anti-Newtonians. These notes, outlined in Table 7.1 below, show how he followed the school of thought from its local origins to its global impact.

In Goethe's view, there was no mystique about how Newton's theory of

Table 7.1. *The Newtonian Epoch*

The adversaries[a]	The school[b]
The Royal Society	
7 first opponents	7 first followers
Edme Mariotte	Wilhelm s'Gravesande
Giovanni Rizzetti	Petrus Musschenbroek
The French Academy	
Philppe de La Hire	Nicola Malebranche
Johann M. Conradi	Bernard de Fontenelle
Melchior de Polignac	Jean J. de Mairan
The public	
Charles F. Dufay (in technology)	Voltaire (writer)
Louis B. Castel (color theorist)	F. Algarotti (writer)
J. Gauthier (chemist)	J. C. Le Blond (chemist)
The international scene	
New Currents	Old School
Johann T. Mayer (chemist)	38 German scientists
Johann H. Lambert (photometry)	6 Gottingen Academy professors
Karl Scherffer (physiology)	1 British textbook
Benjamin Franklin (physiology)	1 French encyclopedia

[a]Nineteen documents were consulted by Goethe.
[b]Sixty-one documents were consulted by Goethe.

color became so successful. With his chapter on the Newtonian paradigm he attempted to show both the scientific and sociopsychological basis of this movement in the history of science; he proceeded from an analysis of Newton's texts on optics to a study of the scientific community's expatiation of the fundamental themes of color theory. To illustrate this development in history Goethe showed the alternating responses to Newton's color theory, both within the scientific community and throughout society in general as summarized in the Table 7.1. Although most of the individuals discussed in the chapter tended to react either favorably (Newtonianer, pp. 366, 370, 400) or unfavorably (Anti-newtonianer, pp. 342, 350) to Newton's color theory, each one did so with varying degrees of intensity, and then usually to only a particular aspect of it.

The first opponent to receive Goethe's critical examination was Mariotte, whom Goethe had difficulty classifying as either a student or as an opponent of Newton. However, Goethe did classify him as an opponent because he had questioned the physical basis of Newton's color theory; that is, Mariotte had observed that Newton had excluded physiological and psychological phenomena in his theory, excluding, for example, "the duration of images and the abatement of color" in the eye (Dauer des Eindrucks and farbiges Abklingen, p. 281).[19]

99

The logocentrism of scientific movements

The second individual opposing Newton in Goethe's history was Rizzetti, an individual who clearly took issue with Newton's disregard for dioptric images and instruments. However, Rizzetti's efforts to advance dioptrics in the scientific community were opposed in most European centers of learning. Also, although Rizzetti had accepted the view of light as a substance, he tempered this view with his own theory that particles separate unwillingly. Thus, colors were not a product of the analysis of light, but a combination of light and darkness, colors were a partial light, a half-light (Halblicht, p. 290).

Goethe ranked Rizzetti, beside Theophrastus and Boyle, as one of the three great contributors to the advancement of color theory, for he like them tried to develop a holistic theory. They all tried to organize the entire range of phenomena on the subject of color rather than to limit the field to a few phenomena in optics as Newton had done. Goethe noted especially Rizzetti's attempt to deal with the physiological colors and in this connection he criticized the experimental philosophy as it was advanced by the Royal Society. Here he observed how individuals like Mariotte and Rizzetti were attacked by Newtonians, such as Sir Hans Sloane (1660–1752) who served as an experimenter for the Society and defended the Newtonian system against conflicting theories.[20] Here Goethe observed a well-organized support system in a society that claimed a nonpartisan approach to science. In Goethe's view particularly proponents like Sloane employed their position for the advancement of Newtonian science and toward the repudiation of other possible viewpoints.[21]

After showing how Newtonian color science had withstood its first opponents, Goethe focused on the explanation of how Newtonian science became dogma. At first followers devoted their efforts to simply understanding Newton's system of thought, particularly in mathematical physics. Among these individuals he listed Samuel Clarke (1675–1729) who translated the *Opticks* (1706) into Latin and rewrote Jacques Rohault's (1620–75) *Traité de physique* (1697) according to Newtonian science. Goethe observed how Rohault had originally written his *Traité de physique* (Paris, 1671), according to Cartesian physics and how Clarke had in the translation introduced Newtonian science by first commenting on Newton's physics in the footnotes: "In this manner Newton's doctrine was first introduced into the lesson parallel to that of Descartes, but after a while the latter was completely suppressed."[22]

After establishing the process by which Newton's students had come to understand the new physics, Goethe expanded his analysis of the epoch to include discussion of scientific efforts abroad, particularly in the French Academy. Here Goethe departed from discussion of Newtonian science and assessed primarily vehicles of popularization in the advancement of normalized science. In general Goethe found fault with the lack of critical thought in the work of popularizers. He thought they would reveal to the audience only that which was sensational and in no manner reflected the complexity of scientific problems. Nor did they represent the intellectual breadth of the master who devised the system. He observed that the public, which enjoys being informed in such matters, is generally not aware of the scope and depth of the system, of the presuppositions and limitations of the system: "The value, worth, and completeness, indeed, the truth about an object is of no concern to the speaker; for him the main question is whether or not the matter is interesting or can be made interesting."[23]

According to Goethe, it was Voltaire who became Newton's greatest popularizer, as he was adept particularly at expressing a point in many different styles; that is, his specific contribution could be attributed to his ability to articulate the language of Newtonian science and this made Voltaire one of the most powerful individuals of his nation. He also was able to suppress effectively all opposition: "With great force and skill he knew how to suppress his opponents; and what he could not force upon the public, that he achieved through flattery, through acclimatization."[24]

In this manner "Newton's gospel" (das Newtonische Evangelium, p. 320) became dogma and found its way into most textbooks, schools, academies of science, courtly societies, and literary circles. Goethe observed that after Voltaire had popularized Newtonian science, it was not easy to find a speaker, artist, or poet who had not at one time or another made use of the division of light into color as a metaphor for the illustration of analysis and synthesis, or principles of unity and diversity. Yet he also observed with a touch of distance and irony that:

once such a curious synthesis has been made for the purpose of such a strange analysis, and when the belief in it is general, no one is to be blamed, if he [the orator] also uses it in his own behalf as an instance or a simile, be it for the purposes of persuading and convincing, or dazzling and inducing.[25]

Goethe traced this school of thought internationally and found not the slightest evidence of independent work. Everywhere he found the same phraseology for the study of color. The procedures were always the same: (1) make a relatively small opening in the window, (2) let a beam of light through the opening, (3) let the beam of light fall through the prism, and (4) see the light separate into seven colors. The steps were the same, whether written in vernacular or Latin, as in Johannes Wenceslaus Caschubius's (d. 1727?) *Elementa Physicae* (Jena, 1718): "Here that refrain began which was to be repeated again and again: *si per foramen rotundem* etc." (Hier fängt schon der Refrain an, den man künftig immer fort hört: si per foramen rotundem etc., p. 345). Nowhere was Goethe able to find followers of the school who permitted themselves, or others, independent thinking or questions about equally important matters in the physiology and the psychology of color perception.

According to Goethe, the scientific community's threshold of tolerance for more flexible modes of representation continued to decline in the course of the eighteenth century. That is, with the increase of "science," there was an

101

increase in the number of participants and in the formalization of terminology and procedures. Thus, he observed in the century a decline in the possibility of a more flexible and personalized language of science, which to him signaled a regression in the history of science. It is not surprising that Goethe would at times become vindictive and label much of science from the eighteenth century as "parrotry" (Nachbeterei), "the same old story" (die alte Leier), or that he would often conclude that "the traditional song is being cranked out" (das hergebrachte Lied wird abgeorgelt, pp. 350–1).

From the tone of Goethe's chapter on Newtonianism in color theory, it becomes clear that Goethe's vindictive moments are grounded in a search for a broader view of color theory than was being presented by the followers of Newton's science. He thought Newton's theory did not account for chemical and physiological color phenomena, and so he was particularly eager to point out that commercially it would not be practical to manufacture dyes based on the scheme of seven primary colors of Newton's theory. He also drew attention to the efforts of those like Lambert in photometry and Scherffer and Franklin in physiology, individuals who were finding new data, for example, on the nature of colored shadows and the measurements of color hues, data not accounted for in the Newtonian color system. With the presentation of these new developments in color science, Goethe closed a chapter that had traced a system of knowledge from its original conception, through a process of student conformation and public popularization, to its eventual acceptance as international dogma.

Achromatism, an epoch in crisis

Goethe marked the final phase of the Newtonian school of thought with an essay on "achromatism" (Achromasie, pp. 361–5). Here he tells the story of how in his opinion the technology of Dollond and the mathematics of Euler eventually unseated Newton's view that the dioptric telescope was not to be improved.[26] Recognizing one of the serendipitous events of the history of science, Goethe recalled how Dollond, a student of Newtonian science, had set out to prove that Euler's mathematical description of an improved dioptric telescope was wrong. Instead, Dollond found it correct and by constructing objectives from crown and flint glass, he made possible a refractor telescope without color aberrations, reinstating a scientific instrument which had come into disuse about a century earlier. Goethe found Euler's status unique in the history of science in that he was one of those few destined to start from the beginning and thereby develop original insights into nature and technology.

Newton had maintained a proportional relationship between refraction and dispersion of light, making it impossible to arrest color dispersion without also terminating refraction. As Goethe pointed out, Euler recognized that the eye was achromatic, allowing refraction without color dispersion, and that the dioptric telescope, like the eye, could be improved through the combination of two different kinds of glass with a liquid contained between them. Thus, Goethe concluded that Euler had disproved a part of the Newtonian optics from the perspective largely ignored by the Newtonian school of science: the physiology of the eye (die Betrachtung des menschlichen Auges, p. 362).[27] But the school continued to support Newton's theory of optics and actually evolved a concept capable of accounting for the Euler–Dollond discovery: "dispersion" (Zerstreuung, p. 363). To the end Goethe was not willing to accept the concept as an improvement upon Newton's language of color theory. He considered it patchwork (Flickwerk, p. 363), as simply another example in the history of science where a new term was invented to heal the wounds of an ailing theory, as a substitute for the direct observation of nature.

Goethe harbored many reservations about the direction of eighteenth-century science, particularly about the directions in physics, and based on these convictions he engaged in an extensive campaign against Newton's theory of optics, specifically.[28] However, despite Goethe's error in a fundamental point of physics, or regardless of what his motive may have been, his analysis of the Newtonian research paradigm represents one of his most significant contributions to the historiography of science, a contribution at least equal to any in his science, for Goethe anticipated by about a century modern views on the psychology and sociology of knowledge.[29]

Into old age Goethe attempted to explain the growth of knowledge as a social and psychological process. In 1829, in some brief notes on the history of geology entitled "Dogmatism and Skepsis" (Dogmatismus und Skepsis, LA, I, 11, 305), he outlined the process by which Werner's theory of the sedimentary forces of geological change had hardened into doctrine. He explained that it had become outdated and eventually did not agree with the concept of granite as a product of crystallization from igneous and aqueous action. Thus, it became vulnerable, for "in the end all dogmatisms of the world become burdensome" (Nun aber wird aller Dogmatismus der Welt am Ende lästig, p. 305).

From this incident in the history of geology, Goethe observed that skepticism emerges as a "natural course of the human mind" (natürlicher Gang des menschlichen Geistes, p. 305), namely, in the case of Werner's theory, it emerged at that point when the theory could survive only as doctrine. It simply rises from the "unexplained problems" (unerklärte Probleme) left in the wake of outdated theories, and once questions are asked about a detail of the theory, the whole system becomes suspect: "Skepticism has many advantages in that it feeds on the natural anxiety and doubt of the human being; one can easily make a dogma suspicious. But then this requires a certain intellectual power, endurance, and talent for persuasion, which is used particularly in inductive reasoning."[30]

Thus, forms of reasoning, persuasion, rhetoric, and other logocentric dimensions of intellectual life inform the thrust of Goethe's theory of the history of science. He found that argumentation by induction alone defies the possibility of communication in ordinary language. From it arises an incredible "scaffolding of steps and ladders" (Gerüste von Stufenleitern, p. 305). And yet the tide of science overcomes all systems, for even when skepticism becomes dogmatic "it too must either let problems lie, or solve them in a manner that shocks common sense" (Denn auch sie muss Probleme entweder ruhen lassen oder auf eine Weise lösen die den Menschenverstand in Alarm setzt, p. 305).

8

Goethe's concept of authority

In talking about transmission we are immediately called upon to speak about authority. For, when looked at closely, every authority is a sort of transmission. We accept the existence, dignity and power of things without clearly understanding and recognizing their origins, descent and value.[1]

Symbols of continuity

Goethe organized his history of science so that color theory was presented as a fine line of thoughts and discoveries, as events informed by a broader scientific movement in which the individual was the prime mover: "How a person thinks about a certain case, will only be properly understood when it is known, how the person is disposed. This matters when one truly wants to understand opinions about scientific events, be they of individuals or entire schools and centuries."[2] For this reason Goethe integrated a broad range of materials from philosophy, biography, and society into his history, following Francis Bacon's insight that the "fusion" (Vereinigung) of "knowledge" (Erkenntnis) and "objects" (Gegenstände) did not progress "in a smooth, graduated and consequent manner" (auf eine gelinde, stufenartige und immer consequente Weise, LA, II, 6, 67).[3]

Goethe recognized with Bacon the sociopsychological basis of science, the range of cultural influences on the path of science, including "idols of the tribe" (Stammgötzen, Idola tribus), "idols of the heart" (Busen- oder Schoosgötzen, Idola specus), "idols of the market" (Marktgötzen, Idola forti), and "idols of the theatre" (Theatergötzen, Idola theatri, p. 68).[4] But he looked beyond these "idols of the mind" into one of the fundamental issues in science and learning in the modern world, into the role of "authority" (Autorität, LA, I, 6, 92–5) in the transmission of texts and ideas.[5] It is in his concept of authority that Goethe explained his view of the driving forces of science, namely, his view of the progress and change of ideas on color over long periods of time.

In his essay on authority, Goethe explained that this force of history is constructed from the fragments of tradition. In his view an authority is a

105

concept in which ideas, experiments, and theories are synthesized by an individual, advanced by groups, at some point becoming yet another piece in the amorphous state of tradition. That is, an authority is not identical with the tradition but adds to it, thus, "every authority is a sort of transmission" (Denn genau betrachtet, so ist jede Autorität eine Art Ueberlieferung, LA, I, 6, 92).[6] In Goethe's view, an authority is formed by "reason" (Vernunft) and "conscience" (Gewissen p. 92), by the powers of cognition. And therefore, authority is impenetrable (unergründlich), for the human mind is not like tradition, that is, fragmentary, but can be forced into systems and patterns of thought that can ignore or permit ambiguity, gaps, and vagueness in the object of study.[7]

In Goethe's view, authority is based on external factors of the mind, on rational and logical forms of thought; but although reason may be used to shape an impenetrable system, it cannot penetrate the essential qualities of events, or the stream of reality.[8] Goethe thought this could only be accomplished with "understanding" (Verstand, LA I, 6, 92), for with understanding one does not build systems of rational structure, but attempts to comprehend the inner being of the object. With reason, on the other hand, we systematize the accidental to our own ends. That is, an authority is developed through reason for its own use (Gebrauch, p. 93), while understanding only generates, or re-creates its own image, forming anarchy rather than authority.

But reason rules over understanding; it explains, interprets, shapes, and organizes the fragments of tradition and eventually has an existence all its own: "Soon we see gathering around an excellent individual friends, students, followers, companions, escorts, cohabitants, and partisans."[9] When such support begins to accumulate, certain documents are canonized and accepted without critical examination. Thus, the external aspects of science, the schools, academies, books, and journals become extremely important in the propagation of an authority.

The concept of authority is primary in Goethe's theory of historiography, for it is at the same time a phenomenon of culture and a construct of the mind. It is an *Urphänomen* of his theory of historiography, grounded in the life of individual scientists and fused with Goethe's ideas of the collective movement of science.[10] In the collective movements he saw a fluctuating response to authority similar to that in the life of the individual, developmental phases in which "the child" (das Kind) is comfortable with the authority of his parents, while "the adolescent" (der Knabe) fights it and "the young adult" (der Jüngling) flees it; "the mature adult" (der Mann) accepts it because he understands that, if he does not, he will get nowhere: "In this manner humanity oscillates in totality" (Eben so schwankt die Menschheit im ganzen, LA, I, 6, 93).[11]

With the concept of authority, Goethe was able to explain the progress of science, on the one hand discussing the continuity and improvement of the laws of chromatics, on the other showing the role certain individuals played in shaping this progress. In a sketch from his research notes, we see how Goethe viewed this progression in color theory, namely, as three epochs of authority, beginning with the ancients who theorized all colors from two sources, light and darkness, that is, as the authority of the "dualists" (Dualisten, LA, II, 6, 72). Moving to the second phase, he showed how writers from the Middle Ages explained that colors came from two chemical elements and a third bonding force, a phase that Goethe called the authority of the "trinitarians" (Trinitarier). And the third phase of authority, the one ending in his own era, was grounded in the view that colors were of a single source, light, and, therefore, appropriately labeled the authority of the "solitarians" (Solitarier).[12] With these concepts Goethe gave shape to three tendencies in the development of color theory, and by selecting concepts with symbolic value, he emphasized both the scientific and social dimensions of historiography.

With these three numerical symbols, Goethe invented concepts for organizing the development of color theory from the time of the Greeks to the present, concepts that showed the fine line connecting theories of color, as well as the relationship of science to life, society, and philosophy. The dualists, trinitarians and solitarians represented the social and intellectual development of color theory, they comprised the individual scientists, students, schools and institutions, indeed, these terms integrated external factors of society with the development of color theory as a system of knowledge. With them Goethe discovered a heuristic device for organizing his historiography of color theory, for explaining the textual centers of progress in science, the individuality and the specificity of a movement in science. Indeed, in this symbolic representation of the historiography of color theory, Goethe found nonmetrical concepts of the type also used in his science, concepts of centrality with "fringes" of meaning, in this case terms useful for painting the broad strokes of history, useful for integrating the knowledge of science with the movement of science.

The dualists

Goethe began his representation of the red thread of authority with the dualists: "They evolved colors from the reciprocal action of light and darkness according to the instruction of Aristotle and especially of Theophrastus."[13] In Aristotle, Goethe found the prototype, the constellation of writings, ideas, and thoughts of the dualists. In Aristotle's students, primarily in Theophrastus, he found the dualists' color theory advanced in greater detail, and under the numerical symbol he included the contributions of those from later centuries.

In the earliest sources of the dualist tradition, Goethe found that color was viewed as a physiological process, that the dualists studied color from the perspective of the viewer. This perspective Goethe observed in Empedocles (495–433), who understood colors as the mutual interaction of the inner eye with its outer environment, following the principle that "a likeness is recognized by a likeness" (Aehnliches wird durch Aehnliches erkannt, LA, I, 6, 2 and 72). However, it was in the writings of Plato that Goethe found the clearest expression of the dualists theory of color and vision, "for he tells us: through white vision is released and through black it is collected."[14] Goethe also found that Plato anticipated the effect of turbid mediums (das trübe Mittel, p. 73), a concept with which Goethe later explained the color blue in his theory of physical colors. Thus, from the beginning the authority of the dualists was grounded in a physiology of sight, a theory in which it was assumed that the eye reciprocated with an object in a process of "contraction" (Zusammenziehen), "expansion" (Ausdehnen), "gathering" (Sammeln), "releasing" (Entbinden), "binding" (Fesseln), and "dissolving" (Lösen, p. 72).

But Goethe united the fragments of the tradition in the name of Aristotle, the prototype of the dualists' color theory: "We can combine everything in Aristotle's name that the ancients knew about this matter" (Wir [können] unter dem Namen des Aristoteles alles versammeln, was den Alten über diesen Gegenstand bekannt gewesen, p. 72). His binary mode of thinking was typical of the ancients, for they recognized reciprocal relations in other phenomena of nature, as in magnetism and electricity. Thus, in their theory yellow developed from a moderated light and blue from a relieved darkness, while red emerged from the effects of shadow on light. The theory essentially explained the process of sight, and was consistent with explanation of other physiological processes; sight was a mixture of white and black, just as tastes varied with the combinations of sweet and sour.

In the name of one of Aristotle's students, Theophrastus, and in the text, *De coloribus,* the authority of the dualists reigned for a millennium. As in all transmissions, this one waxed and waned in significance until the early Renaissance period, when it became the object of critical commentary and philological analysis. Goethe prized the integrity of the text, for it was transmitted whole and without serious change from the original, a condition which he attributed to the binary mode in which it was conceived and presented: "the comprehensible number, its self-contained double symmetry and the resulting convenience made the theory adaptable for propagation."[15]

In Goethe's history the dualists' theory continued into the seventeenth and eighteenth centuries, although by this time the trinitarians and the solitarians had challenged the theory of colors based on the dualism of light and darkness. Kircher, for example, retained the dualistic framework, focusing on specific phenomena such as the duration of an image in the eye (LA, I, 6, 179). Others like Johann Funccius (1680–1729) retained the principles of light and darkness, but approached the field quantitatively, attempting to measure color appearances. Thus, "red would consist of the same quantities of light and darkness, yellow of two parts light and one part shadow, blue of two parts shadow and one part light."[16]

Lazare Nuguet (ca. 1700) and Rizzetti were discussed as recent dualists, as individuals coming closer to Goethe's own theory of color. Indeed, Nuguet came very close for he observed in the solar spectrum that "yellow and blue belong more to light, red and violet more to shadow."[17] Then Goethe, as the most recent dualist, injected his own theory that red emerges as "a turbid double image over light" (ein trübes Doppelbild über das Licht) and violet as "a double image over a shadow" (ein trübes Doppelbild über das Dunkle, LA, I, 6, 216). Although Rizzetti had come close to Goethe's theory, recognizing that red developed from the turbid medium, he did not accept the double image as fact (als Faktum, p. 291). But he did form a link in the fine line of authorities in color theory, connecting the internal system of color science leading to Goethe's work, which failed in physical optics, but contributed to the physiology of colors, the field in which the authority of the dualists had originated.[18]

The trinitarians

The trinitarians approached the study of color from another direction: "According to Paracelsus it is assumed that, in various productive stages, the primordial light created the three chemical elements: salt, sulphur and mercury."[19] Goethe addressed the origins of this system of thought in an essay on the "Pleasure in Mystery" (Lust am Geheimnis, LA, I, 6, 106–8), noting the increase in scientific writing during the Middle Ages, as well as the emerging reception of Greek, Latin, and Arabic texts. But the reception was without criticism, for all writings were judged of equal value, which meant that the writings of the dualists, too, did not have an effect on science in the medieval period. Yet, it was in this neglect of tradition that Goethe located the rise to a new way of looking at nature: "In this way observations on a fresh and newly discovered nature arose" (Eben so drängten sich die Beobachtungen einer erst wieder neu und frisch erblickten Natur auf, p. 107).

In Goethe's view, the trinitarians' "hands-on" approach to the study of nature was a positive trend in the history of science, even though the thoughts and experiences of the individual were often kept secret and were mixed with esoteric aspects of the epoch. Goethe noted that this tendency, to cloak observations on nature in a language of secrecy, lasted well into the seventeenth century, and that "the art of concealment" (Verheimlichungskunst, p. 107) brought confusion to intellectual life, particularly in the period between the Middle Ages and the Renaissance. In this period writings were hidden in codes, symbols, allegory, riddle, and trickery, and not only did this kind of study make the public apprehensive about science, but soon charlatanism and conceit led to complete confusion on the difference between truth and error.

Yet, Goethe observed that it was the trinitarians' enthusiastic manipulation of nature that eventually changed this mystification of learning. The substances of nature were decomposed and analyzed, and from this analysis a new world arose, giving educated people a second realm of experiences to reflect upon. Comprehending this second world, the world created by the manipulation of nature, then became the common effort of physicist and chemist, and with this union the authority of the trinitarians took shape.

In Paracelsus, Philippus Aureolus Theophrastus Bombastus von Hohenheim (1493–1541), Goethe found the prototype representing the development of color theory after the Middle Ages (LA, I, 6, 128–9). Goethe explained how Paracelsus searched for the source of colors in light, although light was for the trinitarians not a substance. It was for them an idea consisting of three principles: salt, sulphur, and mercury (LA, II, 6, 73), concepts with which Paracelsus defined each of the four elements of the ancients: fire, water, earth, and air. Paracelsus then labeled each of these concepts according to an effect of acid on alkali; that is, according to the effects of sulphur on salt. Mercury, the third principle, served only to label that mysterious source of unification (begeistendes Vereinigungs-mittel).[20] In this way Paracelsus also explained the origin of colors, namely, as the effects of an acid on a base and, while he did not have a full understanding of these effects, and thought of them as principles in the mystical sense, he did add scope to the study of color theory: "If every element shares in the more elevated sense of a mystical sulfur, then it can be understood, how in the most diverse instances colors can emerge."[21]

Goethe discussed the continuation of the school of trinitarians in an essay on "alchemists" (Alchymisten, pp. 129–32), where various authorities were mentioned, like Hermes Trismegistus, the reputed author of a collection of occult writings, and Zosimus of Panopolis, the first known alchemist.[22] Goethe collectively represented the students of this doctrine with the number "3" and with this symbol he related the chemical studies of Paracelsus to the ideas of God, virtue, and immortality, as well as to their sensory equivalents – gold, health, and long life. Gold was as powerful on earth as God in the heavens, and from such powerful symmetry arose the search for a single substance with which one could realize the trinity, namely a "virgin soil" (eine jungfräuliche Erde, p. 130), a substance that could not be further decomposed and that could be produced only with universal recipes. Despite detailed study of this symmetry, Goethe found little in the alchemy of the trinitarians that advanced color theory, for colors were only observed to the extent that they described the spiritual trinity.

Goethe presented Giambattista della Porta (1538–1615) and his *Magia naturalis* (1558) as the prototype of the trinitarians in the sixteenth century: "If we would take all of his collected works together, we would see the entire century mirrored in him" (Nähme man seine sämtlichen Schriften zusammen, so würden in ihm das ganze Jahrhundert abgespielt erblicken, p. 141). And

110

from the next generation of scientists he included Pierre Jean Faber (d. 1750), Jean Baptiste du Hamel (1624–1706), Jeremias F. Gülich (1733–1803), and a series of technicians, craftsmen, and manufacturers of dyes, who studied colors in the tradition of the trinitarians.

The work of these individuals was discussed collectively in the essay on "chemists" (Chemiker, pp. 324–6), a chapter in which Goethe connected the contribution of the trinitarians to the early phases of modern chemistry: "The earlier comments on Paracelsus and his school, that colors may be ascribed to the union of sulfur and salts, had remained in fresh memory."[23] But by the eighteenth century, Goethe noted, the sciences had become more formalized through institutional control so that chemical analysis focused less on individual curiosity and more on the common experience possible through study of acids and bases. Thus, the path of the trinitarians became increasingly standardized as well as applied, emphasizing the role of technology, as practiced by dyers, painters and manufacturers in the history of color theory.

Goethe observed from these technical and practical writings the repeated reference to the number "3" specifying yellow, blue, and red as basic colors (p. 327). In du Fay's work he noticed that these three colors were called the "mother colors" (Mutterfarben), and based on Mayer's works, Goethe observed that "all those, who came to color theory from painting and dyeing, found, as history has already instructed us in detail, naturally and comfortably, that only three basic colors can be assumed."[24] From other texts Goethe observed that there are "only three simple primitive colors," "three primordial colors," "fields of this triangle," "three main colors," that "in reality there are only three colors" and "more than three pigments cannot be assumed."[25]

The trinitarians attempted to decompose nature according to three principles, including acids, bases, and a means of bonding. This theory continued into eighteenth-century chemistry, as the science of elective affinities,[26] which also required a third component, a vitalistic means of bonding elements. Indeed, Goethe's own theory of chemical colors was grounded in the tradition of the trinitarians, in "the chemical oppositions" (die chemischen Gegensätze, LA, I, 4, 156), in general functioning like "acids and bases" (Säure und Alkali). However, here Goethe, the most recent trinitarian, again argued that he had advanced the theory of colors, in this case by focusing on a concept of bonding which he called an "intensification" (Steigerung, p. 162) of colors, a process in which colors emerge from a saturation, where, for example, blue turns to violet or yellow to orange, those junctures when opposites reach a "culmination" (Kulmination, p. 164), hence, putting emphasis not on three primary colors, but on three sets of complementary colors. Thus, the project of the dualists and of the trinitarians provided a viable basis for Goethe's own emerging authority, an authority which emerged in conflict with the third phase of the history of chromatics, with that of the solitarians.

The solitarians

The dualists had studied the physiology of colors, dominating the first epoch of Goethe's history of color theory, while the trinitarians, emerging at the end of the Middle Ages, investigated the chemical composition of colors. The third group in this line of authorities researched the physical properties of light, and were given a label representing their approach, the solitarians: "They observed light isolated as a body, which by itself and in relationships could suffer various changes. Here the corpuscular, globular, mechanical and similar explanations of light and the effects of color came forth."[27]

Goethe noted in his history of color theory that the ancients also had studied light, although for them it was not essential, it was accidental: "Light is a clear color 'per accidens' " (Licht ist des Durchsichtigen Farbe *per accidens,* p. 181). But in the watershed between ancient and modern science, during the authority of the trinitarians, at the time of Francis Bacon, light increasingly was viewed as a substance: "They saw it as something original, self-contained, independent, and unconditioned."[28] And from 1600 onward much of the effort in color theory was devoted to the analysis of light. By mid-century, when Marin Cureau de la Chambre's (1594–1669) book on *La Lumière* (1657) appeared, the origins of solitarian authority were established.

Like the theories of the dualists and the trinitarians, those of the solitarians were grounded in assumptions and presuppositions. In the case of the latter, light had "to materialize itself, become material, become matter, present itself as corporeal and finally as a body" (Doch musste diese Substanz, um zu erscheinen, sich materiieren, materiell werden, Materie werden, sich körperlich und endlich als Körper darstellen, pp. 181–2). In this process of defining light as a being, Grimaldi best captured the vitalistic signs: "And thus was ascribed to this being a fluidity, a wave, an agitation, a rolling" (Und so wird denn diesem wirksamen Wesen ein Fliessen (fluidatio), ein Wogen (undulatio, undatio), ein Regen und Bewegen (agitatio), ein Wälzen (volutatio) zugeschrieben, p. 194).

This material view of light was accepted only gradually during the course of the seventeenth century, for it was necessary that light first be viewed as a heterogeneous being of nature, equal to other organized bodies of nature. For this reason Goethe did not think that Newton's theory of decomposed light from 1704 came as a surprise, for preceding it were many studies on the nature of light. And, Goethe observed, between concept and analysis there are not many steps, in this case between the idea of light as a substance and its decomposition in the laboratory. Prior studies in the technical analysis of light also reduced the shock of Newton's theory, including Marcus Antonius de Dominis (1566–1624) determination of the primary and secondary rainbows and Willebrord Snellius (1581–1626) statements on the laws of refraction.

But Newton was without a doubt Goethe's prototype for solitarian authority.[29] In his essay on Newton's personality, Goethe made the anthropological and social basis on an authority especially clear, beginning with his education in England, where individuality was stressed. Then he described the historical period into which Newton was born as "one of the most pregnant in English, in world history" (eine der prägnantesten in der englischen, ja in der Weltgeschichte überhaupt,p. 296), and finally he came to Newton himself. He explained his sense for mathematics and slowly focused on the centrality of his authority, on his logical and consequent approach, his policy not to mingle in controversy, and his inflexible character, "to which the doctrine owed its entire fortune" (Dieser Behandlungsart, diesem unbiegsamen Charakter ist eigentlich die Lehre ihr ganzes Glück schuldig, p. 297).

Goethe found the essential quality of Newton's authority in a trait of his character which he called "to want" (das Wollen, p. 298). In this modality there is no consideration of ordinary human experiences, of an intuitive sense for right and wrong, good and bad, and truth and error. It is a modality that shapes and controls the external world and, when connected with rational faculties of the mind, with reason, it ignores the experiences derived directly from the senses as well as the ethical relationship of man and nature (p. 298–9). In this sense Goethe argued that the doctrine of the solitarians was "unjust toward the world" (treulos gegen die Welt, p. 300), for when the analysis of light is carried out with the tools of optics, distance is created between reason and understanding, a distance grounded in the difference between the sensory experiences of ordinary man and the laboratory designs of the scientist. The solitarians had analyzed light as a substance with an instrumentation no longer controlled by sensory experiences, and for this reason Goethe found the doctrine pernicious and errant in direction and method. This is then the watershed in Goethe's view of the history of science, that point at which the technology of the laboratory mediates between man and nature at a level no longer controlled by sensory experience.

As the most recent dualist, Goethe had considered his concept of polarity in colors an advancement upon the science of Aristotle, Theophrastus, Nuguet, and Rizzetti.[30] He also believed that he had advanced the theories of the trinitarians when he described colors from the bonding of acids and bases as points of saturation (Kulminationspunkt, LA, I, 4, 164–5). However, with the solitarians, with those who mechanized the research on colors and introduced the technology of optics to mediate between man and nature, Goethe had found no agreement. Goethe believed that in achromatism came the end of solitarian authority: "It could no longer remain a secret that the theory has been dealt a death blow" (Niemanden konnte nunmehr verborgen bleiben, dass der Lehre eine tödliche Wunde beigebracht sei, I, 6, 363). And even though he described achromatism correctly, as a dispersion in refraction, he would not let the concept serve as an explanation. He tried to abort what he perceived as the increasing alienation of man from nature through the abstractions of science.[31] But it was perhaps this alienation which prompted his detailed treatment of the history of color theory, and would prompt his friend Knebel to observe that in it "the spirit of true, deep humanity reigns everywhere in reproach as well as in praise, and the scientist himself is called upon, above all to be a human being."[32]

Goethe represented the essential features of the history of color theory in the symbolism of the dualists, trinitarians, and solitarians, and with this scheme he intrinsically related the development of a science to human striving for knowledge in general. Thus, he called his history of color theory "a symbol of the history of all the sciences" (ein Symbol der Geschichte aller Wissenschaften, LA, II, 6, 331).[33] With this symbolism Goethe shaped a "labyrinthine Garden" from the amorphism of tradition, showing the development of theories and discoveries, as well as the development of authorities surrounded by errors, myths, sidetracks, and detours.

Goethe recognized that in a sense the history of science is a "commentary on that which was previously stated" (Kommentar zu dem Vorgesagten, p. 94),[34] for in the history of color theory he found certain authorities whose students and followers repeated for decades and centuries the basic principles of those who came before them. And it was from the commentary that Goethe found in textbooks, schools, and academies, in societies and clubs, that he formed the collective concept of authority and the symbolic labels of change. Therein lies the significance of his historiography of science; a view that scientific traditions were on the one hand amorphous, but that there was also a fine line of progression from one epoch to the next, each one showing individual initiatives and collective effort.

9

Goethe's taxonomy of scientific discourse

> Those theories to which we ascribe originality are not so easily grasped, not
> so quickly epitomized and systematized. An author tends toward this or that
> way of thinking; but it is modified by his individuality, indeed, often simply
> by his presentation, by the peculiarity of the idiom in which he speaks and
> writes, by the change in times, by various considerations.[1]

Modes of conception

Goethe's nature studies had left him with a richness–ambiguity paradox in
scientific language. And in historical studies he faced a second paradox in
which the idiom of the text showed signs both of a symbolic and entropic
language, the former found in the writings of original thinkers and the latter in
those of students in schools of thought. The works of original writers were
rich in metaphors but those embedded in schools of thought were repetitive
and inflicted with standardization. This, too, faced him with a paradox, for
formalized language is both necessary and harmful to the advancement of
knowledge, as he had found the situation in the nomenclature of comparative
anatomy. In historical studies he attended to these paradoxes in the same way
he had in his scientific writings, by examining the linguistic texture of the
field and from it, with the help of the muse, by shaping its "form" and
"content," by seeking "permanence in change." In the symbolic forms of
authority he shaped it chronologically, and in his taxonomy of scientific
discourse he shaped it topically.[2]

  Goethe's history of color theory contains many excerpts from scientific
documents, varying in length from a single paragraph to entire chapters. And
from an analysis of the language of these texts he found that there seem to be
as many forms for expressing scientific information as there are scientists. In
fact, he argued, the individual's fascination with his own particular "mode of
conception" (Vorstellungsart) motivates a great deal of scientific activity:
"Man enjoys his perception of an object more than the object itself."[3] Goethe
perceived science as different ways of re-presenting natural phenomena and
for him the concept "Vorstellungsart" served as a *tertium quid,* a point of

reference for recognizing and discussing the forms of symbolization in the literature of science.

Goethe had found various "modes of conception" in scientific writing, broadly defining them as dynamic, genetic, and atomistic.[4] But in his study of color theory, he concluded that these different ways of thinking were located in linguistic expressions. Here he found that the private language of scientists can be categorized into five "modes of conception," including "metaphysical formulas" (Metaphysische Formeln), which have a great depth and breadth but often ring hollow; "mathematical formulas" (Mathematische Formeln), which have broad applicability but always leave us with a feeling that the application is inadequate, forced, and incommensurable; "mechanical formulas" (Mechanische Formeln), to which the more ordinary mind responds because such forms of symbolization are crude and raw; "corpuscular formulas" (Korpuskular Formeln), which are closely related to mechanical formulas because they change vital forms of life into sterile ones, "they kill the inner life"; and "moral formulas" (Moralische Formeln), which express more gentle relationships, but only as metaphors and hence often get lost in a play of words.[5] Although Goethe discussed other "modes of conception" important to the history of science, he listed these five for the theory of color and specified them as logocentric forms of expression in the field. And like his symbols of authority, they serve as a heuristic device for a survey of his historiography of chromatics.[6]

When Goethe listed five categories of symbolization, he was selecting what appeared to him sets, or groups, of the most commonly used expressions for describing the phenomena of color. In his view it was a classification of the idiom in which authors of scientific texts expressed their opinions on nature. But the language used by a significant scientist did not remain personal, for in the hands of followers it became normalized as the language of an entire school of thought. That is, many of the linguistic expressions used in these five modes of conception have existed in scientific writings since antiquity. Concerning these documents Goethe remarked that, while the language from some of the ancient schools of thought is significant for every epoch, the language of others, such as that of Democritus and Epicurus and the school of atomism, surfaced only occasionally, as in works of sixteenth- and seventeenth-century writers: "How strangely Gassendi adapts himself to Epicurus" (Wie wunderbar verhält sich nicht Gassendi zu Epikur, LA, I, 6, VIII).

Mathematical expressions

The most common "mathematical formulas" found in Goethe's history of color theory come from geometric explanations of color, vision, and light. Writers from Greco-Roman to modern times had approached the field as a problem of optics and for this reason much of the language of color theory was abstract and rigid, as in the Pythagorean view of vision, where images form by reflection, where sight is simply a study in catoptrics. But the mathematical language used to explain phenomena of color, light, and vision improved with time, as it was applied to ever more disciplines and fields of learning. By medieval times Roger Bacon was applying mathematical concepts to most fields of study, to history and religion, as well as to logic, grammar, and music. However, in these fields Goethe observed that mathematical formulations became "a mere symbol" (ein blosses Symbol, p. 97).

Bacon's use of mathematical concepts was central to his way of thinking and Goethe did not find it surprising that he would apply them to theories of light, vision, and color. Thus, Goethe included in his history discussion of the lines, angles, drawings, and concepts basic to Bacon's optics. With them Bacon described optical devices, such as the magic lantern and the solar microscope, although Goethe seriously doubted that Bacon developed an empirical basis for certain concepts such as refraction, or that he had ever seen a *camera obscura*: "The manner in which he expresses himself on these things, shows that the apparatus functioned only in his mind and that from there various imaginary results may have arisen."[7]

In discussions on later epochs of history, Goethe discovered more sophisticated mathematical language and, while he continued to focus on the development of optics, he also drew parallels to the mathematization of nature in other fields. He noted, for example, Galileo's laws of pendular motion (Lehre des Pendels) and in the case of Johann Kepler (1571–1630) observed "how detailed and exact Kepler shows that Euclid copernicized" (Wie umständlich und genau zeigt Kepler, dass Euklides kopernikisiere, p. 156).

Goethe observed that Kepler did not investigate problems of color, primarily because he subjected nature to methods of "measure and number" (Mass und Zahl, p. 157), which he knew would not yield significant results when applied to colors. But Goethe also found that Kepler was not tied to a mathematical language and that his use of ordinary language complemented his mathematical terminology, making him one of the most powerful writers in the history of science: "Since he has language totally in his control, he occasionally ventures bold and strange expressions, but only then, when the event seems to him unattainable."[8] Thus, Kepler demonstrated an approach appropriate to the subject. He used a mathematical language when the subject could be quantified and in other situations he used all forms of ordinary language, including vernacular and classical expressions, thereby complementing his mathematical symbolization with qualitative forms of thought.

It was indeed the quantifying approach to the study of color, vision, and light that continued to develop the most rapidly in the sixteenth and seventeenth century. Goethe believed that Snell came close to explaining the laws of refraction (Gesetze der Refraktion), although he did not discuss refraction in terms of an angle of incidence (Sinus des Einfalls- und Brechungswinkel, p.

158). He did not measure an image that fell through an optical medium (Brechung), instead his optics was largely the measurement of images seen through the optical medium (Hebung): the latter process Goethe called a subjective experiment (subjektiver Versuch), while the former he labeled an objective experiment (objektiver Versuch).[9] And although the latter was recognized by those like Christian Huygens (1629–95), his work in subjective optics was generally ignored until the middle of the eighteenth century.

Goethe also included De Dominis's description of refraction in the rainbow. Using a glass sphere De Dominis showed what happens when light passes through a concave lens. Dominis's perspective drawings of the process intrigued Goethe and were reproduced in the volume of plates to his own color theory. In this discussion Goethe commented that Descartes's more thorough discussion of refraction in a drop of rain is based on the De Dominis model, adding that in his work on geometric optics, Descartes had failed to give recognition to the work of precursors, particularly to De Dominis (p. 163).

Descartes's explanation of the secondary reflection in the rainbow in mathematical terms, Goethe observed, required considerable talent, and set the standard for the study of optics in the seventeenth and eighteenth centuries. Following him, the scientist first had to make a small hole in the door or window, let the light fall through the opening, and then let the light fall on the oblique side of a prism. Goethe observed how the repetition of this procedure eventually led to a refinement in the measurement of angles and to variations in the conditions under which light proceeded through the medium, in some cases leading to innovations such as Johann Marcus Marci de Kronland's (1595–1667) seminal ideas on diverse refrangibility.

According to Goethe it was to Newton's credit that he could employ mathematics with more accuracy and purity than those who came before him. This Newton had demonstrated early in his writings on the concept of refraction, when he presented his ideas on the fabrication of the reflector telescope to the Royal Society. Here Newton had concluded that the dioptric telescope could not be improved and this he based on a key experiment, on an "experimentum crucis," in which he found that light was a heterogeneous mixture of differently refrangible rays (LA, I, 6, 260).

Goethe observed that one of the difficulties in the history of color theory had been explanation of the oblong shape of the color spectrum. Many in the seventeenth century had tried to relate the length and width of the color spectrum to the circular shape of the light entering the prism; that is, the expected shape of the spectrum was circular, because the beam of light and the hole in the window shutters were round. But it was with the concept of diverse refrangibility that Newton provided an answer, which Goethe thought was at the same time true and false; it was true under conditions prescribed by the laboratory, but false for natural conditions in which light appears (p. 261). It was also based on the presupposition that light was a substance, a notion of growing acceptance in the first half of the seventeenth century, but one that involved a different set of terms and concepts, namely, mechanical and metaphysical modes of conception.

Mechanical expressions

Goethe ranked the mechanical modes of expression second in popularity in scientific discourse, following mathematical formulas.[10] In a section on the experimental work of Robert Hooke (1635-1703), Goethe again recalled Descartes's influences on setting the standard of scientific language, this time in the use of mechanical modes of representation: "since Descartes materialized and mechanized the theory of light, writers have not been able to find a way out of the circle: for those who wanted to avoid material conceptions of light and color had to rely on mechanical explanations anyhow."[11]

According to Goethe the problems of the mechanical mode of representation were observed most readily in the study of light and sound, where the subtlety of the phenomena exceeds the boundaries of experience and language. The image of a batted ball, for example, was introduced because the motion of a projected ball follows a curved rather than a rectilinear path, a model which showed how light can be induced out of a rectilinear path (geradlinige Bewegung) into a curved path (krummlinige Bewegung, p. 260) in experiments in refraction. This language Goethe perceived as particularly deceptive, as a "hidden anthropomorphism" (ein versteckter Anthropomorphismus), to which writers in astronomy also subscribe. In a simplified language Goethe argued that "inertia" (Fall) and "acceleration" (Stoss) are really just the motion of a wanderer walking across the field in a process in which "the raised foot sinks, the one left behind strives forwards and falls, and so on from departure to arrival" (Der aufgehobene Fuss sinkt nieder, der zurückgebliebene strebt vorwärts and fällt: und immer so fort, vom Ausgehen bis zum Ankommen, LA, I, 11, 338).

Yet Goethe found some mechanical expressions appropriate, rich in variation and subtle in application, particularly as found in the writings of Malebranche. In his theory of sound he had postulated a vibration of unobservable particles (unmerkliche Teile, p. 204) in resonating bodies, a theory which he then transferred to his study of color. According to Malebranche the brighter colors resulted from more intense vibrations of particles, although the intensity did not change the kind of color. The variations were attributed to the number of vibrations generated at any given moment, making possible an infinite variety and quality of colors. Thus, colors were explained in terms of frequency, vibrations, pressure, and motion. This terminology, explained Goethe, was part of a tradition and, while much of it had been developed by Descartes, it was his followers who entrenched mechanical forms of symbolization in color theory and in science in general.[12]

Goethe observed that the mechanical terminology which came closest to an explanation of the subtlety of light and color was that of Grimaldi. Like Descartes and De La Chambre, he had a materialistic conception of light, although Grimaldi developed this mode of representation with more creativity and delicacy. According to Grimaldi light fatigued as it passed through a labyrinth of pores and a bewildering maze of passages in the material world, never ceasing in the change and shape of its action, flowing, undulating, agitating, and waving through the material world. Grimaldi attributed to his light an outer material and an inner disposition, labeling it an "active being" (wirksames Wesen, p. 194), and in this attempt to comprehend the subtlety of light and color, he came close to what Goethe considered the moral mode of re-presentation.

Although Grimaldi's language was mechanical, it remained free of the atomistic terms and concepts common to the language of Descartes and Malebranche. Instead, Grimaldi took terms from the realm of social experience which "express more subtle relationship" (zartere Verhältnisse) than do the mechanical and corpuscular forms of symbolization. But, Goethe observed, they are in the end "mere similes" (blosse Gleichnisse) that dissipate in "a play of words" (Spiel des Witzes, LA, I, 4, 221).[13]

Corpuscular expressions

Goethe traced corpuscular, or atomistic, forms of symbolization in color theory from antiquity to the eighteenth century.[14] Here he found a continuous tradition that explained color, vision, and light in terms of fundamental units, or particles, and their interactions. Democritus held that vision was due to the compression of the air between the object and the observer, a pressure exerted by object and observer and yielding a shape, or a form (Gestalt, p. 3). This concept of form was the basis of the view that colors are not things in themselves, and that only the "elements" (die Elemente), "plenum" (das Volle), and "void" (das Leere) have qualities; that is, "the form" (die Gestalt), "position" (die Lage), and "direction" (die Richtung, pp. 3–4) of fundamental particles served as a source of colors. Epicurus also denied the existence of colors as essential matter and, like Democritus, considered the shape and position of basic particles to be most important, a view Goethe cited from Diogenes Laertius: "The colors change according to the position of the atoms" (Die Farbe verändre sich nach der Lage der Atomen, p. 4).

Although the revival of ancient atomism was located in the scholarly activities of writers like Pierre Gassendi (1592–1655), variations on the original themes began primarily in the writings of Descartes.[15] He found three levels of fundamental particles which extended the length, breadth, and depth of the universe. According to Goethe, it was to the second level of particles that Descartes ascribed the source of his "light particles" (Lichtkügelchen): "If the particles rotate at a velocity not faster than that of particles in a rectilinear path, then the color yellow is sensed. A faster motion generates red and one slower than the velocity of rectilinear particles produces blue."[16]

Goethe associated Descartes's language with that of the early atomists and considered images of discrete particles, rotation, motion variation, and variation in particle size completely hypothetical.[17] Such terminology, he observed, was present everywhere in eighteenth-century science and was to be found in most handbooks, encyclopedias, and dictionaries. Although the image of light as atomistic, or globular, agreed with the notion that light was heterogeneous, Goethe found no reason to accept either as more than mere hypothesis. That is, there was no empirical evidence for the particles, as the colors produced from a prism were only the result of controlled and manufactured conditions created in a laboratory.

Goethe recognized that most scientists found the images used in corpuscular expressions rich and accessible. Also, the language of corpuscularism seemed to defy standardization, for each writer modified it somewhat, usually through new metaphors and images which varied with the individual's metaphysical views. Thus, matter theory, cosmology, epistemology, and various other branches of philosophy were incorporated into those theories of color expressed in an atomistic language.

Metaphysical expressions

The "metaphysical formulas" appearing in Goethe's history usually involved certain philosophical presuppositions about the nature and structure of the universe. In ancient writings Goethe found that views on the fundamental organization of matter had a bearing on theories of color, as could be observed in Zeno's (335–263) statement that colors are a "primary form of matter" (die ersten Schematismen der Materie).[18] Although the terms vary, the Greek philosophers each presupposed unobservable entities in theories of light, vision, and color, as may be observed in Empedocles' four elements: "The division of original forces of nature into four elements is for primitive sensory experiences conceivable and refreshing, even if they are superficial."[19]

Goethe found that in modern science much of the symbolization centered around the postulation of light as a substance, especially in Newtonian science. The question as to whether light was an essential or accidental quality existed in ancient writings, and in the course of the seventeenth century was finally viewed as a "heterogeneous being" (heterogenes Wesen).[20] In Goethe's view the seventeenth century abounded with "metaphysical formulas," particularly in the writings of Grimaldi, for whom light was an invisible but rarefied vapor.

Goethe showed that Grimaldi generated various expressions that assumed a fluidity of light and colors, including terms used to describe metals, sounds, and magnetism. With these forms of symbolization Grimaldi showed the infinite gradations and subtleties between apparent, discrete, and isolated phenomena. Even transparent bodies contained a "continuous porosity" (continua porositas, p. 194) with magnificent exits, entrances, and passages. Thus, Grimaldi's metaphysical mode of conception led to many expressions that became important only after his time. Indeed, before Newton, Grimaldi postulated colors as occasions of refraction and diffraction, even arguing that colors are light itself. In this Goethe observed that Grimaldi's "metaphysical formulas" directly anticipated Newton's theory of colors, including the idea that light consisted not of a single but of a "bundle of rays" (Strahlenbündel, p. 195).

Malebranche's "aether" (Aether, p. 308) is yet another example by which Goethe illustrated metaphysical modes of representation in theories of light and color. According to Goethe, he had followed closely Cartesian mathematical, mechanical, and corpuscular modes of re-presentation, but occasionally found it necessary to refine Descartes's views on the fundamental organization of matter. Malebranche was dissatisfied particularly with Descartes's theory that particles of light should have the same motion and consistency as those of color. And to relieve the situation he needed to "postulate" (supponieren) additional vortices, a more subtle ether, and a greater variety of particles and "points" (Punkte, p. 206).

Yet, while Goethe found such imagery significant in the development of science, he also argued that in the final analysis "metaphysical formulas" in science are unnecessary, for in the end everything is life and action (Leben und Bewegung).[21] Goethe did not find a great deal of difference between the terms "air" (Luft) and "ether" (Aether) as they were used in Malebranche's theories of sound and light, because the vibrations were not directly observable. That is, because nature is always changing, and because the ether vibrations cannot be observed, what can it benefit the scientist to postulate a new term such as "Aether," when the term "Luft" would serve as well?

Social expressions

The questionable value of some forms of expression became more serious in the fifth and last category of Goethe's taxonomy of scientific discourse. Although social, or moral, forms of symbolization continued in science, even into the eighteenth century, a change came in the sixteenth and seventeenth centuries when scientists consciously began trying to avoid expressions originating from ordinary life.[22] According to Goethe, Kircher was one of the last to express the theory of color in a language also used to describe human and social behavior, although in his writings the expressions often degenerated into naive imagery, such as in his reference to colors as "children of light and darkness" (Kinder des Lichts und des Schattens, p. 181).[23] Yet, because such language still continued to be of value in color theory and in the study of organic and dynamic processes of nature, Goethe devoted an entire chapter of his history to "intentional colors" (Intentionelle Farben).[24]

According to Goethe, intentional colors are those to which a will and a design have been ascribed, usually because of the delicate and gentle effect of colors on the observer. Roger Bacon, for example, had observed these nuances of color and in his writings and concept of intentionality reached a new level of sophistication. Indeed, Bacon could not have found a better simile for describing "active images of nature" (tätige Bilder) than "human wanting" (das menschliche Wollen, p. 169). That is, in order to show the change, variation, becoming and continuation of color and light, Bacon introduced human desire as a *tertium quid* (ein Drittes, p. 169), as an external measure against which to compare colors.

Goethe explained that human actions, like the events of nature, bring with them a great deal of potential and hence a degree of reality before they occur. In nature, and in colors specifically, there is a spirit, or a "virtue" (Tugend, p. 169), which at any moment has the potential of becoming a new reality. Thus intentional forms of symbolization express the view that nature is in process, that phenomena exhibit a force of potentiality. He offered a few examples to clarify the anthropomorphic terminology of intentional colors, including the analogy of a person walking with a specific goal in mind (pp. 170–1), pointing out that, whether the goal is within his sight or only in his mind, there is between the design and its realization the act, an execution. The execution of intent is almost the same as its realization. That is, in human behavior, as in nature, following intention, acting is almost the same as reaching the goal, as long as the subject is resolute and the conditions are normal. Yet Goethe added that the act could only be called intentional because the subject could become paralyzed with the first or last step, and might not fulfill his aim.

As Goethe indicated, many physical events were and could be expressed in such a mode of discourse in order to draw attention to process. In presenting spectral colors with the aid of a prism, for example, one might emphasize the intentionality of light by saying that, when it passes through the prescribed hole, falls through the prism, and finally appears on the wall, it is at every moment fulfilling its intention to be realized, and is hoping at all stages of the process that the conditions are adequately maintained. Thus, Goethe observed that much of the science done in the laboratory is intentional. It is so in the sense that an event is only as real as are the conditions permitting its existence.

Goethe viewed all terminology in the sciences as symbolic, although some was more clearly metaphoric because it reflected images of human behavior. In Friedrich W. Riemer's (1774–1845) record of table talks from 1809, Goethe made a distinction between social and mathematical symbols in science, the former being a reflection of the human disposition (Gemüt) and the latter of the mind (Verstand, GA, 22, 565). In this context Goethe observed that the Cartesian mathematical and corpuscular language was often as in-comprehensible and esoteric as that coming from inspired religions. That is, both social and mathematical modes of conception are a creation of man, and are an extension of his being. Yet, Goethe observed, because most "moral formulas" subscribe to a teleological perception of the world, to notions of design and "final causes" (Endursachen), because of this, the departure from the stream of reality seems more radical, and therefore as a "kind of an-thropomorphism" (eine Art von Anthropomorphism, LA, I, 6, 177).

Goethe attributed the gradual departure from a teleological language to the view that there exists a split between the "body and soul" (Seele and Leib), between "God and world" (Gott und Welt, p. 196).[25] However, this separa-tion, Goethe argued, did not originate in the sciences, rather it emerged from religious and ethical studies, where it was advantageous to ascribe as little as possible to nature's role in human affairs. If an individual wanted to retain moral freedom he had to oppose nature's influence, or if he was striving toward God, he had to leave nature behind. In both cases it was expedient to regard nature as hostile to essential matters in human conduct. Thus, Goethe grounded the disrepute of teleological explanations in religious movements and from there came the broader tendency to separate the world into things spiritual and physical, and eventually to disregard teleological explanations altogether. And with time nothing more was expected from the scientist than mechanistic explanations of matter.

The materials of Goethe's history are rich and varied in modes of scientific discourse. Yet, in Goethe's view, the typical scientist adheres too closely to a particular "formula," generally varying little in the range of possible ex-pressions. Newton, for example, was emotionally and aesthetically attached to a language of atomism, that is, to a "theory of emanations" (Emis-sionssystem, LA, II, 6, 302), although Goethe thought it was the esoteric aspects of this language that captured the imagination of the public, for it was these aspects that served as a "crutch" (Eselsbrücke, p. 302) to understanding his optics. But Goethe did not value any particular mode of conception nega-tively, rather, he found in all of them potential for a better understanding of nature.

In Goethe's view, the scientist's narrow selection of linguistic expressions was an emerging restriction of the profession, one which "scientific man" (der wissenschaftliche Mann, LA, I, 11, 355) had in his century begun to impose upon himself, it was a tendency to separate science from literature, indeed, in his day "neither myths nor legends are tolerated in the sciences" (Weder Mythologie noch Legenden sind in der Wissenschaft zu dulden). That is, in Goethe's view, science had become professionalized, it was being separated from other kinds of intellectual life, and it had imposed upon itself restrictions, rules of behavior, and modes of discourse. He did not see this confinement as a positive trend, urging the development of scientific and poetic sensibilities: "Scientific man is supposed to limit himself to his immediate surroundings. However if he should occasionally want to step forth as a poet, he certainly should not be prevented from doing so."[26]

Part IV

The rhetoric of the guild

In New York there are ninety different Christian denominations; each one confessing God the Lord in its own way without being led astray by the others. In science, indeed in research in general, we must achieve this, for what can it mean when everyone speaks of liberality and then wants to prevent others from thinking and expressing themselves in their own way.[1]

10

Goethe's teleology of science

In 1774 Goethe's Werther cried out against the rationalism of his age, against the logic of his friend Albert:

'O that you people,' I burst out, 'when you mention something, have to say: that is silly, that is wise, that is good, that is bad! And what does it all mean? Has it made you explore the conditions underlying an action? are you able to unfold with precision the reasons why it happened, why it had to happen? If you had, you wouldn't be so ready with your judgments.'[2]

In the course of that letter, written on August 12, located in the middle of the epistolary novel, Werther pursued a discussion with Albert about suicide, a discussion that continued to a point of complete deterioration: "And we parted without having understood each other. As indeed it is not easy in this world for one person to understand the next one."[3]

The novel stands in Goethe's writings as an early statement against those forms of rationalism encroaching upon the freedom of the individual, against the narrow prejudices of society and hasty judgments about a person's worth. It was a cry against those confinements running the depth of personal and social life, inherent in the very language of the age, in the "either-or" (ent-weder-oder) expressions that permit no "shadowing" (schatiren, WA, I, 19, 61). In the pedantry of those like the legate for whom he worked: "No 'and,' no connective may be left out, and he is a mortal foe of all inversions, which I sometimes let slip; if you don't drone out your periods according to the traditional melody, he doesn't understand a word. It is a pain to have to do with such a person."[4] It is against the affected behavior and formalism in his society that Werther reacted, one steeped in the binary language of science, a society that would permit, to Werther's horror, the local preacher's wife to cut down the beautiful walnut trees because the falling leaves make her yard "dirty" (unrein), rob her of "daylight" (Tageslicht), and because little boys throw the walnuts, which disturbs her during study of biblical critics (Ken-nikot, Semler, Michaelis, pp. 122–3).

Goethe's Faust was not much better off, although rather than letting life

129

consume him in suicide, he reversed the process and spent a lifetime striving to overcome the narrow confines of his profession and to dominate his social, economic, and natural environment.[5] But overcoming both his profession and his environment meant first and foremost confronting his past, understanding the tradition of science and medicine that had given him status, honor, and recognition in society, but left him feeling empty with failure in the search for truth. Indeed, he sensed failure, not only in the noble search for truth, but in the ability to solve practical problems of daily life.

In the scene "Before the Gate" (Vor dem Thor), walking amid the people of the community, Faust was greeted first by Wagner, his student assistant, as "Herr Doktor" and then later with the same title by an old farmer, who recalled with respect how Faust had helped his father in hospitals against the ravages of the plague (WA, I, 14, 50–2). But Faust walked only a few steps farther before confiding in his assistant that "my father was an obscure man of honor" (Mein Vater war ein dunkler Ehrenmann), who belonged to "the society of experts" (in Gesellschaft von Adepten), who locked himself "into the black kitchen" (in die schwarze Küche), where he poured together repulsive concoctions "according to endless recipes" (nach unendlichen Recepten, p. 54). He confided in Wagner that the medicine was poison and that he himself poisoned thousands, and now after "They have withered away, I must live to see, that people praise the impudent murderers" (Sie welkten hin, ich muss erleben/ Dass man die frechen Mörder lobt, p. 55).

Wagner responded to Faust's confession with the optimism of the age, with belief in the progress of science, reassuring Faust that "If you, as a man, add to science, then your son can reach a higher goal," a statement that drew from Faust even greater expression of agony for it raised the question of ethical obligations to the past, of responsibility in the "drive" (Trieb) for knowledge: "Two souls, alas! dwell in my breast, / Each struggling to get free of the other. / The one, in gross and passionate desire, / Clutches at the world with greedy limbs; / The other soars, imperious, from the haze / Into realms of the first lofty father."[6] And that is precisely what Faust did, he soared beyond the confines of gross desire and greed of this world and experienced the lofty realms of power and knowledge about to descend upon the world through Western science.

In the Faust story, Goethe's criticism of the world of science looked beyond the themes of the individual and went on to examine the emerging institutions of science, to portray the naive innocence of the student, the bookish pedantry of the assistant, and, through Mephisto, caricatures and postures of the typical professor, in effect satirizing the German university of his day.[7] And although Werther and Faust were only heroes of literary fiction, they nevertheless represented a human drama grounded in Goethe's own personal experiences and observation. Goethe had in his lifetime witnessed a transition in the German university from a scholastic to a research institution and he had personally experienced the growing professionalism along with its departments, disciplines, masses of students; in short, he witnessed the emergence of the German learning enterprise as we know it today.[8]

The new professionals

In a conversation with Johannes D. Falk (1768–1826) in 1809, one year before publishing his history of science, Goethe expressed the deep reservations he held for the German university appearing on the horizon, noting particularly the fragmentation of knowledge inherent in the system:

From our lecterns, the individual disciplines systematically are forced apart into half-year lectures. The list of real discoveries is small, especially when taken together over a couple of centuries. Most of that done today is only repetition of that which this or that famous precursor has said. One can hardly speak of an independent knowledge. They drive the young people into rooms and halls like a herd, and there they feed them, in the absence of real objects, with words and quotations. And the approach, which the teacher is often lacking, the students are supposed to acquire! It does not take much to see that this is a false direction. Moreover, if the professor is in possession of learned instrumentation, it does not make it better, only worse.[9]

Goethe saw in the new age of science a "society of experts" with "endless recipes," professionals who would become the new priests of learning and shaping knowledge.[10] He observed how scientific societies in England, France, and Germany had emerged and begun to control the behavior of the individual scientists, introducing them to models, metaphors, and methods in the study of nature. He saw the impact which these emerging communities had upon science, particularly the power base they were achieving. And it was the ethos of that base he questioned:

Learned societies: as soon as they are certified by the state, and constitute a body, find themselves with respect to pure truth, in an awkward position. They have rank and can bestow it; they have rights and can transfer them; they stand in a specified relationship to their members, to similar corporations, to other branches of government, to the nation and to the world. In some cases not everyone taken in deserves a position, and not everything approved is right and disapproved wrong; for how should they, above all mankind and its societies, possess the privilege to recognize, to examine, to observe, and to anticipate, the past without received opinion, the present without passionate prejudice, the novel without skeptical ways of thinking, and the future without exaggerated hope or apprehension.[11]

Goethe's view of science as a social movement is more than a statement about the details of technical labor, the structure of research, or the by-laws of an organization. He questioned the social fabric of science, asking about the direction of science, referring to its organizations as "the guild" (die Gilde) and to its participants as "specialists" (Männer vom Fach),[12] and observing

131

how he, as an active scientist, was excluded from membership in much of institutionalized science.[13] This lament against the confinement of professionalism went deeper than self-pity, it became an outsider's study of the limits of tolerance in institutionalized art and science. And in the final analysis it was a statement for those existing, or being forced, outside the structure and organization of science.

Goethe had observed the limited tolerance of the scientific guild as various forms of authority throughout the history of science, and he saw it in contemporary life as well. Jean Lerond d'Alembert (1717–83), for example, had unquestioned fame as a mathematician, which at the same time became the grounds for criticism of his attempts at literary development. In Goethe's view it was only a criticism from those "hostile types" (feindselige Naturen) who are eager to label an outstanding person, but then quickly to restrict him to his accomplishments and, in the process, prevent him from "a liberating development" (eine vielseitige Bildung): "And not only the French, who do everything outwardly, but also Germans, who know well how to prize inward consequences, are given to such ways of thinking, whereby, through guilds, writers would be separated from writers and scholars from scholars."[14] Goethe felt particularly the scientific community ought to be free of sectarian and partisan views, that it ought to function more like a "free republic" (freiwirkende Republik) than the "autocratic court" (despotischer Hof), which he had observed in the history of science and was experiencing in the contemporary response to his own science.[15]

The ethos of the academy

Goethe understood the social structure of the scientific profession that had rejected his membership. It was a structure he studied across national boundaries, differentiating scientific communities by cultural and historical origins, but locating its power base in England. An "Anglomania" (Anglomanie), he contended, supported British science, because the people of that nation were able to impress foreigners with an outward appearance of "calm" (Ruhe), "security" (Sicherheit), "activity" (Tätigkeit), qualities which were combined with a certain "stubbornness" (Eigensinn) and "wealth" (Wohlhäbigkeit, p. 324), qualities that exhibited authority. He observed how particularly the French had followed in the image of the British, how the French wished for the "wealth" (Reichtum) and "comforts" (Komforts) of British culture and how this "enthusiasm" (der Enthusiasmus) contributed to the efforts of popularizers, such as Voltaire, in making "Newton's doctrine" (die Newtonische Lehre) into a "kingdom of heaven" (regnum coelorum, p. 324). "Anglomania" was, according to Goethe, a cultural phenomenon that gave force to the activities of the British scientific community, a community with a structure unique in its cultural origins, but typical in its restriction on creativity and innovation in science.

Goethe attributed the particular level of restriction and support in the "French Academy" (Französische Akademie, LA, I, 6, 305–6) and the "London Society" (Londoner Sozietät, p, 238) to the differences in their origins. Goethe observed how the rise of professional science in England was well documented in Thomas Sprat's (1636–1713) *History of the Royal Society* (1667) and in Thomas Birch's (1705–66) expanded study of the same topic, as well as in the society proceedings recorded in the *Philosophical Transactions.* Yet the "uncertain beginnings of the Society" (Ungewisse Anfänge der Sozietät) in England gave rise to some debate on claims to priority for the first professional organizations of science: "The patriotic Englishman would like to set the date of origins for the society early, out of jealousy against certain Frenchmen, who were gathered at the same time in Paris for the same purposes."[16] These political motivations made it difficult to set a date for the beginning of the Society, although Goethe also observed how emerging conflict between church and state in England led to the independence of the organization and to a constitution in 1662, which clearly marked its origins.

In addition to constitutional clarity, Goethe thought professional science advanced quickly in England because of the demographic diversity of the organization. This diversity Goethe considered "External Advantages of the Society" (Aeussere Vorteile der Sozietät, p. 245), a diversity consisting of "princes" (Prinzen), "barons" (Barone), "scholars" (Gelehrte), "researchers" (Forscher), "practicians" (Praktiker), "technicians" (Techniker), as well as "economists" (Ökonomen), "travelers" (Reisende), "merchants" (Kaufleute), and "craftsmen" (Handwerker, p. 249). And in this plurality Goethe found the distinctive feature of the British scientific community, its emphasis on individuality, on experimentation for practical results, but also its lack of systematic focus, and, "the greatest evil" (das gröss Uebel), the premature jump from a "complicated experiment" (verwickelter Versuch, p. 251) to a theory.

Goethe observed a different background and other tendencies in the rise of professional science in France, even though the French Academy was modeled after the London Society. It set the date of its origin in 1634, almost two decades earlier than the one in London, but distinctively as a language society, emphasizing the study of grammar, rhetoric, and poetry. But, as Goethe documented with a letter by Samuel de Sorbière (1615–70) to the king of France (LA, I, 6, 163), while the French praised the English model for political and financial reasons, they continued the integration of science and language societies into one academy.

The French attempt to integrate humanistic and scientific fields into one academy, Goethe observed, did not work and only in 1699 under Louis XIV did the Académie des Sciences emerge with full governmental sanction as an independent organization. Its focus was on the mathematical disciplines, especially on astronomy, although doing so "without any particular theoretical tendency" (ohne sonderliche theoretische Tendenz) and without neglect of disciplines in natural history, preparing the way for Buffon and Louis Daubenton (1716–99). Still, Goethe observed, the emphasis in the French Academy was more focused and centralized, differing markedly from the broad plurality of its counterpart in England. In this difference Goethe observed the positive and negative results of organized science, too much structure leading to limitations and too little structure resulting in confusion, a rephrasing of the richness–ambiguity problem in the very language of science: "Here [France] things are not so confusing as there [England], but they are also not as rich" (Man ist hier nicht so konfus wie dort, aber auch nicht so reich, LA, I, 6, 306).

The litany of physics

Goethe's study of his immediate scientific environment, the one in Germany, also included a structural analysis, but one at each juncture pointing to the authority of French and British models. He began with the broad conceptual "rubric" (Rubrik), "The German aristocratic and busy World" (Deutsche Grosse und Tätige Welt, p. 343),[17] a short essay crediting the German courts with centuries of service to science, but noting from several examples, from the courts of Düsseldorf, Kassel and Gotha, how the physicists' creed in analysis of color and light always began with the same ritual, namely, with letting light fall through a hole in the closed shutter of the window, "das foramen exiguum" (p. 343). In the next rubric, moving from the general to the specific, in the "German academic world" (Deutsche gelehrte Welt), he found adherence to the same language and craft in the works of thirty-seven professional physicists, this time with a summary evaluation, recalling Werther's criticism of the legate: "The usual melody is grinding away" (Das hergebrachte Lied wird abgeorgelt, p. 351).

The third and final rubric enclosing the circle of professional physicists close to Goethe's own scientific work, was the "University of Göttingen" (Akademie Göttingen), the center of experimental physics in Germany. In this group Goethe listed seven names, including Georg Lichtenberg (1742–99) who, as "Professor Extraordinarius," was at first often absent from work. He seemed to occupy himself mostly with mathematics, an emphasis continued after Lichtenberg's death by his successor, Johann T. Mayer, Jr. (1752–1830), who "struck in a new compendium the keynote for the old song."[18]

Goethe concluded this chapter of his history of color theory by searching beyond the closed network of Newtonian physicists, by looking at texts from other fields, emerging but not yet professionalized, at writings by individuals not restricted to the litany of physics, at those by, for example, Lambert, Scherffer, and Franklin. Thus, he introduced the final chapter of his history with an essay on "Achromatism" (Achromasie, pp. 361–5), thinking that in this discovery, in the manufacture of a lens without color aberrations, a design based on study of the physiology of the eye by Euler and Dolland, thinking that here he had observed the end of the litany of the professional physicists and of an era of Newtonianism.

From Goethe's perspective these concluding episodes in the history of color theory showed more than the structure of laws, theories and experiments. They gave him insight into the social fabric of science in his day, into the ethos of science, into that universe of discourse and behavior, which Goethe found decidedly religious in tone. In the poem "Chromatism" (Chromatik, LA, I, 8, 175), he drew the parallel of science and religion, beginning with the privilege of the priestcraft to impart its views, noting the pleasure in having followers, and concluding with the request that he, too, be allowed to announce his theory of color:

Priests will sing the mass
And preachers preach the sermon,
Each one will before all
Free himself of matters of his mind
And will take pleasure in the parish
Which gathers itself around him,
Thus in the past as in the present
Approximative words are stammered.
And so allow me colors
In my way to proclaim
Without wounds, without scars,
With the most pardonable of sins.[19]

In the decades following publication of his color theory he continued to reflect on the value of his research. He continued to comment on the difficulties of language and communication in science, particularly in the environment of professional physicists. Six years after publishing his color theory, in 1816, he wrote to Christoph L. Schultz (1781–1834) that language was the "vehicle" (Organ) with which he had communicated his entire life: "So especially in later years I had to reflect on it."[20] He confessed that even though "correctness" (Correctheit) and "purity" (Reinlichkeit) in the use of language were not his strengths, he nevertheless reflected enough upon language to realize that it was only a "surrogate" (Surrogate, WA, IV, 26, 290) of that which stimulates us inwardly. And even though he often experienced an "inadequacy of language" (Unzulänglichkeit der Sprache), he maintained an optimism in the view that in due time he would be understood by the public, that is, he will be "translated into their languages" (in ihre Sprachen übersetzt werden, p. 290).

The rhetoric of the guild

With similar optimism he held out hope for the guild of physicists, whose work would continue to be sterile, but would continue to advance, because they would continue to be stimulated by a vitalistic and dynamic nature: "And I did not let myself be misled in the fact that the entire physical guild is used to speaking in the traditional, hollow ciphers, whose abracadabra preserves for them a living nature, which everywhere speaks to them, and possibly keeps them from a dry dogmatic corpse."[21] And so in the inadequacy of the scientist and in the power of nature, Goethe saw both the "advantages" (Vorteile) and "deficiencies" (Mängel) of organized science, a paradox kept alive in the motto of the Royal Society of London: "Nullius in Verba," I take no man's word (LA, I, 6, 246).

Confessing alliances

By 1810 Goethe had observed the emergence of modern science with its schools, societies, and professional restrictions, but he did not despair in the litany of experiments, in the demise of creative individuality in approaches and methods, nor in his personal alienation from the mainstream of eighteenth-century physics. Instead of succumbing to the power of the guild, he looked deeper into the structure of science. He examined the language of organized science, gaining insight into the subtle, poetic exchange of ideas and arguments in which the profession is embedded. These elusive activities of the profession he considered an essential part of the historiography of science. Indeed, they were the topic of the postscript to his history of color theory, the final chapter in which Goethe exposed his position as an outsider in the emerging professionalism of science, openly calling attention to his personal experiences in an essay called the "Confession of the Author" (Konfession des Verfassers, LA, I, 6, 412–29).

Goethe's "Confession" is the story of how he came to the topic of color theory, the process by which the professional "physicists" (Physiker) excluded him from their guild (die Gilde, p. 425),[22] and finally, it is the record of how he formed his own network of friends and supporters by going public, by appealing to "a broader public" (das grössere Publikum) as an "author" (Autor, p. 424). He explained how his confrontation with the guild of physicists had begun with an enthusiastic search for guidance in techniques of coloration, but "the less I emerged with a natural talent for the visual arts, the more I looked around for rules and laws; indeed, I paid much more attention to the techniques of painting than to the techniques of poetry."[23] And the more his passion for practical and theoretical clarity in the visual arts grew, the more he realized how little is really known about the "hue" (Kolorit) and "harmony" (Harmonie) of colors, or about "the effect of light and shadow on an object" (Helldunkel, p. 416). A search through art books, dictionaries and compendia offered as little help as discussions with artists, and even living in a colony of artist friends in Italy brought no satisfaction.[24]

Having explored the question of "coloration" with those closest to him in interest, he exposed his lack of expertise a second time, the first when he crossed the threshold from poetry to painting, the next when he decided to take his interests directly to the physicists. He recalled some experiments in electricity from his student days at the University of Leipzig (Akademie), although he remembered none in Newtonian optics, so he read in a handbook of the experiments with a prism. He immediately obtained one from Büttner, a colleague in Jena, although after obtaining it, neglected to follow "the experiments according to prescription" (die Versuche nach der Vorschrift, p. 418), one day simply picking it up and looking through it.[25]

This inadvertent act of looking through the prism rather than letting light fall through it, as prescribed by the scientific community, brought Goethe to a crossroad in his career as a scientist. For later neither the colleague in Jena nor the leading professors of physics at Göttingen would acknowledge that his experiments with the prism had any validity; "the whole school" (die ganze Schule), "the learned journals" (gelehrte Zeitungen), "dictionaries" (Wörterbücher), "compendia" (Kompendien), "no one of the guild" (Keiner von der Gilde) would acknowledge his efforts: "Everywhere I found disbelief in my calling to this matter" (Ueberall fand ich Unglauben an meinen Beruf zu dieser Sache, p. 423).[26]

At this juncture, in the rejection by physicists, Goethe recalled how he began to look beyond the guild, to expertise in other fields, to "anatomists" (Anatomen), "chemists" (Chemiker), "poets" (Literatoren) and "philosophers" (Philosophen). He explained how they became his support group, following his experiments with the naked eye and sifting through texts and documents, much of which eventually led to the collection of materials for his "History of Color Theory."

In retrospect he also observed how he had landed in a foreign field (ein fremdes Feld), almost without realizing it, and how "through the physiological colors" (durch die physiologischen Farben) he found his way back to his primary interest in art. Thus, in the end he recognized that his innocent inquiry into optics, and two decades of research on colors (1790–1810), had brought him to the field of the physiology of colors, the field in which professional scientists have posthumously granted him a measure of success, not necessarily for proofs by demonstrated experiments, but certainly for illustrations by narrated topography.

Goethe observed in the opening paragraphs of his confession that, while "the masses" (die Menge) will recognize talent, it is "to a certain extent" (einigermassen, p. 412) also right, when it restricts this recognition, because cross-disciplinary work brings with it so many difficulties. Still in the end, he continued, one must recognize the importance of viewing cross-disciplinary activities in a higher sense. So that our work does not become fragmented, we should as often as possible share "efforts" (Tüchtigkeiten), practice several "virtues" (Tugenden), and step into an "alliance" with colleagues (Bündnis, p. 413).[27] In the concluding paragraphs of the "Confession," Goethe revealed the names of those with whom he had formed an alliance, mentioning particularly Schiller, who had advanced him intellectually and had guided him in research on colors with "his reflective powers" (seine reflektierende Kraft, p. 429).

In earlier collaboration with Schiller in plant theory, Goethe had come to understand the difference between ideas and experiences. In his "Confession" Goethe pointed to further development of this distinction through the exchange of ideas with Schiller on color theory. At this point the exchange went beyond significance for Goethe's own development and left a mark on the history of German thought, contributing directly to the development of the subject–object categories of thought in philosophy.[28]

The first response to Goethe and Schiller's subject–object distinction came from the next generation. Particularly William Whewell, the British historian and philosopher of science, drew attention to the anecdotal base of this "Fundamental Antithesis of Philosophy," attributing to the Goethe–Schiller collaboration the roots of a distinction which "has been brought into great prominence in the writings of German philosophers, and has conspicuously formed the basis of their systems."[29] In Whewell's view "the combination of the two elements, the subjective or ideal, and the objective or observed, is necessary, in order to give us any insight into the laws of nature. But different persons, according to their mental habits and constitutions, may be inclined to dwell by preference upon the one or the other of these two elements."[30] Goethe recognized that he preferred the subjective investigations into nature, but saw that his own success in this approach came in alliance with a colleague of the opposite persuasion. In the end he confessed that it was both collaboration with Schiller and crossing disciplines that brought significance to his work, and that gave it "a higher meaning" (einem höhern Sinne, p. 413).[31]

Shaping posterity

Goethe's search for "a higher meaning" in his project on color theory began to take shape in 1798, when Schiller observed that "insight into the object" and into "the operation of the mind," that particularly insight into "the tools of the mind" would make man master of mind and body. It was here that Schiller had introduced Goethe to a fundamental principle of the historiography of science, to a "philosophy of the profession" (Philosophie des Geschäfts, LA, II, 6, 304), to a view in which a field of inquiry was not bound by its own subject matter, but one detached from the technology of the discipline, one seeking an understanding of the process of doing science. Indeed, Schiller's concept of detachment might well serve as a marker for setting the origins of the historiography of science, a field that began at that point when the act of science, rather than the results of science, became the focus of study.

The idea of seeking "a higher meaning" through the service of philosophy had been introduced by Kant in 1788 in his essay "On the Use of Teleological Principles," and a year later it was applied to historiography in Schiller's inaugural address on why we study "Universal history."[32] In the former essay, Kant continued the trend of the eighties by secularizing the concept of telos, making the first clear statement on a teleology of life-systems, defining those fields of inquiry marked by conditions of development, by potential, by "purpose" (Zweck, p. 159) and by "a system of final causes" (System von Endursachen, p. 179). Then, in his inaugural address, Schiller argued that histories of mankind must be written according to the principles of teleology, written with a view of the purposiveness in life-systems, with anticipation of the potential and direction of human and cultural development. In his view, a teleological history was one in which the determination of divine providence was removed, one conditioned instead by a concept of "freedom" (Freyheit, p. 375), emphasizing the potential development, the possibility of progress toward improvement, toward the ideals of human achievement and the perfection of organic development.

Goethe's own sense of "a higher meaning" for his project in color theory followed Kant's "doctrine of purpose" (Zwecklehre, p. 182) and Schiller's call for a history of mankind grounded in "rational purpose" (vernünftiger Zweck, p. 374), where "a path to immortality" (eine Bahn zur Unsterblichkeit, p. 376) is open to everyone: "I mean to true immortality, where the deed lives and hurries on, even if the name of its originator should remain behind" (zu der wahren Unsterblichkeit meyne ich, wo die That lebt und weiter eilt, wenn auch der Nahme ihres hinter ihr zurückbleiben sollte, p. 376). It was this sense of historical teleology that informed Goethe's "Confession," a final chapter in his project on color theory, where he explained the conditions from which his theory emerged, and where he projected a view of his achievements, so to speak, guiding the potential outcome of his science. In effect, his "Confession" served to legitimate his entire project on color theory by explaining its origins and by anticipating its impact, even shaping its audience, a public that he hoped would receive his work, interpret it, and judge its value by his terms.[33]

In the opening paragraph of the "Confession," Goethe explained the practical and personal motivation of his strategy for shaping the reception of his color theory. He explained that nothing is more welcome to participants in a political or scientific venture than an account of the conditions and circumstances in which the events originated. And in reporting such events, he thought even seemingly insignificant details may some day be of value to "descendants" (Nachkommenden, LA, I, 6, 412). In addition to friendly participants and receptive descendants, his legitimating strategy focused on a third public, on those who found his project in chromatics "strange" (fremd), that public hostile toward the way in which he crossed the disciplines of physics, chemistry, and physiology, and mixed the approaches of scientists, artists, and historians. Thus, Goethe's "Confession," to a great extent, served as insurance against the influence of future criticism from mainstream scientists who might value his work according to the litany of the profession.

After 1810, legitimating strategies began to play an increasingly important role in Goethe's publications. Indeed, one of the most dominant functions of his autobiography, begun one year after the publication of his color theory, was to set the record straight, to give testimony to the "fiction and truth" (Dichtung und Wahrheit, WA, I, 26–9) in the reconstruction of his past, again an act of designing the future, of shaping his personal life and works for posterity. In fact, after 1810, most of Goethe's publications were framed with essays that reflect a strong sense of historical teleology, with an urge to shape posterity, which he thought was embedded partly in the text, but also in the response to the text. Thus, in 1817, he began to re-issue his scientific writings as collections of "Notebooks" (Hefte), one in morphology and one in science in general (LA, I, 8 and 9), both organized so that his original works were embedded in legitimating essays that framed them for the future.

Perhaps no publication illustrates this sense of historical teleology as clearly as the essays of his first "Notebook" collection in morphology. Here he introduced his treatise on the "Metamorphosis of Plants" (Die Metamorphose der Pflanzen, LA, I, 9, 1–83) with essays on the "intention" (die Absicht), "history" (Geschichte), and "origin" (Entstehen, p. 1) of his botanical studies. And then following the central scientific text, he projected its telos, its possible value for the progress of science, its potency for advancing the state of knowledge about nature. Here he framed the future of his treatise on plant morphology with an essay on the "fate" of the manuscript and the printed publication, concluding the notebook collection with a "happy event" (Glückliches Ereignis, pp. 79–83) a testimony to the "closer connection" (nähere Verbindung, p. 79) with Schiller, a connection which served to legitimate his color theory by naming a participant friendly toward its design and intention.

In the essay on the "Fate of the Manuscript" (Schicksal der Handschrift, pp. 62–5), Goethe recalled the origins of his theory of plant morphology, reflecting upon his reentry into the German intellectual community after a two-year sabbatical leave in Italy from 1786–8. Here he lamented the professional alienation he felt: "nobody understood my language" (niemand verstand meine Sprache, p. 62), a language designed to integrate art and nature as an approach that would show the dynamics of growth and change in organic form.

By 1819 the urge to explain his language, to anticipate the reception of his work and to shape the judgments of posterity, reached a new high. In that year he published his "West–East Divan" (West–östlicher Divan, BA, 3, 1–160), a cycle of love poems in which he integrated motifs and themes from Oriental literary traditions into a web of personal experiences from his life in Western culture. But this time, in 1819, at age seventy, he took no chances with public response to the text, to his cycle of love poems, publishing it together with the materials on the history of Oriental literature with a title that resembles that of his history of color theory, in this case beginning with "Notes and Essays" (Noten und Abhandlungen, p. 161) instead of with the word "Materials" (Materialien, LA, I, 6). But this time the title more clearly reflected his sense of historical teleology, his intention to shape the "path to immortality," for the notes and essays were designed "for better understanding of the West–East Divan" (zu besserem Verständnis des West–östlichen Divans, p. 161).

Goethe began his "Notes and Essays" by observing that there is a time to be silent and another to be vocal, and with the publication of his cycle of love poems, he thought it a time to talk. Here he observed how in his earlier years he published works "without a foreword" (ohne Vorwort, p. 163) in the assumption that they would be understood without explanation. But although some works gained immediate attention as intended, others went unrecognized for years, so that he had to tolerate "the bad images" (die Unbilden) of his first contemporaries into the second and third generation of critics. Thus, in order to protect "the first good impression" (den ersten guten Eindruck, p. 163) of his cycle of poetry, he decided to explain and elucidate, to give background to the text "with the intention" (in der Absicht) that "a reading public with immediate understanding emerges" (ein unmittelbares Verständnis Lesern daraus erwachse). Thus Goethe gave his audience a guide to his cycle of poetry, making it possible to follow the motto to his "Notes and Essays:" "He who wants to understand the poet, must go into the land of the poet" (Wer den Dichter will verstehen,/ Muss in Dichters Lande gehen, BA, 3, 161).

Goethe's attempt to shape posterity was not new, but it was an act of poetry rather than science, for to do so was to integrate events of the past, present, and future. That is, science shaped by a concept of telos called for an approach that, at the same time, recognized the value of tradition and projected the innovations of contemporary science. Goethe realized that this requirement of temporal integration was inconsistent with most scientific writing because a concept of purpose, of potential can not be fixed. That is, an author's intention remains just that, an unfulfilled act, an act that can function within the parameters of the possible, at best shaping a public perception of an event. The rest is an act of faith. Thus, Shakespeare's Hamlet, in his dying breath, says to Horatio, his trusted companion, "report me and my cause aright,"[34] emphasizing the fact that Hamlet can do no more than hope that events of the past and present might have conditioned his friend, the scholar, to give a favorable account of his life story.

But perhaps no one articulated the poet's power of telos as vigorously as Nietzsche, who in 1878, in the emerging age of scientific positivism, used Goethe as a model in writing of "the poet as the pathfinder of the future" (Der Dichter als Wegweiser für die Zukunft).[35] Indeed, here Nietzsche located the power of the poet not in his "depiction of the present" (Abmalung des Gegenwärtigen), nor in the "revitalization and poetization of the past" (Wiederbeseelung und Verdichtung der Vergangenheit), but in "the road signs for the future" (dem Wegweisen für die Zukunft, p. 55). This guidance, Nietzsche explained, was not to be understood in an economic and material sense, but in the sense of the earlier artists who composed the "images of the gods" (Götterbildern), who coaxed from the chaos of life the "beautiful image of man" (dem schönen Menschenbilde, p. 55). In his view the poet reaches into those regions where "the beautiful, great soul" (die schöne grosse Seele) exists, and from these depths the poet "helps create the future" (die Zukunft schaffen hilft). In Nietzsche's view, "many paths" (mancher Weg, p. 56) lead from Goethe's "writings of the future" (Dichtung der Zukunft), writings that rise above the technology of the age, above the fragmentation and disharmony of modern society. In Goethe he found a "good trailblazer" (guter Pfad-finder), a model for his contemporary poets, an alternative to the "mindless presenters of chimaera" (unbedenkliche Darsteller des Halbtiers) in his own era.

When Goethe returned to Weimar from his two-year stay in Italy in 1788, he found that he spoke a new language, one focused on the vitality of nature, one with which he examined the transition in forms, where he found the kinetics of life. Much of his time and energy in the next two decades was devoted to a search through historical sources that would legitimate his approach to color theory in the testimonies of the past, testimonies that could not predetermine the impact of his own chromatics, but could help guide it in a way that would shape interpretation for the next generation of writers on color theory. In his view science could not be separated from the past and it only had value when projected into the future. Thus, the closing chapter on Goethe's historiography of science must ask, how the actors of posterity have received his works,[36] how critics have approached his historiography, whether they have spoken his language, to what extent they have followed his guidance, "understood his language," and "reported his cause aright." That is, to what extent has Goethe been recognized as a "pathfinder for the future" of the historiography of science?

11

The topoi of Goethe scholarship

> It is extremely difficult to report on the opinions of others, especially when they closely agree, border and cross one another. If the reporter goes into detail, he creates impatience and boredom; if he wants to summarize, he risks giving his own point of view; if he avoids judgments, the reader does not know where to begin, and if he organizes his materials according to principles, the presentation becomes one-sided and arouses opposition, and the history itself creates new histories.[1]

From positivism to historicism

The writings on Goethe as a historian also intersect and overlap and at times they diverge beyond any point of reconciliation, for the variations in scholarly opinions often represent basic philosophical differences.[2] The task of sorting out these variations is compounded by the richness of historical materials Goethe collected during his lifetime, for Goethe neither confined his thoughts on history to a single topic, nor did he express them in a single document. Indeed, his thoughts on history appear in journals, letters, conversations, as well as in the arrangement of museum artifacts that number in the thousands.[3] Also, Goethe's literary works deal with topics from various historical periods including antiquity, the Renaissance, and Reformation,[4] so that the range of Goethe's historical interests has given scholarship ample material upon which to agree and disagree. A thorough discussion of this response to Goethe's views on history would represent a book on the history of Western thought, a story by itself, one that can only be briefly sketched here.

The story begins with the positivism of the late nineteenth century, when Franz Wegele (1876) wrote a well-documented description of Goethe's studies in history.[5] He mentioned Goethe's early training in church history and pietism, later meetings with Herder and other philosophers and historians in Strasbourg, personal experience with the changes wrought by the French Revolution, participation in Romantic yearning for the past, and fascination with Oriental literary traditions. Wegele touched on most of the important areas of Goethe's contact with history, including his dramatization of history in literary works such as *Götz von Berlichingen* and *Egmont*. To be sure, the eye of a positivist would not overlook Goethe's two most important pieces of historical writing: the *Materialien zur Geschichte der Farbenlehre* (1810) and the *Noten und Abhandlungen zu besserem Verständnis des West–östlichen Divans* (1819).[6] In short, Wegele documented the entire range of Goethe's work in history and thereby established his relationship to the eighteenth-century German movement in historiography.

Wegele's factual account of Goethe's writings in history sparked reaction from Ottokar Lorenz (1893), who described Goethe's less optimistic views on gaining a realistic picture of the past. Others followed Lorenz's lead in arguing this perspective, although most scholars, like Wilhelm Dilthey (1906), tended to emphasize Goethe's positive, creative, and enthusiastic reception of history and historical study.[7] Yet, whereas some of the earliest scholarship focused on these affective dimensions of Goethe's writing on history, a significant departure from the positivism of Wegele did not really begin until 1907, when Emil Menke–Glückert published his study of Goethe's philosophy of history.[8] He gave special attention to Goethe's place in the tradition of historiography, emphasizing his contact with Herder and their common interest in universal themes such as the history of mankind, principles such as continuity in history and subjectivity and empathy in historical observation. Although the positivism continued in studies on Goethe's biographical relations with contemporary historians and philosophers, such as in George Kass's (1909) dissertation on Goethe and Möser, most of the scholars followed Menke-Glückert's interests and investigated topics in the affective domain of historical studies; they investigated Goethe's response to history, his attitude, appreciation, and empathy.[9]

Menke-Glückert's most important innovation over earlier studies was his recognition that Goethe's nature studies were significant for his philosophy of history. Thus, he introduced to the topic some of Goethe's ideas on organic growth, change and death, and on structure and form.[10] With such notions scholarship began to look at Goethe's total writings, including his biographical works, for information on his philosophy of history, investigating particularly his perception of form and structure in historical developments. This holistic approach reached a high point with Friedrich Meinecke's study in 1936, although it continues to be a line of research in those studies in which scholars hope to sharpen the categories of Goethe's attitude toward history.[11]

Meinecke's study is a synthesis of the specialized research on Goethe's philosophy of history written during the first decades of the twentieth century. Kurt Jahn, for example, approached Goethe's writings with questions concerning the decline of culture, skepticism, the demonic elements in history, and the problem of progress in history.[12] In 1929 Gustav Würtenberg looked more closely at Goethe's views on the tragedy of human history and with similar existential concerns, he demonstrated a radical departure from the positivism of the late nineteenth century.[13] Würtenberg was able to find in Goethe's writings a response to tragic elements in history and from this response he concluded that Goethe's relationship to history was indeed dualistic: subjective and objective, a dualism that emerged from the first two studies on Goethe as a historian. However, Würtenberg made the distinction more pronounced by asking specifically if the modern crisis in history could be observed already in Goethe's writings.[14] Studies in the 1930s then dealt almost exclusively with this question and in Meinecke's essay most of these themes were synthesized into a coherent concept of historicism.

Meinecke's writings on the development of historicism had another side, a side which grew out of studies on Goethe's biography and the effect of his personal life on his view of history. While Walter Lehmann and Wilhelm Dilthey approached the question of Goethe as a historian anthropologically,[15] seeing in Goethe's life support for the view that man is the measure of all things, others like Friedrich Gundolf and Ernst Cassirer looked more to Goethe's poetic writings and saw in them Goethe's unique ability to unite antitheses in historical development, to unite past and present.[16] In Cassirer's view Goethe's intuitive perception of form is the key to his approach to history. He argued that Goethe rejected the bare facts of history (das Historische) except as a medium by which man can discover his *Self*. In this approach Cassirer hoped to find access to explanation of the creative process in the history of culture.[17]

Yet, with this approach scholars invariably came back to the problem which they created, asking how the subjective–objective dualism in Goethe's views on history could be resolved. Particularly Herbert Cysarz (1932) looked to Goethe's writings on history for a clue to reality and for solutions to antinomies in interpretation, such as between being–becoming and truth–fiction.[18] Meinecke's synthesis of criticism on Goethe's theory of history is both biographical and topical; that is, it includes observations on Goethe's attitude toward history and on his documentation of history. Thus, his entire study is skewed in the direction of Goethe's subjective relationship to the past, emphasizing the questions on his negative or positive attitude toward history. Although Meinecke discussed the main points of Goethe's negativism,[19] namely, Goethe's dissatisfaction with a history grounded in divine providence, with the lack of regularity and order in historical transmission, and with the general chaos of information on the past, he was primarily interested in showing that in Goethe there is a synthesis of key points in the development of modern historicism. These include (1) a romantic empathy for distant people and traditions, (2) a pietistic sense of inner life, (3) the revival of a spiritual relationship with antiquity, and (4) a neoplatonic sense for inner form.[20] Meinecke argued that Goethe's historical writings reflected these characteristics, and so they became essential points in his discussion of the rebirth of intellectual and historical life in Western civilization.

A catalog of antinomies

Although Meinecke synthesized Goethe's contribution to historicism, he continued to emphasize the ambivalence in his philosophy of history.[21] That is, Meinecke stood very much in the intellectual climate of the first half of the twentieth century and was influenced by existential questions concerning the tragedy of human history. He also recognized the arbitrary nature of historical truth and recognized in Goethe's writings similar points of interest. Thus, Meinecke's dilemma became the point of departure for scholarship after 1950.

In 1956 Werner Schultz compared Goethe and Hegel's conceptions of history, seeing tragic elements of history particularly in Goethe's dramas, *Egmont* and *Götz von Berlichingen,* although in a study on the same topic a year later, concluding that tragic elements in Goethe's view of history were only a part of his anthropology of life, not necessarily an inherent feature of his philosophy of history. His personal life, he argued, included success and failure, as is represented in the *Faust* story.[22]

Hans-Heinrich Reuter then made it his goal to demonstrate Goethe's unquestionable enthusiasm for life and history.[23] Reuter attempted to resolve that line of research which deals with Goethe's negative–positive attitude toward history and he did this by focusing on Goethe's most important piece of historical writing; the *Materialien zur Geschichte der Farbenlehre* which Thomas Mann had labeled a European novel. Reuter asked the same question that had concerned Cassirer thirty years earlier, namely, how can man learn to know himself through his past achievements, although he avoided the introspective subjectivity of earlier studies by concentrating on Goethe's history of science, on Goethe's study of man's search for knowledge, a search which Goethe recognized as a testament to man's creative urge. According to Reuter, this search, as described by Goethe, was Faustian in nature and, while it did not lack in episodes of failure and error, its character was basically optimistic and enthusiastic. That is, Goethe's history of color theory represents a healthy and persistent attitude toward learning (Aufklärung): "Goethe believes in the 'health' [soundness] of historical reason."[24] Thus, Reuter, along with Thomas Mann, seemed to resolve the discussion on Goethe's attitude toward history, at least with regard to his attitude toward the history of science.

However, scholarship on the question of antinomies in Goethe's historical writings led to another kind of divergence which also began in the 1950s. In 1956 Klaus Ziegler began his study by observing that the negative–positive question on Goethe's attitude toward history was false in both directions.[25] But his interest was not in resolution of dualistic thought patterns, rather it indicated a shift in focus on the cognitive over the affective dimensions of Goethe's history. Thus, he examined the antinomies of Goethe's thinking, opposites like unity–diversity, general–specific, and chaos–order. But he did observe that these "polarities," like those in the affective domain, were false in both directions, for he saw in Goethe's historical thinking an emphasis on human, social and cultural relationships, an emphasis on integrative and synthetic patterns of life. Thus, Meinecke's earlier emphasis on Goethe's attitude toward history was replaced by a new emphasis on the cognitive dimension of Goethe's historical writing, along with a budding interest in his anthropological interpretation of man's past.[26]

The shift in emphasis to study of the cognitive structure of Goethe's history has continued into the most recent scholarship, although some of it does retain the rhetoric of binary language and thinking. In Angelika Groth's study of Goethe as a historian of science (1972) his subjective and intuitive sense for historical development is completely replaced by the rational and structural concepts of history, and these are then forced into an abstract system of codes on history.[27] Groth lists over fifty pages of antinomies from Goethe's writings on the history of science, including, for example, broad philosophical categories such as theory–empiricism, along with subcategories that set up new divisions, such as the differences in scientific approach held by Plato and Aristotle. Further discussion of historical schemes, of cycles and epochs in history, reinforce the classificatory structure of Groth's study. As the study by Groth tends to function like a catalog of concepts, it added to the breach that has come about between studies on Goethe's philosophy on the one hand, and those on his theory of history on the other. Thus, there is today no clear resolution of problems such as the levels of abstraction in Goethe's history, his understanding of the phenomena of history, or his formation of concepts about history. Nor is there any clarity on the distinction between his understanding and empathy for history on the one hand, and his practice of history on the other, a distinction basic to another point of divergence in Goethe scholarship.

In 1932, four years before the appearance of Meinecke's study on Goethe's historicism, Julia Gauss had called into question the studies on Goethe's attitude toward history and labeled the negative–positive polarization an underestimation (Verkennung) of his writings.[28] She thought this line of inquiry was a departure from more important questions, such as about his approach to the writing of history and his theory of historiography. She looked primarily to Goethe's "History of Color Theory" for this shift in emphasis, discussing Goethe's concept of typology in biographical sketches (Idee der Spezifikation), his recognition of national individuality in scientific traditions (Volkscharkter), and his wrestling with questions in the sociology of history (Milieutheorie).[29] According to Gauss these are the themes important to Goethe's historiography. These themes, she argued, come from his nature studies and like Menke–Glückert she brought into the dialogue on Goethe as historian concepts such as "type" and "form" as well as concepts showing the dynamics of growth and change. Thus, Gauss hoped to shift the emphasis of discussion away from the bipolar categories of affective and cognitive thought, and to readdress the question of Goethe's views on the natural, organic, and social development of historic events, a line of criticism that again began to surface in Ziegler's study of 1956.

However, there was no substantive response to Gauss's emphasis on organic development until after the publication of the Leopoldina edition (LA) of Goethe's scientific writings in the 1950s and 1960s. That is, both Menke-Glückert and Gauss had emphasized the importance of Goethe's scientific writings for his views on history, but this emphasis was premature, as the Weimar edition of Goethe's scientific writings was inadequate for the task. But with the appearance of Dorothea Kuhn's essay in 1960, on the form and structure of Goethe's history of color theory, the potential of the new edition was established.[30] Reuter soon followed in 1966 with a reevaluation of Goethe's attitude toward history and Groth (1972) used it to classify abstract cognitive categories of historical thought. With the appearances of new volumes in this edition other topics were soon explored, including Goethe's reception of scientific traditions (Nisbet, 1972; Fink, 1980), style in Goethe's historical and scientific writing (Kuhn, 1960, 1967), and the metalanguage of Goethe's history (Fink, 1979).[31]

The concept of polarity

Yet, the new resources did not solve old problems in conceptions on Goethe's philosophy of history. To this point the lines of research, the overlap and divergences, have been clear enough and the only risk involved in writing the story has been the boredom of detail and the misrepresentation that results from attempting to summarize specific studies. And so at this point it may be worthwhile risking another step in evaluating the past century of scholarship on Goethe's theory of history, a critical step in which scholarship, as Goethe suggests in the opening passage, is evaluated according to certain "principles" (Maximen). Although this step "can create new histories" (die Geschichte macht selbst wieder Geschichten), it seems urgent to examine the question further, particularly in scholarship on Goethe's theory of historiography, where cognitive and affective dimensions of his thought are viewed as mutually exclusive rather than as mutually dependent. The question is which principles and maxims might best be used to explain the dichotomy into which scholarship has placed Goethe's theory of history.

In such situations scholars in other fields have looked to strategies in concept formation as a means of clarifying trends in research.[32] Such strategies call for an analysis of the language of scholarship and a discussion of those concepts which have evolved into patterns of accepted opinion in the field. That is, by searching through the language of scholarship diachronically, it is possible to examine the topoi of scholarship, the "historical topics," critically.[33] Such patterns of thought usually become visible as linguistic formulas which have evolved from a long tradition of research, clarification, interpretation, and criticism. In scholarship on Goethe as a historian several topoi have evolved, including his synthesis of antinomies, his discovery of affective and cognitive polarities, his view of cycles of progress, and his perception of historical types. Because the topos of polarity is central to most studies on Goethe's history, it seems reasonable to examine it with the strategies of concept formation in the hopes that, by this example, some clarity will be achieved in the crisis which has come to exist in the studies on Goethe's theory and philosophy of history.[34]

In his early study on *Göthe als Historiker* (1876) Franz Wegele did not concern himself with the language of Goethe's history. This was left to early Goethe philologists and contemporaries of Wegele, who discovered a number of terms important to Goethean thought, including "Polarität," "Aperçu," "Urphaenomen," and "Typus."[35] Word field studies, at the time called "Semasiologie," and known today as semantics, semiology, and semeiotics, flourished simultaneously with broader efforts to evaluate Goethe's writings critically.[36] And when the comprehensive Weimar edition (WA) of Goethe's works also appeared at this time, along with a number of handbooks, dictionaries, and other research tools, the stage was set for broad studies on Goethe as historian, philosopher and thinker.[37]

From the time of the publication of the Weimar edition to the present, scholarship has tended to organize Goethean thoughts on history around the terms discovered by early Goethe philologists, focusing particularly on the term "Polarität." The cornerstone of this selection and assertion was Ewald Boucke's study of Goethe's "Weltanschauung," in which he traced the development of laws of juxtaposition, such as diastolic and systolic processes of natural and cultural growth.[38] Boucke included in his study manifestations of such duality from throughout Goethe's writings and, indeed, by 1966 Heinz Kindermann devoted around two hundred pages of his survey on a century of Goethe scholarship to what he called the "discovery of polarities" (Entdeckung des Gegenpols).[39] Since Kindermann's survey, there have been additional publications that have rephrased this "discovery," such as Andrew Jaszi's book on the bifurcation and unification of Goethe's "Weltanschauung."[40] However, important for the present study is not the scholarship on Goethe's "Weltanschauung," but the influence that such study has had on the language used to discuss other aspects of Goethean thought, particularly his theory of history.

When Meinecke claimed in 1936 that Goethe could only be understood in his polarities, he was taking over a term from studies on Goethe's "Weltanschauung" and applying it to Goethe's view of history. However, Boucke had stated that, although Goethe was well acquainted with the laws of juxtaposition, he did not occupy himself with them in questions dealing with history. This, argued Boucke, was due to his general lack of interest in historical studies. Although Meinecke, on the other hand, showed Goethe's extensive interest in history, he nevertheless took Bouckian polarity and asserted that it was basic to Goethe's conception of history. In Meinecke's study, Goethe's attitude toward history became synonymous with his theory of history: "Goethe can only be understood in his polarities."[41] Polarity having become a familiar topos of Goethe scholarship, Angelika Groth can write a half century later (1972) concerning Goethe's history of color theory:

> Thus, the doctrines of Plato and Aristotle, for example, are judged positive and that of Newton negative. All three, however, present an authority; therefore, correct and false doctrines can have the effect of authority. That means that a pole and the opposite pole of one polarity can emerge as one and the same pole of another polarity, and conversely, a pole can once converge with one polarity, and the next time with a juxtaposed pole of a second polarity.[42]

Although this quotation from Groth is an extreme example of the abstractions that can occur in the scholarly writing on Goethe's history, it does magnify the view that Goethe's history and his thought can be confined to, and understood through, a set of juxtaposed terms. However, such constraints are contrary to Goethe's theory of history, which is admirably free of abstract systems of organization. Not only is such language a misrepresentation of Goethe's own language of history, it also advances a system of polarities invented by scholarship, postponing points of view and avoiding materials that cannot be classified and cataloged as discrete entities and thoughts. Also, to use a binary language to discuss Goethe's history is to resort to a basic notion of science which holds that "all communicable information may be stated in a binary code."[43] That is, language and thought are both creations of man and just as binary languages have existed for centuries, so has bi-valued logic been the standard medium of rational thought, at least since the time of Aristotle.[44] In binary languages and bi-valued logic everything is either X or not–X (exclusive or) and all different operations are subjected to the law of the excluded middle. When Groth suggested that Goethe viewed trends in the history of science as either empirical or theoretical, traditional or original, and synthetic or analytic, she was in effect reaffirming the use of binary language and bi-valued logic for her methods of evaluation, and at the same time was claiming this method as the one used by Goethe for his composition of the history of science.

The inadequacy of a binary language as a means of communication has been apparent since the 1930s, when Jan Lukasiewicz and Alfred Tarski invented a workable, consistent, many-valued logic, and at the same time initiated discussion on the semantic values and structure of a "metalanguage" in scientific discourse.[45] This form of discourse and type of logic allows events and processes, namely Goethe's discussion of history, to be couched in a linguistic medium with more-so and less-so qualities. Although the advantages of a binary language for cataloging information are clear, it should be equally clear that binary language and thought systems are not capable of representing life processes, creative experiences, irrational and random events, as Goethe found them in the history of science. The inadequacy of the binary language is particularly apparent in the evaluation of Goethe's history, for this kind of language gives the impression that Goethe quantized and quantified history, a tendency against which he struggled most of his life. Groth's classification of Goethe's history as systems of cycles, and particularly as a catalog of antinomies, reduces his entire code of history to yes-no questions and either-or conclusions. A closer look at Goethe's history of color theory will show that he was concerned with displaying drama and life in history, without giving the impression that these events necessarily fall into, or arose from, a systematic intelligible and rational plan.

Although a binary language has for centuries been used as a convenient device for organizing and cataloging information in a logical and accessible format, it seems inappropriate to use Goethe's polarity formula in this manner.[46] Goethe's polarity comes to us from his studies in nature, which he viewed as a unity, as a totality in which form, process, and continuity could be observed. Historical transmission (Ueberlieferung) lacked this completeness and was viewed by Goethe as fragmented, chaotic, and disorganized, as an amorphous mass open to chance and accidental modes of transmission, which are in turn open to interpretation by the observer.

Although Goethe certainly saw antinomies in history, there is insufficient evidence to support the view that the polarity which he observed in organic processes was also applied to historical studies, a caution expressed already in the writings of Boucke at the turn of the century. As Hugh Nisbet has argued, Goethe applied the polarity formula to striking and unique instances, to original phenomena (Urphänomene), such as those in color, where traditionally opposite instances like light and dark intensify toward new formations, namely, toward purple and violet.[47] Thus, it would follow that his concept of "intensification" (Steigerung), a corollary in his polarity formula, could be translated into conceptions of historical synthesis, crediting Goethe with preemptive statements concerning Hegelian dialectics, another topos of Goethe scholarship.[48]

The Weimar edition revisited

Scholarship has taken the concept of polarity from Goethe's nature studies and has used it to catalog its thoughts on his historical studies. It has done so without regard for Goethe's understanding of the term as a sign for primal phenomena of nature, rather than for metaphysical abstractions of the mind. But critics have done so for reasons other than for the convenience of cataloging their thoughts. In part scholarship has only conformed to the way Goethe's science was embedded in the late nineteenth century Weimar edition of his collected works. The editorial principles used in the organization of Goethe's scientific writings in this edition were largely the product of Rudolf Steiner's personal interpretation of Goethe's views on nature.[49] His emphasis on the dynamic qualities of Goethe's science, for example, gave cause to organize materials around that term in an arbitrary fashion. And only after the East German publication of Goethe's scientific writings in the new Leopoldina edition (1947–), has it been possible to examine critically the influence Steiner has had on the interpretation of Goethe's science.

The East Germans' neopositivistic approach to editing a text, and their interest in the contextual origins of a text, have contributed significantly to the reappraisal of Goethe's science. Indeed, at the heart of the polarity problem in historiography lies the difference in philological principles of two different schools of thought, the neopositivism of the East Germans and the anthroposophy of Rudolf Steiner.

Both the Weimar and the Leopoldina editions include writings in which Goethe expressed various forms of binary thoughts and phenomena, such as "the polarization of light" (Polarisation des Lichts), "the opposition of extremes" (Gegensatz der Extreme), and "two ends of a specific body" (Zwei Enden eines spezifischen Körpers, LA, I, 11, 342, 46, 40–1). However, in reference specifically to the term polarity, there is one significant difference in the editorial presentation. In Steiner's presentation, that is, in the Weimar edition, the term "Polarität" was arbitrarily placed at the head of some notes and observations to Goethe's "Outline of Lectures on Physics" (Physikalische Vorträge Schematisiert) of 1805–6, a section which in the Leopoldina edition was more appropriately labeled "Introduction" (Einleitung).[50] The significance of this editorial divergence lies in the fact that in these notes Goethe never used the term "Polarität," and, furthermore, he organized the notes with another term, "Dualität," and thirdly, in these notes he made a distinction between "Dualisms" of the mind, such as "God and the World" (Gott und die Welt) and "Spirit and Matter" (Geist und Materie), and "Dualisms" of the body, such as "right and left" (Recht und Links, LA, I, 11, 55).

Based on the content and language of these introductory notes to Goethe's "Lectures on Physics," it might have been appropriate to use the heading "Dualism" (Dualität), for here Goethe is discussing more generally (Einiges Allgemeine) the various environments in which "binary appearances" (Dualität der Erscheinung) and "bifurcating processes" (Dualität als Auseinandergehen der Einheit, LA, I, 11, 55) can be observed. Yet, even the improved editorial presentation of the Leopoldina edition seems to have had a minor impact on Goethe scholarship, for discussions of polarity continue to be based on the Steiner version in the Weimar edition. Indeed, on occasion critics will show quotations from the Leopoldina edition, but, when dealing specifically with polarity, there is a switch to the Weimar edition, conforming to Steiner's correlation of dualism of the mind with polarities of nature.[51]

Although much of the writing on Goethe as a historian has drawn sources from the Weimar edition, there is also a thin line of research that has not conformed to the anthroposophy of Steiner, particularly that line of research that has been focused specifically on the *Materialien zur Geschichte der Farbenlehre*. The need to study the work for its own merits, as a document with a particular view of the history of science, was perhaps first expressed by George Sarton in an article on "Montucla," in which he noted Goethe's pioneer efforts in writing a history of optics.[52] Later, in 1952, John Hennig wrote on "Goethe's interest in the history of British physics" and in 1960 Dorothea Kuhn emphasized the literary qualities of the history, particularly the narrative qualities, the balance of form and content in some of the essays.[53] Then, in Reuter's essay from 1966, a new emphasis was placed on the substance of Goethe's history, on "the phenomenology of thought" (gegenständliches Denken), opening the door to the study of Goethe's "History of Color Theory" as a "Novel of European Thought" (Roman des europäischen Gedankens),[54] a possibility formerly reserved for classical works such as Goethe's *Faust*.

The present study is an attempt to forge a departure from the topoi of Goethe scholarship, which has been dominated by binary forms of criticism since the beginning of the twentieth century. It is an attempt to look beyond the "storehouse of trains of thought," beyond the "shared exemplars" of scholarship, and to develop a line of thinking from Goethe's own philosophy of language, in which the emphasis is on the *expanded middle,* rather than on the *excluded middle.* That is, the pages of this book are an attempt to shift the focus of Goethe scholarship on those junctures at which Goethe saw growth and change take place; hence, the emphasis is on his tropes of transition, on the language of the intensified middle, on the borders between opposition, for it is at the joints of nature where Goethe discovered the kinetics of life, both in science and in history. This book is an attempt to shift discussion from the topoi of Goethe scholarship, and to follow Goethe's search for thresholds of change in life processes, and in pursuing his line of thinking, the author has tried to follow a dictum from Goethe's writings on the historiography of science: "Authority, namely, that something previously has occurred, has been said or decided, has great value; however, only the pedant everywhere demands authority."[55]

Notes

Introduction

1. Bernhard Gajek and Franz Götting, *Goethes Leben und Werk in Daten und Bildern* (Frankfurt: Insel, 1966), give a detailed chronicle of Goethe's life by year, month, and day. For a good picture biography of the main periods of Goethe's life, see Jörn Göres, *Goethes Leben in Bilddokumenten* (Munich: Beck, 1981), and for a brief critical study with a guide for further reading, see Terence J. Reed, *Goethe* (Oxford University Press, 1984).

2. Goethe's major works are translated into most languages of the modern world, including the recent twelve-volume edition of *Goethe in English*, 12 vols., ed. V. Lange (Boston: Suhrkamp-Insel, 1982–).

3. Hans Pyritz, *Goethe-Bibliographie*, 2 vols. (Heidelberg: Winter, 1965), covers research on Goethe to 1964, including reference tools and editions, his philosophy and world views, his scientific, poetic, and literary writings, his works as statesman and theatre director, and the impact of his life and works on western civilization. See also Hans Henning, "Goethe–Bibliographie 1987," *Goethe-Jahrbuch*, 106 (1989): 377–410, an annual bibliography of primary and secondary sources published since 1951.

4. See Karl J. Fink, "Johann Wolfgang Goethe," in *Read More About It. An Encyclopedia of Information Sources on Historical Figures and Events*, 3 vols., C. Kohoyda-Inglis (Ann Arbor, Mich.: Pierian Press, 1989), vol. 3, pp. 252–4, for a guide to recordings, video tapes, movies, plays, museums, and popular discussions of Goethe's life and works.

5. Dorothea Kuhn, "Goethe's Relationship to the Theories of Development of His Time," in *Goethe and the Sciences: A Reappraisal*, ed. F. Amrine, F. Zucker, and H. Wheeler (Dordrecht: Reidel, 1987), p. 4.

6. See Erich Trunz, "Goethe als Sammler," in *Weimarer Goethe-Studien*, ed. Erich Trunz (Weimar: Böhlau, 1980), pp. 7–47.

7. Dorothea Kuhn, "Goethes Schriften zur Naturwissenschaft," *Goethe-Jahrbuch*, 33 (1971): 123–46, discusses the content and structure of the Leopoldina edition, commemorating the completion of the eleventh and last volume of his primary writings and projecting plans for the corresponding volumes of archival and explanatory materials designed for the second part of the edition.

8. During the 1980s three separate collections of essays on Goethe as a scientist have

154

appeared, the first by scholars in the former East Germany, organized by Helmut Brandt, ed., *Goethe und die Wissenschaften* (Jena: Friedrich-Schiller-Universität, 1984), and another by West Europeans, organized by Horst Glaser, ed., *Goethe und die Natur* (Bern: Peter Lang, 1986). The most recent volume, organized by Amrine, et al., *Goethe and the Sciences* (1987), includes new materials by American scholars and reprints of earlier essays by European colleagues, an anthology on the state of the art in research on Goethe's scientific writings.

1. Goethe's romantic science

1. Goethe, "Ueber Naturwissenschaft im Allgemeinen. Einzelne Betrachtungen und Aphorismen," in *Aufsätze, Fragmente, Studien zur Naturwissenschaft im Allgemeinen*, ed. D. Kuhn and W. Engelhardt, LA, pt. I, vol. 11, p. 357. "Grundeigenschaft der lebendigen Einheit: sich zu trennen, sich zu vereinen, sich ins Allgemeine zu ergehen, im Besondern zu verharren, sich zu verwandeln, sich zu spezifizieren, und wie das Lebendige unter tausend Bedingungen sich dartun mag, hervorzutreten und zu verschwinden, zu solideszieren und zu schmelzen, zu erstarren und zu fliessen, sich auszudehnen und zusammenzuziehen. Weil nun alle diese Wirkungen im gleichen Zeitmoment zugleich vorgehen, so kann alles und jedes zu gleicher Zeit eintreten." The English translation is taken from *Johann Wolfgang Goethe. Scientific Studies*, ed. and trans. D. Miller (New York: Suhrkamp, 1988), pp. 303–4.
2. Gajek and Götting, *Goethes Leben und Werk*, p. 19. To place Goethe's confrontation with German higher education into context, see Charles E. McClelland, *State, Society, and University in Germany, 1700–1914* (Cambridge University Press, 1980): "The crisis in student enrollments was only the quantitative sign of a deep qualitative malaise in the German universities. Scholasticism was the method and orthodoxy the content of most instruction" (p. 28).
3. Ernst Traumann, *Goethe der Strassburger Student*, 2d ed. (Leipzig: Klinkhardt & Biermann, 1923), quotes the passage from a letter written by a Professor Metzger on August 7, 1771: "Jesus autor et judex sacrorum, dans laquelle il avance entre autres que Jesus Christ n'était pas le fondateur de notre religion, mais que quelques autres savants l'avaient faite sous son nom. Que la religion chrétienne n'était autre chose qu'une saine politique etc." (p. 287). For German and English versions of the letter, see George Brandes, *Wolfgang Goethe*, trans. A. W. Porterfield (New York: Frank-Maurice, 1924), p. 112.
4. Traumann, *Goethe der Strassburger Student*, "Ce jeune homme enflé de son érudition et principalement de quelques chicanes de Monsieur de Voltaire alla faire une soutenance qui devait avoir pour titre" (p. 287); Brandes, *Wolfgang Goethe*, p. 19.
5. Gertrud Schubart-Fikentscher, *Goethes Sechsundfünfzig Strassburger Thesen vom 6. August, 1771* (Weimar: Böhlau, 1949), organized them into five thematic groups, arguing that the topics themselves were commonplaces of formal law education at the time (pp. 8–9).
6. Johann W. Ritter (1776–1810), discoverer of ultraviolet rays and a representative of romantic science, repeated this assertion in his lecture on the history of science at the dedication of the Bavarian Academy of Science on March 28, 1806, stating

that nature does not seem to have any greater purpose than to serve as "the teacher of human beings" (die Lehrerin des Menschen, p. 4); Johann W. Ritter, *Die Physik als Kunst. Ein Versuch, die Tendenz der Physik aus iher Geschichte zu deuten* (Munich: Lindauer, 1806). Alexander G. H. Gode-Von Aesch, *Natural Science in German Romanticism* (New York: Columbia University Press, 1941), saw in Goethe the epitome of romantic science, arguing that, when we speak of the "age of Goethe," we accept him as "the fullest representative of his entire era," and thus we take his "biotic" world view as a benchmark of romantic science (pp. 3–4). More recently D. M. Knight, "The Physical Sciences and the Romantic Movement," *History of Science* 9 (1970): 54–75, and idem, "German Science in the Romantic Period," in *The Emergence of Science in Western Europe*, ed. M. Crosland (New York: Science History Publications, 1976), pp. 161–78, explored the science of individuals from the era independent of Goethe's views on nature, giving a broader base to romantic natural philosophy in Germany. Timothy Lenoir, *The Strategy of Life* (Chicago: University of Chicago Press, 1989; repr., 1982), as a third alternative, avoided the association of romantic science with Goethe's world view as well as the list of accomplishments by individuals and disciplines during his era; instead he looked at the period before Darwin as one in which "a very coherent body of theory based on a teleology was worked out," a thesis he located in the last decade of the eighteenth century, in "the writings of the philosopher Imannuel Kant" (p. 2).

7. McClelland, *State, Society, and University in Germany*, argues in the opening statement of his study, that law faculties in German universities were "caught in a decline," because "the traditional Roman law that had served since the late fifteenth century as the basis of instruction and had had some relevance to the law of the Holy Roman Empire was now becoming comparatively useless as the new enlightened despots created their own legal traditions and needs" (p. 30).

8. Wilhelm Scherer, "Die Litteratur-revolution," in *Sturm und Drang*, ed. M. Wacker (Darmstadt: Wiss. Buchgesellschaft, 1985; repr., 1870), pp. 17–24, 20. Roy Pascal, "The 'Sturm and Drang' Movement," *Modern Language Review* 47 (1952): 129–51, also pointed to the dynamics of the group, observing that they were more successful in "grasping problems than asserting principles" (p. 131).

9. Friedrich Schiller, "Versuch über den Zusammenhang der thierischen Natur des Menschen mit seiner Geistigen," in *Schillers Werke*, ed. K. H. Hahn, National-ausgabe (NA), 42 vols. (Weimar: Böhlau, 1943–), vol. 20, pp. 37–75. See Wolfgang Riedel, *Die Anthropologie des jungen Schiller. Zur Ideengeschichte der medizinischen Schriften und der 'Philosophischen Briefe'* (Würzburg: Königshausen and Neumann, 1985).

10. Johann Gottfried Herder, "Abhandlung über den Ursprung der Sprache," in *Sämtliche Werke*, ed. B. Suphan, Suphan-Ausgabe (SA), 33 vols. (Hildesheim: Georg Olm, 1967, repr., 1891), vol. 5, pp. 1–148.

11. Herder, "Auch eine Philosophie der Geschichte zur Bildung der Menschheit," SA, vol. 5, pp. 475–594.

12. Immanuel Kant, "Von den verschiedenen Racen der Menschen," in *Kant's Gesammelte Schriften*, publ. by the Preussische Akademie der Wissenschaften (Akad.), 29 vols. (Berlin: Reimer and de Gruyter, 1910–), vol. 2, pp. 427–43.

13. Kant, "Von den verschiedenen Racen," Akad., vol. 2, p. 429.

14. Johann Blumenbach, *De generis humani varietate nativa* (Göttingen: Vandenhoeck, 1776). For an introduction to Blumenbach's place in the history of anthropology, for an English translation, and for comparative editions of the dissertation, see idem, *The Anthropological Treatises of Johann Friedrich Blumenbach*, ed. and trans. T. Bendyshe (Boston: Milford House, 1973; repr., 1865).

15. François M. A. Voltaire, *The Philosophy of History*, trans. T. Kiernan (New York: Philosophical Library, 1965), p. 5.

16. Johann Blumenbach, *Ueber den Bildungstrieb und das Zeugungsgeschäft* (Göttingen: Dietrich, 1781).

17. See also Manfred Wenzel, "Johann Wolfgang von Goethe und Samuel Thomas Soemmerring: Morphologie und Farbenlehre," in *Samuel Thomas Soemmerring und die Gelehrten der Goethezeit*, ed. G. Mann and F. Dumant (Stuttgart: Fischer, 1985), pp. 11–33, for further discussion of the web of events and scientists that informed Goethe's early interests in physical anthropology.

18. Goethe, "Zur Morphologie," in *Morphologische Hefte*, ed. D. Kuhn, LA, pt. I, vol. 9, pp. 85–189.

19. Timothy Lenoir, "Kant, Blumenbach, and Vital Materialism in German Biology," *ISIS* 71 (1980): 77–108, too, explains that Kant and Blumenbach's concept of the "force of formation" was "conceived as an organic version of a Newtonian force, a mechanico-teleological drive operating materially within organic bodies to give rise to their determinate structures" (p. 77). In his book on *The Strategies of Life* (1989), he argues that from these ideas nineteenth-century biologists constructed "a consistent body of unified theory for the life sciences" (p. 2).

20. Goethe, "Mailied," ed. G. Loeper, WA, pt. I, vol. 1, p. 72. Quotations from Goethe's poetry in English translation are taken from *Johann Wolfgang Goethe. Selected Poems*, ed. and trans. C. Middleton (Boston: Suhrkamp, 1983), pp. 11–12. Recently scholars have attempted to examine Goethe's science and poetry as twin manifestations of the same urge to explain nature, as for example, Helmut Brandt, "Natur in Goethes Dichten und Denken," *Goethe und die Wissenschaften*, pp. 156–78. Ivan Supek, "Wissenschaft und Dichtung," *Goethe und die Natur Referate des Triestiner Kongresses*, ed. H. A. Glaser (Frankfurt: Peter Lang, 1986), pp. 217–31, also focuses the theme on the juncture between science and art, however, with emphasis on the ethical values that emerge from Goethe's nature poetry.

21. Goethe, "Auf dem See," trans. C. Middleton, p. 41, *Gedichte*, ed. G. Loeper, WA, pt. I, vol. 1, p. 78.

22. Goethe, "Auf dem See," trans. Middleton, p. 41; WA, pt. I, vol. 1, p. 78, "Und frische Nahrung, neues Blut / Saug' ich aus freier Welt; / Wie ist Natur so hold und gut, Die mich am Busen hält!"

23. Goethe, "Auf dem See," trans. Middleton, p. 41; WA, pt. I, vol. 1, p. 78, "Und im See bespiegelt / Sich die reifende Frucht." Here Goethe has moved beyond simple subject–object distinctions, and has begun to explore the processes within critical thought itself, examining the way observations and judgments are made, a focus current in questions raised particularly by Thomas Kuhn, "Objectivity, Value, Judgement, and Theory Choice," in *Critical Theory Since 1965*, ed. H. Adams and L. Searle (Tallahassee: University Presses of Florida, 1986), pp. 383–

93: "My argument has so far been directed to two points. It first provided evidence that the choices scientists make between competing theories depend not only on shared criteria – those my critics call objective – but also on idiosyncratic factors dependent on individual biography and personality" (p. 388).

24. Goethe, "Dauer im Wechsel," trans. C. Middleton, p. 169; *Gedichte,* ed. G. Loeper, WA, pt. I, vol. 1, p. 119.

25. Goethe, "Dauer im Wechsel," trans. Middleton, p. 169; WA, pt. I, vol. 1, p. 119, "Ach, und in demselben Flusse / Schwimmst du nicht zum zweitenmal."

26. Goethe, "Allerdings: Dem Physiker," trans. Middleton, p. 237; G. Loeper, ed., WA, pt. I, vol. 3, p. 105. Gode-Von Aesch, *Natural Science in German Romanticism,* calls the search for a unified nature "the quest for a new Lucretius" (p. 31). He devotes an entire chapter to "The New Lucretius" (pp. 32–52), treating primarily Wieland's effort to overcome the mechanisms of Leibnitz's monadology and to replace it with more subtle "spiritualities" (p. 48), the basis of the German concept of a harmony of nature.

27. Goethe, "Allerdings: Dem Physiker," trans. Middleton, p. 237; WA, pt. I, vol. 3, p. 105, "'In's Innre der Natur—' / O du Philister!— / 'Dringt kein erschaffner Geist.'"

28. Ibid., "Dich prüfe du nur allermeist, / Ob du Kern oder Schale seist."

29. There is the consensus among historians of science that Goethe's studies in geology and mineralogy "form no milestone in the history of these sciences," Rudolf Magnus, *Goethe as a Scientist,* trans. H. Norden (New York: Schuman, 1949), p. 205; and that his writings are of interest primarily because they "reflect the intellectual milieu of his time" (p. 163), W. Scott Baldridge, "The Geological Writings of Goethe," *American Scientist* 72 (1984): 163–7.

30. Baldridge, "Geological Writings of Goethe," p. 167, reports that Goethe did receive the honor of having a mineral, Goethite, an orthorhombic mineral with the formula FeO.OH, named after him, as well as the fact that a number of professional societies and institutions recognized his activities during his lifetime. Goethe also continues to attract attention among historians for his "explanation for basalt," a fine-grained rock consisting mostly of feldspar and pyroxene, and for his innovative discussion of a general "ice age"; idem, pp. 165–7. Otfried Wagenbreth, "Goethes Stellung in der Geschichte der Geologie," *Goethe und die Wissenschaften,* ed. H. Brandt (Jena: Friedrich-Schiller-Universität, 1984) pp. 59–71, and Hans Wolff, "Goethes Kenntnisse der Alpen im Lichte der modernen Geologie," *Sudhoffs Archiv* 70 (1986): 144–52, discuss Goethe's research on erratic granite deposits, moraine lines and rock fissures, pointing out his miscalculations, but reminding us that his work reflects the level of science at the time and that in some points, such as in glacial drift theories, he anticipated science of the nineteenth century.

31. Goethe, "Ueber den Granit," *Schriften zur Geologie und Mineralogie, 1770–1810,* ed. G. Schmid, LA, pt. I, vol. 1, p. 62, "So sieht man doch offenbar, dass der Granit durch eine lebendige, bei ihrem Ursprung innerlich sehr zusammengedrängte Kristillisation entstanden ist."

32. Baldridge, "Geological Writings of Goethe," discusses Goethe's concept of granite as an "Urgestein" (p. 164–5), although the concept of a primal phenomenon,

an Urphänomen, was not fully developed until later studies in comparative anatomy and botany. See also Hugh Nisbet, *Goethe and the Scientific Tradition* (London: Maney, 1972), pp. 39–47, for a full discussion of the concept, particularly as applied to color theory.

33. Baldridge, "Geological Writings of Goethe," observed that "Goethe proposed a unique compromise between an origin as an aqueous precipitate and as a solid crystallized from a hot melt" (p. 165), a compromise of the two schools of thought which led him to another innovative concept with currency in the annals of geology, a "general volcanic ocean" (p. 165).

34. Goethe, "Der Dynamismus in der Geologie," *Schriften zur Geologie und Mineralogie, 1770–1810,* ed. G. Schmid LA, pt. I, vol. 1, p. 379, "Sie lässt endlich im bereits Gebildeten noch eine innere Bildung, d. h. eine Sammlung und Anziehung des Aehnlichen und Entsprechenden gelten."

35. Ibid., p. 380, "Dieses Aufgeben seines Charakters im Granite, diese Metamorphose, kann man als ein Aussichschreiten, ein Ueberschreiten ansehen."

36. Ronald Brady, "Form and Cause in Goethe's Morphology," *Goethe and the Sciences,* ed. F. Amrine, F. Zucker, and H. Wheeler (Dordrecht: Reidel, 1987), pp. 257–300, devoted several sections of his essay to the question of "Form as Movement" (pp. 279–81), also signaling "difficulties of expression" in portraying "form in the context of movement," which is "a 'making' principle rather than a 'thing made' " (p. 281).

37. See Magnus, *Goethe as a Scientist,* pp. 202–4, for a brief discussion of Goethe's work on Müller's mineral collection and its value as a pedagogical and scientific description of the geology of the Karlsbad region.

38. Gode-Von Aesch, *Natural Science in German Romanticism,* is particularly rich in discussion of the themes comprising the idea of the harmony of nature, including a chapter on "The Unity of Organic Nature: Man and Animal" (pp. 53–73).

39. For a review of the origins, distribution, and ensuing controversy on the date of the original manuscript, see Hermann Bräuning-Oktavio's essay on "Goethes naturwissenschaftliche Schriften und die Freiheit von Forschung und Lehre," *Jahrbuch des Freien Deutschen Hochstifts,* D. Lüders, ed. (Tübingen: Niemeyer, 1982), pp. 110–215, where he focuses on the textual and editorial origin of key documents in comparative anatomy (pp. 111–38), as well as in botany and plant theory and optics and color theory. The story of the textual life of Goethe's essays on the intermaxillary bone is also thoroughly discussed by D. Kuhn, ed., LA, pt. II, vol. 9A, pp. 474–92.

40. See Bräuning-Oktavio, "Goethes naturwissenschaftlichen Schriften," p. 127, and D. Kuhn, LA, pt. II, vol. 9a, pp. 474–87, for the details of the reception and history of the original manuscript.

41. Bräuning-Oktavio, "Goethes naturwissenschaftlichen Schriften," discusses the reception of Goethe's essay among twelve of the leading comparative anatomists of the day, including that of the Frenchman, Felix Vicq d'Azyr (1748–96) to whom priority in the discovery is ascribed: "Schon 1780 hatte er in einer Sitzung der Pariser Academie des Sciences sein Memoire vorgetragen. . . . Darin betont er die 'grande analogie entre la structure de l'homme et alle des animaux' " (p. 120).

42. Goethe, "Dem Menschen wie den Tieren ist ein Zwischen Knochen der obern Kinnlade zuzuschreiben." *Morphologische Hefte,* ed. D. Kuhn, LA, pt. I, vol. 9, p. 155, "Es hatte solche Schwierigkeiten, wenn sie auf alle Tiere passen sollte."

43. Gode-Von Aesch, *Natural Science in German Romanticism,* also discusses the concept of "type," but relates it to romantic "ideas of infinity" (pp. 136–57), rather than following the transition in Goethe's science from the rhapsodic diffusion of his early work to the controlled order of his mature writing.

44. Goethe's view of organic life was fundamentally teleological, although he did not assume a divine creator as the source of change and variety, but like many of his contemporaries, grounded his views of biological teleology in concepts of analogy. Compare Karl J. Fink, "Ontogeny Recapitulates Phylogeny: A Classical Formula of Eighteenth-century Organicism," in *Approaches to Organic Form,* ed. F. Burwick (Dordrecht: Reidel, 1987), pp. 87–112.

2. Goethe's classical science

1. Goethe, "Ueber Naturwissenschaften im Allgemeinen," LA, pt. I, vol. 11, p. 339, "Kein Phänomen erklärt sich an und aus sich selbst; nur viele zusammen überschaut, methodisch geordnet, geben zuletzt etwas was für Theorie gelten könnte."

2. Adolf Portmann, "Goethe and the Concept of Metamorphosis," *Goethe and the Sciences,* ed. Amrine, et al. (Dordrecht: Reidel), pp. 113–45, correctly observes that "none of Goethe's other writings on natural science approaches the inner unity and intellectual scope of this treatise, with which only the *Theory of Color* can compare" (p. 133).

3. Portmann, "Concept of Metamorphosis," attempts to capture "the drama of the life of plants" by discussing Goethe's theory of plants in the language of "the stage of life" (p. 139). This approach is not uncommon to the reception of Goethe's plant theory, as discussed by Richard H. Eyde, "The Foliar Theory of the Flower," *American Scientist* 63 (1975): 430–7, who includes in his essay various visual representations of the drama as viewed by scientific illustrators such as P. J. F. Turpin (p. 432).

4. Portmann, "Concept of Metamorphosis," observed how Goethe limited his study to "flowering plants," "dicotyledons," "annual grasses," and to "blossoming shoots," and explained this restriction as grounded in "a deep-seated, unconscious need for a clear theme" (p. 134).

5. Goethe, "Die Metamorphose der Pflanzen," *Morphologische Hefte,* ed. D. Kuhn, LA, pt. I, vol. 9, p. 53, "Alles was wir bisher nur mit der Einbildungskraft und dem Verstande zu ergreifen gesucht, zeigt uns das Beispiel einer durchgewachsenen Rose auf das deutlichste."

6. See Bräuning-Oktavio, "Die naturwissenschaftlichen Schriften," pp. 138–45, for a survey of the reviews and Goethe's response to them.

7. Theodor Butterfass, "Goethe und die Wissenschaft von der Pflanze," in *Allerhand Goethe,* ed. D. Kimpel and J. Pompetzki (Bern: Peter Lang, 1985), pp. 165–80, examines Goethe's reference to Wolff, observing that Goethe had found Wolff's forgotten study of plant morphology from 1768 in search of support for his

theory, but in doing so, ironically had jeopardized his own priority in the discovery (p. 168).

8. Scholarship on Goethe's "errors in physical optics" is typically framed in a discussion of the Goethe–Newton controversy and on this topic Werner Heisenberg's essay "The Teachings of Goethe and Newton on Colour in the Light of Modern Physics," in *Philosophic Problems of Nuclear Science,* trans. F. C. Hayes (New York: Pantheon, 1952), pp. 60–76, has become a classic. First published in German as "Die Goethesche und Newtonsche Farbenlehre im Lichte der modernen Physik, *Geist der Zeit,* 19 (1941): 261–75, the essay has set the standard on the question of emphasizing the differences in approach and goals: "Newton's theory makes possible a certain control over the phenomena of light and their practical use but it is plainly of no assistance to a better appreciation of the world of color surrounding us" (p. 63). In more recent scholarship, Jürgen Blasius, "Zur Wissenschaftstheorie Goethes," *Zeitschrift für philosophische Forschung* 33 (1979): 371–88, has given sharper definition to the differences, finding in Goethe's "Gesetz über den Zusammenhang von Phänomenen" (p. 384), anticipation of modern physics: "Goethes Kritik impliziert das wissenschaftstheoretische Postulat, dass die Struktur der Theorie die relevanten Bedingungen der Erscheinung des Erklärungsobjektes der Theorie und damit die Voraussetzungen ihrer eigenen Gültigkeit umfassen muss" (p. 386), ironically anticipating Heisenberg's own uncertainty principle. Paul Feyerabend, "Classical Empiricism," in *The Methodological Heritage of Newton,* ed. R. E. Butts and J. W. Davis (Toronto: University of Toronto Press, 1970), pp. 150–70, examines the basis of Newton's "greater control over the phenomena of light," also explaining how his ray theory has "much in common with contemporary argument in microphysics" (p. 160). And where Feyerabend emphasizes Newton's concept of the "experimentum crucis," the view that "not all experiments are given equal value" (p. 163), Blasius focuses on Goethe's contextual approach, "die Gültigkeit der Gesetze auf den Rahmen ihrer Bedingungen zu relativieren" (p. 384).

9. Goethe, "Beiträge zur Optik," *Beiträge zur Optik und Anfänge der Farbenlehre, 1790–1808,* ed. R. Matthaei, LA, pt. I, vol. 3, p. 17, "Man nehme also zuerst das Prisma vor, betrachte durch dasselbe die Gegenstände des Zimmers und der Landschaft, man halte den Winkel, durch den man sieht, bald oberwärts, bald unterwärts, man halte das Prisma horizontal oder vertikal und man wird immer dieselbigen Erscheinungen wahrnehmen."

10. M. H. Wilson, "Goethe's Colour Experiments," *Year Book of the Physical Society* (1958): 12–21, recasts Goethe's prismatic colors in terms of modern physics, focusing on "boundary colours or edge spectra, unknown in Goethe's time and often unnoticed today" (p. 12). More recently, Gernot Böhme, "Is Goethe's Theory of Color Science?" in *Goethe and the Sciences,* ed. Amrine et al. (Dordrecht: Reidel, 1987), pp. 147–73, focused on the differences between the science of Goethe and that of the tradition from Newton to modern physics, asking specifically whether or not Goethe's "alternative science will serve a useful purpose" (p. 170). Both of these studies, Wilson's interpretation of Goethe's color theory with the tools of modern physics and Böhme's examination of Goethe's color theory as an alternative science, give a sympathetic reading of Goethe's

theory of colors, although both essays are grounded in the fact that Goethe made some fundamental errors in his research in physical optics, if this research is judged from the perspective of the Newtonian tradition.

11. The text of 1791 relates to the one of 1810 as does a "primer" (Fibel) to a "bible" (Bibel, LA, pt. II, vol. 3, p. 165), a cliche from scholarship that has come to characterize not just the growth and development of two decades of Goethe's research in optics and color theory, but also the status to which these documents rose in the Goethe–Newton polemics, a controversy grounded in two significantly different approaches to science in the eighteenth century.

12. Wilson, "Goethe's Colour Experiments," praises particularly Goethe's "beautiful experiment with the Coloured Shadows," observing that his exact descriptions "have stimulated much of our science of physiological optics" (p. 13).

13. Goethe, *Zur Farbenlehre. Didaktischer Teil.* ed. R. Matthaei, LA, pt. I, vol. 4, p. 62, "So finden wir, dass die katoptrischen Farben sich nahe an die physiologischen anschliessen, die paroptischen sich schon etwas mehr ablösen und gewissermassen selbständig werden, die dioptrischen sich ganz eigentlich physisch erweisen und eine entschieden objektive Seite haben; die epoptischen, obgleich in ihren Anfängen auch nur apparent, machen den Uebergang zu den chemischen Farben."

14. Wilson, "Goethe's Colour Experiments," concludes that "the basic concept of light–dark polarity leads to a study of colour in the forms in which we see and use it," although most of his essay is a demonstration of the argument that Goethe's physical optics can be explained by modern methods of physics and that they are "by no means inconsistent with quantitative treatment" (p. 21).

15. Goethe, *Zur Farbenlehre*, LA, pt. I, vol. 4, p. 38, "So fordert Gelb das Violette, Orange das Blaue, Purpur das Grüne, und umgekehrt."

16. Frederick Burwick, *The Damnation of Newton: Goethe's Color Theory and Romantic Perception* (Berlin: de Gruyter, 1986), argued that Goethe continued working on the polarity problem after publishing this theory in 1810, by 1817 accepting Schopenhauer's arguments that "his account of color opposition belonged to physiology rather than to physics" (p. 58).

17. Wilson, "Goethe's Colour Experiments," explains that Goethe's prismatic colors have only recently been investigated and that most of the "edge-spectra" can be illustrated with the modern techniques of "additive and subtractive Mixing" (pp. 19–20).

18. Werner Abraham, "Bemerkungen zu Goethes Farbenlehre im Lichte der Wahrnehmungspsychologie und der kognitiven Psychologie," *Euphorion* 77 (1985): 144–75, looks at Goethe's color theory for evidence in the debate between cross-cultural universals and Whorfian relativity in language, arguing on the basis of recent studies in psycholinguistics and ethnolinguistics that Goethe's theory is grounded in universal concepts of color and can be used to refute "den Whorf-Sapirischen Relativismus" (p. 174).

19. M. Norton Wise, "On the Relation of Physical Science to History in late Nineteenth-Century Germany," in *Functions and Uses of Disciplinary Histories*, ed. L. Graham, W. Lepenies, and P. Weingart (Dordrecht: Reidel, 1983), pp. 3–34, introduced his study with a quotation from Goethe's color theory, stating that "the

history of science is science itself," a quotation emphasizing "the priority of an historical mode of knowing over an abstract, analytical mode," a point of view Wise places at the center of Goethe's polemics with Newton and that has served "as a reference mark for the two culture debate since the beginning of the nineteenth century," a debate between the "Geisteswissenschaften" and the "Naturwissenschaften" (p. 3).

20. Wise, "On the Relation of Physical Science to History," traces Goethe's view, that "one could know nature only directly, by experiencing it as a participant" (p. 3), to Heisenberg's uncertainty principle, finding in Goethe the origins of a view that raised "a wholly modern objection to the concept of a material world definable outside our thought and action" (p. 4).

21. Ronald Brady, "Goethe's Natural Science. Some Non-Cartesian Meditations," in *Toward a Man-Centered Medical Science,* ed. K. E. Schaefer, H. Hensel, and R. Brady (vol. 1 of *A New Image of Man in Medicine*) (Mt. Kisco, N.Y.: Futura, 1977), pp. 137–65, argued that Goethe's rejection of the Cartesian separation of mind and body is grounded in the same "growing dissatisfaction with the Cartesian world view" that has led to the present success of Thomas Kuhn's *The Structure of Scientific Revolutions,* 2nd ed. (Chicago: University of Chicago Press, 1970), and to "a sudden reprieve" for views that are not based on the premise of a divorce between subject and object, mind and body, and spirit and matter (pp. 139–40).

22. Blasius, "Zur Wissenschaftstheorie Goethes," argues that Goethe's linkage of the design of the experiment with the experimenter is a structure, "die seit der Relativitätstheorie für die ganze moderne Physik charakteristisch ist: die Messgeräte, mit denen die Eigenschaften der Natur bestimmt werden, sind selbst Gegenstände dieser Natur" (p. 384).

23. John A. McCarthy, "The Philosopher as Essayist: Leibniz and Kant," in *The Philosopher as Writer,* ed. R. Ginsberg (Selinsgrove, Pa.: Susquehanna University Press, 1987), pp. 48–74, argues that the kind of philosophy that gave rise to the essay is skeptical, "consequently, the attempts to get at the truth of the matter are tentative," an approach others have referred to as a "process of encirclement," "weighing the possibilities," or as "processuality" (p. 50). Joachim Wohlleben, *Goethe als Journalist und Essayist* (Bern: Peter Lang, 1981), affirms the tentative status of Goethe's science by arguing that his essays are fragments of knowledge, that most of his scientific work is presented in essays and as such they are incomplete projects, so that one could hardly say, "Goethes Arbeiten zur Naturwissenschaft hätten ein System errichtet" (p. 130).

24. Feyerabend, "Classical Empiricism," refers to this measure of the self as a "rule of faith" (p. 154), arguing that the Baconian creed of experience had no more measures of objectivity than did Protestantism, and for like nature, the Bible does not contain "a grammar and a dictionary of the language in which it is written" (p. 153). Karl J. Fink, "Private and Public Authority," in *Goethe as a Critic of Literature,* ed. K. J. Fink and M. L. Baeumer (Lanham, Md.: University Press of America, 1984), pp. 182–214, observes how Goethe also compared biblical criticism to science, recognizing that the scriptures, like nature, did not bring with them " 'a standard by which their independence, originality, many sides, totality,

indeed, by which the infinite contents could be measured' " (p. 188), a condition that required external instrumentation, namely, a critical approach, which Feyerabend considers a "practice of post-Galilean science" (p. 150).

25. Brady, "Some Non-Cartesian Meditations," speculates that an awareness of the "ontological implications" of Goethe's holistic science may be an indication that we are "outgrowing the mechanistic discreteness that structures the Cartesian view" (pp. 162–3).

26. Heisenberg, "Goethe and Newton on Colour," emphasized that "exact measurements" and "mathematics" were *not* a feature distinguishing Goethe's science from Newton's, for "mathematical symmetries" can be found throughout his theory of colors (pp. 64–5).

27. Dennis Sepper, *Goethe contra Newton, Polemics and the Project for a New Science of Color* (Cambridge University Press, 1988), argues that these intuitive sensibilities are defined by Goethe's concept of an "aperçu," a concept that describes prior conditions in the rational process of science, one conditioned by "interest" (p. 184), a point in the process of experience that is "speculative" and "anticipatory": "it is a seeing through a set of given phenomena to a higher or more elemental level of (putative) truth" (p. 185).

28. Susan H. Krueger, "Allegory, Symbol, and Symbolic Representation" (Ph.D. diss., Yale University, 1984), argues that the breakdown of antimony in Goethe's symbolism developed over the course of his career, reaching a point in his late literary style, confirmed in scientific writings, where "our best and only access to the truth is by indirection and irony," *Dissertation Abstracts International* 46 (1985): 711–A.

3. Goethe's re-presentation of nature

1. Goethe, "Geschichtliches," in *Naturwissenschaftliche Hefte,* ed. D. Kuhn, LA, pt. I, vol. 8, pp. 220–32, "Symbolik. Anthropomorphismus der Sprache. In der Geschichte überhaupt, besonders aber der Philosophie, Wissenschaft, Religion, fällt es uns auf, dass die armen beschränkten Menschen ihre dunkelsten subjektiven Gefühle, die Apprehensionen eingeengter Zustände in das Beschauen des Weltalls und dessen hoher Erscheinungen überzutragen nicht unwürdig finden" (p. 225). Joseph Agassi, "Anthropomorphism in Science," in *Dictionary of the History of Ideas,* 5 vols., ed. Philip Wiener (New York: Scribner, 1973), vol. 1, pp. 87–91, surveys the topic, beginning with Aristotle and including "the 'locus classicus' of the critique of anthropomorphism," Bacon's doctrine of the idols (p. 91). However, he does not discuss the view that the symbolism of scientific language is located in anthropomorphism, namely, in Goethe's sense, that scientific language is the product of rational experience.

2. See Karl J. Fink, "The Metalanguage of Goethe's History of Color Theory," in *The Quest for the New Science, Language and Thought in Eighteenth Century Science,* ed. K. J. Fink and J. W. Marchand (Carbondale, Ill.: SIU Press, 1979), pp. 41–55. More recently Uwe Pörksen, "Goethes Kritik naturwissenschaftlicher Metaphorik und der Roman 'Die Wahlverwandtschaften,' " *Jahrbuch der deutschen Schiller-Gesellschaft* 25 (1981): 285–315, has looked at Goethe's linguistic observations, particularly at the question of "diversification" (Sphärenver-

mengung, p. 285) as a "seduction of the mind" (Sprachverführung des Denkens, p. 290). The recent trend has been for scholars to study Goethe's views of language, as opposed to those of the 1960s and early 1970s, who looked at the language of Goethe's science, as Dorothea Kuhn, *Empirische und ideelle Wirklichkeit* (Köln: Böhlau, 1967), who divides the development of his language into three periods: "Weimarer Zeit bis 1810," "Die naturwissenschaftliche Hefte 1817–24," "Vom Dornburger Aufenthalt 1828 bis zu Goethes Tod" (pp. 14–63). In this line of research see also Uwe Pörksen, "Zur Wissenschaftssprache und Sprachauffassung bei Linné and Goethe," in *Sprache und Welterfahrung,* ed. J. Zimmermann (Munich: Fink, 1978), pp. 110–41, where he contrasts Linnaeus's "Weg der Analyse" with Goethe's "Weg der Synthese" (p. 111), before providing a detailed study of the language of Goethe's morphology of plants (pp. 120–31).

3. Goethe, "Zwischenknochen," trans. Miller, p. 112; LA, pt. I, vol. 9, p. 155, "Eine lateinische Terminologie, die ich mit Beihülfe des Herrn Hofrat Loders verfertiget habe und hier beilege, wird dabei zum Leitfaden dienen können. Es hatte solche viele Schwierigkeiten, wenn sie auf alle Tiere passen sollte. Da bei dem einen gewisse Teile sich sehr zurückziehen, zusammenfliessen und bei andern gar verschwinden: so wird auch gewiss, wenn man mehr in's Feinere gehen wollte, diese Tafel noch manche Verbesserung zulassen."

4. Goethe, *Materialien zur Geschichte der Farbenlehre,* ed. D. Kuhn, LA, pt. I, vol. 6, p. 127, "Dadurch entspringt eine Individualisierung bis ins Grenzenlose, wohin keine Sprache, ja alle Sprachen der Welt zusammengenommen, nicht nachreichen." Pörksen, "Zur Sprachauffassung bei Linné und Goethe," points out that Goethe's appreciation for, and criticism of, technical language has not yet been sufficiently researched (p. 137), to which he responded in Pörksen, "Goethes Kritik naturwissenschaftlicher Metaphorik," where he examined the question of "diversification" (Sphärenvermengung) as represented in the novel "Die Wahlverwandtschaften."

5. On Goethe's concept of authority see Karl J. Fink, "'Dualisten,' 'Trinitarier,' 'Solitarier': Formen der Autorität in Goethes 'Geschichte der Farbenlehre,'" *Goethe-Jahrbuch* 99 (1982): 230–49. Rudolf Eucken, *Geschichte der Philosophischen Terminologie* (Hildesheim: Olm, 1960, 1st ed. 1879), credits Christian Wolff with creating the concept of "Vorstellung," as well as "Begriff," and provides detailed references on discussion of its use in eighteenth-century Germany (pp. 208–11).

6. Goethe, "Der Versuch als Vermittler von Objekt und Subjekt, 1793," *Naturwissenschaftliche Hefte,* ed. D. Kuhn, trans. C. Miller, p. 14; LA, pt. I, vol. 8, pp. 305–15, "Der Mensch erfreut sich nämlich mehr an der Vorstellung als an der Sache, oder wir müssen vielmehr sagen: der Mensch erfreut sich nur einer Sache, in so fern er sich dieselbe vorstellt" (p. 310).

7. Goethe, "Kirchers Pyrophylacium wieder hergestellt," *Aufätze, Fragmente, Studien zur Naturwissenschaft im Allgemeinen,* ed. D. Kuhn and W. Engelhardt, LA, pt. I, vol. 11, pp. 269–70, "Bei Betrachtung der Natur, im Grossen wie im Kleinen, hab ich unausgesetzt die Frage gestellt: Ist es der Gegenstand oder bist du es, der sich hier ausspricht? Und in diesem Sinne betrachtete ich auch Vorgänger und Mitarbeiter" (p. 269).

8. Maurice P. Crosland, *Historical Studies in the Language of Chemistry* (New York: Dover, 1978; 1st ed., 1962), locates the introduction of "systematic nomenclature into chemistry" (pp. 133–224), in the decades at the turn of the century, specifically in the reforms from 1787, about the time when Goethe began to develop his ideas about the metalanguage of science and history.

9. See Wilda C. Anderson, *Between the Library and the Laboratory: The Language of Chemistry in Eighteenth-century France* (Baltimore: Johns Hopkins University Press, 1984), for a discussion of French discourse on chemistry, a development parallel to French debates on zoology studied by Goethe.

10. Goethe, "Principes de philosophie zoologique. Discutés en mars 1830 au sein de l'Académie Royale des Sciences par Mr. Geoffroy de Saint-Hilaire Paris," *Aufsätze Fragmente, Studien zur Morphologie,* ed. D. Kuhn, LA, pt. I, vol. 10, pp. 373–403, "Wir wollen suchen, diesen Umstand bescheidentlich aufzuklären. Denn wir möchten diese Gelegenheit nicht versäumen, bemerklich zu machen, wie ein bedenklicher Wortgebrauch bei französischen Vorträgen, ja bei Streitigkeiten vortrefflicher Männer zu bedeutenden Irrungen Veranlassung gibt. Man glaubt in reiner Prosa zu reden und man spricht schon tropisch; den Tropen wendet einer anders an als der andere, führt ihn in verwandtem Sinne weiter und so wird der Streit unendlich und das Rätsel unauflöslich" (p. 398). Andrew Ortony, "Metaphor: A Multidimensional Problem," in *Metaphor and Thought,* ed. A. Ortony (Cambridge University Press, 1979), pp. 1–16, argues that, although the study of metaphors all but disappeared in most disciplines, it did remain important to at least one area of literary theory, namely, rhetoric: "thus, literary scholars vary in the extent to which the study of metaphors and other tropes is central to their enterprise. Even so, until very recently, few would have denied that tropes (of which the metaphor is the archetype) are in some way special to literature. However, in many of the chapters that follow, it is implied that all language is tropological, the language of the scientist included" (p. 3).

11. Goethe, "Schlussbetrachtung. Ueber Sprache und Terminologie," *Zur Farbenlehre. Didaktischer Teil,* ed. R. Matthaei, LA, pt. I, vol. 4, pp. 221–3, "Man bedenkt niemals genug, dass eine Sprache eigentlich nur symbolisch, nur bildlich sei und die Gegenstände niemals unmittelbar, sondern nur im Widerscheine ausdrücke" (p. 221).

12. In the scene in Faust's study, Goethe, *Faust. I. Teil, II. Teil,* ed. E. Schmidt, WA, pt. I, vol. 14, p. 62, where Faust attempts to translate the story of Genesis from the Bible, and gets stuck on the term "Logos," Goethe illustrates the difficulty of bringing into harmony a particular concept and the historical event it signifies. On this problem see also Hans R. Schweizer, *Goethe und das Problem der Sprache* (Bern: Francke, 1959), pp. 67–117, and Christa Dill, *Bedeutungsentfaltung der Wörter Tat, tätig und Tätigkeit bei Goethe* (Berlin: Humboldt Universität, 1957). August Langen, "Der Wortschatz des 18. Jahrhunderts," in *Deutsche Wortgeschichte,* 3 vols., 3d ed. edited by F. Maurer and H. Rapp (Berlin: De Gruyter, 1974), vol. 2, pp. 128ff., also points out the importance of the concept of "Tätigkeit" for Goethe's writing and that the emphasis on a dynamic language characterizes more his later writings, particularly his *Faust* and *Wilhelm Meister,* but was decidedly absent in *Werther.*

13. Goethe, "Physikalische Vorträge Schematisiert 1805–1806," *Aufsätze,*

Fragmente, Studien zur Naturwissenschaft im Allgemeinen, ed. D. Kuhn and W. Engelhardt, LA, pt. I, vol. 11, pp. 55–102, "Durch Worte sprechen wir weder die Gegenstände noch uns selbst völlig aus. Durch die Sprache entsteht gleichsam eine neue Welt, die aus Notwendigem und Zufälligem besteht" (p. 56).

14. Anderson, *Between the Library and the Laboratory,* explored the French reaction to terms of convention in chemistry, observing how Lavoisier "attacked the followers of Stahl on two grounds. First, their concept of phlogiston is an empty one, and second, they are partisans of a school" (p. 82).

15. For more recent studies on the tropological source of the language of science, see Crosland, *Historical Studies in the Language of Chemistry,* which includes a chapter on "Chemical Symbolism" (pp. 227–81), and Anderson, *Between the Library and the Laboratory,* which has a chapter on "Rhetorical and Chemical Figures" (pp. 19–34).

16. Goethe, *Materialien zur Geschichte der Farbenlehre,* ed. D. Kuhn, LA, pt. II, vol. 6, p. 186, "Alle Erscheinungen sind unaussprechlich denn die Sprache ist auch eine Erscheinung für sich die nur ein Verhältniss zu den übrigen hat, aber sie nicht herstellen (identisch ausdrücken) kann."

17. Ortony, "Metaphor: A Multidimensional Problem," pp. 1–16, contrasts literal from metaphoric language, arguing that "faith in literal language as the only adequate and appropriate tool for objective characterization of reality" reached its peak "in the doctrine of logical positivism," but that "a different approach is possible – an approach in which any truly veridical epistemological access to reality is denied" (p. 1).

18. Thomas Kuhn, "Metaphor in Science," in *Metaphor and Thought,* ed. A. Ortony (Cambridge University Press, 1979), pp. 409–19, makes the distinction between "the instrumental effectiveness" of science and its "ontology, about what really exists in nature, about the world's real joints. And in this area I see no historical evidence for a process of zeroing in" (p. 418).

19. Thomas Kuhn, *The Essential Tension* (Chicago: University of Chicago Press, 1977), p. 307; Ernst R. Curtius, *European Literature and the Latin Middle Ages,* W. Trask, trans. (New York: Harper & Row, 1963, repr., 1953; 1st German ed., 1948), p. 70; and Max Black, *Models and Metaphors* (Ithaca, N.Y.: Cornell University Press, 1962), p. 241, and idem, "More about Metaphor," in *Metaphor and Thought,* ed. A. Ortony (Cambridge University Press, 1979), pp. 36–40.

20. See Pörksen, "Goethes Kritik naturwissenschaftlicher Metaphorik," for a discussion of Goethe's understanding and appreciation for "Diskontinuität" in Linnaeus's binary and analytical language, and Goethe's own emphasis on a prose of synthesis. Goethe's virtues are "Einbildungskraft und Witz, Phantasie und Kombinationsgabe. Er betont die Einheit der Natur, die Analogien zwischen ihren Reichen" (pp. 289–90). Schweizer, *Goethe und das Problem der Sprache,* studied the problem of the relationship of language to life under the concepts of "Wort und Tat" (pp. 67–116), also focusing on Goethe's interests in the problem after arriving in Weimar: "von nun an ringt er unablässig um die Einheit des Lebens in der inneren Bezogenheit von Wort und Tat" (p. 5).

21. Goethe, "Nomenklatur," *Zur Farbenlehre. Didaktischer Teil,* ed. R. Matthaei, LA, pt. I, vol. 4, p. 183, "Auch die Farbenterminologie der neuern Sprachen werden wir gelegentlich aufführen; wobei sich denn zeigen wird, dass man immer

auf genauere Bestimmungen ausgegangen, und ein Fixiertes, Spezifiziertes auch durch die Sprache festzuhalten und zu vereinzeln gesucht hat."

22. William Whewell, *The Philosophy of the Inductive Sciences,* in *The Historical and Philosophical Works of William Whewell,* 10 vols., ed. G. Buchdahl and L. Laudan (London: F. Cass, 1967; repr., 3rd ed., 1857), reporting on progress in *The Philosophy of the Inductive Sciences* (1840), considered German and Greek to be those languages that have a great advantage in scientific discourse, because they possess a power of "forming words of composition": "Of modern European languages, the German possesses the greatest facility of composition; and hence scientific authors in that language are able to invent terms it is impossible to imitate in the other languages of Europe" (vol. 6, p. 486). Winifred P. Lehman, "Session 7. The Dictionary," *Proceedings of the National Symposium on Machine Translation,* ed. H. P. Edmundson (Englewood Cliffs, N.J.: Prentice-Hall, 1961), pp. 309–53, more recently has reported that 40 percent of German compound nouns used in scientific discourse cannot be found in a dictionary (p. 344), adding to the evidence of the flexibility of the German language for concept formation.

23. Anderson, *Between the Library and the Laboratory,* makes the same case for Lavoisier, and in general for the French Enlightenment philosophers, who were "preoccupied with the relationship between 'language and the world,' that is, between the symbols of a language and the objects they signify" (p. 1).

24. Goethe, *Materialien,* LA, pt. I, vol. 6, p. 75, "Sehen wir uns aber nach den eigentlichen Ursachen um, wodurch die Alten in ihren Vorschritten gehindert worden; so finden wir sie darin, dass ihnen die Kunst fehlt, Versuche anzustellen, ja sogar der Sinn dazu. Die Versuche sind Vermittler zwischen Natur und Begriff, zwischen Natur und Idee, zwischen Begriff und Idee."

25. Goethe, "Verhältnis zur Philosophie," LA, pt. I, vol. 4, p. 210, "Er soll sich hüten, das Anschauen in Begriffe, den Begriff in Worte zu verwandeln, und mit diesen Worten, als wären's Gegenstände, umzugehen und zu verfahren."

26. Eva Fiesel, *Die Sprachphilosophie der deutschen Romantik* (Tübingen: Mohr, 1927), labels these two traditions classicism-romanticism, distinguishing the "zentrierende Begriffe" of the Romantics from the "systematisierende Abstraktion" of the Classicists: "Novalis aber sagt einmal von Lessing, dass er zu scharf gesehen und darüber das Gefühl 'des undeutlichen Ganzen' verloren habe" (p. 4). That is, Lessing, like most rationalists, preferred concepts that were well-defined, whereas those like Novalis felt that concepts should have an inner focus, an essence with fringes of ambiguity. In more recent discussion on the language of science these two traditions have resurfaced under different names but with similar distinguishing features, the one prizing the language of science for its literal and the other for its "metaphoric" value, the former bringing with it clarity, the latter flexibility; Ortony, "Metaphor: A Multidimensional Problem," pp. 3 and 15.

27. For a discussion of the methods of definition by division and differentiation see Kenneth Burke, *A Grammar of Motives* (New York: Prentice-Hall, 1945), p. 408. Eric A. Blackall, *The Emergence of German as a Literary Language,* (Ithaca, N.Y.: Cornell University Press, 1978), p. 45, notes the monotonous style of Wolff's sentence rhythm that resulted from this method of definition. As Jean-Jacques Rousseau pointed out in his *Essay on the Origin of Languages,* trans. J. Moran and A. Gode (New York: Ungar, 1966), all written languages will change

their character and lose vigor when gaining clarity: "To the degree that needs multiply, that affairs become complicated, that light is shed, language changes its character. It becomes more regular and less passionate. It substitutes ideas for feelings. It no longer speaks to the heart but to reason. Similarly, accent diminishes, articulation increases. Language becomes more exact and clearer, but more prolix, duller and colder" (p. 16).

28. Günter Altner, "Goethe as a Forerunner of Alternative Science," in *Goethe and the Sciences: A Reappraisal,* ed. F. Amrine, F. Zucker, and H. Wheeler (Dordrecht: Reidel, 1987), defines Goethe's alternative science as an "ecology" of the "interrelationships between living creatures and their environment" (p. 341), arguing that following Heisenberg's uncertainty principle (p. 345), the scientist "must remain plastic in contemplating natural forms" (p. 348), a flexibility he places in "the biographies of individual scientists" (p. 348).

29. Pörksen, "Zur Sprachauffassung bei Linné und Goethe," in *Sprache und Welterfahrung,* p. 137, emphasizes Goethe's balanced view toward these two traditions in the language of science: "Er war gegenüber der wissenschaftlichen Terminologie und Nomenklatur an sich nicht kritisch eingestellt, im Gegenteil: er sah in der Analyse, dem Unterscheiden ein der Synthese gleichwertiges und gleichnotwendiges wissenschaftliches Verfahren."

30. Eucken, *Geschichte der Philosophischen Terminologie,* p. 150, notes in the "Begriffssprache" of Fichte, Schelling, and Hegel that: "specielle Zergliederungen finden sich sehr selten, und daher ebensowenig scharfe Definitionen." Fiesel, *Sprach-philosophie der Deutschen Romantik,* also states that the concepts of the Romantics do not meet the "terminologische Determination einer Fachsprache" (p. 3), and tend, as the Romantic mind itself, to express an "Unendlichkeit" (p. 7). In more recent philosophy William James, *The Principles of Psychology,* 2 vols. (New York: Dover, 1950; 1st ed., 1890), vol. 1, pp. 258, 281–2, 471–82, tries to define the process by which nonmetrical terms are understood: "It is the overtone, halo, or fringe of the word, as spoken in that sentence. It is never absent; no word in an understood sentence comes to consciousness as a mere noise. We feel its meaning as it passes; although our object differs from one moment to another as to its verbal kernel or nucleus, yet it is similar throughout the entire segment of the stream" (p. 281).

31. Eucken, *Geschichte der Philosophischen Terminologie,* p. 138.

32. The logocentrism of Vico's theory of history and its importance in the theories of late eighteenth-century German writers is the point of James W. Marchand's "Introduction," *The Quest for the New Science: Language and Thought in Eighteenth Century Science,* ed. K. J. Fink and J. W. Marchand (Carbondale, Ill.: SIU Press, 1979): "In fact, the entire eighteenth century in Germany can be looked upon from Vico's point of view as a process of developing a language which was adequate to the task of articulating the universe of science and philosophy" (p. 2). Karl O. Apel, "Die Idee der Sprache in der Tradition des Humanismus von Dante bis Vico," in *Archiv für Begriffsgeschichte* 8 (1963): 1–398, focuses his survey on the more systematic contribution of Leibniz and others up to the middle of the eighteenth century, although he did introduce ideas from the second half of the century, including Goethe's emphasis on the symbolic nature of language (p. 353). Rudolf Eucken, *Geschichte der Philosophischen Terminologie,* begins his

discussion of the development of scientific language with ancient and medieval writers: "obschon die deutsche Terminologie erst im 18. Jahrhundert allgemeine Verwendung erlangt hat" (p. 114).

33. Johann G. Eichhorn, *Allgemeine Geschichte der Cultur und Litteratur des neueren Europa,* 2 vols. (Göttingen: Rosenbusch, 1796–99), vol. 1, p. vi, "Die Geschichte der Künste und Wissenschaften, ihres Anfangs und Fortgangs und ihrer manchfaltigen Veränderungen kann nie von der Geschichte des gesellschaftlichen Zustandes abgesondert vorgetragen werden. Denn Cultur und Litteratur sind Zwillingsschwestern eines gemeinschaftlichen Vaters, die durch gegenseitige Hülfleistung einander unablässig unterstützen." Max Black, *Models and Metaphors,* observes that "If we have been on the right track in my diagnosis of the part played in scientific method by models and archetypes, some interesting consequences follow for the relations between the sciences and the humanities" (p. 242). These relations Goethe found in the historiography of science and literature, relations that, Black adds, may to some extent be learned "from the industry of literary critics" (p. 243), especially in "excavating the presuppositions and latent archetypes of scientists" (p. 243).

34. Franz C. Horn, *Geschichte und Kritik der deutschen Poesie und Beredsamkeit* (Berlin: Unger, 1805), pp. 12–13, "Der Geist einer Sprache ist nicht in dem quantitativen Umfange derselben, sondern gleich dem lebenden Prinzip im Menschen, in dem Mittelpunkt derselben zu finden, von wo aus er ihren ganzen Cyklus bestimmt, und in gleicher Art und Farbe erhält."

35. See K. Michael Seibt, "Einfühlung, Language, and Herder's Philosophy of History," in *The Quest for the New Science. Language and Thought in Eighteenth Century Science,* ed. K. J. Fink and J. W. Marchand (Carbondale, Ill.: SIU Press, 1979), pp. 17–27.

36. Johann Gottfried Herder, "Ueber die neuere deutsche Literatur. Erste Sammlung von Fragmenten," SA, vol. 1, p. 147, "Die Sprache ist ein Werkzeug der Wissenschaften, und ein Theil derselben: wer über die Litteratur eines Landes schreibt, muss ihre Sprache auch nicht aus der Acht lassen."

37. On Goethe's relationships to Herder's language philosophy see Blackall, *Emergence of German,* pp. 494–525. The influence of Herder's language study upon Goethe is documented by Goethe himself in *Aus meinem Leben. Dichtung und Wahrheit,* ed. J. Baechthold and G. Loeper, WA, pt. I, vol. 27, pp. 302–20, where he comments on reading Herder's essay on the origin of language: "Ich las die Abhandlung mit grossem Vergnügen und zu meiner besondern Kräftigung" (p. 310).

38. Samuel Miller, *A Brief Retrospect of the Eighteenth Century,* 2 vols. (New York: Swords, 1803), reported in his survey of the accomplishments of the century "that Germany has lately become literary," that in the second half of the eighteenth century the Germans, and the world, began to realize the potential of the German language for "many new combinations of words" (vol. 2, p. 111), which led to the transition in general intellectual discourse from Latin to German and eventually to contributions in the sciences, including "mechanical philosophy," "natural history," "medicine," and to a lesser degree, "historical work" (pp. 319–21).

39. Crosland, *Historical Studies in the Language of Chemistry,* reviving the concept of a logocentric historiography of science, quoted from M. M. Pattison Muir, *A*

History of Chemical Theories and Laws (New York, 1907), asserting that " 'to write a full description of the origin, growth and misadventures of the language of chemistry is to write a history of that science' " (p. xiii).

40. Goethe, "Nachträge," *Morphologische Hefte,* ed. D. Kuhn, LA, pt. I, vol. 9, pp. 167–86, "Fortgesetzte vieljährige Versuche haben mich eines andern belehrt, mich belehrt: dass immerfort wiederholte Phrasen sich zuletzt zur Ueberzeugung verknöchern und die Organe des Anschauens völlig verstumpfen" (p. 172).

41. Goethe, *Materialien,* LA, pt. I, vol. 6, p. ix, "Mögen sie nur dastehen, um zu erinnern, wie höchst bedeutend es sei, einen Autor als Menschen zu betrachten; denn wenn man behauptet hat: schon der Stil eines Schriftstellers sei der ganze Mann, wie vielmehr sollte nicht der ganze Mensch den ganzen Schriftsteller enthalten."

42. José M. López Piñero, "Eighteenth Century Medical Vitalism: The Paracelsian Connection," in *Revolutions in Science: Their Meaning and Relevance,* ed. W. R. Shea (Canton, Mass.: Science History Publications, 1988), pp. 117–32, traces the eighteenth-century search for an "intermediate line between mechanism and animism" from two historical lines, the first from the systems of Georg E. Stahl and the second from Albrecht von Haller's concept of "irritabilitas" (p. 117).

43. Chaim Perelman and L. Olbrechts-Tyteca, *The New Rhetoric, A Treatise on Argumentation,* trans. J. Wilkinson and P. Weaver (Notre Dame, Ind.: Notre Dame University Press, 1969; 1st ed., 1958), corroborate this estimation of the language of science, observing that "we must not indeed lose sight of the fact that logic, in the first half of the 19th century, enjoyed no prestige either in scientific circles or with the public at large. Whately [Richard Whately, *Elements of Rhetoric* (New York: Harper and Brothers, 1893), p. iii] could write in 1828 that, if rhetoric no longer enjoyed the esteem of the public, logic was some degrees lower in popular estimation" (p. 10). See also Feyerabend, "Classical Empiricism," who describes this kind of science as "critical" (p. 150), as a "fascinating, tortuous, schizophrenic combination of a conservative ideology and a progressive practice" (p. 151), a practice he finds "indistinguishable from party lines" (p. 169), a practice of "trial by a competition of opposing opinions which allows examination of the most fundamental assumption and the most convincing expert testimony" (p. 170).

44. Wise, "On the Relation of Physical Science to History," studied the question, "under what conditions does historiography become significant for scientists" (p. 31), seeking an answer in the physics of Mach and Ostwald whose operations suggest "a kind of historical logic," contrasting it with "Helmholtz and his party," who "promoted their program of materialist reduction in opposition to existing research schemes that were linked closely to historicist ideas" (p. 27).

45. A. Rupert Hall, *Philosophers at War* (Cambridge University Press, 1980), emphasized in the introduction to his book that in earlier epochs, success in science depended far more on "a militant combativeness" (p. 2), because "in the absence of a sociological theory of the growth of knowledge," greater value was attached to "personal merit," to "innovation and the creation of an individual talent" (p. 6).

46. Burwick, *Damnation of Newton,* argues that Goethe's polemics with Newton "was prompted in large part by his inability to understand the methods of physical

optics," that it served "as a counter-measure to the mathematical and mechanistic approach to optics," indeed, that in the publication of the "polemics" Goethe "enacted his 'damnation of Newton' " (p. 5), a metaphor by which Burwick seeks a parallel to the sixteenth-century religious damnation of Faust. Albrecht Schöne, *Goethes Farbentheologie* (Munich: Beck, 1987), also emphasizes the passion with which Goethe pursued his study of color theory, however, avoiding the implication that Goethe's attack on Newtonian optics represented the criticism of established science, arguing rather, that Goethe was the renegade, the scientific rebel, the perpetrator of heresy in the sense of the sectarian movements in "Kirchen- und Ketzerhistorie" (pp. 45–62).

47. Particularly Blasius, "Zur Wissenschaftstheorie Goethes," examines Goethe's criticism of Newton's "experimentum crucis" as a "Vertauschung von Hypothese und Beobachtungsdatum" (p. 376), a criticism, he argues, that ultimately led to an emphasis on a science of relations in modern physics, and on "eine symbolische Darstellung" of these relationships (p. 384).

48. Goethe, *Materialien*, LA, pt. I, vol. 5, p. 194, "dass niemand sich aus seinem Vorteil herausschmeicheln oder herauskomplimentieren lässt, sondern dass er, wenn es nicht anders sein kann, wenigstens herausgeworfen sein will."

49. Fink, "Private and Public Authority," discusses Goethe's view of canonization as the product of "a tensile force" in the life of a critic, who develops an authority by following his own experiences at the same time responding to the experiences of others, to those of the public (p. 184). T. Kuhn, *Essential Tension*, writes of the scientist as a "convergent thinker," at the same time a "traditionalist" and an "iconoclast" (p. 227).

50. Hall, *Philosophers at War*, tells this "story of the bitter quarrel between two of the greatest men in the history of thought, the most notorious of all priority disputes" (p. ix).

51. Sepper, *Goethe contra Newton*, observed how Goethe, too, in older age, regretted his "polemicizing," and how he thought the volume of polemics with Newton could be eliminated in future editions, because "the historical part on its own contained sufficient polemical material" to loosen the stranglehold of Newton's color theory (p. 183), a reference to the value Goethe saw in his polemics as linkage to history.

52. Between 1766–90, over two thousand new periodicals were founded in Germany (Margot Lindemann, *Deutsche Presse bis 1815* [Berlin: Colloquium, 1969], p. 183), many of them functioning as review journals, as a dialogue between an author and a critic, who often wrote anonymously, but with the support of publishing houses and with the authority of a professional in a discipline.

53. Others, particularly Sepper, *Goethe contra Newton*, have studied Goethe's polemical writings as a link to the logic of his science, treating "Goethe and Newton in some sense as contemporaries" (p. xi), in the first part concentrating on Goethe's "efforts to amplify, by comprehensively outlining the scope of color phenomena, the narrow base on which the modern sciences of color had been founded" (p. 21), concluding that, in the end, "the manifold project of *Zur Farbenlehre* remained a science in search of an audience that never developed" (p. 170).

54. See Fink, "Private and Public Authority," for a study of Goethe's view of Newton "standing on the shoulders of giants" (pp. 200–5), namely, as a scientist embed-

ded in a tradition, as one following and at the same time advancing the mathe-matical-mechanical approaches to the study of chromatics.

55. Goethe, *Materialien*, LA, pt. I, vol. 6, p. 87, "Der Konflikt des Individuums mit der unmittelbaren Erfahrung und der mittelbaren Ueberlieferung, ist eigentlich die Geschichte der Wissenschaften: denn was in und von ganzen Massen geschieht, bezieht sich doch nur zuletzt auf ein tüchtigeres Individuum, das alles sammeln, sondern, redigieren und vereinigen soll; wobei es wirklich ganz einerlei ist, ob die Zeitgenossen ein solch Bemühen begünstigen oder ihm wiederstreben."

56. John A. McCarthy, *Crossing Boundaries, A Theory and History of Essay Writing in German, 1680–1815* (Philadelphia: University of Pennsylvania Press, 1989), might have added polemical texts as a category of essay writing, for he argues that the essay is a genre of innovation, that by definition it "bridges the gap between the systematization of scientific information, the searching inquisitiveness of phi-losophy, and the innovative expression of the aesthetic experience" (p. 3).

4. Goethe's narrative strategies

1. Goethe, *Materialien*, LA, pt. I, vol. 6, p. 149, "Dass die Weltgeschichte von Zeit zu Zeit umgeschrieben werden müsse, darüber ist in unsern Tagen wohl kein Zweifel übrig geblieben. Eine solche Notwendigkeit entsteht aber nicht etwa daher, weil viel Geschehenes nachentdeckt worden, sondern weil neue Ansichten gegeben werden, weil der Genosse einer fortschreitenden Zeit auf Standpunkte geführt wird, von welchen sich das Vergangene auf eine neue Weise überschauen und beurteilen lässt." I. Bernard Cohen, *Revolution in Science* (Cambridge, Mass.: Harvard University Press, 1985), studied the history of this revisionist posture in the historiography of science, looking specifically at the writers who viewed events in science as "revolutionary." In Goethe's writings Cohen found statements about "radical change" in individuals, but a more cautious language with regard to historical change and periods: "But Goethe did endorse a cyclical theory of scientific change, although in his discussion of this topic in the *Science of Colors* he does not use the actual word 'revolution' in this context. He argues that history, like living organisms, never stands still: 'Nothing stands still' (Nichts ist stillstehend)" (p. 259).

2. Georges Buffon, *Histoire naturelle, générale et particulière*, 44 vols. (Paris: De l'imprimerie royale, 1749–1803) and Charles Lyell, *Principles of Geology*, 3 vols. (New York: Johnson, 1969; repr., 1st ed., 1830–3). For a study of the changing conception of time found in these works, see Stephen Toulmin and June Goodfield, *The Discovery of Time* (New York: Harper & Row, 1965), pp. 125–70.

3. Kant, *Allgemeine Naturgeschichte und Theorie des Himmels*, in *Kant's gesam-melte Schriften*, 29 vols., Preussische Akademie der Wissenschaften (Akad.) (Berlin: Reimer and de Gruyter, 1910–) vol. 1, pp. 215–368; Gotthold Lessing, *Die Erziehung des Menschengeschlechts*, in *Sämtliche Schriften*, 23 vols., ed. Karl Lachmann (Berlin: de Gruyter, 1968; repr., Leipzig: Göschen, 1886–1924), vol. 13, pp. 413–36; August Ludwig von Schlözer, *Vorstellung seiner Universal-historie*, 2 vols. (Göttingen: Dieterich. 1772–3); and Johann Herder, *Ideen zur Philosophie der Geschichte der Menschheit*, SA, vols. 13 and 14.

4. Kant, *Theorie des Himmels*, Akad., vol. 1, p. 315, quotes from Albrecht Haller's

poem "Ueber die Ewigkeit" (1736): "Unendlichkeit! wer misset dich? Vor dir sind Welten Tag und Menschen Augenblicke; Vielleicht die tausendste der Sonnen wälzt jetzt sich, und tausend bleiben noch zurücke." The importance of these conceptions of time for later theories of evolution is discussed by Loren Eiseley, *Darwin's Century: Evolution and the Men who Discovered It* (Garden City, N.Y.: Doubleday, 1958), pp. 327–34.

5. When Goethe's history appeared in 1810, Karl Knebel wrote to Goethe, "Ich kenne kein revolutionäreres Buch im guten Sinne als das Deinige," August 10, 1810; Goethe, *Materialien,* LA, pt. II, vol. 6, p. 404.

6. Goethe, "An Merck," *Goethes Briefe,* ed. E. Hellen, WA, pt. IV, vol. 4, p. 202, "Die Epochen *de la nature* von Buffon sind ganz vortrefflich. Ich *acquiescire* dabei, und leide nicht, dass jemand sagt, es sei eine Hypothese oder ein Roman. Es soll mir keiner etwas gegen ihn im Einzelnen sagen, als der ein grösseres und zusammenhängenderes Ganze machen kann. Wenigstens scheint mir das Buch weniger Hypothese als das erste Capitel Mosis zu seyn."

7. Goethe, "Epochen bei der Weltbildung," *Schriften zur Geologie und Mineral-ogie,* ed. G. Schmid, LA, pt. I, vol. 2, pp. 102–3. It was not uncommon to express the passing of life as a function of mathematical form; see, for example, Karl J. Fink, "Herder's Life Stages as Forms in Geometric Progression," *Eighteenth-Century Life* 6 (1981): 39–59.

8. Toulmin and Goodfeld, *Discovery of Time,* p. 138, argue that individuals preceding Darwin preempted only certain aspects of the theory of evolution, for as conceived by Darwin it included the doctrine of progression, the doctrine of transformation, and the view that both transformation and progression were a result of the principle of natural selection. Eiseley, *Darwin's Century,* p. 117, refers to those preceding Darwin as "minor evolutionists," as structuralists, who attempted to "change the scale into a moving chain."

9. See Julia Gauss, "Goethe und die Patriarchenwelt," *Goethe-Studien* (Göttingen: Vandenhoeck, 1961), pp. 67–77, "So war es zunächst Herder, der Goethes früherwachte Liebe zum alten Testament leitete," and also "Ein wohl ebenbürtiger, doch nahezu verborgener Einfluss auf Goethes Bibelstudien ging von dem Orientalisten und Theologen Johann Gottfried Eichhorn (1752–1827) aus" (pp. 67–8). For a survey of Goethe's biblical studies see Willy Schottroff, "Goethe als Bibelwissenschaftler," *Allerhand Goethe,* ed. D. Kempel and J. Pompetzki (Bern: Peter Lang, 1985), pp. 111–37, an essay examining studies from his youthful pietism to later orientalism.

10. See Johann Fück, *Die arabischen Studien in Europa, Bis in den Anfang des 20. Jahrhunderts* (Leipzig: Harrassowitz, 1955), pp. 108–24, on the secularization of history and the change that Oriental studies brought to *sacra philologia* (p. 122). Karl J. Fink "Goethe's West-östlicher Divan: Orientalism Restructured," *International Journal of Middle East Studies* 14 (1982): 315–28, examines the way in which German writers like Goethe overcame the myth of orientalism and represented a view more detached and politically disinterested than did cultural counterparts in England and France.

11. See Fink, "Private and Public Authority in the Life of a Critic," for a study of Goethe's theoretical views on biblical criticism as "textual models of authority" (pp. 185–9).

12. Katharina Mommsen, *Goethe und Diez, Quellenuntersuchungen zu Gedichten der Divan-Epoche* (Berlin: Akademie, 1961), argues that the debate centered on the art of translation, "Diskussion des Uebersetzungsideal" (p. 21).

13. See particularly his letters to Schiller between April 12–May 23, 1797, *Briefe, WA*, pt. IV, vol. 12, pp. 86–127, and his autobiographical writings, *Tagebücher, WA*, pt. III, vol. 2, pp. 64–77.

14. Goethe, "Vorstufen und Vorarbeiten zu einzelnen Abschnitten," *West-östlicher Divan, BA*, vol. 3, p. 394, "Schriften, in welchen alte Traditionen zusammengestellt sind, bleiben immer eine Art von Poesie, nicht gerechnet, dass ihr grösster Teil selbst der Form nach Lied war, so ist ihr Inhalt meist poetisch, das heisst, es ist gerade nur der Sinn *wahr,* das ausgesprochne Faktum ist meist nur Fabel."

15. Wolfgang Lentz, *Goethes Noten und Abhandlungen zum West-östlichen Divan* (Hamburg: Augustin, 1958), pp. 99–100, "Soweit der Text gereinigt wird, . . . hält sich Goethe im Rahmen dessen, was wir philologisch-historische Methode zu nennen gewohnt sind," p. 100.

16. Goethe used as his source the *Lebens-Beschreibung des Herrn Gözens von Berlichingen,* ed. W. F. Pistorius (Nürnberg, 1731), a work with which Goethe became familiar in his younger student days in Leipzig, Frankfurt, and Strasbourg.

17. Hayden White, "The Historical Text as Literary Artifact," in *The Writing of History: Literary Form and Historical Understanding,* ed. R. H. Canary and H. Kozicki (Madison: University of Wisconsin Press, 1978), pp. 41–62, observes that "historical narratives are not only models of past events and processes, but also metaphorical statements that suggest a relation of similitude between such events and process and the story types that we conventionally use to endow the events of our lives with culturally sanctioned meanings" (p. 51).

18. Friedrich Schiller, "Ueber Egmont, Trauerspiel von Goethe," in *Goethe im Urteil seiner Kritiker,* 3 vols., ed. Karl R. Mandelkow (Munich: Beck, 1975–9), vol. I, pp. 104–11. See also Karl-Heinz Hahn, "Geschichtsschreibung als Literatur: Zur Theorie deutschsprachiger Historiographie im Zeitalter Goethes," in *Studien zur Goethezeit. Erich Trunz zum 75. Geburtstag,* ed. H. J. Mähl and E. Mannack (Heidelberg: Winter, 1981), pp. 91–101, who points out that Schiller's own historical writing is "ein Musterbeispiel" for "diese künstlerische Tendenz," to narrate materials of history in epic form (p. 96).

19. Schiller, "Ueber Egmont," vol. 1, p. 105, "In der Geschichte ist Egmont kein grosser Charakter, er ist es auch in dem Trauerspiele nicht." See also idem, *Geschichte des Abfalls der Vereinigten Niederlande von der Spanischen Regierung,* in *Schiller Werke. Nationalausgabe, NA,* vol. 17, pp. 1–356, which includes a chapter on the life and death of Egmont: "Ein historisches Detail seiner Geschichte, aus glaubwürdigen Quellen geschöpft, dürfte manchen Leser vielleicht interessieren, und diess um so mehr, da das öffentliche Leben dieses Mannes in die Geschichte seines Volks auf's genaueste eingreift" (p. 290).

20. Schiller, "Ueber Egmont," vol. 1, p. 108.

21. Ibid., p. 111, "Je höher die Illusion in dem Stück getrieben ist, desto unbegreiflicher wird man es finden, dass der Verf. selbst sie mutwillig zerstört." Georg Lukács, "Goethe und seine Zeit," in *Georg Lukács Werke,* 17 vols. (Berlin: Luchterhand, 1964–), vol. 7, pp. 41–184, restated Schiller's point more

broadly, focusing on the realistic illusion created in Goethe's literary works, in this case in Goethe's *Werther;* "So wie die Helden der Französischen Revolution, von heroischen, geschichtlich notwendigen Illusionen erfüllt, heldenhaft strahlend in den Tod gingen, so geht auch Werther in der Morgenröte der heroischen Illusionen des Humanismus vor der Französischen Revolution tragisch unter" (p. 67).

22. The morphological principles Goethe discovered in plant and animal life have been applied to a number of Goethe's fictive characters; see, for example, Larry D. Wells, "Organic Structure in Goethe's 'Novelle'," *German Quarterly* 53 (1980): 418–31: "Finding it more illuminating to interpret the story chiefly in literary terms, critics have failed to consider if and to what extent 'Urphänomene' such as polarity, metamorphosis, and 'Steigerung' and other organic concepts relevant to plant growth do in fact structure the thematic 'Werden' of the story" (p. 418). See also Elizabeth Wilkinson, "The Relation of Form and Meaning in Goethe's 'Egmont'," in *Goethe. Poet and Thinker,* ed. E. Wilkinson and L. Willoughby (London: Arnold, 1962), pp. 55–74, who concludes her essay by observing that Egmont's "lyrical conclusion" follows the principle of "Steigerung" (p. 71), a principle extrapolated from Goethe's nature studies, namely, the ascent of all plant forms to their fulfillment and moment of rebirth. Alfred G. Steer, *Goethe's Science in the Structure of the Wanderjahre* (Athens: University of Georgia Press, 1979), has organized a chapter on "The Goethean Series" (pp. 119–25), a collection of individuals and institutions thought to live by the principles of Goethe's metamorphosis.

23. Goethe, "Schicksal der Druckschrift," *Morphologische Hefte,* LA, pt. I, vol. 9, pp. 66–72, "Der Künstler versicherte mich später: in Gefolg der Naturgesetze, wie ich sie ausgesprochen, sie ihm geglückt Natürliches und Unmögliches zu verbinden, und etwas erfreulich Wahrscheinliches hervorzubringen" (p. 67). Wilhelm Emrich, *Die Symbolik von Faust II,* 3d ed. (Frankfurt: Athenäum, 1964), wrote that the strength of Goethe's representation of reality lies in his art because it existed as a mediator between nature and history, it existed in the symbols which Goethe used in his writings (pp. 57–8). E. H. Gombrich, "Evidence of Images," in *Interpretation: Theory and Practice,* ed. C. Singleton (Baltimore: Johns Hopkins Press, 1969), pp. 35–104, observes how important visual theory and practice is to the "process of reconstruction" (p. 37). He sees interpretation as a process of "construction" and "creativity," and particularly in visual stimuli he observes the process of selectivity, which goes on when an individual begins to form impressions of an event: "The redundancies decrease progressively and increase the need to supplement the information from the store of our imagination" (p. 47).

5. Goethe's reconstruction of amorphous states

1. Goethe, *Materialien,* LA, pt. I, vol. 6, p. 88, "Weniges gelangt aus der Vorzeit her über als vollständiges Denkmal, vieles in Trümmern; manches als Technik, als praktischer Handgriff; einiges, weil es dem Menschen nahe verwandt ist, wie Mathematik; anderes, weil es immer wieder gefordert und angeregt wird, wie

Himmel- und Erd-Kunde; einiges, weil man dessen bedürftig bleibt, wie die Heilkunst; anderes zuletzt, weil es der Mensch, ohne zu wollen, immer wieder selbst hervorbringt, wie Musik und die übrigen Künste."

2. This point of view has been expanded in more recent writing by May Brodbeck, "Explanation, Prediction, and 'Imperfect' Knowledge," in *Readings in the Philosophy of the Social Sciences,* ed. May Brodbeck (London: Macmillan, 1968), pp. 363–98: "Perfect knowledge is the ideal, actualized only in certain branches of physical science. Elsewhere, as in biology, economics, sociology, psychology, and the social sciences generally, knowledge is conspicuously 'imperfect.' We do not know the variables that affect, say, a person's resistance to disease, or his behavior under certain circumstances" (p. 375). Alasdair MacIntyre, "Epistemological Crisis, Dramatic Narrative and the Philosophy of Science," in *Paradigms and Revolutions, Appraisals and Applications of Thomas Kuhn's Philosophy of Science,* ed. G. Gutting (Notre Dame, Ind.: University of Notre Dame Press, 1980), pp. 54–74, also examines "the connection between narrative and tradition," making the point that a tradition "is only to be recovered by an argument retelling of that narrative which will itself be in conflict with other argumentative retellings. Every tradition therefore is always in danger of lapsing into incoherence, and when a tradition does so lapse it sometimes can only be recovered by a revolutionary reconstitution. Precisely such a reconstitution of a tradition which had lapsed into incoherence was the work of Galileo" (p. 63).

3. Goethe, *Materialien,* LA, pt. I, vol. 6, p. 85, "Der betrachtende Mensch aber kommt oft in den Fall beide mit einander zu verwechseln, wie sich besonders an parteiischen Historikern bemerken lässt, die zwar meistens unbewusst, aber doch künstlich genug, sich eben dieser Unsicherheit zu ihrem Vorteil bedienen." Karl Mannheim, *Ideology and Utopia: An Introduction to the Sociology of Knowledge,* trans. Louis Wirth and Edward Shils (New York: Harcourt, Brace & Co., 1936, 1st German ed., 1929), argues that "It has become uncontrovertibly clear to-day that all knowledge which is either political or which involves a world-view, is inevitably partisan" (p. 148). This view Mannheim bases on the "state of atomization" of our thought (p. 252), and on the "amorphous aspects of life": "Whereas Marxism focussed its attention too sharply on and overemphasized the purely structural foundation of the political and historical realm, fascism turned its attention to the amorphous aspects of life, to those 'moments' in critical situations which are still present and still have significance, in which class forces become disjointed and confused" (pp. 150–1).

4. Johann Wolfgang Goethe, *Goethes Gespräche,* GA, vol. 22, p. 403, "Könnte man die geschichtliche Wahrheit demonstrieren, wie die mathematische, so wäre aller Unterschied verschwunden; solange man das nicht kann, so lange wird wohl ein Unterschied bleiben, nicht zwischen dem, was wirklich wahr ist, sondern zwischen dem, was hier also wahr demonstriert, dort als wahr angenommen wird." In a similar idiom Karl Popper, *The Poverty of Historicism* (London: Kegan Paul, 1957), argues that there can be no "scientific method" in history nor can there be "prediction of the course of human history by scientific method. . . . This means that we must reject the possibility of a theoretical history; that is to say, of a historical social science that would correspond to a theoretical

physics" (pp. vii–x). More recently MacIntyre, "Crisis, Narrative and Science," argued that also Thomas Kuhn "did of course recognize very fully how a scientific tradition may lapse into incoherence" (p. 67).

5. See Wilhelm Bietak, "Goethe und die Geschichte," *Jahrbuch des Wiener Goethe-Vereins* 68 (1964): 101–11, for a summary of the criticisms on historical continuity that Goethe expressed in his discussion with Luden.

6. Goethe, *Goethes Gespräche,* GA, vol. 22, p. 403, "Der Unterschied ist, dass die Mathematik jeden Menschen zwingen kann, anzuerkennen, dass alle rechte Winkel gleich sind; dass Sie hingegen in historischen Dingen mich niemals zwingen können, Ihrer Meinung zu sein."

7. Julia Gauss, "Die methodische Grundlage von Goethes Geschichtsforschung," in *Jahrbuch des Freien Deutschen Hochstifts,* ed. Ernst Beutler (Halle: Niemeyer, 1932), pp. 163–283, attempted to draw close parallels between Goethe's studies in natural morphology and history: "So rechtfertigte sich ein biologisches Prinzip: die Idee der organischen Entwicklung. Es war in der Geschichte der Standpunkt zu erreichen, der Goethe als der höchste galt, derjenige nämlich, einen Entwicklungszusammenhang anzusehen wie ein 'Lebendiges,' 'ein organisches Wesen,' das seinen 'notwendigen' Gang durchläuft, vom 'Wachstum' zur 'Vollendung' und 'Abnahme' " (p. 207).

8. Jane Brown, "History and Historicity in Act II of Faust, Part II," *Goethe Yearbook* 2 (1984): 69–90, makes a similar point in a study of Goethe's *Faust,* arguing that the "chaotic" historical background in Act I, that the "succession of meaningless violence" in much of *Faust II,* sets the stage for Faust's search for "a meaningful past": "The temporal flux can only be given shape, history can only be fixed by an effort of the mind" (p. 86).

9. See John E. Sandys, *A History of Classical Scholarship,* 3 vols. (New York: Hafner, 1958; 1st ed. 1903–8), vol. 3, pp. 47–87, on early German philology and on Goethe's collaborations with leading German philologists of the period such as Friedrich August Wolf; see also Michael Bernays, ed., *Goethes Briefe an Friedrich August Wolf* (Berlin: Reimer, 1868), pp. 1–89.

10. A record of Goethe's use of the library in Weimar is available in Elise Keudell, *Goethe als Benutzer der Weimarer Bibliothek* (Weimar: Böhlau, 1931). Goethe's own accounts of interest in the Göttingen School of history is documented in book six of *Dichtung und Wahrheit,* ed. J. Baechtold, WA, pt. I, vol. 27, p. 42ff.

11. Johann S. Pütter, *Versuch einer akademischen Gelehrten-Geschichte der Universität Göttingen* (Göttingen: Vandenhök, 1765–88). In his contact with Göttingen Goethe studied works by professional historians such as those by Johann C. Gatterer, *Handbuch der Universalhistorie* (Göttingen: Vandenhök, 1761) and Ludwig von Spittler, *Entwurf der Geschichte der Europäischen Staaten,* 2 vols. (Berlin: Mylius, 1793–4). Goethe fondly recalls the experiences in Göttingen: "So fand ich nebenher allseitig so viel Anlockendes, dass ich bei meiner ohnehin leicht zu erregenden Bestimmbarkeit und Vorkenntnis in vielen Fächern, hier und da hingezogen ward und meine Collectaneen eine bunte Gestalt anzunehmen drohten," Johann Wolfgang Goethe, *Tag- und Jahres-Hefte als Ergänzung Meiner Sonstigen Bekenntnisse, von 1749–1806,* ed. W. Biedermann, WA, pt. I, vol. 35, p. 110.

12. Goethe, *Materialien,* LA, pt. I, vol. 6, p. 80, "Worin er sich aber vom wahren

Physiker am meisten unterscheidet, sind seine beständigen, oft sehr gezwungen herbeigeführten Nutzanwendungen und die Verknüpfung der höchsten Naturphänomene mit dem Bedürfnis, dem Genuss, dem Wahn und dem Uebermut der Menschen."

13. For more recent collections see Hermann Diels, *Die Fragmente der Vor-sokratiker. Grieschisch und Deutsch*, 2d ed., 2 vols. (Berlin: Weidmann, 1906–10), and Kathleen Freeman, *The Pre-Socratic Philosophers: A Companion to Diels, Fragmente der Vorsokratiker*, 2d ed. (Oxford: Blackwell, 1949).

14. See Karl J. Fink, "Atomism: A Counterpoint Tradition in Goethe's Writings," *Eighteenth-century Studies* 13 (1980): 377–95.

15. Goethe, *Materialien*, LA, pt. II, vol. 6, p. 6–13. For his source Goethe used the French edition, *Les vies des hommes illustres de Plutarque*, J. Amyot, trans. (Paris, 1783–7), which was available in the Weimar library.

16. On Goethe's understanding of the process by which a text becomes canonized see Fink, "Private and Public Authority," particularly sections on "The Rise and Fall of a Text," "Legitimatizing Personal Protest," and "Standing on the Shoulders of Giants" (pp. 190–203).

17. Goethe, *Materialien*, LA, pt. I, vol. 6, pp. 13–14. Brent Berlin and Paul Kay, *Basic Color Terms* (Berkeley and Los Angeles: University of California Press, 1969), pp. 17–45, discovered that black and white are primary colors in the language of primitive societies today, recapitulating from field study what Goethe had discovered in historical societies through textual analysis.

18. Goethe, *Materialien*, LA, pt. II, vol. 6, pp. 319–20, "Mit Wolf habe ich schon das Büchlein von den Farben durchgegangen. Das Hauptresultat: dass, auch nach seinen Kriterien, das Werk echt, alt und der peripatetischen Schule wert sei, hat mich, wie Sie denken können, sehr gefreut, ja er mag es lieber dem Aristotles als einem Nachfolger zuschreiben." On Goethe's relationship to Wolf see Bernays, *Goethes Briefe an Friedrich August Wolf*, pp. 90–120, which documents an exchange of views beginning with October 5, 1795, and ending with June 4, 1819; the most intense exchange of letters came in the years during which Goethe wrote his history of color theory, 1800–10.

19. Goethe, *Materialien*, LA, pt. I, vol. 6, p. 121, "Wir gedachten es zu übersetzen, fanden aber bald, dass man in einer Sprache nicht die Etymologie der andern behandeln könne, und so entschlossen wir uns, es in der Urschrift wieder abdrucken zu lassen." Eric Lenneberg, "Language and Cognition," in *Semantics: An Interdisciplinary Reader in Philosophy, Linguistics, and Psychology*, ed. Danny D. Steinberg and Leon A. Jakobovits (Cambridge University Press, 1971), pp. 536–57, argues that the "recognition of colors is an entirely intrapersonal process," making the articulation of colors nearly impossible because "communication accuracy is a distinctly social phenomenon" (p. 551).

20. Goethe, *Materialien*, LA, pt. I, vol. 6, p. 126, "Die lateinische Sprache dagegen wird durch den Gebrauch der Substantiven entscheidend und befehlshaberisch. Der Begriff ist im Wort fertig aufgestellt, im Worte erstarrt, mit welchem nun als einem wirklichen Wesen verfahren wird."

21. Ibid., p. 124, "Die Form des Vortrags, Noten zu einem Text zu schreiben, nötigt zum Wiederholen, zum Zurückweisen, alles Gesagte wird aber und abermals durch und über einander gearbeitet, so dass es dem Ganzen zwar an innerer

Klarheit und Konsequenz nicht fehlt, wie irgend einem Kartenspiel und Steinspiel; hat man jedoch alles gelesen und wieder gelesen, so weiss man wohl etwas mehr als vorher, aber gerade das nicht, was man erwartete und wünschte."

22. Carl Prantl, *Aristotles Ueber die Farben* (Munich: Kaiser, 1849), p. 85.

23. See, for example, Aristotle, *De Colorbus*, trans. T. Loveday and E. S. Forster in *The Works of Aristotle*, 12 vols., ed. W. D. Ross (Oxford: Oxford University Press [Clarendon Press], 1910–52), vol. 6, p. i, "Both the method and the style of this treatise are unlike Aristotle's, and its contents differ considerably from his known views. But it is very likely a Peripatetic product."

24. Goethe, *Materialien*, LA, pt. I, vol. 6, pp. 83–108. See Johann G. Sulzer, *Allgemeine Theorie der schönen Künste*, 5 vols. (Hildesheim: Olm, 1967–70; repr., 2d ed., 1792–9) for the definitions of "Lüke" (vol. 3, pp. 297–8) and of "Zwischenzeit" (vol. 4, pp. 760–1), and for the significance of drama terminology for Goethe's concept of history: "Es würde für einen grossen Fehler gehalten werden, wenn zwischen zwey Auftritten eine Lüke, oder Zwischenzeit bleibe. Darum ist es eine durchgehende aufgenommene Regel, dass während einem Aufzug die Schaubühne nie soll leer gelassen werden" (vol. 4, pp. 760–1). More recently in the historiography of science MacIntyre, "Crisis, Narrative and Science," argues with Goethe "that the best account that can be given of why some scientific theories are superior to others presupposes the possibility of constructing an intelligible dramatic narrative" (p. 73).

25. Sulzer, *Theorie der schönen Künste*, vol. 3, p. 73.

26. See Steven D. Martinson, "Filling in the Gaps: 'The Problem of World-Order' in Schiller's Essay on Universal History," *Eighteenth-Century Studies* 22 (1988): 24–45, for a discussion of Schiller's observation that because of the "many gaps" and "empty stretches," there is an "incongruity that forces artificial connecting links," namely, the gaps of history force "the invention of linkage" (p. 36).

27. Goethe, *Materialien*, LA, pt. I, vol. 6, p. 83. For a more recent discussion of the view that language, or a code system, does not fully represent the details of its object see Alfred Korzybski, *Science and Sanity. An Introduction to Non-Aristotelian Systems and General Semantics*, 4th ed. (Lakeville, Conn.: Non-Aristotelian Library, 1973), p. 58, "Two important characteristics of maps should be noticed. A map is not the territory it represents, but, if correct, it has a similar structure to the territory, which accounts for its usefulness. If the map could be ideally correct, it would include, in a reduced scale, the map of the map; the map of the map of the map; and so on, endlessly, a fact first noticed by Royce."

28. Johann Wolfgang Goethe, "Das Göttliche," trans. C. Middleton, *Gedichte*, ed. G. Loeper, p. 81; WA, pt. I, vol. 2, pp. 83–4, "Nur allein der Mensch / Vermag das Unmögliche: / Er unterscheidet, / Wählet und richtet; / Er kann dem Augenblick / Dauer verleihen" (p. 84).

6. Goethe's transition from history to historiography

1. Goethe, *Materialien*, LA, pt. II, vol. 6, p. 61, "Wünschenswerth wäre gewesen, dass Baco das Kind nicht mit dem Bade ausgeschüttet hätte, dass er den Werth des vorhandenen Ueberlieferten eingesehen und diese Einsicht fortgepflanzt hätte,

dass er die vorhandenen Erfahrungen hätte zu schätzen und fortzusetzen gewusst, anstatt durch seine Manier ins Unbestimmte und ins Unendliche hinzuweisen. So kannte er z.B. Gilberts Bemühungen über den Magneten, ohne dass man auch nur eine Ahndung bemerkt des ungeheuern Werthes, der schon in diesem Entdeckten lag."

2. Goethe, "Konfession des Verfassers," *Materialien zur Geschichte der Farben-lehre*, ed. D. Kuhn, LA, pt. I, vol. 6, p. 427, "doch nirgends bin ich auf einmal soviel gefördert worden, als in Göttingen durch den mit grosser Liberalität und tätiger Beihülfe gestatteten Gebrauch der unschätzbaren Büchersammlung."

3. Karl Vorländer, *Kant-Schiller-Goethe*, 2d ed. (Leipzig: Meiner, 1923), discusses how Goethe mentioned in his letter of January 10, 1798, that he sent Schiller a copy of his essay from five years earlier on "Der Versuch als Vermittler von Objekt und Subjekt" as an indication of how he saw things at that time, a difference he located in a new view of empiricism, one that Schiller had defined for him as a "rationelle Empiricism" (p. 173).

4. Vorländer, *Kant-Schiller-Goethe*, traces Goethe's studies in philosophy through each of the phases of his life, emphasizing that "auf keinen Fall also hat Goethe in der Zeit bis zur Rückkehr aus Italien [1788] eindringendem Studium Kants obgelegen" (p. 137). He locates Goethe's first serious appreciation of Kantian philosophy between 1788–90, in his "Kritik der teleologischen Urteilskraft" (p. 144), which Ernst Cassirer, *Rousseau-Kant-Goethe. Two Essays,* trans. J. Gut-mann, P. Kristeller, and J. Randall (Hamden, Conn.: Archon Books, 1961; origi-nal published, 1944), linked to Goethe's morphological studies, quoting from Goethe that: "Here I saw my most diverse interests brought together, artistic and natural production handled the same way; the power of aesthetic and teleological judgement mutually illuminated each other" (p. 64). Cassirer pointed out that "in the eighteenth century the force of this type of explanation was still unbroken" (p. 64), although not until recently did Monika Firla, *Untersuchungen zum Verhältnis von Anthropologie und Moralphilosophie bei Kant* (Bern: Peter Lang, 1981), study more closely the link between Kant's teleological judgments and his science of man, which is essentially an anthropology of the mind, namely, Goethe's study of "the characteristics of the human mind" (pp. 47–55).

5. Kant, "Ueber den Gebrauch teleologischer Principien in der Philosophie," Akad. (1910), vol. 8, pp. 159–84, makes this distinction, defending his essays on the definition of the human races and a probable history of mankind against the criticism of Georg Forster, who was arguing a global ethnography based on the present state of man.

6. Friedrich Schiller, "Was heisst und zu welchem Ende studiert man Universal-geschichte?" NA, vol. 17, pp. 359–76.

7. Martinson, "Filling in the Gaps," observes that "it has gone unrecognized that Schiller did not give free rein to the philosophical mind. Because he loves truth more than his own system of thought, Schiller says, the 'philosophischer Kopf' is critically aware of the movement of his own thinking" (p. 31).

8. Cassirer, *Rousseau-Kant-Goethe*, pointed out that Kant "by no means wishes to exclude the conception of 'end', especially in biological phenomena" and in "knowledge of organized being" (p. 65), namely, that Goethe was "in complete

agreement with Kant" on teleology, an argument Cassirer supported with a distich by Goethe on "The Teleologist:" "What reverence is due the world's Creator, / Who when creating the cork tree graciously also invented the cork" (p. 68).

9. However, in his discussion Goethe is not distinguishing between "history" and "historiography," indeed, his concept of "a history of the human mind" comes much closer to "a description of the mind" in the sense of Kant's anthropology published in 1798, namely, as described by Mareta Linden, *Untersuchung zum Anthropologiebegriff des 18. Jahrhunderts* (Bern: Peter Lang, 1976) in her study of the tradition of "Anthropologie als Psychologie" (pp. 63–104).

10. Cassirer, *Rousseau-Kant-Goethe,* pointed out that Goethe's copy of Kant's *Kritik der reinen Vernunft,* Akad., vol. 3, "shows the intensive study he devoted to it," but adding that the work never had the significance it had for Schiller, and that scholarship generally views Goethe's interest in the work as "a compromise" forced upon him by "his friendship with Schiller" (p. 63). Based on this consensus, scholars have focused discussion on Goethe's greater interest in Kant's *Kritik der Urteilskraft* (p. 64).

11. Schiller has here applied "Allheit," one of the three categories of "Quantität," to Goethe's collection of materials on chromatics, Kant, *Kritik der reinen Vernunft,* 2d ed. (1787), *Schriften,* Akad., vol. 3, p. 93.

12. A comparison of the structure and organization of Goethe's color theory, *Didaktischer Teil,* LA, pt. I, vol. 4, with Kant's category "Of Relation," Kant, *Kritik der reinen Vernunft* vol. 3, p. 93, shows the influence of Schiller's lessons, particularly in Goethe's version of the three categories of "Relation," "Of Inherence and Subsistence," "Of Causality and Dependence," and "Of Community," Immanuel Kant, *Immanuel Kant's Critique of Pure Reason,* trans. N. K. Smith (New York: Macmillan, 1982), p. 113. Particularly Part IV of Goethe's color theory shows an effort to establish cause and effect relationships in the question "Wie energisch die Farbe sei?" (pp. 204–5), whereas Part V on "Nachbarliche Verhältnisse" (pp. 210–32), seems to be organized according to the category of "community," namely, on the "reciprocity between the agent and patient" (p. 113), at least if taken in the broadest sense to include those individuals engaged in observation as part of the physiology of colors.

13. In this distinction, Cassirer, *Rousseau-Kant-Goethe,* finds "a very strange analogy to Kant's way of thinking," for "Kant was always the philosopher of the a priori, but for him a priori knowledge disclosed no distinctive and independent realm beyond experience" (p. 94).

14. Goethe, *Materialien,* LA, pt. II, vol. 6 p. 306, "In welcher Ordnung und Abteilung die Geschichte der Farbenlehre vorgetragen werden sollte, ward epochenweise durchgedacht und die einzelnen Schriftsteller studiert, auch die Lehre selbst genau erwogen und mit Schillern durchgesprochen."

15. Goethe, *Materialien,* LA, pt. II, vol. 6, p. 307, "Das Schema zur Geschichte der Farbenlehre weiter bearbeitet und geheftet. Sodann den Charakter einzelner Naturforscher aus dem Gedächtnis summarisch aufgezeichnet."

16. Abraham G. Kästner, *Geschichte der Mathematik,* 4 vols. (Göttingen: Rosenbusch, 1796–1800), Johann F. Gmelin, *Geschichte der Chemie,* 3 vols. (Göttingen: Rosenbusch, 1797–9), Johann K. Fischer, *Geschichte der Physik,* 8 vols.

(Göttingen: Röwer, 1801–08), and Jean Etienne Montucla, *Histoire des mathématiques,* new ed., 4 vols. (Paris: Agasse, 1799–1802).

17. Goethe's use of contemporary histories of science for their scientific value agrees with the historiography of D. Ludwig Wachler, who excluded the Göttingen histories of science from his *Geschichte der historischen Forschung und Kunst, seit der Wiederherstellung der litterärischen Cultur in Europa,* 2 vols. (Göttingen: Röwer, 1812–18), as these late eighteenth-century histories were really studies in a branch of science. Wachler's study of the branches of history appeared in the same series, namely in the *Geschichte der Künste und Wissenschaften,* as did the histories of science by Kästner, Gmelin, and Fischer.

18. For a discussion of these two kinds of history of science see Ernan McMullin, "The History and Philosophy of Science: A Taxonomy," in *Historical and Philosophical Perspectives of Science,* ed. Roger H. Stuewer (Minneapolis: University of Minnesota Press, 1970), pp. 12–67. Helge Kragh, *An Introduction to the Historiography of Science* (Cambridge University Press, 1987), discusses a broader range of types of history, including "hypothetical history" (pp. 70–4), and "scientists' histories" (pp. 150–8), but in the final analysis seems to prefer distinguishing primarily between an "anachronical and diachronical history of science" (pp. 89–107), the former viewing science relative to the present and the latter relative to the period in which it occurred.

19. Joseph Agassi, "Towards a Historiography of Science," *History and Theory,* Beiheft 2 (1963), 1–117, pp. 3–6.

20. Ibid., p. 7.

21. Agassi, "Towards a Historiography of Science," finds the state of the field today as Goethe found it in 1810: "Almost every classical or contemporary history of science bears the stamp of Francis Bacon's philosophy of science. Bacon's philosophy divides thinkers into two categories variously characterized as right and wrong, scientific and superstitious, open-minded and dogmatic, observer of facts and speculant" (p. 1).

22. Joseph Priestley, *The History and Present State of Discoveries Relating to Vision, Light and Colours* (London: Johnson, 1772), p. i.

23. Montucla, *Histoire des mathématiques,* p. iii, ". . . je me suis particulièrement attaché à présent idée distincte et les véritables principes de toutes les théories de quelque considération qui composent le système des mathématiques."

24. Goethe, *Materialien,* LA, pt. I, vol. 6, p. 88, "Leider besteht der ganze Hintergrund der Geschichte der Wissenschaften bis auf den heutigen Tag aus lauter solchen beweglichen, in einander fliessenden und sich doch nicht vereinigenden Gespenstern, die den Blick dergestalt verwirren, dass man die hervortretenden, wahrhaft würdigen Gestalt kaum recht scharf ins Auge fassen kann."

25. Ibid., p. 4, "Wie man tappend hin und wiederschwankt, indem man sich das Wissen zueignen will, wie man in der Wissenschaft das hinterste fürs vörderste, das unterste fürs oberste zu nehmen geneigt ist, wird in der Geschichte der Farbenlehre darzustellen seyn, die, indem sie von einem besondern Kreise handelt, zugleich die Schicksale vieler andren menschlichen Bemühungen symbolisch dartstellen muss."

26. Goethe's correspondence with these individuals has been included in the Leopoldina edition (LA) of his scientific writings, ibid., pp. 279–407.

27. On Goethe's reception of atomism see Fink, "Atomism," 379–84.
28. Goethe, *Materialien,* LA, pt. I, vol. 6, p. 69, "So begreift sich die Geschichte der Farbenlehre auch nur in Gefolg der Geschichte aller Naturwissenschaften. Denn zur Einsicht in den geringsten Teil ist die Uebersicht des Ganzen nötig."
29. Thomas Kuhn, "The History of Science," in *International Encyclopedia of the Social Sciences,* 18 vols., ed. David Sills (New York: Macmillan, 1968), vol. 14, p. 81.
30. A. Rupert Hall, "Merton Revisited," *History of Science: An Annual Review of Literature, Research and Teaching* 2 (1963): 1–16, "Social and economic relations are rather concerned with the scientific movement than with science as a system of knowledge" (p. 13).
31. See, for example, Ortony, "Metaphor: A Multidimensional Problem," pp. 1–16, who asks some questions that are central to the role language and metaphors play in historiography: "How can metaphorical language be distinguished from literal language? How literal is literal language? Is the problem of metaphor one to be handled by a theory of language, a theory of language use, or both? Are the comprehension processes for metaphorical uses of language the same as those for literal uses? Can metaphors be reduced to comparisons? Is the reduction of metaphors to comparisons a fruitful approach to understanding the nature of metaphor? Are the comparisons to which one might attempt to reduce a metaphor themselves in need of explanation? Are metaphors necessary for the transmission of new scientific concepts? Are metaphors necessary for the transmission of new ideas in general? What dangers are there associated with the use of metaphors to describe new or problematical situations?" (p. 16).
32. Ortony, "Metaphor: A Multidimensional Problem," reviews the development of language centrality in twentieth-century philosophy of science: "It reached one of its peaks in the doctrine of logical positivism, which was so pervasive amongst philosophers and scientists fifty years ago. A basic notion of positivism was that reality could be precisely described through the medium of language in a manner that was clear, unambiguous, and, in principle, testable – reality could, and should, be literally describable" (p. 1). See also Thomas Kuhn, "Metaphor in Science," pp. 409–19, where he critically examines Richard Boyd's view of theory change as one in which language is accommodated to the world: "Does it obviously make better sense to speak of accommodating language to the world than of accommodating the world to language?" (p. 418).
33. Thomas Kuhn, *The Structure of Scientific Revolutions,* pp. 43–51.
34. Margaret Masterman, "The Nature of a Paradigm," in *Criticism and the Growth of Knowledge,* ed. I. Lakotos and A. Musgrave (Cambridge University Press, 1970), pp. 59–89, cites from textual analysis "twenty-nine senses of 'paradigm' " used by Kuhn (p. 65). It is significant that Kuhn's multiple uses of the term, and the linguistic and philosophical problems of dealing with the concept of "paradigm," have converged with Max Black's "interaction view of a metaphor," which was also formulated in the early 1960s, a view that has become the subject of much discussion in the past two decades, and has recently come under his own closer examination in "More about Metaphors," pp. 19–43, "I shall add some suggestions about the relations of a metaphor to its grounding resemblances and

analogies, with the hope of also shedding some further light on the connections between metaphors and models" (p. 19).

35. See Hans-Werner Schütt, "Lichtenberg als 'Kuhnianer,' " *Sudhoffs Archiv* 63 (1979): 87–90, who footnotes some of Goethe's statements on paradigms, but focuses on Lichtenberg's view of radical breaks in paradigm shifts: "Aus einem immer verbesserten, aber nach seinen Grundsätzen verbesserten Katholizismus konnte nie Protestantismus, und aus einer verbesserten Populär-Philosophie nie Kantische Philosophie werden. Aus einer allmählig verbesserten Cartesianischen Physik konnte nie die wahre Newtonische werden" (p. 89).

36. Goethe, "Die Geschichte seiner botanischen Studien," LA, pt. I, vol. 10, p. 319, "Um die Geschichte der Wissenschaften aufzuklären, um den Gang derselben genau kennen zu lernen, pflegt man sich sorgfältig nach ihren ersten Anfängen zu erkundigen; man bemüht sich zu forschen: wer zuerst irgend einem Gegenstand seine Aufmerksamkeit zugewendet, wie er sich dabei benommen, wo und zu welcher Zeit man zuerst gewisse Erscheinungen in Betracht gezogen, dergestalt dass von Gedanke zu Gedanken neue Ansichten sich hervorgetan, welche durch Anwendung allgemein bestätigt endlich die Epoche bezeichnen."

37. Eugenio Coseriu, *Die Geschichte der Sprachphilosophie von der Antike bis zur Gegenwart,* 2 vols. (Tübingen: Tübinger Beiträge, 1972), vol. 2, pp. 244–7, outlines the main concerns addressed in Rousseau's language philosophy, particularly his interest in relating the development of language to that of society.

38. See Paul Cantor, "The Metaphysics of Botany, Rousseau and the New Criticism of Plants," *Southwest Review* 70 (1985): 362–80, who also locates the "new criticism" in Rousseau's rejection of the analysis of plants and in his interest in the structure of plants as "living wholes," as "organisms" (p. 367), making us "witness to the aestheticisms of nature" (p. 372).

39. Goethe, "Die Geschichte seiner botanischen Studien," LA, pt. I, vol. 10, p. 325, "Wir mussten öfters hören: die ganze Botanik, deren Studium wir so emsig verfolgten, sei nichts weiter als eine Nomenklatur, und ein ganzes auf Zahlen, und das nicht einmal durchaus, gegründetes System." Ortony, "Metaphor: A Multidimensional Problem," to a certain extent explains Goethe's reaction to the Linnean terminology when he points out that one of the dominant presuppositions of our culture is "faith in literal language as the only adequate and appropriate tool for the objective characterization of reality," and that "knowledge occasioned of reality, whether it is by perception, language, memory, or anything else, is a result of going beyond the information given" (p. 1). Robert R. Sokal and Peter H. A. Sneath, *Principles of Numerical Taxonomy* (San Francisco: Freeman, 1963), observe in their chapter on the "Critique of Current Taxonomy" (pp. 5–36), that "recent years have witnessed increasing dissatisfaction with the principles and practices of biological classification. . . . As our knowledge of the organic world increases there are continuing stresses and strains in the frame of the taxonomic system to accommodate these new discoveries, and the inadequacies of the present system become ever more apparent" (p. 5).

40. Goethe, "Die Geschichte seiner botanischen Studien," LA, pt. I, vol. 10, p. 330, "Wie er sich nun, befreit von allem nationalen Starrsinn, an die auf jeden Fall vorschreitenden Wirkungen Linnés hielt, so dürfen wir auch wohl von unsrer Seite

bemerken, dass es ein grosser Vorteil sei, wenn wir beim Eintreten in ein für uns neues wissenschaftlisches Fach, es in einer Krise und einen ausserordentlichen Mann beschäftigt finden, hier das Vorteilhafte durchzuführen. Wir sind jung mit der jungen Methode, unsre Anfänge treffen in eine neue Epoche." Kuhn, *The Structure of Scientific Revolutions* (1970), makes the notion of a crisis fundamental to his historiography of science, placing it in two chapters central to his idea of paradigm change, one on "Crisis and the Emergence of Scientific Theories" (pp. 66–76), and the other on "The Response to Crisis" (pp. 77–91): "The proliferation of competing articulations, the willingness to try anything, the expression of explicit discontent, the recourse to philosophy and to debate over fundamentals, all these are symptoms of a transition from normal to extraordinary research" (p. 91).

41. Goethe, "Principes de philosophie zoologique," LA, pt. I, vol. 10, p. 374, "jener geht aus dem Einzelnen in ein Ganzes, welches, zwar vorausgesetzt, aber als nie erkennbar betrachtet wird; dieser hegt das Ganze im innern Sinne und lebt in der Ueberzeugung fort: das Einzelne könne daraus nach und nach entwickelt werden."

42. Stephen Jay Gould, "Archetype and Adaptation," *Natural History* 95 (1986): 16–27, locates the modern version of the dichotomy in the tension between theories of form and function, quoting from Goethe's discussion of the debate between Cuvier and Saint-Hilaire, and arguing with him that the more these two modes of discourse are related, the better science will be, hence, the motto to Gould's essay, "The truly great intellectual dichotomies are not battles to the death, but struggles to find partial truths" (pp. 16, 27).

43. Goethe, "Principes de philosophie zoologique," LA, pt. I, vol. 10, p. 399, "da denn der forterbende Sprachgebrauch zwar im gemeinen Dialog hinreicht, sobald aber die Unterhaltung sich ins Geistige erhebt, den höheren Ansichten vorzüglicher Männer offenbar widerstrebt." Hans Eichner, "The Rise of Modern Science and the Genesis of Romanticism," *Publications of the Modern Language Association* 97 (1982): 8–30, attempts to "isolate some of the implications of the mechanical philosophy that made it unacceptable to the Romantics and that prompted them to branch out on new paths" (p. 24), emphasizing the classic schism between methods and approaches of the humanities (Geisteswissenschaft) and the sciences (Naturwissenschaft) (p. 25).

44. Goethe, "Principes de philosophie zoologique," LA, pt. I, vol. 10, p. 399, "Weil sich, um die Materialien wohl zu komponieren, eine gewisse voraus überdachte Anordnung nötig macht, so bedienen jene sich des Wortes Plan, werden aber sogleich dadurch auf den Begriff eines Hauses, einer Stadt geleitet, welche, noch so vernünftig angelegt, immer noch keine Analogie zu einem organischen Wesen darbieten können."

45. Johann Gottfried Herder, "Vom Erkennen und Empfinden der menschlichen Seele," SA, vol. 8, pp. 164–202, "Was wir wissen, wissen wir nur aus Analogie" (p. 170).

46. Goethe, *Materialien*, LA, pt. II, vol. 6, p. 292; Goethe, *Gedichte*, WA, pt. I, vol. 2, p. 231, "Noch spukt der Babylon'sche Thurm, Sie sind nicht zu vereinen! Ein jeder Mann hat seinen Wurm, Copernicus den seinen."

7. Goethe's theory of biography

1. Goethe, *Materialien*, LA, pt. I, vol. 6, p. 71, "Betrachten wir nun Epikur und Lukrez, so gedenken wir einer allgemeinen Bemerkung, dass die originellen Lehrer immer noch das Unauflösbare der Aufgabe empfinden, und sich ihr auf eine naive gelenke Weise zu nähern suchen. Die Nachfolger werden schon didaktisch, und weiterhin steigt das Dogmatische bis zum Intoleranten. Auf diese Weise möchten sich Demokrit, Epikur und Lukrez verhalten. Bei dem Letztern finden wir die Gesinnung der Erstern, aber schon als Ueberzeugungsbekenntnis erstarrt und leidenschaftlich parteiisch überliefert."

2. Ibid., p. 85, "Der schwache Faden, der sich aus dem manchmal so breiten Gewebe des Wissens und der Wissenschaften durch alle Zeiten, selbst die dunkelsten und verworrensten, ununterbrochen fortzieht, wird, durch Individuen durchgeführt." Thomas L. Hankins, "In Defence of Biography," *History of Science* 17 (1979): 1–16, points out today's enthusiasm for the Hegelian approach to the study of historical "movements" and then he appeals for a return to the biographical approach to history: "A fully integrated biography of a scientist, which includes not only, personality but also his scientific work and the intellectual and social context of his times, is still the best way to get at many of the problems that beset the writings of the history of science" (p. 13–14).

3. Goethe, *Materialien*, LA, pt. I, vol. 6, p. 87; J. W. N. Watkins argues in his "Historical Explanations in the Social Sciences," in *Theories of History*, ed. P. Gardiner (Glencoe, Ill.: Free Press, 1959), pp. 503–15, that "rock bottom explanations" in history must be deduced from "the disposition, beliefs, resources and inter-relations of individuals" (p. 505).

4. Goethe, "Der Versuch," trans. H. G. Haile, unpublished, LA, pt. I, vol. 8, pp. 305–15, "Es lässt sich bemerken, dass die Kenntnisse, gleichsam wie ein eingeschlossenes aber lebendiges Wasser, sich nach und nach zu einem gewissen Niveau erheben, dass die schönsten Entdeckungen nicht sowohl durch Menschen als durch die Zeit gemacht worden" (p. 307). Later statements by Germans who contributed to the sociological perspective on the history of science include those by Karl Marx and Friedrich Engels, "Concerning the Production of Consciousness," pp. 97–108, and Karl Mannheim, "The Sociology of Knowledge," pp. 109–30, collected in *The Sociology of Knowledge: A Reader*, ed. J. Curtis and J. Petras (New York: Praeger, 1970).

5. Recent writers in social psychology have expressed the difficulties in grasping a process located in the individual who is in turn located in cultural change, as for example, Erik Erikson, *Identity: Youth and Crisis* (New York: Norton, 1968), p. 23: "At its best it is a process of increasing differentiation, and it becomes ever more inclusive as the individual grows aware of a widening circle of others significant to him." See also Emile Durkheim and Marcel Mauss, *Primitive Classification*, trans. Rodney Needham (Chicago: University of Chicago Press, 1963; 1st ed., 1903), who point out that there is a "fluid" and "contagious" aura spreading out from the individual and which extends to unknown points of proximity, making it difficult to demark the limits of an individual's efficacy (p. 87).

6. Goethe, "Von der Physiognomik Ueberhaupt," *Antheil an Lavaters Physiog-*

nomischen Fragmenten, ed. V. Valentin, et al., WA, pt. I, vol. 37, pp. 329–61, "Man wird sich öfters nicht enthalten können, die Worte Physiognomie, Physiognomik in einem ganz weiten Sinne zu brauchen. Diese Wissenschaft schliesst vom Aeussern aufs Innere . . . Stand, Gewohnheit, Besitzthümer, Kleider, alles modificirt, alles verhüllt ihn [den Menschen] . . . So lassen Kleider und Hausrath eines Mannes sicher auf dessen Character schliessen" (p. 329).

7. According to Joachim Campe, *Wörterbuch der deutschen Sprache*, 5 vols. (Braunschweig: Schulbuchhandlung, 1807–11), vol. 2, pp. 301–2, both terms, "Gemeinort" and "Gemeinplatz," were in common use during Goethe's day, both, according to Campe, coming from the Latin "locus communis." Goethe used the term more as an expression of stereotyping both in ordinary and scientific life, whereas Curtius, *European Literature and the Latin Middle Ages*, pp. 70, 79–105, went to the original Greek term, "topos," for study of the history of literary topology.

8. Goethe, *Materialien*, LA, pt. I, vol. 6, p. 296, "Newton war ein wohlorganisierter, gesunder wohltemperierter Mann, ohne Leidenschaft, ohne Begierden. Sein Geist war konstruktiver Natur und zwar im abstraktesten Sinne; daher war die höhere Mathematik ihm als das eigentliche Organ gegeben, durch das er seine innere Welt aufzubauen und die äussere zu bewältigen suchte."

9. Ibid., p. 96, "Obgleich Roger nur ein Mönch war und sich in dem Bezirk seines Klosters halten mochte, so dringt doch der Hauch solcher Umgebungen durch alle Mauern, und gewiss verdankt er gedachten nationellen Anlagen, da sein Geist sich über die trüben Vorurteile der Zeit erheben und der Zukunft voreilen konnte."

10. Ibid., p. 78, "Wir gedenken hier des Lucius Annäus Seneca nicht sowohl insofern er von Farben etwas erwähnt, da es nur sehr wenig ist und bloss beiläufig geschieht, als vielmehr wegen seines allgemeinen Verhältnisses zur Naturforschung." Other biographies were introduced with the same comment: "Wenn gleich Porta für unser Fach wenig geleistet, so können wir ihn doch, wenn wir im Zusammenhange der Naturwissenschaften einigermassen bleiben wollen, nicht übergehen," Ibid., p. 138. Goethe's prototypes are somewhat like those of Carl Becker, as described by Don Martindale, "Sociological Theory and the Ideal Type," in *Symposium on Sociological Theory*, ed., Llewellyn Gross (Evanston, Ill.: Row, Peterson, 1959), pp. 57–91, as "dated and localized," useful in characterizing features of a particular epoch in history (p. 76).

11. Reinhard Schuler, *Das Exemplarische bei Goethe* (Munich: Fink, 1973), explained with the examples of Aristotle, Plato, Roger Bacon, and Francis Bacon, how Goethe could write on the general without extinguishing the richness of the individual: "Goethes Richtung auf das Allgemeine hebt hervor, ohne zu vereinfachen. Sie löscht die Beziehungsvielfalt des individuellen Daseins nicht aus" (p. 11).

12. Goethe, *Materialien*, LA, pt. I, vol. 6, p. 152, "Das Leben jedes bedeutenden Menschen, das nicht durch einen frühen Tod abgebrochen wird, lässt sich in drei Epochen teilen, in die der ersten Bildung, in die des eigentümlichen Strebens, und in die des Gelangens zum Ziele, zur Vollendung."

13. See Robert K. Merton, "Behavior Patterns of Scientists," in *The Sociology of Science: Theoretical and Empirical Investigations*, ed. N. W. Storer (Chicago: University of Chicago Press, 1973), pp. 325–42, concerning modern notions of

role stratification, rank achievement, competition, and identity. An interesting interpretation of the relationship of young and old scientists can be found in the same volume in an essay on "The Matthew Effect in Science," pp. 439–59, where Merton suggests that in cases in which research results from the common effort of beginning and established scientists, recognition usually goes to the established scientist; that is, the rich get richer and the poor get poorer.

14. Goethe, *Materialien*, LA, pt. I, vol. 6, p. 153, "Diese Epoche ist also gewöhnlich die des Konflikts, und man kann niemals sagen, dass diese Zeit Ehre von einem Manne habe. Die Ehre gehört ihm selbst an und zwar ihm allein und den wenigen, die ihm begüngstigen und mit ihm halten."

15. Ibid., p. 297, "Eigentlich kontrovertiert er nicht, sondern wiederholt nur immer seinen Gegnern: greift die Sache an wie ich; geht auf meinem Wege; richtet alles ein wie ichs eingerichtet habe; seht wie ich, schliesst wie ich, und so werdet ihr finden, was ich gefunden habe."

16. Ibid., p. 94, "Die Epochen der Naturwissenschaften im allgemeinen und der Farbenlehre insbesondre, werden uns ein solches Schwanken auf mehr als eine Weise bemerklich machen. Wir werden sehen, wie dem menschlichen Geist das aufgehäufte Vergangene höchst lästig wird zu einer Zeit, wo das Neue, das Gegenwärtige gleichfalls gewaltsam einzudringen anfängt."

17. Geoffrey N. Cantor, *Optics after Newton, Theories of light in Britain and Ireland, 1704–1840* (Manchester: Manchester University Press, 1983), examines "the problem of communities" in his "historiographical introduction," questioning Kuhn's concept of "scientific communities," because he finds little evidence of an "institutional framework" for research in theories of light, particularly among "the projectile, fluid, and vibration theorists" (p. 22). He also questions "role theories, as developed by sociologists," arguing that this alternative "cannot be employed until we know much more about the social history of science in the eighteenth century" (p. 22). In practice this leaves Cantor with an approach grounded in the reception of texts, although one in which he chose to use "a small number of research papers and monographs" and to "make little use of textbooks or their authors" (p. 52), an important ingredient of Goethe's study of Newtonianism and of his concept of "schools of thought."

18. Goethe, *Materialien*, LA, pt. II, vol. 6, p. 189, "Patriotismus der Engländer. Wer im Kreise der Physik und Mathematik gegen Newton auftritt wird nicht als Gegner, sondern als Rebell behandelt. Die Streitigkeiten über die Farbenlehre, wie über den Differenzial und Integralcalcul werden von der Academie, ja von der Nation als eigene betrachtet, die ganze Masse ist wie Newton selbst ein *noli me tangere.*"

19. For a detailed eighteenth-century study on psychophysiological aspects of the eye see William Porterfield, *A Treatise on the Eye, the Manner and Phenomena of Vision* (London: Miller, 1759), while today's understanding of vision is represented in Richard L. Gregory, *The Intelligent Eye* (New York: McGraw-Hill, 1970), including a chapter on "pictures, symbols, thought and language" (pp. 137–54), in which he concludes with a question typical of Goethe's concern in science in general: "How far are human brains capable of functioning with concepts detached from sensory experience?" (p. 154).

20. See David A. Kronick, "Authorship and Authority in the Scientific Periodicals of

the Seventeenth and Eighteenth Centuries," *The Library Quarterly* 48 (1978): 255–75, on the role of editors and society leadership in establishing authority in scientific communities, particularly with regard to the role of scientific societies in processing information in the eighteenth century, pp. 258–66.

21. V. Ronchi, *The Nature of Light*, trans. V. Barocas (Cambridge, Mass.: Harvard University Press, 1970), also points out that Newton was able to sustain all polemics through the help of his followers; he suggests that when examining the foremost of these followers, we must ask ourselves about the extent to which corpuscular theory had shaped optics and whether acceptance of this shape was "purely rhetorical" (pp. 212–13). G. N. Cantor, *Optics after Newton*, argues against "accepting a monolithic corpuscular theory" as an approach to the reception of Newtonian science, proposing instead to make "some suggestions about the social dynamics of optical knowledge, particularly concentrating on the groups who held the various theories and styles and on their audiences" (p. 23).

22. Goethe, *Materialien*, LA, pt. I, vol. 6, p. 302, "Auf diesem Wege führte man die Newtonische Lehre, neben der des Cartesius, in den Unterricht ein und verdrängte jene nach und nach." Eventually Samuel Clarke's revision of *Rohaults Physik* appeared with a new title: *Rohault's System of Natural Philosophy* (London: Knapton, 1723), reflecting a complete transition from Cartesian to Newtonian physics. See, also Schütt, "Lichtenberg als 'Kuhnianer,' " 87–90, who observes from Lichtenberg's comments in the "Sudelbücher" a radical form of the paradigm shift: "Aus einer allmählig verbesserten Cartesianischen Physik konnte nie die wahre Newtonische werden" (p. 89).

23. Goethe, *Materialien*, LA, pt. I, vol. 6, p. 310, "Dem Redner kommt es auf den Wert, die Würde, die Vollständigkeit, ja die Wahrheit seines Gegenstandes nicht an; die Hauptfrage ist, ob er interessant sei, oder interessant gemacht werde."

24. Ibid., p. 320, "Voltairens grosses Talent sich auf alle Weise, sich in jeder Form zu kommunizieren, machte ihn für eine gewisse Zeit zum unumschränkten geistigen Herrn seiner Nation. Was er ihr angebot musste sie aufnehmen; kein Widerstreben half: mit aller Kraft and Künstlichkeit wusste er seine Gegner bei Seite zu drängen, und was er dem Publikum nicht aufnötigen konnte, das wusste er ihm aufzuschmeicheln, durch Gewöhnung anzueignen."

25. Ibid., p. 323, "Und es ist freilich niemand zu verargen, wenn einmal so eine wunderliche Synthese zum Behuf einer so wunderlichen Analyse gemacht worden, wenn der Glaube daran allgemein ist, dass er sie auch zu seinem Behuf, es sei nun des Belehrens und Ueberzeugens, oder des Blendens und Ueberredens, als Instanz oder Gleichnis beibringe."

26. Modern versions of this story are similar to the one by Goethe as for example, by Ronchi, *The Nature of Light*, p. 214, who states that the Euler/Dollond discovery brought about a revolution in the design of optical instruments, but that the event "did not receive the attention it deserved because it was striking at the roots of an idea which was already dead" (p. 214). Cantor, *Optics after Newton*, observes that the event "had a small but significant effect on optical writers of the period," but that, while Dolland's paper ("Philosophical Transactions," 1758) "affected the theory of dispersion it did not involve major revision in the theory of light" (p. 51).

27. Cantor, *Optics after Newton*, suggests that Euler's *Nova theoria lucis et colorum*

(1746) is "probably the most important single publication of the period," a work that "attacked the projectile theory and propounded a vibration theory of light" (p. 50). See Karl J. Fink, "Johann Krüger on Electricity: 'Cui bono,' For Whom to What Good?" *Electric Quarterly* 12 (1990): no. 1:2–3; no. 2:2–4; and 3:2–4, for a note on one of the earliest attempts to link a global force of physics, electricity, to the human body, in this case for possible medical purposes, a connection more fully established in the course of the century in Albrecht Haller's theory of irritability. See also Jörg Meya and Otto Sibum, *Das fünfte Element. Wirkungen und Deutungen der Elektrizität* (Hamburg: Rowohlt, 1987), who look to the writings of Johann Winkler for the metaphor that adds electricity to the classical elements, fire, water, earth, and air (p. 57), and who document the process by which electricity was found common to the organic and synthetic world.

28. Most of the recent studies on the Goethe–Newton conflict treat the irreconcilable differences in points of view, in philosophies of science, and in approaches to the study of nature. See Karl R. Mandelkow, "Die Rezeption der natur-wissenschaftlichen Schriften," *Goethe in Deutschland. Rezeptionsgeschichte eines Klassikers* (Munich: Beck, 1980), pp. 174–200, for a survey of the changing ideological basis of response to Goethe's science. Central to most of the differences, particularly to the conflict with Newton, is a passage taken from Hermann Helmholtz, "Ueber Goethe's naturwissenschaftliche Arbeiten," in *Goethe im Urteil seiner Kritiker*, 3 vols., ed. Karl R. Mandelkow (Munich: Beck, 1975–9), vol. 2, pp. 401–16, "Seine Farbenlehre müssen wir als den Versuch betrachten, die unmittelbare Wahrheit des sinnlichen Eindrucks gegen die Angriffe der Wissenschaft zu retten" (pp. 413–14).

29. Other works from the Goethe period on the history of knowledge and learning are surveyed by Otto Dahlke, "The Sociology of Knowledge," in *Contemporary Social Theory*, ed. Harry E. Barnes and Howard Becker (New York: Appleton-Century, 1940), pp. 64–89. He does not include discussion of Goethe's views, but does examine the approach of those preceding Goethe, for example, the works by Johann M. Chladenius, *Einleitung zur Richtigen Auslegung Vernünftigen Reden und Schriften* (Leipzig: Friedrich Lanck, 1742) and his *Allgemeine Geschichtswissenschaft. Worinnen der Grund zu einer nueun Ensicht in aller Arten der Gelahrheit gelegt wird* (Leipzig: Friedrich Lanck, 1752).

30. Goethe, "Zur Geologie November 1829," *Aufsätze, Fragmente, Studien zur Naturwissenschaft im Allgemeinen,* ed. D. Kuhn and W. Engelhardt, LA, pt. I, vol. 11, p. 305, "Die Skepsis fängt mit dem Ausnahmen an das Dogma zu befeinden, welches auf einem gesetzlichen Fuss gefasst hat. Die Skepsis hat grosse Vorteile in der natürlichen Unruhe und Zweifelsucht der Menschen, man macht ihnen ein Dogma gar leicht verdächtig. Dazu gehört denn aber doch eine gewisse Kraft des Geistes, Anhaltsamkeit und Ueberredungsgabe die sich besonders der Induktion zu bedienen weiss."

8. Goethe's concept of authority

1. Goethe, *Materialien*, LA, pt. I, vol. 6, pp. 92–3, "Indem wir nun von Ueberlieferung sprechen, sind wir unmittelbar aufgefordert, zugleich von Autor-

ität zu reden. Denn genau betrachtet, so ist jede Autorität eine Art Ueberlieferung. Wir lassen die Existenz, die Würde, die Gewalt von irgend einem Dinge gelten, ohne dass wir seinen Ursprung, sein Herkommen, seinen Wert deutlich einsehen und erkennen."

2. Ibid., p. 68, "Wie irgend jemand über einen gewissen Fall denke, wird man nur recht einsehen, wenn man weiss, wie er überhaupt gesinnt ist. Dieses gilt, wenn wir die Meinungen über wissenschaftliche Gegenstände, es sei nun einzelner Menschen oder ganzer Schulen und Jahrhunderte, recht eigentlich erkennen wollen."

3. Blasius, "Zur Wissenschaftstheorie Goethes," argues that Goethe's concept of science not only overcame "eine empiristische Illusion der Newtonischen Wissenschaftsauffassung" (p. 371), but also anticipated T. S. Kuhn's paradigm, which rejects "die Illusion der linearen Begründungsstruktur der Natur-wissenschaften" (p. 381).

4. See also Irving Horowitz, *Philosophy, Science, and the Sociology of Knowledge* (Springfield, Ill.: Thomas, 1961), pp. 18–24, who prizes Bacon's pioneer contri-bution to the analysis of the relationship of science, society, and philosophy: "Francis Bacon was responsible for major landmarks in the pre-history of the sociology of knowledge on two counts. He developed the first typology of the sources of distortion in human understanding; and he also attempted a social explanation of philosophical errors" (p. 18). Carl Becker, *The Heavenly City of the Eighteenth-century Philosophers* (New Haven, Conn.: Yale University Press, 1932), recalls that "Professor Whitehead has recently restored to circulation a seventeenth-century phrase – 'climate of opinion.' The phrase is much needed. Whether arguments command assent or not depends less upon the logic that conveys them than upon the climate of opinion in which they are sustained" (p. 5).

5. Fink, "Private and Public Authority," studied Goethe's view of how the text shapes the authority of a critic, examining Theophrastus's *De Coloribus* in "the rise and fall of a text," Bacon's *Cogitata et Visa* in "legitimatizing personal protest," Newton's *Opticks* in "standing on the shoulders of giants," and Moham-med's *Koran* in "criticism and the fabrication of fables." Leonard Krieg, "Au-thority," in *Dictionary of the History of Ideas,* 5 vols. ed. P. Wiener (New York: Scribner, 1973), vol. 1, pp. 141–62, offers a broad critical survey of writings on "authority," adding a note to his bibliography that "no comprehensive history or bibliography of authority exists" (p. 162). Robert Loy, "Attitudes Toward Author-ity in European Literature to the Eighteenth Century," *Proceedings of the IXth Congress of the International Comparative Literature Association* 9 (1981): 65–9, places the recognition of ancient literary authorities and the urge to overcome them in Diderot and Richardson, "rather than in Goethe": "it is somewhat earlier in the century in England and in France that we can most clearly see a turning point from authority to what some of us may call modern literature" (p. 65). Thomas L. Hankins, *Science and the Enlightenment* (Cambridge University Press, 1985), finds the rejection of classical authority the mark of the entire era in which writers thought of themselves as members of a "republic of letters," which valued "freedom of thought and action and rejected authority," which he too thinks "appeared in literature before it appeared in natural science" (p. 8).

6. Goethe's reference to the history of science as the "history of opinions" (Geschichte der Meynungen, LA, pt. II, vol. 6, p. 3), drew attention to the fact that an authority is grounded in the amorphous state of knowledge, in the range of possible interpretations, in the room to maneuver. More recently Lancelot Hogben, *Science in Authority* (London: Unwin, 1963), pointed out "that the scientific worker of today does in fact take more and more of his science on trust," a tendency due less to an "accumulation of facts previously unknown," than to the "logical instruments at our own disposal for coordinating them" (pp. 139–40).

7. John P. Kirscht and Ronald C. Dillehay, *Dimensions of Authoritarianism: A Review of Research* (Lexington: University of Kentucky Press, 1967), pp. 42–6, discuss "cognitive functioning" in terms closely associated to Goethe's view that authority is based on reason and logic and that it ignores the ambiguities of qualitative processes in history: "Investigators have explored the relationship of authoritarianism to certain psychological variables, including aspects of cognitive functioning (especially rigidity and intolerance of ambiguity)" (p. 42). Kronick, "Authority and Authorship," argues that science is "consensus" formed by periodicals and journals and, as Ziman (*Public Knowledge,* 1968) reminds us, is nevertheless "full of ambivalence and ambiguity" (p. 255).

8. Kenneth D. Benne, *A Conception of Authority* (New York: Bureau of Publications, 1943), devotes a chapter to "External and Internal Authority" (pp. 114–37), also commenting in the preface of his book that "authority operates in situations in which a person, fulfilling some purpose or end, requires guidance from a source outside himself. He grants obedience to another person, to a group, or to a method or rule, with a claim to be able to assist him in mediating this field of conduct or belief, as a condition of the grant of such assistance" (p. 2). In literary criticism Edward Said, *Orientalism* (New York: Random House, 1979), emphasizes the "exteriority" of Western authority in the representation of Eastern culture: "And these representations rely upon institutions, traditions, conventions, agreed-upon codes of understanding for their effects, not upon a distant and amorphous Orient" (p. 22). Isolde Stark, "Despot und Tyrann bei Johann Wolfgang Goethe," in *Das Fortleben altgriechischer sozialer Typenbegriffe in der deutschen Sprache,* ed. E. C. Welskopf (Berlin: Akademie, 1981), pp. 169–82, studied political forms of authority as represented in Goethe's poetic writings, emphasizing Goethe's talent for giving internal expression to the "exteriority" of political life. Kenneth Burke, *Attitudes toward History* (Los Altos, Calif.: Hermes, 1959), rephrased Goethe's distinction between internal and external forms of authority by distinguishing between "the authority of words" and "delegated authority," emphasizing that "it is precisely because the authority of words cannot be delegated, . . . that one must watch the 'poetry exchange' to learn what is really going on in the world" (p. 334).

9. Goethe, *Materialien,* LA, pt. I, vol. 6, p. 93, "Bald sehen wir um einen vorzüglichen Mann sich Freunde, Schüler, Anhänger, Begleiter, Mitlebende, Mitwohnende, Mitstreitende versammeln. Bald fällt eine solche Gesellschaft, ein solches Reich wieder in vielerlei Einzelnheiten auseinander." T. Kuhn, *Structure of Scientific Revolutions,* refers to these support groups as "secondary workers."

10. According to Nisbet, *Goethe and the Scientific Tradition,* Goethe's concept of an "Urphänomen" is a union of empirical and ideal realms of knowledge: "The

'Urphänomen' is not, as has been claimed, a Platonic idea. It represents the fusion of two traditions, the Platonic and the empirical, in Goethe's mind (p. 42). Dorothea Kuhn, *Empirische und ideelle Wirklichkeit,* expresses this relationship even more clearly as "der empirische, der die Realität umgreift, der ideelle, der sich öffnet zu Typus Gestalt und Gesetz, ohne zu transzendieren zu einem Reich reiner Ideen" (p. 155).

11. Max Weber, "Ideal Types and Theory Construction," in *Readings in the Philosophy of the Social Sciences,* ed. May Brodbeck (London: Macmillan, 1968), pp. 496–507, discusses various kinds of ideal-type presentations, including the one used by Goethe where an individual scientist served as a representative for an entire epoch, that is, "model types" that are "always close at hand whenever the descriptive historian begins to develop his 'conception' of a personality of an epoch" (p. 503).

12. See also Karl J. Fink, " 'Dualisten,' 'Trinitarier,' 'Solitarier,' " 230–49.

13. Goethe, *Materialien,* LA, pt. II, vol. 6, p. 72, "Dualisten, nach Anleitung des Aristoteles und besonders des Theophrasts lassen sie die Farben aus einer Wechselwirkung des Lichtes und der Finsterniss entstehen."

14. Ibid. "Er kennt den Hauptpunkt der ganzen Farben- und Lichtschatten-Lehre; denn er sagt uns: durch das Weiss werde das Gesicht entbunden, durch das Schwarze gesammelt."

15. Ibid., p. 128, "Die fassliche Zahl, die in ihr enthaltene doppelte Symmetrie, und die daraus entspringende Bequemlichkeit machte eine solche Lehre zur Fortpflanzung geschickt." Colin Cherry, *On Human Communication,* 2d ed. (Cambridge, Mass.: MIT Press, 1971), p. 36, explains the adequacy of binary thought in expressing the basic ideas of primitive societies as in Celtic culture. For other studies on the history of binary thought see W. Dobbek, "Die coincidentia oppositorum als Prinzip der Weltdeutung bei J. G. Herder wie in seiner Zeit," *Herder-Studien,* ed. W. Wiora (Würzburg: Holzner, 1960), pp. 16–47, and Rolf Zimmermann, "Goethes Polaritätsdenken im geistigen Kontext des 18. Jahrhunderts," *Jahrbuch der deutschen Schillergesellschaft* 18 (1974): 304–47, who argues that "das Polaritätsdenken entartete nun förmlich zu einer geistigen Epidemie," against which eventually even Hegel wrote polemical essays (p. 304).

16. Goethe, *Materialien,* LA, pt. I, vol. 6, p. 207, "Er wendet sich aber, um die Sache näher zu bestimmen, und die verschiedenen Farben entstehen zu lassen, zu einer quantitativen Erklärung, auf welche Aristoteles schon hingedeutet, und nimmt an, dass vom Weiss dass reine gedrängte Lichte zurückstrahle, dass Rot aus gleichen Teilen von Licht und Schatten bestehe, Gelb aus zwei Teilen Licht und einem Teil Schatten, Blau aus zwei Teilen Schatten und einem Teile Licht."

17. Ibid., p. 216, "In seinem fünften Punkte bemerkt er ganz richtig, dass im prismatischen Bilde Gelb und Blau mehr dem Lichte, Rot und Violett mehr dem Schatten angehören; dass das Rote sich von dem Schatten entfernt, dass das Violette sich gegen den Schatten bewegt."

18. Böhme, "Is Goethe's Theory of Color Science?" pp. 147–73, observes that "Goethe's theory of colors is regarded as a questionable scientific attempt because it enters into the realms of subjective perception," but then he also observes that "it is precisely here that Goethe's theory of colors has attained results which have found the greatest recognition" (p. 148).

19. Goethe, *Materialien*, LA, pt. II, vol. 6, p. 72, "Trinitarier. Nach Paracelsus wird angenommen das Urlicht habe durch verschiedene productive Stufen die drey physisch chemischen Elemente erzeugt. Salz. Schwefel und Merkurius."

20. Ibid., p. 129. Goethe was also familiar with T. O. Bergman, *Kleine physische und chymische Werke*, 5 vols., trans. Heinrich Tabor (Frankfurt: Garbe, 1782–9), in which such mystic connections were set up as tables of elective affinities. To date, Jeremy Adler, *"Eine fast magische Anziehungskraft," Goethe's "Wahlverwandtschaften" und die Chemie seiner Zeit* (Munich: Beck, 1987), has provided the most detailed study of Goethe's research in the history of chemistry, particularly "Zur Geschichte der chemischen 'Verwandtschaft' " (pp. 32–83).

21. Goethe, *Materialien*, LA, pt. I, vol. 6, p. 129, "Hat sodann jedes Element seinen Anteil an dem höher verstandenen mystischen Schwefel, so lässt sich auch wohl ableiten, wie in den verschiedensten Fällen Farben entstehen können."

22. See also Goethe, *Aus meinem Leben. Dichtung und Wahrheit*, ed. J. Baechtold and G. Loeper, WA, pt. I, vol. 27, pp. 199–222, and Rolf Zimmermann, *Das Weltbild des Jungen Goethe, Studien zur Hermetischen Tradition des Deutschen 18. Jahrhunderts*, 2 vols. (Munich: Fink, 1969–79), for the source and background to Goethe's study of alchemical and mystical writings, particularly those sections on "Symbolik" (vol. 1, pp. 32–7), and "Analogiedenken" (pp. 37, 127, 147, 302).

23. Goethe, *Materialien*, LA, pt. I, vol. 6, p. 325, "Die frühern Bemerkungen des Paracelsus und seiner Schule, dass die Farben aus dem Schwefel und dessen Verbindung mit den Salzen sich herschreiben möchten, waren auch noch in frischem Andenken geblieben."

24. Ibid., pp. 327, 353, "Alle diejenigen, die von der Malerei und Färberei an die Farbenlehre herantraten, fanden dagegen, wie uns die Geschichte umständlich unterrichtet, naturgemäss und bequem, nur drei Grundfarben anzunehmen."

25. Goethe, *Materialien*, LA, pt. I, vol. 6, "Es seien nur drei einfache primitive Farben," "Die drei Urfarben machen Grau" (p. 354); "Die Felder dieses Dreiecks sollen nun nach ihren Zahlbezeichnungen koloriert werden" (p. 355); "Er findet bald, dass er, um alle Farben hervorzubringen, nur drei Hauptfarben bedarf" (p. 371); "Eigentlich gibt es nur drei Farben, Gelb, Rot and Blau" (p. 389); und "Mehr als drei Pigmente dürfe man nicht annehmen" (p. 355).

26. See Adler, *"Eine fast magische Anziehungskraft,"* for a detailed study of Goethe's understanding of the concept in chemistry and use of it as a metaphor in his novel by the same title.

27. Goethe, *Materialien*, LA, pt. II, vol. 6, p. 72, "Solitarier. Diese betrachten das Licht isolirt als Körper der an sich und in Verhältnissen mancherley Veränderungen erleiden kann. Hier kommen nun korpuscular, globular, mechanische und ähnliche Erklärungen der Licht- und Farbenwirkungen zum Vorschein." Ronchi, *The Nature of Light*, is essentially a history of the doctrines of the solitarians, in Goethe's sense of the term.

28. Goethe, *Materialien*, LA, pt. I, vol. 6, p. 181, "Man schrieb ihm vielmehr eine Substanz zu, man sah es als etwas Ursprüngliches, für sich Bestehendes, Unabhängiges, Unbedingtes an." I. Sabra, *Theories of Light from Descartes to Newton* (London: Oldbourne, 1967), focuses his book on this epoch in the development of theories of light, emphasizing in his preface "that Newton's belief in

atomism is the key to his interpretation of the 'experimentum crucis' " (p. 9).

29. Henry Guerlac, "Some Areas for Further Newtonian Studies," *History of Science,* 17 (1979): 75–101, might have included Goethe's work in his discussion of "a phase of Newtonian scholarship which has attracted renewed interest and which we may call the 'influence,' the 'reception,' or the 'legacy' of Newton" (p. 75). Goethe focuses primarily on the French reception of Newtonianism, *Materialien,* LA, pt. I, vol. 6, pp. 305–24, also emphasizing the "cool reception" of Newton's color theory, as did Guerlac, "Some Areas for Further Newtonian Studies," p. 77, beginning with Edme Mariotte (1620–84) as the first opponent of Newton and one of the first to introduce Newton to the French scientific world.

30. Goethe, "Didaktischer Teil," LA, pt. I, vol. 4, p. 206, discusses the concept as a principle of his theory of colors: "Diese Steigerung ist unaufhaltsam schnell und stetig; sie ist allgemein und kommt sowohl bei physiologischen als physischen und chemischen Farben vor."

31. Goethe's conversations with Johannes Falk on February 28, 1809, shortly before publishing his history, *Goethes Gespräche,* GA, vol. 22, pp. 538–42, are particularly useful in understanding Goethe's views on a mathematically inspired science. This theme is also found in Goethe's novel, *Die Wahlverwandtschaften,* WA, pt. I, vol. 20, pp. 53–7, where Charlotte resists in the fourth chapter a comparison of human relationships to scientific relationships. Nisbet, *Goethe and the Scientific Tradition,* also observes in his conclusion how Goethe at the beginning of the nineteenth century no longer saw any unity in science: "As knowledge increases, it becomes more and more difficult to relate the details to a comprehensive view of nature, without which, as Goethe sees it, science must become an aimless and stultifying activity" (p. 71). Also see Hans J. Schrimpf, "Ueber die geschichtliche Bedeutung von Goethes Newton-Polemik und Romantik-Kritik," in *Der Schriftsteller als Oeffentliche Person, Von Lessing bis Hochhuth,* ed. H. J. Schrimpf (Berlin: Schmidt, 1977), pp. 126–43, where he writes that "Goethes Kampf gegen den romantischen Subjektivismus der Innerlichkeit in der Kunst und wirklichkeitsflüchtigen Religiösität entspricht genau seiner entschlossenen Polemik gegen die moderne mathematisch-abstrakte Naturwissenschaft" (p. 143).

32. Goethe, *Materialien,* LA, pt. II, vol. 6, p. 404, "Der Geist wahrer tiefer Humanität herrscht dabei überall, sowohl im Tadel wie im Lobe, und der wissenschaftliche Mensch selbst wird gleichsam aufgerufen, vor allem ein Mensch zu sein."

33. Particularly Hans-Heinrich Reuter, "Roman des Europäischen Gedankens," *Goethe-Jahrbuch* 28 (1966): 1–49, saw the symbolic value of Goethe's history as a statement on human striving toward enlightenment: "Der geschichtswissenschaftliche Charakter der Geschichte der Farbenlehre erlaubt es uns, dabei ebenfalls 'symbolisch' vorzugehen" (p. 26). H. Hamm, *Der Theoretiker Goethe* (Berlin: Akademie Verlag, 1980), finds his symbolism to be a general characteristic of his presentation of reality after 1800: "Mit dem 'symbolischen' Verfahren entdeckt er in der 'Erscheinung' die 'Idee' und formt sie zum 'Bild' " (p. 212).

34. See August Boeckh, *Encyklopädie und Methodologie der philologischen Wissenschaft,* 2d ed. (Leipzig: Teubner, 1886), p. 15, who understood the entire

field of philology to be a study of commentary on the past, "Erkennen des Erkannten."

9. Goethe's taxonomy of scientific discourse

1. Goethe, *Materialien,* LA, pt. I, vol. 6, p. viii, "Alle Lehren, denen man Originalität zuschreiben kann, sind nicht so leicht gefasst, nicht so geschwind epitomiert und systematisiert. Der Schriftsteller neigt sich zu dieser oder jener Gesinnung; sie wird aber durch seine Individualität, ja oft nur durch den Vortrag, durch die Eigentümlichkeit des idioms, in welchem er spricht und schreibt, durch die Wendung der Zeit, durch mancherlei Rücksichten modifiziert."
2. Hayden White, *Metahistory. The Historical Imagination in Nineteenth-Century Europe* (Baltimore: Johns Hopkins University Press, 1973), emphasizes that the "tropological mode" and "linguistic protocol" comprise the "'metahistorical' basis of every historical work" and that "it is no accident that the principal philosophers of history were also (or have lately been discovered to have been) quintessentially philosophers of language" (p. xi).
3. Goethe, "Der Versuch als Vermittler," LA, pt. I, vol. 8, p. 310. Although the concept of "Vorstellung" was important to various eighteenth-century thinkers, see particularly Ernst Hohenemser, "Die Lehre von den kleinen Vorstellungen bei Leibniz" (Ph.D. diss., Heidelberg University, 1899), Carl Knüfer, "Grundzüge der Geschichte des Begriffs Vorstellung von Wolff bis Kant. Ein Beitrag zur Geschichte der philosophischen Terminologie" (Ph.D. diss., Berlin University, 1911), and Hans Naegelsbach, "Das Wesen der Vorstellung bei Schopenhauer," *Beiträge zur Philosophie* 12 (1927): 1–188, Goethe seems to be the first to apply it to discussion in the historiography of science.
4. For more exhaustive lists of "Vorstellungsarten" see Angelika Groth, *Goethe als Wissenschaftshistoriker* (Munich: Fink, 1972), pp. 49–112, and Manfred Kleinschneider, *Goethes Naturstudien, wissenschaftliche und geschichtliche Untersuchungen* (Bonn: Bouvier, 1971), pp. 91–196, who discuss the concept as a system of polarities, including for example, the opposition that Goethe saw between atomism and dynamism, or between synthesis and analysis.
5. Goethe, "Ueber Sprache und Terminologie," LA, pt. I, vol. 4, p. 221.
6. There is a close parallel between Thomas Kuhn's use of the term "paradigm," *The Structure of Scientific Revolutions,* and Goethe's modes of conception (Vorstellungsart) in the language of science. Indeed, Masterman argues in "The Nature of a Paradigm," pp. 59–89, that Kuhn's twenty-one uses of the term paradigm may be grouped into three categories: metaphysical paradigms, sociological paradigms, and construct or artifact paradigms (p. 65). These paradigms, Goethe would argue, are based on the use of language and represent different forms of symbolization. See also White, *Metahistory,* where "Following the analysis of Stephen C. Pepper in his *World Hypotheses,* I have differentiated four paradigms of the form that a historical explanation, considered as a discursive argument, may be conceived to take: Formist, Organicist, Mechanistic, and Contextualist" (p. 13).
7. Goethe, *Materialien,* LA, pt. I, vol. 6, p. 103, "Aber die Art, wie er sich über

diese Dinge äussert, zeigt dass sein Apparat nur in seinem Geiste gewirkt und dass daher manche imaginäre Resultate entsprungen sein mögen."

8. Ibid., p. 156, "Da er die Sprache völlig in seiner Gewalt hat, so wagt er gelegentlich kühne, seltsame Ausdrücke, aber nur dann, wenn der Gegenstand ihm unerreichbar scheint."

9. Ibid., p. 158.

10. This view has been confirmed by modern scholarship as can be judged by the many excellent studies on the mechanical conception of the universe. See, for example, Edward J. Dijksterhuis, *The Mechanization of the World Picture,* trans. C. Dikshoorn (Oxford: [Clarendon Press], 1961), and also Dudley Shapere's survey of concepts and literature on "Newtonian Mechanics and Mechanical Explanation," in *Encyclopedia of Philosophy,* 8 vols., ed. Paul Edwards (New York: Macmillan, 1967), vol. 5, pp. 491–6.

11. Goethe, *Materialien,* LA, pt. I, vol. 6, p. 203, "Seitdem Descartes die Lehre von dem Lichte materialisiert und mechanisiert hatte, so können sich die Dichter nicht wieder aus diesem Kreise heraus finden: denn die jenigen welche Licht und Farben nicht materiell nehmen wollen, müssen doch zur mechanischen Erklärung greifen."

12. For a study of seventeenth- and eighteenth-century mechanical philosophy in England see Robert Schofield, *Mechanism and Materialism: British Mechanical Philosophy in the Age of Reason* (Princeton, N.J.: Princeton University Press, 1970), who also includes in his study chapters on the "Diffusion of the Creed" (pp. 19–39), and "Newtonian Pagans and Heretics" (pp. 115–33).

13. See also Goethe's review of the "Principes de philosophie zoologique," LA, pt. I, vol. 10, pp. 373–403, where he elaborates on the problems caused by mechanical symbols in discussion of living, vital, and organic processes. Joseph H. Woodger, *Biology and Language* (Cambridge University Press, 1952) and John S. Haldane, *Mechanism, Life and Personality,* 2d ed. (New York: Dutton, 1923), have criticized a mechanistic language in organic studies, suggesting new approaches to concept formation in the life sciences.

14. See Fink, "Atomism," 377–95, for a study of Goethe's reception of the philosophy of the atomists and the effect that it had in his own writings, particularly in literary works.

15. There are various studies on this epoch of atomism like those by Kurd Lasswitz, *Geschichte der Atomistik vom Mittelalter bis Newton,* 2 vols. (Hildesheim: Olm, 1963; 1st ed. 1890), and Robert H. Kargon, "Atomism in the Seventeenth Century," in *Dictionary of the History of Ideas,* 5 vols., ed. P. Wiener (New York: Scribner, 1973), vol. 1, pp. 132–41, which list a number of original sources on the concept of atomism. Still a standard work on the topic is Joshua C. Gregory, *A Short History of Atomism, From Democritus to Bohr* (London: Black, 1931).

16. Goethe, *Materialien,* LA, pt. I, vol. 6, p. 173, "Bewegen sich die Kügelchen rotierend, aber nicht geschwinder als die gradlinigen; so entsteht die Empfindung von Gelb. Eine schnellere Bewegung derselben bringt Rot hervor; und eine langsamere als die der gradlinigen Blau."

17. Ibid., pp. 174, 308. For a study of "Die Atomistik als Fiktion," see Hans Vaihinger, *Die Philosophie des Als Ob: System der theoretischen, praktischen und religiösen Fiktionen der Menschheit auf Grund eines idealistischen Positivismus,*

7th and 8th eds. (Leipzig: Meiner, 1922), pp. 429–51. Vaihinger was writing in the tradition of Friedrich Nietzsche, *Die Fröhliche Wissenschaft, in Nietzsche Werke*, 8 pts., ed. G. Colli and M. Montinari (Berlin: De Gruyter, 1967–), pt. V, vol. 2, who wrote that without bodies, divisible time, lines, surfaces and many such articles of faith, nobody would be able to endure life (pp. 155–6). In Goethe's own time, the idea of the fictions of atomism was expressed most clearly by Jeremy Bentham, *Bentham's Theory of Fictions*, ed. C. K. Ogden (Paterson, N.J.: Littlefield, 1959; 1st ed. 1789), p. 110. For a study of the criticism of fiction in science see also Karl J. Fink, "Actio in Distans, Repulsion, Attraction. The Origin of an Eighteenth-century Fiction," *Archiv für Begriffsgeschichte* 25 (1982): 69–87.

18. Goethe, *Materialien*, LA, pt. I, vol. 6, pp. 2, 72. For varying notions on the organization of matter see, for example, Ernan McMullin, ed., *The Concept of Matter in Greek and Medieval Philosophy* (Notre Dame, Ind.: Notre Dame University Press, 1963), or the historical survey by Friedrich A. Lange, *Geschichte des Materialismus und Kritik seiner Bedeutung in der Gegenwart*, 3d ed., 2 vols. (Iserlohn: Baedeker, 1876), who includes a brief discussion on Goethe (vol. 1, pp. 406–8), emphasizing Goethe's resistance to abstract conceptions of matter: "Auch Göthe verwahrte sich dagegen, dass man den Gott Spinoza's als einen abstracten Begriff, das heisst, als eine Null auffasse" (vol. 1, p. 406).

19. Goethe, *Materialien*, LA, pt. I, vol. 6, p. 74, "Die Einteilung der ursprünglichen Naturkräfte in vier Elemente ist für kindliche Sinnen fasslich und erfreulich, ob sie gleich nur oberflächlich gelten kann."

20. Ibid., p. 182. See Karl Bärthlein, "Zur Entstehung der aristotelischen Substanz-Akzidenz-lehre," *Archiv für Geschichte der Philosophie* 50 (1968): 196–253, for a fuller discussion and critique of the Substanz-Akzidenz concepts in Greek thought.

21. Goethe, *Materialien*, LA, pt. I, vol. 6, p. 308. It is interesting to note that in modern physics this search for empirical evidence of fundamental particles continues, reaffirming Goethe's notion that in the end everything is life and activity. Werner Heisenberg, *Das Naturbild der heutigen Physik* (Hamburg: Rowolt, 1955), reformulates this view when he writes that all particles consist of the same substance and that they are only various stationary moments of one and the same matter, informing us that the life expectancy of particles such as mesons is extremely short (one millionth of a second) (p. 32).

22. Goethe's term "moral" may be broadly interpreted as social, or human-centered, as used in the theory of culture by a contemporary, Daniel Jenisch, *Universalhistorischer Ueberblick der Entwicklung des Menschengeschlechts, als eines sich fortbildenden Ganzen, Eine Philosophie der Culturgeschichte*, 2 vols (Berlin: Voss, 1801). For a taxonomy of the term as used by Jenisch see Fink, "Ontogeny Recapitulates Phylogeny" (1987), pp. 100–12. Today these "moral" or social concepts are discussed as "Panpsychism," Paul Edwards, in *The Encyclopedia of Philosophy*, 8 vols., ed. Paul Edwards (New York: Macmillan, 1967), vol. 6, pp. 22–31.

23. Agassi, "Anthropomorphism in Science," vol. 1, pp. 87–91, discusses the negative aspect of anthropomorphism as "parochialism," but shows also that much of technology and instrumentation is imitation of human characteristics, concluding,

like Goethe, that "it is very hard to draw a very clear line between parochial and nonparochial anthropomorphisms," and that "we do better to speak against parochialism" (p. 90).

24. Goethe, *Materialien*, LA, pt. I, vol. 6, pp. 168–72. Today the concept of "intentionality" is receiving considerable attention as in Jitendranath Mohanty, *The Concept of Intentionality* (St. Louis, Mo.: Green, 1972), particularly in studies on phenomenology as in the one by Herbert Spiegelberg, "Intention und Intentionalität in der Scholastik, bei Brentano und Husserl," *Studia Philosophica* 29 (1969): 189–216, who points out that in antiquity and through the scholastic period "intentio" had the meaning of "Hinstreben" (p. 192). Although Goethe's understanding of intentionality is not included, one could position him somewhere in the comparative scheme between scholasticism and Husserl as outlined by Spiegelberg (pp. 201–3).

25. Ernest Nagel, "Teleological Explanations and Teleological Systems," in *Readings in the Philosophy of Science,* Baruch A. Brody, ed. (Englewood Cliffs, N.J.: Prentice Hall, 1970), pp. 106–20, recently observed that almost any biological treatise is concerned with vital processes and the activities of living things and in that sense is directed toward inquiry into certain "end-products"; that is, the language is teleological (p. 106). Fink, "Ontogeny Recapitulates Phylogeny," pp. 87–112, asks in his review of purposive designs in late eighteenth-century theories of anthropology "if a science in which it is claimed that ontogeny recapitulates phylogeny could be anything other than teleological" (p. 105).

26. Goethe, "Ueber Naturwissenschaft im Allgemeinen," LA, pt. I, vol. 11, p. 355, "Weder Mythologie noch Legenden sind in der Wissenschaft zu dulden. Lasse man diese den Poeten, die berufen sind sie zu Nutz und Freude der Welt zu behandeln. Der wissenschaftliche Mann beschränke sich auf die nächste klarste Gegenwart. Wollte derselbe jedoch gelegentlich als Rhetor auftreten, so sei ihm jenes auch nicht verwehrt."

10. Goethe's teleology of science

1. Goethe, "Ueber Naturwissenschaft im Allgemeinen," LA, pt. I, vol. 11, p. 337, "In New-York sind neunzig verschiedene christliche Konfessionen, von welchen jede auf ihre Art Gott und den Herrn bekennt, ohne weiter an einander irre zu werden. In der Naturforschung, ja in jeder Forschung, müssen wir es so weit bringen; denn was will das heissen, dass jedermann von Liberalität spricht und den andern hindern will nach seiner Weise zu denken und sich auszusprechen!"

2. Goethe, *Die Leiden des jungen Werthers,* trans. B. Q. Morgan (New York: Ungar, 1957), p. 62; B. Seuffert, ed., WA, pt. I, vol. 19, pp. 1–191, "Dass ihr Menschen, rief ich aus, um von einer Sache zu reden, gleich sprechen müsst: das ist thöricht, das ist klug, das ist gut, das ist bös! Und was will das alles heissen? Habt ihr desswegen die inneren Verhältnisse einer Handlung erforscht? Wisst ihr mit Bestimmtheit die Ursachen zu entwickeln, warum sie geschah, warum sie geschehen musste? Hättet ihr das, ihr würdet nicht so eilfertig mit euren Urtheilen sein" (pp. 65–6).

3. Goethe, *Werther,* trans. Morgan (1957), p. 67; WA, pt. I, vol. 19, p. 72, "Und

wir gingen aus einander, ohne einander verstanden zu haben. Wie denn auf dieser Welt keiner leicht den andern versteht."

4. Ibid., p. 82; WA, pt. I, vol. 19, pp. 91–2, "Kein Und, kein Bindewörtchen darf aussenbleiben, und von allen Inversionen, die mir manchmal entfahren, ist er ein Todfeind; wenn man seinen Perioden nicht nach der hergebrachten Melodie herab-orgelt, so versteht er gar nichts drin. Das ist ein Leiden, mit so einem Menschen zu thun zu haben."

5. Ingeborg Kluge, *Wissenschaftskritik in Goethes "Faust"* (Bern: Peter Lang, 1982), views the various stages of the development of the Faust text "als Paradigma der wissenschaftlichen Entwicklung Goethes," proceeding from the irrationalism of the "Urfaust" to the synthesis of science, ethics, and art in the mature "Faust" (p. 1). Some of the parallels are interesting but not many are convincing.

6. Goethe, *Faust,* trans. Randall Jarrell (New York: Farrar, 1976), p. 5; WA, pt. I, vol. 14, p. 55, "Zwei Seelen wohnen, ach! in meiner Brust, / Die eine will sich von der andern trennen; / Die eine hält, in derber Liebeslust, / Sich an die Welt mit flammernden Organen; / Die andre hebt gewaltsam sich vom Dunst / Zu den Gefilden hoher Ahnen."

7. McClelland, *State, Society, and University in Germany,* notes that "mockery of the traditional German universities became almost a staple of the budding German literature of the period" (p. 79), an observation that he discusses as part of "the second eighteenth-century reform movement" that led to the founding of the University of Berlin in 1810.

8. Martha Ornstein, *The Role of Scientific Societies in the Seventeenth Century* (Chicago: University of Chicago Press, 1928), noted that until the end of the seventeenth century German scientific societies were devoted to "the development and cultivation of the German tongue," whereas much of the enthusiasm in other countries "was bestowed upon cultivation of experiment" (p. 166). Her view of science in the German universities to that point was equally disparaging, although she noted at least one university (Halle) that used the vernacular and a second (Altdorf) in which "pure science" was encouraged (p. 235). McClelland, *State, Society, and University in Germany,* argues that the eighteenth-century German university went through two reforms before the French Revolution, in whose wake "The Humboldt Era" (pp. 101–49) and "New Concepts of Research" (p. 122) emerged. Rolf Klima and Ludgen Viehoff, "The Sociology of Science in West Germany and Austria," in *The Sociology of Science in Europe,* ed. R. K. Merton and J. Gaston (Carbondale, Ill.: SIU Press, 1977), pp. 145–92, begin their review of the German scientific institutions with "the classical German university" (pp. 149–52), the institution Goethe saw emerging in the last decade of the eighteenth century and first decades of the nineteenth century. Magali Sarfatti Larson, *The Rise of Professionalism. A Sociological Analysis* (Berkeley and Los Angeles: University of California Press, 1977), follows this line of thought, showing that, after the French Revolution, the three traditional professions supported by litigating, preaching, and teaching expanded with the industrialization of the West.

9. Goethe, *Gespräche,* GA, vol. 22, pp. 538–42, "Auf unsern Kathedern werden die einzelnen Fächer planmässig zu halbjährigen Vorlesungen mit Gewalt ausei-

nandergezogen. Die Reihe von wirklichen Erfindungen ist gering, besonders, wenn man sie durch ein paar Jahrhunderte im Zusammenhange betrachtet. Das meiste, was getrieben wird, ist doch nur Wiederholung von dem, was dieser oder jener berühmte Vorgänger gesagt hat. Von einem selbstständigen Wissen ist kaum die Rede. Man treibt die jungen Leute herdenweise in Stuben und Hörsäle zusammen und speist sie in Ermangelung wirklicher Gegenstände mit Zitaten und Worten ab. Die Anschauung, die oft dem Lehrer selbst fehlt, mögen sich die Schüler hinterdrein verschaffen! Es gehört eben nicht viel dazu, um einzusehen, dass dies ein völlig verfehlter Weg ist. Besitzt nun der Professor vollends gar einen gelehrten Apparat, so wird es dadurch nicht besser, sondern nur noch schlimmer" (p. 538).

10. Hogben, *Science in Authority,* writes in his chapter on "The New Authoritarianism" (pp. 136–51), of "the emergence of a new scientific priestcraft" (p. 141), pointing out "that the scientific worker of today does in fact take more and more of his science in trust" (p. 139).

11. Goethe, *Materialien,* LA, pt. I, vol. 6, p. 316, "Gelehrte Gesellschaften, sobald sie vom Gouvernement bestätigt, einen Körper ausmachen, befinden sich in Absicht der reinen Wahrheit in einer misslichen Lage. Sie haben einen Rang und können ihn mitteilen; sie haben Rechte und können sie übertragen; sie stehen gegen ihre Glieder, sie stehen gegen gleiche Korporationen, gegen die übrigen Staatszweige, gegen die Nation, gegen die Welt in einer gewissen Beziehung. Im einzelnen verdient nicht jeder den sie aufnehmen, seine Stelle; im einzelnen kann nicht alles was sie billigen, recht, nicht alles was sie tadeln, falsch sein: denn wie sollten sie vor allen andern Menschen und ihren Versammlungen das Privilegium haben, das Vergangene ohne hergebrachtes Urteil, das Gegenwärtige ohne leidenschaftliches Vorurteil, das Neuauftretende ohne misstrauische Gesinnung, und das Künftige ohne übertriebene Hoffnung oder Apprehension, zu kennen, zu beschauen, zu betrachten, und zu erwarten."

12. Campe, *Wörterbuch der Deutschen Sprache,* vol. 2, p. 379, includes "Gilde" in his dictionary, defining it as "eine geschlossene Gesellschaft, die auf gemeinschaftliche Kosten zu gewissen Zeiten schmauset, daher in weiterer Bedeutung auch wol eine jede zu dieser Absicht versammelte Gesellschaft, ein Schmaus, eine Zeche, ein Gelag, eine Gilde genannt wird. Dann überhaupt, eine zur Erreichung einer gemeinschaftlichen Absicht verbundene Gesellschaft."

13. Goethe, "Konfession des Verfassers," LA, pt. I, vol. 6, p. 425, and Goethe, "Ueber Naturwissenschaft im Allgemeinen," LA, pt. I, vol. 11, pp. 339, 341. Indeed, William Whewell, *History of the Inductive Sciences,* in *The Historical and Philosophical Works of William Whewell,* 10 vols., ed. G. Buchwald and L. Laudan (London: F. Coss, 1967; repr. 3d. ed., 1857) vol. 3, p. 370, included Goethe in the survey for his work in color theory, comparative anatomy, and plant morphology, although he confirmed Goethe's perception that he was excluded from science of the professions: "I do not pretend that Göthe's anatomical works have had any influence on the progress of science comparable with that which has been exercised by the labours of professional anatomists; but the ingenuity and value of the views which they contained was acknowledged by the best authorities." However, Bräuning-Oktavio, "Goethes Naturwissenschaftliche

Schriften," examining the scientific communities' reception of Goethe's research on the intermaxillary bone (pp. 111–38), observed how he, as a thirty-five-year-old lay scientist, failed to gain recognition for discovery of "the inner relationship" of the bone in man and animal, a connection rejected by leading comparative anatomists like Petrus Camper in Holland and Johann Friedrich Blumenbach at the University of Göttingen. Thus, Goethe had to wait almost half a century, until 1831, one year before his death, for the essay to be published in a reputable scientific journal, the *Nova Acta Leopoldina* in Berlin.

14. Goethe, "Anmerkungen über Personen und Gegenstände, deren in dem Dialog Rameau's Neffe erwähnt wird," *Rameau's Neffe. Ein Dialog von Diderot*, ed. R. Schösser, WA, pt. I, vol. 45, pp. 159–217, "Und nicht allein Franzosen, welche alles nach aussen thun, sondern auch Deutsche, welche die Wirkung nach innen recht gut zu schätzen wissen, geben solche Gesinnungen zu erkennen, wodurch der Schriftsteller vom Schriftsteller, der Gelehrte vom Gelehrten gildenmässig abgetrennt würde," p. 163. McClelland, *State, Society, and University in Germany*, too, observes "that is would be fair to conclude that the professoriate was entrenched in a conservative posture, unwilling and unable to change age-old customs even when they had become corrupt" (p. 80).

15. Goethe, "Der Versuch," LA, pt. I, vol. 3, p. 291. Goethe's image of a "republic of science," like that of most eighteenth-century writers who commented on the rise of modern institutions of science, was a response to Francis Bacon's mythical "House of Salomon" as described in his *New Atlantis* (ca. 1622). Goethe, *Materialien*, LA, pt. I, vol. 6, pp. 248–9, observed that Bacon's "Salomon's College" (das Salomonische Kollegium) was a "romantic palace" (ein romantischer Palast) (p. 248), and that his ideal separation and cooperation of scientific functions had not surfaced in the actual life and proceedings of the Royal Society in England: "Von dieser glücklichen Sonderung und Zusammenstellung ist keine Spur in dem Verfahren der Sozietät" (p. 249). For another German eighteenth-century response to Bacon's mythical "House" and to British realization of "a republic of science" see Otto Sonntag, "Albrecht von Haller on Academies and the Advancement of Science: The Case of Göttingen," *Annals of Science* 32 (1975): 379–91: "He [Haller] attributed to Bacon, whose *New Atlantis* he had read as a young man, the original idea of a society with the exclusive task of experimenting" (p. 380).

16. Goethe, *Materialien*, LA, pt. I, vol. 6, p. 241, "Der patriotische Engländer möchte den Ursprung der Sozietät gern früh festsetzen, aus Eifersucht gegen gewisse Franzosen, welche sich gleichzeitig zu solchem Zwecke in Paris versammelt."

17. Larson, *The Rise of Professionalism*, confirms Goethe's isolation of this rubric in the structure of science at the turn of the century, for in a chapter on "The Historical Matrix of Modern Professions" (pp. 2–8), she observes how "in the pre-industrial days, the professions were closely bound to the stratification system. For learned professions, establishment and social standing were equivalent to their association with the elites and with the state" (p. 3).

18. Goethe, *Materialien*, LA, pt. I, vol. 6, p. 352, "Mayer nach Lichtenbergs Tod, stimmt in einem neuen Kompendium das alte Lied an." Sonntag, "The Case of

Göttingen," confirms Goethe's observation, pointing out that Haller "could be persuaded only with difficulty" to accept philology as a branch of study, for he argued that "'the taste of the world is not at all disposed toward languages, but solely toward mathematics and physics'" (p. 381).

19. Goethe, "Chromatik," LA, pt. I, vol. 8, p. 175, "Priester werden Messe singen / Und die Pfarrer werden pred'gen, / Jeder wird vor allen Dingen / Seiner Meinung sich entled'gen / Und sich der Gemeine freuen / Die sich um ihn her versammelt, / So im Alten wie im Neuen / Ohngefähre Worte stammelt. / Und so lasset auch die Farben / Mich nach meiner Art verkünden / Ohne Wunden, ohne Narben, / Mit der lässlichsten der Sünden."

20. Goethe, *Goethes Briefe,* ed. Carl Alt, WA, pt. IV, vol. 26, p. 289, "Da die Sprache das Organ gewesen, wodurch ich mich während meines Lebens am meisten und liebsten den Mitlebenden mittheilte; so musste ich darüber, besonders in spätern Zeiten, reflectiren."

21. Goethe, *Briefe,* WA, pt. IV, vol. 26, p. 290, "Und ich liess mich nicht irren dass die ganze physische Gilde in hergebrachten hohlen Chiffern zu sprechen gewohnt ist, deren Abracadabra ihnen die Geister der lebendigen Natur, die überall zu ihnen spricht, möglichst vom trocknen dogmatischen Leichnam abhält."

22. Bräuning-Oktavio, "Goethes Naturwissenschaftliche Schriften," concluded from his study that the response was not as bad as perceived by Goethe, "Selbst die günstigsten Urteile sind nicht ohne Tadel, und die ungünstigsten (fast) nie ohne Lob" (p. 169).

23. Goethe, "Konfession," LA, pt. I, vol. 6, p. 414, "Je weniger also mir eine natürliche Anlage zur bildenden Kunst geworden war, desto mehr sah ich mich nach Gesetzen und Regeln um; ja ich achtete weit mehr auf das Technische der Malerei, als auf das Technische der Dichtkunst."

24. Charles Lock Eastlake, "The Translator's Preface," in *Goethe's Theory of Colors,* trans. C. L. Eastlake (Cambridge, Mass.: MIT Press, 1970; repr., 1840), pp. xxvii–xxxv, who was distinguished primarily in the fine arts but with scientific interests, observed that "sufficient time" had elapsed "to allow a calmer and more candid examination of his [Goethe's] claims" (p. xxx), which he found useful "in all that relates to harmony of colours" (p. xxxi), including the connection discovered between ancient and Italian Renaissance painting, "one of the most interesting features of Goethe's theory" (p. xxxii).

25. Most early studies on Goethe's science recall this anecdote in explaining Goethe's fundamental error in exhibiting the state of the arts in physical optics; see, for example, Magnus, *Goethe as a Scientist,* pp. 137–8, and Charles Sherrington, *Goethe on Nature and on Science* (Cambridge University Press, 1949), p. 7.

26. Bräuning-Oktavio, "Goethes Naturwissenschaftliche Schriften," concludes in his survey of professional responses to Goethe's color theory that the criticisms and judgments then were the same as they are today: "Goethes Hauptthese gegen Newton wird als falsch abgelehnt; dagegen werden anerkannt, ja gerühmt, seine Verdienste im didaktischen Teil, seine Erkenntnisse über die physiologischen Farben, seine Darstellung der sinnlich-sittlichen Wirkung der Farbe, die Lehre von der Harmonie der Farben und, besonders wichtig für den Künstler, der Abschnitt über die Farbe als ästhetisches Mittel" (p. 203). However, Stephen

Toulmin, *Human Understanding* (Princeton, N.J.: Princeton University Press, 1972), does not see Goethe's conflict with the guild as a question of physics, but of historiography, namely, as an example of the differences between scientific paradigms and "genuine parallels" in the history of science: "Whereas there is a direct intellectual conflict between the electromagnetic theories of (say) Maxwell and Heisenberg, the colour theories of Goethe and Newton were largely at cross-purposes" (pp. 124–5).

27. Sonntag, "The Case of Göttingen," concludes his study of Albrecht Haller's leadership in forming scientific institutions in Göttingen, observing "his trust in the powers of specialized empirical inquiry" and that he was not "altogether unique in fixing on competition rather than on co-operation as the motive force in academies" (p. 391).

28. See Kleinschneider, *Goethes Naturstudien*, who studied "Goethes Objektivismus" and "Subjektivismus" as categories of his "Vorstellungsarten" (pp. 123–9).

29. Whewell, *The Philosophy of the Inductive Sciences*, vol. 5, p. 29.

30. Ibid., p. 30.

31. Heisenberg, "Die Goethesche und Newtonsche Farbenlehre," also notes the elevated perception that was gained, not through the Goethe–Schiller, but through the Goethe–Newton controversy, noting the same antithesis: "In der Naturwissenschaft der neuen Zeit beginnt sehr bald die Scheidung der Wirklichkeit in eine objektive und eine subjektive . . . Es sieht zunächst so aus, als ob diese beiden Wirklichkeiten für immer als unüberbrückbare Gegensätze einander gegenüberstehen müssten. Der Kampf Goethes gegen die Newtonsche Farbenlehre wäre dann nur ein Ausdruck für diesen nicht zu schlichtenden Gegensatz" (p. 425).

32. Kant, "Ueber den Gebrauch teleologischer Principien," Akad., vol. 8, pp. 157–84. Schiller, "Was heisst und zu welchem Ende studiert man Universalgeschichte?" NA, vol. 17, pp. 359–76. Lenoir, *The Strategy of Life*, observes that "perhaps no area of endeavor better exhibits the hold that the notion of goal-directedness as a mode of natural causation has over the human mind than the writing of history" (p. 17), a discipline that emerged in tandem with interest in the origin of the human species and in general with anthropology. Wolf Lepenies, "Naturgeschichte und Anthropologie im 18. Jahrhundert," in *Deutschlands kulturelle Entfaltung, Neubestimmung des Menschen*, ed. B. Faber (Munich: Kraus, 1980), pp. 211–26, argues that studies from the eighteenth century remained "fixed on the human being" (auf den Menschen fixiert, p. 212), and, in his view, modern anthropology did not emerge until man lost this privileged position, and was integrated into research on processes of nature in general. Lenoir, *Strategy of Life* (1989), finds such a "unified theory for the life sciences" (p. 2), in the writings of Kant, Blumenbach, and the German biologists from the period before Darwin.

33. Wolf Lepenies and Peter Weingart, "Introduction," in *Functions and Uses of Disciplinary Histories*, ed. L. Graham, W. Lepenies, and P. Weingart (Dordrecht: Reidel, 1983), p. viii, discuss some of the "legitimating functions" of a history of science, although Goethe's strategy of defining a public, which would shape the

future reception of his work, seems to have escaped modern critics more concerned with social theory of the present, with theory, Goethe might argue, wanting in telos.

34. William Shakespeare, *Hamlet,* in *The London Shakespeare,* 5 vols., ed. J. Munro (New York: Simon & Schuster, 1957), vol. 5, p. 568.

35. Friedrich Nietzsche, *Menschliches, Allzumenschliches II,* in *Nietzsche Werke,* (1967–), pt. IV, vol. 3, pp. 55–6.

36. Mandelkow, *Goethe im Urteil seiner Kritiker* (1975–9), includes samples of reviews of Goethe's science by his contemporaries, including texts by rather obscure critics such as Leopold von Henning, who reviewed Goethe's *Farbenlehre* in 1822, and classical reviews such as Carl G. Carus's review of the French translation of the *Metamorphose der Pflanzen* in 1832, vol. 1, pp. 335–43, 496–502. Volumes 2 and 3, respectively, treat the reception of Goethe's works in the nineteenth and twentieth centuries.

11. The topoi of Goethe scholarship

1. Goethe, *Materialien,* LA, pt. I, vol. 6, p. viii, "Es ist äusserst schwer, fremde Meinungen zu referieren, besonders wenn sie sich nachbarlich annähern, kreuzen und decken. Ist der Referent umständlich, so erregt er Ungeduld und lange Weile; will er sich zusammenfassen, so kommt er in Gefahr, seine Ansicht für die fremde zu geben; vermeidet er zu urteilen, so weiss der Leser nicht, woran er ist; richtet er nach gewissen Maximen, so werden seine Darstellungen einseitig und erregen Widerspruch, und die Geschichte macht selbst wieder Geschichten."

2. Ernst Laslowski, "Goethes Stellung zur Geschichte," *Historisches Jahrbuch* 53 (1933): 480–9, was the first to study the writings on Goethe as a historian seriously and to observe that from the beginning studies on the topic were polarized. Whereas Franz Wegele, *Göthe als Historiker* (Würzburg: Stuber, 1876), viewed Goethe's writings on history as positive, the next study, by Ottokar Lorenz, "Goethe als Historiker," in *Goethes politische Lehrjahre* (Berlin: Hertz, 1893), pp. 160–80, dealt more with Goethe's negative attitude toward history.

3. Erich Trunz, "Goethe als Sammler," *Weimar Goethe-Studien,* ed. Erich Trunz (Weimar: Böhlau, 1980) emphasized the relationship between Goethe's work as curator and historian by introducing his discussion of Goethe's collections with observations on his "historisches Denken" (pp. 8–10).

4. Hans Reiss, ed. *Goethe und die Tradition* (Frankfurt: Athenäum, 1972), included in his volume essays on Goethe's writings on antiquity, the Renaissance, baroque, and Orientalism.

5. Wegele, *Göthe als Historiker,* is criticized for his positivistic approach, although the work is written clearly and is well documented, making it a readable text today.

6. Ibid., pp. 20–1.

7. Lorenz, "Goethe als Historiker," p. 162, based his reaction to the topic on Goethe's conversation with Heinrich Luden, a professor of history at the University of Jena, *Goethes Gespräche,* GA, vol. 22, p. 403. Bietak, "Goethe und die Geschichte," pp. 101–11, found twelve negative criticisms in Goethe's conversa-

tion with Luden, grouping them into three problems relating to historical continuity: (1) that cultural transmission is at best fragmentary, (2) that the chronicler is a subjective participant in history, and (3) that critical historical methods are inadequate for overcoming subjectivity in history (p. 106). See Wilhelm Dilthey, "Goethe und die dichterische Welt," in *Das Erlebnis und die Dichtung* (Leipzig: Teubner, 1906), pp. 137–200, for an interpretation of Goethe's inner, subjective view of life: "In dieser Weise wirken in Goethe die Vertiefung in das eigene Innere und eine mächtige Begabung für Phantasiebilder zusammen" (p. 188).

8. Emil Menke-Glückert, *Goethe als Geschichtsphilosoph und die geschichtsphilosophische Bewegung seiner Zeit* (Leipzig: Voigtländer, 1907), pp. 35–55.

9. Georg Kass, *Möser und Goethe* (Berlin: Paul, 1909), shows that Möser's influence on Goethe may have equalled that of Herder, at least on points such as the dramatization of history, notions about individuality, and the focus on biography in history.

10. Menke-Glückert, *Goethe als Geschichtsphilosoph*, pp. 56–67. See also Julia Gauss, "Die methodische Grundlage von Goethes Geschichtsforschung," pp. 163–283, particularly on Goethe's morphology and history (pp. 187–206).

11. Friedrich Meinecke, *Goethe und die Geschichte* (Munich: Leibniz, 1949; 1st ed., 1936). Ludwig Landgrebe, "Die Geschichte in Goethes Weltbild," in *Beiträge zur Einheit von Bildung und Sprache im geistigen Sein,* ed. G. Haselbach and G. Hartmann (Berlin: de Gruyter, 1957), pp. 371–84, for example, hopes to improve upon Meinecke's attempt to show Goethe's synthesis of historical events and to show more clearly Goethe's challenge to mathematically inspired theories of history (pp. 373–5).

12. Kurt Jahn, "Goethes Stellung zur Geschichte," in *Goethes Dichtung und Wahrheit* (Halle: Niemeyer, 1908), pp. 49–77.

13. Gustav Würtenberg, *Goethe und der Historismus* (Leipzig: Teubner, 1929). Werner Schultz, "Die Bedeutung des Tragischen für das Verstehen der Geschichte bei Hegel und Goethe," *Archiv für Kulturgeschichte* 38 (1956): 92–115, distinguishes between two kinds of anthropology at the time of Goethe and Hegel; the one was Promethean and the other humanistic. The former assumed an a priori unity of God and man and permitted no tragedy, decline, evil, and failure, whereas humanistic anthropology permitted the polarities of good and evil, that is, the source of tragedy (p. 93).

14. Würtenberg, *Goethe und der Historismus,* p. 3.

15. Walter Lehmann, *Goethes Geschichtsauffassung in ihren Grundlagen* (Langensalza: Beyer, 1930), pp. 137–200. More recently Klaus Ziegler, "Zu Goethes Deutung der Geschichte," *Deutsche Vierteljahrsschrift für Literaturwissenschaft und Geistesgeschichte* 30 (1956): 232–67, attempted to explain Goethe's history as philosophical anthropology: "erst in der Geschichte, nur mit der Geschichte gelangt das Wesen des Menschen überhaupt zu sich selbst" (p. 232).

16. Friedrich Gundolf, "Geschichte und Politik," in *Goethe* (Berlin: Bondi, 1916), pp. 400–12, and Ernst Cassirer, *Goethe und die geschichtliche Welt* (Berlin: Cassirer, 1932): "Und wie diese Art der dichterischen Intuition für Goethe erst das eigene Sein erschliesst, so ist sie es auch, die ihn zur Kenntnis und zum Verständnis alles fremden Seins hinführt" (p. 18).

17. Cassirer, *Goethe und die geschichtliche Welt,* pp. 25–6.
18. Herbert Cysarz, *Goethe und das geschichtliche Weltbild* (Brünn: Rohrer, 1932), pp. 38–49.
19. Meinecke, *Goethe und die Geschichte,* pp. 90–119.
20. Ibid., pp. 197–8.
21. Victor Lange, "Goethe's View of History," in *Goethe Proceedings, Essays Commemorating the Goethe Sesquicentennial at the University of California, Davis,* ed. C. Bernd, et al. (Columbia, S.C.: Camden, 1984), pp. 107–19, revives Meineckean ambivalence, pointing out that Goethe was "from beginning to end profoundly skeptical toward any suggestion that the historical process . . . might yield a coherent scheme of progression" (p. 107), or that with Lessing's "optimistic view of history Goethe was increasingly to disagree" (p. 110), or that "the relentless assertions of the disjointedness of history are the pronouncements of a man who never ceased to reflect upon temporality and tradition" (p. 113). The same article was translated into German as "Goethes Geschichtsauffassung," *Etudes Germaniques* 38 (1983): 3–16.
22. Schultz, "Die Bedeutung des Tragischen," p. 103, and idem, "Der Sinn der Geschichte bei Hegel und Goethe," *Archiv für Kulturgeschichte* 39 (1957): 209–27. In the latter essay Schultz makes the point that tragic elements are actually a minor part of Goethe's view on history: "Prüft man abschliessend die positiven Aussagen Goethes über die Geschichte, so ergibt sich, dass sie die negativen Aussagen nicht ausschliessen, sondern nur ergänzen und einschränken" (p. 226).
23. Reuter, "Roman des europäischen Gedankens" (1966), 1–49.
24. Reuter, "Roman des europäischen Gedankens," p. 48, "Goethe glaubt an die 'Gesundheit' historischer Vernunft."
25. Ziegler, "Goethes Deutung der Geschichte," "In der Tat ist die Antithese, welche die bisherige Forschung weithin beherrscht, nach beiden Seiten hin falsch" (p. 234), namely, Goethe's attitude toward the historical past can hardly be reduced to bi-valued judgments.
26. See Nikolai Wilmont, "Goethes Geschichts- und Kulturauffassung," in *Kolloquium über Probleme der Goethe-Forschung, Weimarer Beiträge* 6 (1960): 978–92: "Goethes Denken ist durch und durch geschichtlich; er ist durch und durch Historiker der Menschheit" (p. 978).
27. Groth, *Goethe als Wissenschaftshistoriker,* pp. 49–117.
28. Gauss, "Die methodische Grundlage," p. 186.
29. Ibid., pp. 180–7.
30. Dorothea Kuhn, "Goethes Geschichte der Farbenlehre als Werk und Form," *Deutsche Vierteljahrsschrift* 34 (1960): 356–77.
31. Nisbet, *Goethe and the Scientific Tradition* (1972); Fink, "Atomism," 377–95; Kuhn, *Empirische und ideelle Wirklichkeit,* pp. 64–89; and Fink, "The Metalanguage of Goethe's History of Color Theory," pp. 41–55.
32. Examples of such strategies may be found in discussions on "vagueness," Francis Zartman, *Definition and Open Texture* (Ph.D. diss., University of Illinois, 1964), on "overtones" and "haloes", James, *The Principles of Psychology,* vol. 1, pp. 258, 281, 471; and on "nonmetrical ordering," Carl G. Hempel, *Fundamentals of Concept Formation in Empirical Science* (Chicago: University of Chicago Press,

1952), section III. On the history of concept formation, see Morris Weitz, *Theories of Concepts, A History of the Major Philosophical Tradition* (London: Routledge, 1988).

33. Curtius, *European Literature and the Latin Middle Ages,* (1963) p. 82. On the relationships of thought and linguistic form embedded in the concept of topos, see August Obermayer, "Zum Toposbegriff der modernen Literaturwissenschaft," in *Toposforschung,* ed. Max Baeumer (Darmstadt: Wiss. Buchgesellschaft, 1973), pp. 252–67, "Hier sei der Versuch unternommen, die grosse Konfusion, die sich um diesen Begriff gebildet hat, zu entwirren," p. 252. More recently Thomas Kuhn, "Reflections on My Critics," in *Criticism and the Growth of Knowledge,* ed. I. Lakotos and A. Musgrave (Cambridge University Press, 1970), pp. 231–78, argued that scientific communities may be viewed as "language communities" that share the use of particular sets of linguistic formulas: "When I speak of knowledge embedded in terms and phrases learned by some non-linguistic process like ostension, I am making the same point that my book aimed to make by repeated reference to the role of paradigms as concrete problem solutions, the exemplary objects of an ostension" (p. 271).

34. Compare studies by Tadeusz Pawlowski, *Concept Formation in the Humanities and the Social Sciences* (Dordrecht: Reidel, 1980); William Outhwaite, *Concept Formation in Social Science* (London: Routledge & Kegan Paul, 1983); and Guy Oakes, *Weber and Rickert: Concept Formation in the Cultural Sciences* (Cambridge, Mass.: MIT Press, 1988).

35. Early studies include those by Richard Meyer, "Studien zu Goethes Wortgebrauch," *Archiv für das Studium der neueren Sprachen und Litteraturen* 96 (1896): 1–42; Otto Pniower, "Zu Goethes Wortgebrauch," *Goethe Jahrbuch* 19 (1898): 229–47; and Ewald Boucke, *Wort und Bedeutung in Goethes Sprache* (Berlin: Felber, 1901).

36. Most of the Goethe philologists such as Ewald Boucke cited Hermann Paul, *Principles of the History of Language,* H. A. Strong, trans. (College Park, Md.: McGrath, 1970), on the theoretical foundations of word field studies. On the history and development of this field see Jost Trier, *Aufsätze und Vorträge zur Wortfeldtheorie,* ed. A. van der Lee and O. Reichmann (The Hague: Mouton, 1973), pp. 9–39.

37. These tools along with a history of the Weimar edition are discussed by Heinz Kindermann, *Das Goethebild des 20. Jahrhunderts,* 2d ed. (Darmstadt: Wiss. Buchgesellschaft, 1966), pp. 22–50.

38. Ewald Boucke, *Goethes Weltanschauung auf historischer Grundlage. Ein Beitrag zur Geschichte der dynamischen Denkrichtung und Gegensatzlehre* (Stuttgart: Frommann, 1907).

39. Kindermann, *Das Goethebild* (1966), pp. 512–704.

40. Andrew Jaszi, *Entzweiung und Vereiningung. Goethes symbolische Weltanschauung* (Heidelberg: Stiehm, 1973), discusses many of the polarized terms in Goethe's language and thought; for a comparison of the polarized terms in Goethe's language with antonyms generally found in the German language see Morris Stockhammer, "Kurzes dualistisches Wörterverzeichnis," *Archiv für Begriffsgeschichte* 4 (1959): 158–81.

41. Meinecke, *Goethe und die Geschichte,* p. 118, "Goethe kann nur in seinen Polaritäten verstanden werden."

42. Groth, *Goethe als Wissenschaftshistoriker,* p. 113, "So wird beispielsweise die Lehre des Plato und des Aristoteles positiv, die Newtons dagegen negativ beurteilt. Alle drei aber stellen eine Autorität dar; also sowohl richtige als auch falsche Lehren können als Autorität wirken. Das heisst aber, Pol and Gegenpol einer Polarität können als ein und derselbe Pol einer anderen Polarität auftreten, beziehungweise umgekehrt kann ein Pol einmal mit dem einen, zum anderen mit dem entgegengesetzten Pol einer zweiten Polarität zusammenfallen." This study offers the most comprehensive list of polarities discovered in Goethe's history to date.

43. Cherry, *On Human Communication,* p. 93.

44. Ibid., p. 36, discusses some of these languages including the Ogam script of the ancient Celts and the famous dot-dash code introduced by Samuel F. B. Morse in 1832. These coding systems are similar to the typical punched card (hole / no-hole) formerly used for the computer that operates with electrical impulses (pulse / no-pulse). A good survey of the development of alternative forms of thought may be found in Stuart Chase's chapter on "Turn with the Logicians," in *The Tyranny of Words* (New York: Harcourt, Brace and Co., 1938), pp. 226–43.

45. For a discussion of the literature on nonstandard logic see Robert Ackermann, *Introduction to Many-valued Logics* (London: Routledge & Kegan Paul, 1967), pp. 21–6. Alfred Tarski, *Logic, Semantics, Metamathematics, Papers from 1923–1938,* ed. J. H. Woodger (Oxford: Oxford University Press [Clarendon Press], 1956), pointed out that "semantical concepts," "those concepts which, roughly speaking, express certain connexions between the expressions of language and the objects and states of affairs referred to by these expressions," "have often led to paradoxes and antinomies" (p. 401). He goes on to argue that generally speaking "people have proceeded as though there was only one language in the world," not realizing "that the language about which we speak need by no means coincide with the language in which we speak" (p. 402).

46. On the "Ills of Modern Taxonomy" see Sokal and Sneath, *Principles of Numerical Taxonomy,* pp. 5–11: "Taxonomy, more than most other sciences, is affected by subjective opinions of its practitioners" (p. 11).

47. Nisbet, *Goethe and the Scientific Tradition,* pp. 39–47, points out that Goethe's concept of an "Urphänomen" is a synthesis of complementary concepts such as idea-experience, and indeed, of the separate Platonic and empirical traditions: "It represents the fusion of two traditions, the Platonic and the empirical, in Goethe's mind" (p. 42).

48. See Meinecke, *Goethe und die Geschichte,* p. 196, "So kam es in ihm zu der vielleicht einzig möglichen Synthese von relativierendem und absolutierendem, von idealisierendem und individualisierendem Denken," as well as sections from Groth, *Goethe als Wissenschaftshistoriker,* such as "Kreislauf und Fortschreiten" (p. 118). But close examination of the distinction between Hegelian dialectics and Goethe's concept of intensification may be found in Werner Schultz, "Der Sinn der Geschichte bei Hegel und Goethe," where in the final analysis the question is discounted: "Es wird nicht einmal auf eine steigende positive Linie in diesem Kampf hingewiesen" (p. 225).

49. Rudolf Steiner, *Goethe the Scientist,* trans. O. Wannamaker (New York: Anthroposophic Press, 1950), explains in a chapter on "The Arrangement of Goethe's Scientific Writings" (pp. 99–101), that "in the editing of Goethe's writings on natural science, for which I have been responsible, I have been guided by the idea of giving life to the study of details by the exposition of the magnificent realm of ideas upon which these details rest" (p. 99). One of these "ideas" emerged as another title in the same volume, "Goethe against Atomism" (pp. 243–63), a Steiner reaction to the chemist Wilhelm Ostwald's assertion "that things are composed of atoms in motion and that these atoms and the forces operating among them are the ultimate realities of which the single phenomena consist" (p. 243). See Fink, "Atomism," a study designed to overcome Steiner's bias by showing how Goethe integrated basic principles of the atomistic tradition into his descriptive novels on life, as in *Wilhelm Meister.*

50. Goethe, "[Polarität]," in *Naturwissenschaft. Allgemeine Naturlehre,* ed. R. Steiner, WA, pt. II, vol. 11, p. 164; Goethe, "Einleitung," in *Aufsätze, Fragmente, Studien zur Naturwissenschaft im Allgemeinen,* ed. D. Kuhn and W. Engelhardt, LA, pt. I, vol. 11, p. 55.

51. See, for example, Nisbet, *Goethe and the Scientific Tradition,* p. 45.

52. George Sarton, "Montucla," *OSIRIS* 1 (1936): 519–67, saw the scope of Goethe's "history of optics from the 'Urzeit' to his own time" (p. 553).

53. John Hennig, "Goethe's interest in the history of British physics," *OSIRIS,* 10 (1952): 43–66, and D. Kuhn, "Goethes Geschichte der Farbenlehre als Werk und Form," both emphasized a new look at the content and language of Goethe's history.

54. Reuter, "Roman des europäischen Gedankens," begins and concludes his essay with an emphasis on the need to focus the study of Goethe as historian on the events, the materials, the stuff of his historical writing (pp. 1–5, 41–9), a shift away from an era of scholarship influenced by a "Geistesgeschichte."

55. Goethe, "Ueber Naturwissenschaft im Allgemeinen," LA, pt. I, vol. 11, p. 353, "Autorität, dass nämlich etwas schon einmal geschehen, gesagt oder entschieden worden sei, hat grossen Wert; aber nur der Pedant fordert überall Autorität."

Histories of science from the Goethe period

Recent taxonomies of the historiography of science cover a wide range of approaches to the field, including types that are intrinsic and extrinsic to a particular branch of science (Agassi, 1963; McMullin, 1970; Kragh, 1987). This range is in evidence already in histories written during the Goethe era, 1770–1820, some of which emphasize the chronology of discoverers and discoveries (Portal, 1770–3; Wiegleb, 1790–1), others showing the impact of a few individuals on a course of study (Bailly, 1779; Gmelin, 1797–9). Many of the works from this era are strictly disciplinary, intended to serve the cutting edge of research (Montucla, 1758; Priestley, 1767, 1772), although those of this persuasion, too, struggled with a definition of history, with problems of periodization, with questions about the parameters of a field and the external influences on science (Bailly, 1777; Goethe, 1810).

Works from the Goethe period also explored the development of science from an ethnocentric (Pulteney, 1790) and a global (Sprengel, 1817–18) point of view, particularly in botany, where geographic questions had conditioned the course of research and the sources of history. And whereas some traced the study of a very narrow topic across several periods and cultures (Sprengel, 1787), others integrated several disciplines in the attempt to show the development of a unified theory of science (Saverien, 1766; 1775). Indeed, a taxonomy of approaches from the Goethe era encompasses the field of historiography itself, including studies with a sociolinguistic view of writing history (Chladenius, 1752) and a biobibliographic organization of the history of historiography (Wachler, 1812–18) as a discipline in its own right.

Bailly, Jean Sylvain. *Histoire de l'astronomie ancienne, depuis son origine jusqu'à l'éstablissement de l'école Alexandrie.* Paris: Debure, 1775.
Histoire de l'astronomie moderne depuis la fondation de l'école d'Alexandrie, jusqu'à l'époque de M.D.CC.XXX. Paris: de Bure, 1779–82.
Lettres sur l'origine des sciences, et sur celle des peuples de l'Asie. London: Elmesly, 1777.
Beckmann, Johann. *Beyträge zur Geschichte der Erfindungen.* 5 vols. Leipzig: Kummer, 1782–1805.

Birch, Thomas. *The History of the Royal Society of London for improving of Natural Knowledge, From its first rise, in which the most considerable of those Papers communicated to the Society, which have hitherto not been published, are inserted in their proper order, as a supplement to The Philosophical Transactions.* 4 vols. London: Millar, 1756–7.

Breitkopf, Johann G. I. *Ueber die Geschichte der Erfindung der Buchdruckerkunst.* Leipzig: Breitkopf, 1779.

Chladenius, Johann M. *Allgemeine Geschichtswissenschaft, Worinnen der Grund zu einer neuen Ensicht in aller Arten der Gelahrheit gelegt wird.* Leipzig: Friedrich Lanck, 1752.

Einleitung zur Richtigen Auslegung Vernüftigen Reden und Schriften. Leipzig: Friedrich Lanck, 1742.

Condorcet, Marie-Jean-Antoine-Nicolas. *Esquisse d'un tableau historique des progrès de l'esprit humain. Ouvrage Posthume de Condorcet.* Paris: Agasse, 1793.

Fischer, Johann K. *Geschichte der Physik.* 8 vols. Göttingen: Röwer, 1801–8. (Series: Geschichte der Künste und Wissenschaften seit der Wiederherstellung derselben bis an das Ende des 18.Jahrhunderts)

Fourcroy, Antoine. *Leçons élémentaires d'histoire naturelle et de chimie.* 2 vols. Paris: n. p., 1782.

Gmelin, Johann F. *Allgemeine Geschichte der Gifte.* Leipzig: Weygand, 1776.

Geschichte der Chemie. 3 vols. Göttingen: Rosenbusch, 1797–9. (Series: Geschichte der Künste und Wissenschaften seit der Wiederherstellung derselben bis an das Ende des 18. Jahrhunderts)

Goethe, Johann W. *Materialien zur Geschichte der Farbenlehre.* Tübingen: Cotta, 1810.

Hissmann, Michael. *Anleitung zur Kenntniss der auserlesenen Litteratur in allen Theilen der Philosophie.* Göttingen: Meyer, 1778.

Kästner, Abraham G. *Geschichte der Mathematik.* 4 vols. Göttingen: Rosenbusch, 1796–1800. (Series: Geschichte der Künste und Wissenschaften seit der Wiederherstellung derselben bis an das Ende des 18. Jahrhunderts)

Kühn, Karl G. *Geschichte der medizinischen und physikalischen Elektricität und der neuesten Versuche.* 2 vols. Leipzig: Weygand, 1783–85.

Meiners, Christoph. *Geschichte des Ursprungs und Verfalls der Wissenschaften in Griechenland und Rom.* 2 vols. Lemgo: Meyer, 1781–2.

Montucla, Jean E. *Histoire des mathématiques, dans laquelle on rend compte de leurs progrès depuis leur origine jusqu'à nos jours; où l'on expose le tableau & le développement des principales découvertes, les contestations qu'elles ont fait naître, & les principaux traits de la vie des mathématiciens les plus célebres.* 2 vols. Paris: Jombert, 1758.

Poppe, Johann H. M. *Ausführliche Geschichte der Anwendung aller krummen Linien in mechanischen Künsten und in der Architektur, seit der ältesten Zeiten bis zu Anfange des neunzehnten Jahrhunderts.* Nürnberg: Raspe, 1802.

Geschichte der Technologie. 3 vols. Göttingen: Röwer, 1807–11. (Series: Geschichte der Künste und Wissenschaften seit der Wiederherstellung derselben bis an das Ende des achtzehnten Jahrhunderts)

Portal, Antoine. *Histoire de l'anatomi et de la chirurgie.* 6 vols. Paris: Didot, 1770–3.

Histories of science from the Goethe period

Priestley, Joseph. *The history and present state of discoveries relating to vision, light, and colours.* London: Johnson, 1772.

The history and present state of electricity, with original experiments. London: Dodsley, 1767.

Pulteney, Richard. *Historical and Biographical Sketches of the Progress of Botany in England, from Its Origins to the Introduction of the Linnean System.* 2 vols. London: Cadell, 1790.

Pütters, Johann S. *Versuch einer academischen Gelehrten-Geschichte von der Georg-Augustus-Universität zu Göttingen.* Göttingen: Vandenhoek, 1765–88.

Ritter, Johann W. *Die Physik als Kunst. Ein Versuch, die Tendenz der Physik aus ihrer Geschichte zu deuten. Zur Stiftungsfeyer der Königlichen-baierischen Akademie der Wissenschaften am 28sten März 1806.* Munich: Lindauer, 1806.

Saverien, Alexander. *Histoire des progrès de l'esprit humain, dans les sciences exactes, et dans les arts qui en dépendent.* Paris: Lacombe, 1766.

Histoire des progrès de l'esprit humain, dans les sciences naturelles et dans les arts qui en dépendent. Paris: Lacombe, 1775.

Spix, Johannes. *Geschichte und Beurtheilung aller Systeme in der Zoologie nach ihrer Entwiklungsfolge von Aristoteles bis auf die gegenwärtige Zeit.* Nürnberg: Schrag, 1811.

Sprengel, Kurt P. J. *Beiträge zur Geschichte des Pulses, nebst einer Probe seiner Commentarien über Hippokrates Aphorismen.* Leipzig: Meyer, 1787.

Geschichte der Botanik. Neu bearbeitet. 2 vols. Leipzig: Brockhaus, 1817–18.

Versuch einer pragmatischen Geschichte der Arzneikunde. Halle: Gebauer, 1794.

Wachler, D. Ludwig. *Geschichte der historischen Forschung und Kunst, seit der Wiederherstellung der litterärischen Cultur in Europa.* 2 vols. Göttingen: Röwer, 1812–18. (Series: Geschichte der Künste und Wissenschaften seit der Wiederherstellung derselben bis an das Ende des 18. Jahrhunderts)

Wiegleb, Johann C. *Geschichte des Wachstums und der Erfindungen in der Chemie in der neuern Zeit.* 2 vols. Berlin: Nicolai, 1790–1.

Historisch-kritische Untersuchung der Alchemie, oder der eingebildeten Goldmacherkunst; von ihrem Ursprunge sowohl als Fortgange, und was nun von ihr zu halten sey. Weimar: Hoffman, 1777.

References

Abraham, Werner. "Bemerkungen zu Goethes Farbenlehre im Lichte der Wahrnehmungspsychologie und der kognitiven Psychologie." *Euphorion* 77 (1985): 144–75.

Ackermann, Robert. *Introduction to Many-valued Logics*. London: Routledge & Kegan Paul, 1967.

Adler, Jeremy. *'Eine fast magische Anziehungskraft,' Goethe's 'Wahlverwandtschaften' und die Chemie seiner Zeit*. Munich: Beck, 1987.

Agassi, Joseph. "Anthropomorphism in Science." In *Dictionary of the History of Ideas*. 5 vols. Ed. Philip Wiener. New York: Scribner, 1973, vol. 1, pp. 87–91.

Agassi, Joseph. "Towards a Historiography of Science." *History and Theory* Beiheft 2 (1963): 1–117.

Altner, Günter. "Goethe as a Forerunner of Alternative Science." In *Goethe and the Sciences: A Reappraisal*. Ed. F. Amrine, F. Zucker, and H. Wheeler. Dordrecht: Reidel, 1987, pp. 341–50.

Amrine, Frederick, Francis Zucker, and Harvey Wheeler, eds. *Goethe and the Sciences: A Reappraisal*. Dordrecht: Reidel, 1987.

Anderson, Wilda C. *Between the Library and the Laboratory: The Language of Chemistry in Eighteenth-century France*. Baltimore: Johns Hopkins University Press, 1984.

Apel, Karl O. "Die Idee der Sprache in der Tradition des Humanismus von Dante bis Vico." *Archiv für Begriffsgeschichte* 8 (1963): 1–398.

Aristotle. *De Coloribus*. Trans. T. Loveday and E. S. Forster. In *The Works of Aristotle*. 12 vols. Ed. W. D. Ross. Oxford: Oxford University Press (Clarendon Press), 1910–52.

Baldridge, W. Scott. "The Geological Writings of Goethe." *American Scientist* 72 (1984): 163–7.

Bärthlein, Karl. "Zur Entstehung der aristotelischen Substanz-Akzidenz-lehre." *Archiv für Geschichte der Philosophie* 50 (1968): 196–253.

Becker, Carl. *The Heavenly City of the Eighteenth-century Philosophers*. New Haven, Conn.: Yale University Press, 1932.

Benne, Kenneth D. *A Conception of Authority*. New York: Bureau of Publications, 1943.

Bentham, Jeremy. *Bentham's Theory of Fictions*. Ed. C. K. Ogden. Paterson, N.J.: Littlefield, 1959; 1st ed. 1789.

References

Berlin, Brent and Paul Kay. *Basic Color Terms*. Berkeley and Los Angeles: University of California Press, 1969.

Bernays, Michael, ed. *Goethes Briefe an Friedrich August Wolf* Berlin: Reimer, 1868.

Bietak, Wilhelm. "Goethe und die Geschichte." *Jahrbuch des Wiener Goethe-Vereins* 68 (1964): pp. 101–11.

Black, Max. *Models and Metaphors*. Ithaca, N.Y.: Cornell University Press, 1962.
"More about Metaphors." *Metaphor and Thought*. Ed. A. Ortony. Cambridge University Press, 1979, pp. 19–43.

Blackall, Eric A. *The Emergence of German as a Literary Language*. 2d ed. Ithaca, N.Y.: Cornell University Press, 1978.

Blasius, Jürgen. "Zur Wissenschaftstheorie Goethes." *Zeitschrift für philosophische Forschung* 33 (1979): 371–88.

Blumenbach, Johann. *The Anthropological Treatises of Johann Friedrich Blumenbach*. Trans. and Ed. T. Bendyshe. Boston: Milford House, 1973; repr., 1865.
De generis humani varietate nativa. Göttingen: Vandenhoeck, 1776.
Ueber den Bildungstrieb und das Zeugungsgeschäft. Göttingen: Dietrich, 1781.

Boeckh, August. *Encyklopädie und Methodologie der philologischen Wissenschaft*. 2d ed. Leipzig: Teubner, 1886.

Böhme, Gernot. "Is Goethe's Theory of Color Science?" In *Goethe and the Sciences*. Ed. F. Amrine, et al. Dordrecht: Reidel, 1987, pp. 147–73.

Boucke, Ewald. *Wort und Bedeutung in Goethes Sprache*. Berlin: Felber, 1901.

Boucke, Ewald. *Goethes Weltanschauung auf historischer Grundlage. Ein Beitrag zur Geschichte der dynamischen Denkrichtung und Gegensatzlehre*. Stuttgart: Frommann, 1907.

Brady, Ronald. "Goethe's Natural Science. Some Non-Cartesian Meditations." In *Toward a Man-Centered Medical Science*. Ed. K. E. Schaefer, H. Hensel and R. Brady. Mt. Kisco, N.Y.: Futura, 1977, pp. 137–65.

Brady, Ronald. "Form and Cause in Goethe's Morphology." In *Goethe and the Sciences*. Ed. F. Amrine, F. Zucker, and H. Wheeler. Dordrecht: Reidel, 1987, pp. 257–300.

Brandes, Georges. *Wolfgang Goethe*. Trans. A. W. Porterfield. New York: Frank-Maurice, 1924.

Brandt, Helmut. "Natur in Goethes Dichten und Denken." In *Goethe und die Wissenschaften*. Ed. H. Brandt. Jena: Friedrich-Schiller-Universität, 1984, pp. 156–78.

Bräuning-Oktavio, Hermann. "Goethes naturwissenschaftliche Schriften und die Freiheit von Forschung und Lehre." In *Jahrbuch des Freien Deutschen Hochstifts*. Ed. D. Lüders. Tübingen: Niemeyer, 1982, pp. 110–215.

Brodbeck, May. "Explanation, Prediction, and 'Imperfect' Knowledge." In *Readings in the Philosophy of the Social Sciences*. Ed. May Brodbeck. London: Macmillan, 1968, pp. 363–98.

Brown, Jane. "History and Historicity in Act II of Faust, Part II." *Goethe Yearbook* 2 (1984): 69–90.

Buffon, Georges. *Histoire naturelle, générale et particulière*. 44 vols. Paris: De l'imprimerie royale, 1749–1803.

Burke, Kenneth. *Attitudes toward History*. Los Altos, Calif.: Hermes, 1959.
A Grammar of Motives. New York: Prentice-Hall, 1945.

Burwick, Frederick. *The Damnation of Newton: Goethe's Color Theory and Romantic Perception*. Berlin: de Gruyter, 1986.

Butterfass, Theodor. "Goethe und die Wissenschaft von der Pflanze." In *Allerhand Goethe*. Ed. D. Kimpel and J. Pompetzki. Bern: Peter Lang, 1985, pp. 165–80.

Campe, Joachim. *Wörterbuch der deutschen Sprache*. 5 vols. Braunschweig: Schulbuchhandlung, 1807–11, vol. 2, pp. 301–2.

Cantor, Paul. "The Metaphysics of Botany, Rousseau and the New Criticism of Plants." *Southwest Review* 70 (1985): 362–80.

Cantor, Geoffrey N. *Optics after Newton, Theories of Light in Britain and Ireland, 1704–1840*. Manchester: Manchester University Press, 1983.

Cassirer, Ernst. *Rousseau-Kant-Goethe. Two Essays*. Trans. J. Gutmann, P. Kristeller, and J. Randall. Hamden, Conn.: Archon Books, 1961, 1st ed., 1944.

Goethe und die geschichtliche Welt. Berlin: Cassirer, 1932.

Chase, Stuart. *The Tyranny of Words*. New York: Harcourt, Brace, and Co., 1938.

Cherry, Colin. *On Human Communication*. 2d ed. Cambridge, Mass.: MIT Press, 1971.

Cohen, I. Bernard. *Revolution in Science*. Cambridge, Mass.: Harvard University Press, 1985.

Coseriu, Eugenio. *Die Geschichte der Sprachphilosophie von der Antike bis zur Gegenwart*. 2 vols. Tübingen: Tübinger Beiträge, 1972.

Crosland, Maurice P. *Historical Studies in the Language of Chemistry*. New York: Dover, 1978; 1st ed. 1962.

Curtius, Ernst R. *European Literature and the Latin Middle Ages*. Trans. W. Trask. New York: Harper & Row, 1963, repr. 1953, 1st German ed., 1948.

Cysarz, Herbert. *Goethe und das geschichtliche Weltbild*. Brünn: Rohrer, 1932.

Dahlke, Otto. "The Sociology of Knowledge." *Contemporary Social Theory*. Ed. Harry E. Earnes and Howard Becker. New York: Appleton-Century, 1940, pp. 64–89.

Diels, Hermann. *Die Fragmente der Vorsokratiker. Grieschisch und Deutsch*. 2 vols. 2d ed. Berlin: Weidmann, 1906–10.

Dijksterhuis, Edward J. *The Mechanization of the World Picture*. Trans. C. Dikshoorn. Oxford: Oxford University Press (Clarendon Press), 1961.

Dill, Christa. *Bedeutungsentfaltung der Wörter Tat, tätig und Tätigkeit bei Goethe*. Berlin: Humboldt University, 1957.

Dilthey, Wilhelm. "Goethe und die dichterische Welt." In *Das Erlebnis und die Dichtung*. Leipzig: Teubner, 1906.

Dobbek, W. "Die coincidentia oppositorum als Prinzip der Weltdeutung bei J. G. Herder wie in seiner Zeit." In *Herder-Studien*. Ed. W. Wiora. Würzburg: Holzner, 1960, pp. 16–47.

Durkheim, Emile and Marcel Mauss. *Primitive Classification*. Trans. Rodney Needham. Chicago: University of Chicago Press, 1963; 1st ed., 1903.

Eastlake, Charles Lock. "The Translator's Preface." In *Goethe's Theory of Colors*. Trans. C. L. Eastlake. Cambridge, Mass.: MIT Press, 1970; repr., 1840, pp. xxvii–xxxv.

Edwards, Paul, "Panpsychism." In *The Encyclopedia of Philosophy*. 8 vols. Ed. Paul Edwards. New York: Macmillan, 1967, Vol. 6, pp. 23–31.

References

Eichhorn, Johann G. *Allgemeine Geschichte der Cultur und Litteratur des neueren Europa.* 2 vols. Göttingen: Rosenbusch, 1796–9.

Eichner, Hans. "The Rise of Modern Science and the Genesis of Romanticism." *Publication of the Modern Language Association* 97 (1982): 8–30.

Eiseley, Loren. *Darwin's Century: Evolution and the Men who Discovered it.* Garden City, N.Y.: Doubleday, 1958.

Emrich, Wilhelm. *Die Symbolik von Faust II.* 3d ed. Frankfurt: Athenäum, 1964.

Erickson, Erik. *Identity: Youth and Crisis.* New York: Norton, 1968.

Eucken, Rudolf. *Geschichte der Philosophischen Terminologie.* Hildesheim: Olm, 1960; 1st ed. 1879.

Eyde, Richard H. "The Foliar Theory of the Flower." *American Scientist* 63 (1975): 430–7.

Feyerabend, Paul. "Classical Empiricism." In *The Methodological Heritage of Newton.* Ed. R. E. Butts and J. W. Davis. Toronto: University of Toronto Press, 1970, pp. 150–70.

Fiesel, Eva. *Die Sprachphilosophie der deutschen Romantik.* Tübingen: Mohr, 1927.

Fink, Karl J. "Actio in Distans, Repulsion, Attraction. The Origin of an Eighteenth-Century Fiction." *Archiv für Begriffsgeschichte* 25 (1982): 69–87.

"Atomism: A Counterpoint Tradition in Goethe's Writings." *Eighteenth-century Studies* 13 (1980): 377–95.

"'Dualisten,' 'Trinitarier,' 'Solitarier': Formen der Autorität in Goethe's 'Geschichte der Farbenlehre'." *Goethe-Jahrbuch* 99 (1982): 230–49.

"Goethe's West-östlicher Divan: Orientalism Restructured." *International Journal of Middle East Studies* 14 (1982): 315–28.

"Herder's Life Stages as Forms in Geometric Progression." *Eighteenth-Century Life* 6 (1981): 39–59.

"Johann Krüger on Electricity: 'Cui bono,' For Whom to What Good?" *Electric Quarterly* 12 (1990), no. 1, 2–3; no. 2, 2–4; and no. 3, 2–4.

"Johann Wolfgang Goethe." In *Read More About It. An Encyclopedia of Information Sources on Historical Figures and Events.* Ed. C. Kohoyda-Inglis. 3 vols. Ann Arbor, Michigan: Pierian Press, 1989, vol. 3, pp. 252–4.

"The Metalanguage of Goethe's History of Color Theory." In *The Quest for the New Science. Language and Thought in Eighteenth Century Science.* Ed. K. J. Fink and J. W. Marchand. Carbondale, Ill.: SIU Press, 1979, pp. 41–55.

"Ontogeny Recapitulates Phylogeny: A Classical Formula of Eighteenth-century Organicism." In *Approaches to Organic Form.* Ed. F. Burwick. Dordrecht: Reidel, 1987, pp. 87–112.

"Private and Public Authority in the Life of a Critic." In *Goethe as a Critic of Literature.* Ed. K. J. Fink and M. L. Baeumer. Lanham, Md.: University Press of America, 1984, pp. 182–214.

Firla, Monika. *Untersuchungen zum Verhältnis von Anthropologie und Moralphilosophie bei Kant.* Bern: Peter Lang, 1981.

Fischer, Johann K. *Geschichte der Physik.* 8 vols. Göttingen: Röwer, 1801–8.

Freeman, Kathleen. *The Pre-Socratic Philosophers: A Companion to Diels, Fragmente der Vorsokratiker.* 2d ed. Oxford: Blackwell, 1949.

Fück, Johann. *Die arabischen Studien in Europa, Bis in den Anfang des 20. Jahrhunderts.* Leipzig: Harrassowitz, 1955.

218

Gajek, Bernhard, and Franz Götting. *Goethes Leben und Werk in Daten und Bildern.* Frankfurt: Insel, 1966.

Gauss, Julia. "Goethe und die Patriarchenwelt." In *Goethe-Studien.* Göttingen: Vandenhoeck, 1961, pp. 67–77.

Gauss, Julia. "Die methodische Grundlage von Goethes Geschichtsforschung." *Jahrbuch des Freien Deutschen Hochstifts.* Ed. Ernst Beutler. Halle: Niemeyer, 1932, pp. 163–283.

Glaser, Horst, ed. *Goethe und die Natur.* Bern: Peter Lang, 1986.

Gleick, James. *Chaos. Making a New Science.* New York: Viking Penguin, 1987.

Gode-Von Aesch, Alexander G. H. *Natural Science in German Romanticism.* New York: Columbia University Press, 1941.

Goethe, Johann Wolfgang. "Allerdings: Dem Physiker." In *Gedichte.* Ed. G. Loeper. WA. Pt. I, vol. 3, p. 105.

"An C. L. F. Schultz." *Goethes Briefe.* Ed. Carl Alt. WA. Pt. IV, vol. 26, pp. 289–91.

"An Merck," *Goethes Breife.* Ed. E. Hellen. WA. Pt. IV, vol. 4, pp. 200–5.

"Anmerkungen über Personen und Gegenstände, deren in dem Dialog Rameau's Neffe erwähnt wird." In *Rameaus Neffe. Ein Dialog von Diderot.* Ed. R. Schösser. WA. Pt. I, vol. 45, pp. 159–217.

"Auf dem See." In *Gedichte.* Ed. G. Loeper. WA. Pt. I, vol. 1, p. 78.

Aus meinem Leben. Dichtung und Wahrheit. Ed. J. Baechtold and G. Loeper. WA. Pt. I, vols. 26–9.

"Beiträge zur Optik." In *Beiträge zur Optik und Anfänge der Farbenlehre, 1790–1808.* Ed. R. Matthaei. LA. Pt. I, vol. 3, pp. 1–108.

"Bildungstrieb." In *Morphologische Hefte.* Ed. D. Kuhn. LA. Pt. I, vol. 9, pp. 99–100.

"Chromatik." In *Naturwissenschaftliche Hefte.* Ed. D. Kuhn. LA. Pt. I, vol. 8, p. 175.

"Dauer im Wechsel." In *Gedichte.* Ed. G. Loeper. WA. Pt. I, vol. 1, pp. 119–20.

"Der Dynamismus in der Geologie." In *Schriften zur Geologie und Mineralogie, 1770–1810.* Ed. G. Schmid. LA. Pt. I, vol. 1, pp. 378–81.

"Einwirkung der neueren Philosophie." In *Morphologische Hefte.* Ed. D. Kuhn. LA. Pt. I, vol. 9, pp. 90–4.

Enthüllung der Theorie Newtons. Ed. R. Matthaei. LA. Pt. I, vol. 5.

"Epochen bei der Weltbildung." In *Schriften zur Geologie und Mineralogie.* Ed. G. Schmid. LA. Pt. I, vol. 2, pp. 102–3.

Faust. Trans. R. Jarrell. New York: Farrar, 1976.

Faust. I. Teil, II. Teil. Ed. E. Schmidt. WA, Pt. I, vols. 14, 15.

"Geschichtliches." In *Naturwissenschaftliche Hefte.* Ed. D. Kuhn. LA. Pt. I, vol. 8, pp. 220–32.

"Das Göttliche." In *Gedichte.* Ed. G. Loeper. WA. Pt. I, vol. 2, pp. 83–4.

Johann Wolfgang Goethe. Scientific Studies. Ed. and trans. D. Miller. New York: Suhrkamp, 1988.

Johann Wolfgang Goethe. Selected Poems. Ed. and trans. C. Middleton. Boston: Suhrkamp, 1983.

"Kirchers Pyrophylacium wieder hergestellt." In *Aufsätze, Fragmente, Studien zur*

References

Naturwissenschaft im Allgemeinen. Ed. D. Kuhn and W. Engelhardt. LA. Pt. I, vol. 11, pp. 269–70.

"Konfession des Verfassers." In *Materialien zur Geschichte der Farbenlehre.* Ed. D. Kuhn. LA. Pt. I, vol. 6, pp. 412–29.

Die Leiden des jungen Werthers. Ed. B. Seuffert and E. Hellen. WA. Pt. I, vol. 19, pp. 1–191.

"Mailied." In *Gedichte.* Ed. G. Loeper. WA. Pt. I, vol. 1, pp. 72–3.

Materialien zur Geschichte der Farbenlehre. Ed. D. Kuhn. LA. Pt. I, vol. 6.

"Dem Menschen wie den Tieren ist ein Zwischenknochen der obern Kinnlade zuzuschreiben." In *Morphologische Hefte.* Ed. D. Kuhn. LA. Pt. I, vol. 9, pp. 154–66.

"Die Metamorphose der Pflanzen." In *Morphologische Hefte.* Ed. D. Kuhn. LA. Pt. I, vol. 9, pp. 23–61.

"Nachträge." In *Morphologische Hefte.* Ed. D. Kuhn. LA. Pt. I, vol. 9, pp. 167–86.

"Nomenklatur." In *Zur Farbenlehre. Didaktischer Teil.* Ed. R. Matthaei. LA. Pt. I, vol. 4, pp. 182–84.

"Physikalische Vorträge Schematisiert, 1805–1806." In *Aufsätze, Fragmente, Studien zur Naturwissenschaft im Allgemeinen.* Ed. D. Kuhn and W. Engelhardt. LA. Pt. I, vol. 11, pp. 55–102.

"[Polarität]." In *Zur Naturwissenschaft. Allgemeine Naturlehre.* Ed. R. Steiner. WA. Pt. II, vol. 11, pp. 164–6.

"Principes de philosophie zoologique. Discutés en mars 1830 au sein de l'Académie Royale des Sciences par Mr. Geoffroy de Saint-Hilaire Paris 1830." In *Aufsätze, Fragmente, Studien zur Morphologie.* Ed. D. Kuhn. LA. Pt. I, vol. 10, pp. 373–403.

"Schicksal der Druckschrift." In *Morphologische Hefte.* Ed. D. Kuhn. LA. Pt. 1, vol. 9, pp. 65–72.

"Schlussbetrachtung. Ueber Sprache und Terminologie." In *Zur Farbenlehre. Didaktischer Teil.* Ed. R. Matthaei. LA. Pt. I, vol. 4, pp. 221–3.

The Sufferings of Young Werther. Trans. B. Q. Morgan. New York: Ungar, 1957.

"1801." In *Tag- und Jahres- Hefte als Ergänzung meiner sonstigen Bekenntnisse, von 1749–1806.* Ed. W. Biedermann. WA. Pt. I, vol. 35, pp. 87–120.

"Ueber den Granit." In *Schriften zur Geologie und Mineralogie, 1770–1810.* Ed. G. Schmid. LA. Pt. I, vol. 1, pp. 57–63.

"Ueber Naturwissenschaft im Allgemeinen. Einzelne Betrachtungen und Aphorismen." In *Aufsätze, Fragmente, Studien zur Naturwissenschaft im Allgemeinen.* Ed. D. Kuhn and W. Engelhardt. LA. Pt. I, vol. 11, pp. 337–66.

"Der Verfasser teilt Die Geschichte seiner botanischen Studien mit." In *Aufsätze, Fragmente, Studien zur Morphologie.* Ed. D. Kuhn. LA. Pt. I, vol. 10, pp. 319–38.

"Vernhältnis zur Philosophie." In *Zur Farbenlehre. Didaktischer Teil.* Ed. R. Matthaei. LA. Pt. I, vol. 4, pp. 210–11.

"Der Versuch als Vermittler von Objekt und Subjekt, 1793." In *Naturwissenschaftliche Hefte.* Ed. D. Kuhn. LA. Pt. I, vol. 8, pp. 305–15.

"Von der Physiognomik Ueberhaupt." In *Antheil an Lavaters Physiognomischen Fragmenten.* Ed. V. Valentin, et al. WA. Pt. I, vol. 37, pp. 329–30.

"Vorstufen und Vorarbeiten zu einzelnen Abschnitten." In *West-östlicher Divan.* BA. Vol. 3, pp. 381–403.

Die Wahlverwandtschaften. Ed. M. Waldberg. WA. Pt. I, vol. 20.

"Zur Geologie November 1829." In *Aufsätze, Fragmente, Studien zur Natur-wissenschaft im Allgemeinen.* Ed. D. Kuhn and W. Engelhardt. LA. Pt. I, vol. 11, pp. 305–8.

"Zur Morphologie. Ersten Bandes. Zweites Heft." In *Morphologische Hefte.* Ed. D. Kuhn. LA. Pt. I, vol. 9, pp. 85–189.

Gombrich, E. H. "Evidence of Images." In *Interpretation: Theory and Practice.* Ed. C. Singleton. Baltimore, Md.: Johns Hopkins Press, 1969, pp. 35–104.

Göres, Jörn. *Goethes Leben in Bilddokumenten.* Munich: Beck, 1981.

Gould, Stephen Jay. "Archetype and Adaptation." *Natural History* 95 (1986): 16–27.

Gregory, Joshua C. *A Short History of Atomism, From Democritus to Bohr.* London: Black, 1931.

Gregory, Richard L. *The Intelligent Eye.* New York: McGraw-Hill, 1970.

Groth, Angelika. *Goethe als Wissenschaftshistoriker.* Munich: Fink, 1972.

Guerlac, Henry. "Some Areas for further Newtonian Studies." *History of Science* 17 (1979): 75–101.

Gundolf, Friedrich. "Geschichte und Politik." *Goethe.* Berlin: Bondi, 1916, pp. 400–12.

Hahn, Karl-Heinz. "Geschichtsschreibung als Literatur: Zur Theorie deutschsprachiger Historiographie im Zeitalter Goethes." In *Studien zur Goethezeit. Erich Trunz zum 75. Geburtstag.* Ed. H. J. Mähl and E. Mannack. Heidelberg: Winter, 1981, pp. 91–101.

Haldane, John S. *Mechanism, Life and Personality.* 2d ed. New York: Dutton, 1923.

Hall, A. Rupert. "Merton Revisited." *History of Science: an Annual Review of Literature, Research and Teaching* 2 (1963): 1–16.

Philosophers at War. Cambridge University Press, 1980.

Hamm, H. *Der Theoretiker Goethe.* Berlin: Akademie Verlag, 1980.

Hankins, Thomas L. *Science and the Enlightenment.* Cambridge University Press, 1985.

Hankins, Thomas L. "In Defence of Biography." *History of Science* 17 (1979): 1–16.

Heisenberg, Werner. "Die Goethesche und Newtonsche Farbenlehre im Lichte des modernen Physik." *Geist der Zeit* 19 (1941): 261–75.

Das Naturbild der heutigen Physik. Hamburg: Rowolt, 1955.

"The Teachings of Goethe and Newton on Colour in the Light of Modern Physics." *Philosophic Problems of Nuclear Science.* Trans. F. C. Hayes. New York: Pantheon, 1952. pp. 60–76.

Helmholtz, Hermann. "Ueber Goethe's naturwissenschaftliche Arbeiten." In *Goethe im Urteil seiner Kritiker.* Ed. Karl R. Mandelkow. 3 vols. Munich: Beck, 1975–9, vol. 2, pp. 401–16.

Hempel, Carl G. *Fundamentals of Concept Formation in Empirical Science.* Chicago: University of Chicago Press, 1952.

Hennig, John. "Goethe's interest in the history of British physics." *OSIRIS* 10 (1952): 43–66.

Herder, Johann G. "Abhandlung über den Ursprung der Sprache." In *Sämtliche Werke.* Ed. B. Suphan. Suphan-Ausgabe (SA). 33 vols. Hildesheim: Georg Olm, 1967; repr., 1891, vol. 5, pp. 1–148.

References

"Auch eine Philosophie der Geschichte zur Bildung der Menschheit." SA. Vol. 5, pp. 475–594.

Ideen zur Philosophie der Geschichte der Menschheit. SA. Vols. 13, 14.

"Ueber die neuere deutsche Literatur. Erste Sammlung von Fragmenten." SA. Vol. 1, pp. 139–240.

"Vom Erkennen und Empfinden der menschlichen Seele." SA. Vol. 8, pp. 164–202.

Hogben, Lancelot. *Science in Authority.* London: Unwin, 1963.

Hohenemser, Ernst. *Die Lehre von den kleinen Vorstellungen bei Leibniz.* Ph.D. diss. Heidelberg University, 1899.

Horn, Franz C. *Geschichte und Kritik der deutschen Poesie und Beredsamkeit.* Berlin: Unger, 1805.

Horowitz, Irving. *Philosophy, Science, and the Sociology of Knowledge.* Springfield, Ill.: Thomas, 1961.

Jahn, Kurt. "Goethes Stellung zur Geschichte." *Goethes Dichtung und Wahrheit.* Halle: Niemeyer, 1908, pp. 49–77.

James, William. *The Principles of Psychology.* 2 vols. New York: Dover, 1950; 1st ed., 1890.

Jaszi, Andrew. *Entzweiung und Vereinigung. Goethes symbolische Weltanschauung.* Heidelberg: Stiehm, 1973.

Jenisch, Daniel. *Universalhistorischer Ueberblick der Entwicklung des Menschenge schlechts, als eines sich fortbildenden Ganzen, Eine Philosophie der Culturgeschichte.* 2 vols. Berlin: Voss, 1801.

Kant, Immanuel. *Allgemeine Naturgeschichte und Theorie des Himmels.* In *Kant's gesammelte Schriften.* 29 vols., Preussische Akademie der Wissenschaften (Akad.). Berlin: Reimer and de Gruyter, 1910–, vol. 1, pp. 215–368.

Immanuel Kant's Critique of Pure Reason. Trans. N. K. Smith. New York: Macmillan, 1982.

Kritik der reinen Vernunft. Akad. Vol. 3.

"Ueber den Gebrauch teleologischer Principien in der Philosophie." Akad. Vol. 8, pp. 159–84.

"Von den verschiedenen Racen der Menschen." Akad. Vol. 2, pp. 427–43.

Kargon, Robert H. "Atomism in the Seventeenth Century." In *Dictionary of the History of Ideas.* Ed. P. Wiener. 5 vols. New York: Scribner, 1973, vol. 1, pp. 132–41.

Kass, Georg. *Möser und Goethe.* Berlin: Paul, 1909.

Keudell, Elise. *Goethe als Benutzer der Weimarer Bibliothek.* Weimar: Böhlau, 1931.

Kindermann, Heinz. *Das Goethebild des 20. Jahrhunderts.* 2d ed. Darmstadt: Wiss. Buchgesellschaft, 1966.

Kirscht, John P. and Ronald C. Dillehay. *Dimensions of Authoritarianism: A Review of Research.* Lexington: University of Kentucky Press, 1967.

Kleinschneider, Manfred. *Goethes Naturstudien, wissenschaftliche und geschichtliche Untersuchungen.* Bonn: Bouvier, 1971.

Klima, Rolf and Ludgen Viehoff. "The Sociology of Science in West Germany and Austria." In *The Sociology of Science in Europe.* Ed. R. K. Merton and J. Gaston. Carbondale, Ill.: SIU Press, 1977, pp. 145–92.

Kluge, Ingeborg. *Wissenschaftskritik in Goethes "Faust."* Bern: Peter Lang, 1982.

Knight, David M. "German Science in the Romantic Period." In *The Emergence of Science in Western Europe*. Ed. M. Crosland. New York: Science History Publications, 1976, pp. 161–78.

"The Physical Sciences and the Romantic Movement." *History of Science* 9 (1970): 54–75.

Knüfer, Carl. *Grundzüge der Geschichte des Begriffs Vorstellung von Wolff bis Kant. Ein Beitrag zur Geschichte der philosophischen Terminologie*. Ph.D. diss. Berlin University, 1911.

Korzybski, Alfred. *Science and Sanity. An Introduction to Non-Aristotelian Systems and General Semantics*. 4th ed. Lakeville, Conn.: Non-Aristotelian Library, 1973.

Kragh, Helge. *An Introduction to the Historiography of Science*. Cambridge University Press, 1987.

Krieg, Leonard. "Authority." In *Dictionary of the History of Ideas*. Ed. P. Wiener. 5 vols. New York: Scribner, 1973, vol. 1, pp. 141–62.

Kronick, David A. "Authorship and Authority in the Scientific Periodicals of the Seventeenth and Eighteenth Centuries." *The Library Quarterly* 48 (1978): 255–75.

Krueger, Susan H. "Allegory, Symbol, and Symbolic Representation." Ph.D. diss. Yale University, 1984.

Kuhn, Dorothea. *Empirische und ideelle Wirklichkeit*. Köln: Böhlau, 1967.

"Goethes Geschichte der Farbenlehre als Werk und Form." *Deutsche Vierteljahrsschrift* 34 (1960): 356–77.

"Goethe's Relationship to the Theories of Development of His Time." In *Goethe and the Sciences: A Reappraisal*. Ed. F. Amrine, F. Zucker, and H. Wheeler. Dordrecht: Reidel, 1987, pp. 3–15.

"Goethes Schriften zur Naturwissenschaft." *Goethe-Jahrbuch* 33 (1971): 123–46.

Kuhn, Thomas. *The Essential Tension*. Chicago: University of Chicago Press, 1977.

"The History of Science." In *International Encyclopedia of the Social Sciences*. Ed. David Sills. 18 vols. New York: Macmillan, 1968, vol. 14, pp. 74–83.

"Metaphor in Science." *Metaphor and Thought*. Ed. A. Ortony. Cambridge University Press, 1979, pp. 409–19.

"Objectivity, Value, Judgement, and Theory Choice." In *Critical Theory Since 1965*. Ed. H. Adams and L. Searle. Tallahassee: University Presses of Florida, 1986, pp. 383–93.

"Reflections on My Critics." In *Criticism and the Growth of Knowledge*. Ed. I. Lakotos and A. Musgrave. Cambridge University Press, 1970, pp. 231–78.

The Structure of Scientific Revolutions. 2d ed. Chicago: University of Chicago Press, 1970.

Landgrebe, Ludwig. "Die Geschichte in Goethes Weltbild." In *Beiträge zur Einheit von Bildung und Sprache im geistigen Sein*. Ed. G. Haselbach and G. Hartmann. Berlin: de Gruyter, 1957, pp. 371–84.

Lange, Friedrich A. *Geschichte des Materialismus und Kritik seiner Bedeutung in der Gegenwart*. 2 vols. 3d ed. Iserlohn: Baedeker, 1876.

Lange, Victor, ed. *Goethe in English*. 12 vols. Boston: Mass.: Suhrkamp-Insel, 1982–.

"Goethes Geschichtsauffassung." *Etudes Germaniques* 38 (1983): 3–16.

References

"Goethe's View of History." In *Goethe Proceedings. Essays Commemorating the Goethe Sesquicentennial at the University of California, Davis*. Ed. C. Bernd, T. Lulofs, H. Nerjes, F. Semmern-Frankenegg and P. Schäffer. Columbia, S.C.: Camden, 1984, pp. 107–19.

Langen, August. "Der Wortschatz des 18. Jahrhunderts." *Deutsche Wortgeschichte*. 3 vols. 3d ed. Ed. F. Maurer and H. Rupp. Berlin: De Gruyter, 1974, vol. 2, pp. 31–244.

Larson, Magali Sarfatti. *The Rise of Professionalism. A Sociological Analysis*. Berkeley and Los Angeles: University of California Press, 1977.

Laslowski, Ernst. "Goethes Stellung zur Geschichte." *Historisches Jahrbuch* 53 (1933): 480–9.

Lasswitz, Kurd. *Geschichte der Atomistik vom Mittelalter bis Newton*. 2 vols. Hildesheim: Olm, 1963; 1st ed., 1890.

Lehman, Winifred P. "Session 7. The Dictionary." In *Proceedings of the National Symposium on Machine Translation*. Ed. H. P. Edmundson. Englewood Cliffs, N.J.: Prentice-Hall, 1961, pp. 309–53.

Lehmann, Walter. *Goethes Geschichtsauffassung in ihren Grundlagen*. Langensalza: Beyer, 1930.

Lenneberg, Eric. "Language and Cognition." In *Semantics: An Interdisciplinary Reader in Philosophy, Linguistics, and Psychology*. Ed. Danny D. Steinberg and Leon A. Jakobovits. Cambridge University Press, 1971, pp. 536–57.

Lenoir, Timothy. "Kant, Blumenbach, and Vital Materialism in German Biology." *ISIS* 71 (1980): 77–108.

The Strategy of Life. Chicago: University of Chicago Press, 1989; repr., 1982.

Lentz, Wolfgang. *Goethes Noten und Abhandlungen zum West-östlichen Divan*. Hamburg: Augustin, 1958.

Lepenies, Wolf and Peter Weingart. "Introduction." In *Functions and Uses of Disciplinary Histories*. Ed. L. Graham, W. Lepenies and P. Weingart. Dordrecht: Reidel, 1983, pp. ix–xx.

"Naturgeschichte und Anthropologie im 18. Jahrhundert." In *Deutschlands kulturelle Entfaltung, Neubestimmung des Menschen*. Ed. B. Faber. Munich: Kraus, 1980, pp. 211–26.

Lessing, Gotthold. *Die Erziehung des Menschengeschlechts*. In *Sämtliche Schriften*. 23 vols. Ed. Karl Lachmann. Berlin: de Gruyter, 1968; repr., 1886–1924, vol. 13, pp. 413–36.

Lindemann, Margot. *Deutsche Presse bis 1815*. Berlin: Colloquium, 1969.

Linden, Mareta. *Untersuchung zum Anthropologiebegriff des 18. Jahrhunderts*. Bern: Peter Lang, 1976.

Lorenz, Ottokar. "Goethe als Historiker." *Goethes politische Lehrjahre*. Berlin: Hertz, 1893, pp. 160–80.

Loy, Robert. "Attitudes toward Authority in European Literature to the Eighteenth Century." *Proceedings of the IXth Congress of the International Comparative Literature Association* 9 (1981): 65–9.

Lukács, Georg. "Goethe und seine Zeit." In *George Lukács Werke*. 17 vols. Berlin: Luchterhand, 1964–, vol. 7, pp. 41–184.

Lyell, Charles. *Principles of Geology*. 3 vols. New York: Johnson, 1969; repr., 1st ed., 1830–3.

MacIntyre, Alasdair. "Epistemological Crisis, Dramatic Narrative and the Philosophy of Science." In *Paradigms and Revolutions. Appraisals and Applications of Thomas Kuhn's Philosophy of Science*. Ed. G. Gutting. Nortre Dame, Ind.: University of Notre Dame Press, 1980, pp. 54–74.

Magnus, Rudolf. *Goethe as a Scientist*. Trans. H. Norden. New York: Schuman, 1949.

Mandelkow, Karl R. "Die Rezeption der naturwissenschaftlichen Schriften." In *Goethe in Deutschland. Rezeptionsgeschichte eines Klassikers*. Munich: Beck, 1980, pp. 174–200.

Mandelkow, Karl R., ed. *Goethe im Urteil seiner Kritiker*. 3 vols. Munich: Beck, 1975–9.

Mann, Thomas, ed. *The Permanent Goethe*. New York: Dial Press, 1948.

Mannheim, Karl. *Ideology and Utopia: An Introduction to the Sociology of Knowledge*. Trans. Louis Wirth and Edward Shils. New York: Harcourt, Brace & Co., 1936; 1st German ed., 1929.

"The Sociology of Knowledge." In *The Sociology of Knowledge: A Reader*. Ed. J. Curtis and J. Petras. New York: Praeger, 1970, pp. 109–30.

Marchand, James W. "Introduction." In *The Quest for the New Science. Language and Thought in Eighteenth Century Science*. Ed. K. J. Fink and J. W. Marchand. Carbondale, Ill.: SIU Press, 1979, pp. 1–5.

Martindale, Don. "Sociological Theory and the Ideal Type." In *Symposium on Sociological Theory*. Ed. Llewellyn Gross. Evanston, Ill.: Row, Peterson, 1959, pp. 57–91.

Martinson, Steven D. "Filling in the Gaps: 'The Problem of World-Order' in Schiller's Essay on Universal History." *Eighteenth-century Studies* 22 (1988): 24–45.

Marx, Karl. "Concerning the Production of Consciousness." In *The Sociology of Knowledge: A Reader*. Ed. J. Curtis and J. Petras. New York: Praeger, 1970, pp. 97–108.

Masterman, Margaret. "The Nature of a Paradigm." In *Criticism and the Growth of Knowledge*. Ed. I. Lakotos and A. Musgrave. Cambridge University Press, 1970, pp. 59–89.

McCarthy, John A. *Crossing Boundaries, A Theory and History of Essay Writing in German, 1680–1815*. Philadelphia: University of Pennsylvania Press, 1989.

"The Philosopher as Essayist: Leibniz and Kant." In *The Philosopher as Writer*. Ed. R. Ginsberg. Selinsgrove, Pa.: Susquehanna University Press, 1987, pp. 48–74.

McClelland, Charles E. *State, Society, and University in Germany, 1700–1914*. Cambridge University Press, 1980.

McMullin, Ernan, ed. *The Concept of Matter in Greek and Medieval Philosophy*. Notre Dame, Ind.: Notre Dame University Press, 1963.

"The History and Philosophy of Science: A Taxonomy." In *Historical and Philosophical Perspectives of Science*. Ed. Roger H. Stuewer. Minneapolis: University of Minnesota Press, 1970, pp. 12–67.

Meinecke, Friedrich. *Goethe und die Geschichte*. Munich: Leibniz, 1949; 1st ed., 1936.

Menke-Glückert, Emil. *Goethe als Geschichtsphilosoph und die geschichtsphilosophische Bewegung seiner Zeit*. Leipzig: Voigtländer, 1907.

References

Merton, Robert K. "Behavior Patterns of Scientists." In *The Sociology of Science: Theoretical and Empirical Investigations*. Ed. N. W. Storer. Chicago: University of Chicago Press, 1973, pp. 325–42.

"The Matthew Effect in Science." In *The Sociology of Science: Theoretical and Empirical Investigations*. Ed. N. W. Storer. Chicago: University of Chicago Press, 1973, pp. 439–59.

Meya, Jörg and Otto Sibum. *Das fünfte Element. Wirkungen und Deutungen der Elektrizität*. Hamburg: Rowohlt, 1987.

Meyer, Richard. "Studien zu Goethes Wortgebrauch." *Archiv für das Studium der neueren Sprachen und Litteraturen* 96 (1896): 1–42.

Miller, Samuel. *A Brief Retrospect of the Eighteenth Century*. 2 vols. New York: Swords, 1803.

Mohanty, Jitendranath. *The Concept of Intentionality*. St. Louis, Mo.: Green, 1972.

Mommsen, Katharina. *Goethe und Diez, Quellenuntersuchungen zu Gedichten der Divan-Epoche*. Berlin: Akademie, 1961.

Montucla, Jean Etienne. *Histoire des mathématiques*. New ed. 4 vols. Paris: Agasse, 1799–1802.

Naegelsbach, Hans. "Das Wesen der Vorstellung bei Schopenhauer." *Beiträge zur Philosophie* 12 (1927): 1–188.

Nagel, Ernest. "Teleological Explanations and Teleological Systems." In *Readings in the Philosophy of Science*. Ed. Baruch A. Brody. Englewood Cliffs, N.J.: Prentice Hall, 1970, pp. 106–20.

Nietzsche, Friedrich. *Die Fröhliche Wissenschaft*. In *Nietzsche Werke*. 8 pts. Ed. G. Colli and M. Montinari. Berlin: de Gruyter, 1967, pt. V, vol. 2, pp. 11–335.

Menschliches, Allzumenschliches II. In *Nietzsche Werke*. 8 pts. Ed. G. Colli and M. Montinari. Berlin: de Gruyter, 1967, pt. IV, vol. 3, pp. 1–342.

Nisbet, Hugh. *Goethe and the Scientific Tradition*. London: Maney, 1972.

Oakes, Guy. *Weber and Rickert: Concept Formation in the Cultural Sciences*. Cambridge, Mass.: MIT Press, 1988.

Obermayer, August. "Zum Toposbegriff der modernen Literaturwissenschaft." In *Toposforschung*. Ed. Max Baeumer. Darmstadt: Wiss. Buchgesellschaft, 1973, pp. 252–67.

Ornstein, Martha. *The Role of Scientific Societies in the Seventeenth Century*. Chicago: University of Chicago Press, 1928.

Ortony, Andrew. "Metaphor: A Multidimensional Problem." In *Metaphor and Thought*. Ed. A. Ortony. Cambridge University Press, 1979, pp. 1–16.

Outhwaite, William. *Concept Formation in Social Science*. London: Routledge & Kegan Paul, 1983.

Pascal, Roy. "The 'Sturm und Drang' Movement." *Modern Language Review* 47 (1952): 129–51.

Paul, Hermann. *Principles of the History of Language*. Trans. H. A. Strong. College Park, Md.: McGrath, 1970.

Pawlowski, Tadeusz. *Concept Formation in the Humanities and the Social Sciences*. Dordrecht: Reidel, 1980.

Perelman, Chaim and L. Olbrechts-Tyteca. *The New Rhetoric, A Treatise on Argu-*

mentation. Trans. J. Wilkinson and P. Weaver. Notre Dame, Ind.: Notre Dame University Press, 1969; 1st ed., 1958.

Piñero, José M. López. "Eighteenth Century Medical Vitalism: The Paracelsian Connection." In *Revolutions in Science: Their Meaning and Relevance.* Ed. W. R. Shea. Canton, Mass.: Science History Publications, 1988, pp. 117–32.

Pniower, Otto. "Zu Goethes Wortgebrauch." *Goethe-Jahrbuch* 19 (1898): 229–47.

Popper, Karl. *The Poverty of Historicism.* London: Kegan Paul, 1957.

Pörksen, Uwe. "Goethes Kritik naturwissenschaftlicher Metaphorik und der Roman 'Die Wahlverwandtschaften.' " *Jahrbuch der deutschen Schiller-Gesellschaft* 25 (1981): 285–315.

"Zur Wissenschaftssprache und Sprachauffassung bei Linné und Goethe." In *Sprache und Welterfahrung.* Ed. J. Zimmermann. Munich: Fink, 1978, pp. 110–41.

Porterfield, William. *A Treatise on the Eye, the Manner and Phenomena of Vision.* London: Miller, 1759.

Portmann, Adolf. "Goethe and the Concept of Metamorphosis." In *Goethe and the Sciences.* Ed. F. Amrine, et al. Dordrecht: Reidel, 1987, pp. 113–45.

Prantl, Carl. *Aristotles Ueber die Farben.* Munich: Kaiser, 1849.

Priestley, Joseph. *The History and Present State of Discoveries Relating to Vision, Light and Colours.* London: Johnson, 1772.

Pyritz, Hans. *Goethe-Bibliographie.* 2 vols. Heidelberg: Winter, 1965.

Reed, Terence J. *Goethe.* Oxford: Oxford University Press, 1984.

Reiss, Hans, ed. *Goethe und die Tradition.* Frankfurt: Athenäum, 1972.

Reuter, Hans-Heinrich. "Roman des europäischen Gedankens." *Goethe-Jahrbuch* 28 (1966): 1–49.

Riedel, Wolfgang. *Die Anthropologie des jungen Schiller. Zur Ideengeschichte der medizinischen Schriften und der "Philosophischen Briefe."* Würzburg: Königshausen and Neumann, 1985.

Ritter, Johann W. *Die Physik als Kunst. Ein Versuch, die Tendenz der Physik aus ihrer Geschichte zu deuten.* Munich: Lindauer, 1806.

Ronchi, V. *The Nature of Light.* Trans. V. Barocas. Cambridge, Mass.: Harvard University Press, 1970.

Rousseau, Jean-Jacques. *Essay on the Origin of Languages.* Trans. J. Moran and A. Gode. New York: Ungar, 1966.

Sabara, I. *Theories of Light from Descartes to Newton.* London: Oldbourne, 1967.

Said, Edward. *Orientalism.* New York: Random House, 1979.

Sandys, John E. *A History of Classical Scholarship.* 3 vols. New York: Hafner, 1958; 1st ed. 1903–8.

Sarton, George. "Montucla." *OSIRIS* 1 (1936): 519–67.

Scherer, Wilhelm. "Die Litteratur-revolution." In *Sturm und Drang.* Ed. M. Wacker. Darmstadt: Wiss. Buchgesellschaft, 1985; repr., 1870, pp. 17–24.

Schiller, Friedrich. *Geschichte des Abfalls der Vereinigten Niederlande von der Spanischen Regierung.* In *Schillers Werke.* Nationalausgabe (NA). 42 vols. Ed. Karl-Heinz Hahn. Weimar: Böhlau, 1943–, vol. 17, pp. 1–356.

"Ueber Egmont, Trauerspiel von Goethe." In *Goethe im Urteil seiner Kritiker.* 3 vols. Ed. Karl R. Mandelkow. Munich: Beck, 1975–9, vol. 1, pp. 104–11.

References

"Versuch über den Zusammenhang der thierischen Natur des Menschen mit seiner Geistigen." NA. Vol. 20, pp. 37–75.

"Was heisst und zu welchem Ende studiert man Universalgeschichte?" NA. Vol. 17, pp. 359–76.

Schlözer, August Ludwig. *Vorstellung seiner Universal-historie*. 2 vols. Göttingen: Dieterich. 1772–3.

Schofield, Robert. *Mechanism and Materialism: British Mechanical Philosophy in the Age of Reason*. Princeton, N.J.: Princeton University Press, 1970.

Schöne, Albrecht. *Goethes Farbentheologie*. Munich: Beck, 1987.

Schottroff, Willy. "Goethe als Bibelwissenschaftler." In *Allerhand Goethe*. Ed. D. Kempel and J. Pompetzki. Bern: Peter Lang, 1985, pp. 111–37.

Schrimpf, Hans J. "Ueber die geschichtliche Bedeutung von Goethes Newton-Polemik und Romantik-Kritik." In *Der Schriftsteller als Öffentliche Person, Von Lessing bis Hochhuth*. Ed. H. J. Schrimpf. Berlin: Schmidt, 1977, pp. 126–43.

Schubart-Fikentscher, Gertrud. *Goethes Sechsundfünfzig Strassburger Thesen vom 6. August, 1771*. Weimar: Böhlau, 1949.

Schuler, Reinhard. *Das Exemplarische bei Goethe*. Munich: Fink, 1973.

Schultz, Werner. "Der Sinn der Geschichte bei Hegel und Goethe." *Archiv für Kulturgeschichte* 39 (1957): 209–27.

Schultz, Werner. "Die Bedeutung des Tragischen für das Verstehen der Geschichte bei Hegel und Goethe." *Archiv für Kulturgeschichte* 38 (1956): 92–115.

Schütt, Hans-Werner. "Lichtenberg als 'Kuhnianer.' " *Sudhoffs Archiv* 63 (1979): 87–90.

Schweizer, Hans R. *Goethe und das Problem der Sprache*. Bern: Francke, 1959.

Seibt, K. Michael. "Einfühlung, Language, and Herder's Philosophy of History." In *The Quest for the New Science, Language and Thought in Eighteenth Century Science*. Ed. K. J. Fink and J. W. Marchand. Carbondale, Ill.: SIU Press, 1979, pp. 17–27.

Sepper, Dennis. *Goethe contra Newton, Polemics and the Project for a New Science of Color*. Cambridge University Press, 1988.

Shakespeare, William. *Hamlet*. In *The London Shakespeare*. 5 vols. Ed. J. Munro. New York: Simon & Schuster, 1957, vol. 5, pp. 361–571.

Shapere, Dudley. "Newtonian Mechanics and Mechanical Explanation." Ed. Paul Edwards. In *Encyclopedia of Philosophy*. 8 vols. New York: Macmillan, 1967, vol. 5, pp. 491–6.

Sherrington, Charles. *Goethe on Nature and on Science*. Cambridge University Press, 1949.

Sokal, Robert R. and Peter H. A. Sneath. *Principles of Numerical Taxonomy*. San Francisco: Freeman, 1963.

Sonntag, Otto. "Albrecht von Haller on Academies and the Advancement of Science: The Case of Göttingen." *Annals of Science* 32 (1975): 379–91.

Spiegelberg, Herbert. "Intention und Intentionalität in der Scholastik, bei Brentano und Husserl." *Studia Philosophica* 29 (1969): 189–216.

Stark, Isolde. "Despot und Tyrann bei Johann Wolfgang Goethe." In *Das Fortleben altgriechischer sozialer Typenbegriffe in der deutschen Sprache*. Ed. E. C. Welskopf. Berlin: Akademie, 1981, pp. 169–82.

Steer, Alfred G. *Goethe's Science in the Structure of the Wanderjahre.* Athens: University of Georgia Press, 1979.

Steiner, Rudolf. *Goethe the Scientist.* Trans. O. Wannamaker. New York: Anthroposophic Press, 1950.

Stockhammer, Morris. "Kurzes dualistisches Wörterverzeichnis." *Archiv für Begriffsgeschichte* 4 (1959): 158–81.

Sulzer, Johann G. *Allgemeine Theorie der schönen Künste.* 5 vols. Hildesheim: Olm, 1967–70; repr., 2d ed., 1792–9.

Supek, Ivan. "Wissenschaft und Dichtung." In *Goethe und die Natur: Referate des Triestiner Kongresses.* Ed. H. A. Glaser. Frankfurt: Peter Lang, 1986, pp. 217–31.

Tarski, Alfred. *Logic, Semantics, Metamathematics, Papers from 1923–1938.* Ed. J. H. Woodger. Oxford: Oxford University Press (Clarendon Press), 1956.

Toulmin, Stephen. *Human Understanding.* Princeton, N.J.: Princeton University Press, 1972.

Toulmin, Stephen and June Goodfield. *The Discovery of Time.* New York: Harper & Row, 1965.

Traumann, Ernst. *Goethe der Strassburger Student.* 2d ed. Leipzig: Klinkhardt & Biermann, 1923.

Trier, Jost. *Aufsätze und Vorträge zur Wortfeldtheorie.* Ed. A. van der Lee and O. Reichmann. The Hague: Mouton, 1973.

Trunz, Erich. "Goethe als Sammler." In *Weimarer Goethe-Studien.* Ed. Erich Trunz. Weimar: Böhlau, 1980, pp. 7–47.

Vaihinger, Hans. *Die Philosophie des Als Ob: System der theoretischen, praktischen und religiösen Fiktionen der Menschheit auf Grund eines idealistischen Positivismus.* 7th and 8th eds. Leipzig: Meiner, 1922.

Voltaire, François M. A. *The Philosophy of History.* Trans. T. Kiernan. New York: Philosophical Library, 1965.

Vorländer, Karl. *Kant-Schiller-Goethe.* 2d ed. Leipzig: Meiner, 1923.

Wachler, D. Ludwig. *Geschichte der historischen Forschung und Kunst, seit der Wiederherstellung der litterärischen Cultur in Europa.* 2 vols. Göttingen: Röwer, 1812–18.

Wagenbreth, Otfried. "Goethes Stellung in der Geschichte der Geologie." In *Goethe und die Wissenschaften.* Ed. H. Brandt. Jena: Friedrich-Schiller-Universität, 1984, pp. 59–71.

Watkins, J. W. N. "Historical Explanations in the Social Sciences." In *Theories of History.* Ed. P. Gardiner. Glencoe, Ill.: Free Press, 1959, pp. 503–15.

Weber, Max. "Ideal Types and Theory Construction." In *Readings in the Philosophy of the Social Sciences.* Ed. May Brodbeck. London: Macmillan, 1968, pp. 496–507.

Wegele, Franz. *Göthe als Historiker.* Würzburg: Stuber, 1876.

Weitz, Morris. *Theories of Concepts. A History of the Major Philosophical Tradition.* London: Routledge, 1988.

Wells, Larry D. "Organic Structure in Goethe's 'Novelle.' " *German Quarterly* 53 (1980): 418–31.

Wenzel, Manfred. "Johann Wolfgang von Goethe und Samuel Thomas Soemmerring:

Morphologie und Farbenlehre." In *Samuel Thomas Soemmerring und die Gelehrten der Goethezeit*. Ed. G. Mann and F. Dumont. Stuttgart: Fischer, 1985, pp. 11–33.

Whewell, William. *History of the Inductive Sciences*. In *The Historical and Philosophical Works of William Whewell*. 10 vols. Ed. G. Buchdahl and L. Laudan. London: F. Cass, 1967, repr., 3d ed., 1857, vols. 2, 3, and 4.

The Philosophy of the Inductive Sciences. In *The Historical and Philosophical Works of William Whewell*. 10 vols. Ed. G. Buchdahl and L. Laudan. London: F. Cass, 1967, repr., 3d ed., 1857, vols. 5 and 6.

White, Hayden. "The Historical Text as Literary Artifact." In *The Writing of History: Literary Form and Historical Understanding*. Ed. R. H. Canary and H. Kozicki. Madison: University of Wisconsin Press, 1978, pp. 41–62.

Metahistory. The Historical Imagination in Nineteenth-Century Europe. Baltimore: Johns Hopkins University Press, 1973.

Wilkinson, Elizabeth. "The Relation of Form and Meaning in Goethe's 'Egmont.'" In *Goethe. Poet and Thinker*. Ed. E. Wilkinson and L. Willoughby. London: Arnold, 1962, pp. 55–74.

Wilmont, Nikolai. "Goethes Geschichts- und Kulturauffassung." *Kolloquium über Probleme der Goethe-Forschung, Weimarer Beiträge* 6 (1960): 978–92.

Wilson, M. H. "Goethe's Colour Experiments." *Year Book of the Physical Society* (1958): 12–21.

Wise, M. Norton. "On the Relation of Physical Science to History in Late Nineteenth-Century Germany." In *Functions and Uses of Disciplinary Histories*. Ed. L. Graham, W. Lepenies and P. Weingart. Dordrecht: Reidel, 1983, pp. 3–34.

Wohlleben, Joachim. *Goethe als Journalist und Essayist*. Bern: Peter Lang, 1981.

Wolff, Hans. "Goethes Kenntnisse der Alpen im Lichte der modernen Geologie." *Sudhoffs Archiv* 70 (1986): 144–52.

Woodger, Joseph H. *Biology and Language*. Cambridge University Press, 1952.

Würtenberg, Gustav. *Goethe und der Historismus*. Leipzig: Teubner, 1929.

Zartman, Francis. *Definition and Open Texture*. Ph.D. diss. University of Illinois, 1964.

Ziegler, Klaus. "Zu Goethes Deutung der Geschichte." *Deutsche Vierteljahrsschrift für Literaturwissenschaft und Geistesgeschichte* 30 (1956): 232–67.

Zimmermann, Rolf. "Goethes Polaritätsdenken im geistigen Kontext des 18. Jahrhunderts." *Jahrbuch der deutschen Schillergesellschaft* 18 (1974): 304–47.

Zimmermann, Rolf. *Das Weltbild des Jungen Goethe, Studien zur Hermetischen Tradition des Deutschen 18. Jahrhunderts*. 2 vols. Munich: Fink, 1969–79.

Index

Index

Index

Index

Index

Index

Index

in historical records, 66
mathematical versus historical, 67
search for, 130
type
    construction of, 25
    definition of, 24
    historical, 147, 149
    theory of, 24, 25

Ussher, James (1581–1656), 61

Vesalius, Andreas (1514–64), 24, 61
Voltaire, François, M. A. (1694–1778), 11, 101, 132
vulcanism and neptunism, 17–18

Wachler, D. Ludwig (1767–1838), 61
Weimar
    and science, 88

circle of thinkers, 90
community of intellectuals, 85
Werner, Abraham G. (1750–1817), 14, 103
Whewell, William (1794–1866), 138
Wolf, Friedrich A. (1759–1824), 70
Wolff, Caspar F. (1734–94), 30
words
    and concepts and objects, 47–9, 71
    and correspondence rules, 86
    as discrete entities, 48
    environments of, 54
    field studies, 149
    of centrality, 49
    see also concepts; models and metaphors; symbolism
Wünsch, Christian E. (1744–1828), 76

Zeno (335–263), 121